Philosophy For Dummies®

P9-EMH-669

Glossary of Basic Terms

It's good to understand up front some of the lingo of philosophers.

- **Philosophy:** Love of wisdom. (Part I)
- **Wisdom:** Practical insight for living. (Ditto)
- **Epistemology:** The study of belief, truth, knowledge, and rationality. (Part III)
- **Metaphysics:** The study of 'being,' or what really exists. All the 'ultimate stuff' questions. *Meta* means 'after' or 'transcending.' (Parts IV, V, VI, and VII)
- **Ethics:** The study of good and evil, right and wrong, rules and virtues, character and vice, success and happiness (Parts III and VIII). Lots of subareas, like:

  - *Business ethics:* What is it okay to do?

  - *Legal ethics:* Who is it okay to sue?

  - *Medical ethics:* When is it okay to clone?

  - *Techno ethics:* Why is it okay to tap a phone?

- **Aesthetics:** The study of beauty, ugliness, and maybe even the sublime. What is art? *Meta-aesthetics tip:* If a theoretical aesthetician can't match a suit and tie or a skirt and shirt, take anything they say with a grain of salt. (Chapter 8)

The Problems of Philosophy: A Sampler

The problems posed by the great philosophers can enhance our experience of the world.

- Can we really ever know anything? (Part II)
- What is the good in life? (Part III)
- Are we actually free, as we seem to be, or are we just robots programmed by nature or God? (Part IV)
- Are we just bodies, or do we have souls? (Part V)
- Do we survive death? (Part VI)
- Is there a God? (Part VII)
- Does life have meaning? (Part VIII)

Philosophy For Dummies®

Cheat Sheet

A Few Big Names in the Ancient Game

It's important to become acquainted with some of the early founding philosophers.

- **Presocratics:** Anaximines, Anaxamander, Anaxagoras. Strange and famous names. Among the earliest philosophers on record. Costarring such luminaries as Thales, who believed that everything is made of water, once almost drowned, and got rich from getting a corner on the olive oil market. The Presocratics did speculative protoscience. Of course, they didn't know they were Presocratics. But we do.

- **Socrates:** Did philosophy using The Socratic Method (Duh). Hit the streets in search of wisdom. Executed by popular demand. Taught Plato.

- **Plato:** Hung around with Socrates. Wrote dialogues featuring his teacher. Maybe the most famous philosopher of all time. Taught the other contender for this accolade, Aristotle.

- **Aristotle:** Student of Plato. Codified logic. Said everyone seeks happiness. Taught Alexander the Great. Plato emphasized the next world; Aristotle concentrated on this one.

- **The Stoics:** Seneca, Epictetus, and Marcus Aurelius were the best known of the Roman Stoics. Main advice for handling any difficult thing in life: Put it in perspective and get over it.

The Questions of Philosophy

Some of the great questions raised by students of philosophy:

- Why?
- What?
- Will this be on the test?

...For Dummies®: Bestselling Book Series for Beginners

PHILOSOPHY
FOR
DUMMIES®

PHILOSOPHY FOR DUMMIES®

by Tom Morris, Ph.D.

IDG Books Worldwide, Inc.
An International Data Group Company

Foster City, CA ◆ Chicago, IL ◆ Indianapolis, IN ◆ New York, NY

Philosophy For Dummies®

Published by
IDG Books Worldwide, Inc.
An International Data Group Company
919 E. Hillsdale Blvd.
Suite 400
Foster City, CA 94404
www.idgbooks.com (IDG Books Worldwide Web site)
www.dummies.com (Dummies Press Web site)

Library of Congress Catalog Card No.: 99-65870

ISBN: 0-7645-5153-1

Printed in the United States of America

10 9 8 7 6 5 4 3 2

1B/QT/QZ/ZZ/IN

Distributed in the United States by IDG Books Worldwide, Inc.

Distributed by CDG Books Canada Inc. for Canada; by Transworld Publishers Limited in the United Kingdom; by IDG Norge Books for Norway; by IDG Sweden Books for Sweden; by IDG Books Australia Publishing Corporation Pty. Ltd. for Australia and New Zealand; by TransQuest Publishers Pte Ltd. for Singapore, Malaysia, Thailand, Indonesia, and Hong Kong; by Gotop Information Inc. for Taiwan; by ICG Muse, Inc. for Japan; by Intersoft for South Africa; by Eyrolles for France; by International Thomson Publishing for Germany, Austria and Switzerland; by Distribuidora Cuspide for Argentina; by LR International for Brazil; by Galileo Libros for Chile; by Ediciones ZETA S.C.R. Ltda. for Peru; by WS Computer Publishing Corporation, Inc., for the Philippines; by Contemporanea de Ediciones for Venezuela; by Express Computer Distributors for the Caribbean and West Indies; by Micronesia Media Distributor, Inc. for Micronesia; by Chips Computadoras S.A. de C.V. for Mexico; by Editorial Norma de Panama S.A. for Panama; by American Bookshops for Finland.

For general information on IDG Books Worldwide's books in the U.S., please call our Consumer Customer Service department at 800-762-2974. For reseller information, including discounts and premium sales, please call our Reseller Customer Service department at 800-434-3422.

For information on where to purchase IDG Books Worldwide's books outside the U.S., please contact our International Sales department at 317-596-5530 or fax 317-596-5692.

For consumer information on foreign language translations, please contact our Customer Service department at 1-800-434-3422, fax 317-596-5692, or e-mail rights@idgbooks.com.

For information on licensing foreign or domestic rights, please phone +1-650-655-3109.

For sales inquiries and special prices for bulk quantities, please contact our Sales department at 650-655-3200 or write to the address above.

For information on using IDG Books Worldwide's books in the classroom or for ordering examination copies, please contact our Educational Sales department at 800-434-2086 or fax 317-596-5499.

For press review copies, author interviews, or other publicity information, please contact our Public Relations department at 650-655-3000 or fax 650-655-3299.

For authorization to photocopy items for corporate, personal, or educational use, please contact Copyright Clearance Center, 222 Rosewood Drive, Danvers, MA 01923, or fax 978-750-4470.

is a registered trademark or trademark under exclusive license to IDG Books Worldwide, Inc. from International Data Group, Inc.

About the Author

Tom Morris has recently become one of the most active business speakers in America due to his unusual ability to bring the greatest wisdom of the past into the challenges we face now. A native of North Carolina, Tom is a graduate of the University of the North Carolina (Chapel Hill) and has been honored, along with Michael Jordan, as a recipient of its "Distinguished Young Alumnus Award." He holds a Ph.D. in both Philosophy and Religious Studies from Yale University and for 15 years served as a Professor of Philosophy at the University of Notre Dame, where he quickly became its most popular teacher, in many years having as much as an eighth of the entire student body in his classes. He is now Chairman of the Morris Institute for Human Values in Wilmington, NC.

Tom's twelfth book, *True Success: A New Philosophy of Excellence,* catapulted him over the walls of academia and launched him into a new adventure as a public philosopher and advisor to the corporate world. Recent audiences include General Motors, Ford Motor Company, Merrill Lynch, GTE, IBM, the U.S. Air Force, Price Waterhouse, Arthur Andersen, Campbell's Soup, Target Stores, The Dayton Hudson Corporation, Schlotzky's Delis, NBC Sports, *Business Week Magazine,* The Bayer Corporation, Deloitte and Touche, Federated Investors, American Funds, Taco Bell, The American Heart Association, the Young Presidents Organization, and the World Presidents Organization, along with many of the largest national and international associations. His most recent book, prior to *Philosophy For Dummies,* is called *If Aristotle Ran General Motors*: *The New Soul of Business.*

Known by his Notre Dame students as "TV Morris," this modern scholar is a former rock guitarist. He is also the first philosopher in history to appear in network TV commercials, where he has served as the national spokesman for Winnie the Pooh, Disney Home Videos, as well as being the only thinker ever to engage in early morning philosophy with Regis and Kathie Lee. He has appeared on CNBC's early morning show *Business Today,* as well as on the NBC *Today Show* with Matt Lauer. Tom is known for bringing the insights of the great thinkers into the drama of everyday life with high energy and good humor. His message is helping to change lives and revolutionize business practices everywhere.

ABOUT IDG BOOKS WORLDWIDE

Welcome to the world of IDG Books Worldwide.

IDG Books Worldwide, Inc., is a subsidiary of International Data Group, the world's largest publisher of computer-related information and the leading global provider of information services on information technology. IDG was founded more than 30 years ago by Patrick J. McGovern and now employs more than 9,000 people worldwide. IDG publishes more than 290 computer publications in over 75 countries. More than 90 million people read one or more IDG publications each month.

Launched in 1990, IDG Books Worldwide is today the #1 publisher of best-selling computer books in the United States. We are proud to have received eight awards from the Computer Press Association in recognition of editorial excellence and three from Computer Currents' First Annual Readers' Choice Awards. Our best-selling *...For Dummies®* series has more than 50 million copies in print with translations in 31 languages. IDG Books Worldwide, through a joint venture with IDG's Hi-Tech Beijing, became the first U.S. publisher to publish a computer book in the People's Republic of China. In record time, IDG Books Worldwide has become the first choice for millions of readers around the world who want to learn how to better manage their businesses.

Our mission is simple: Every one of our books is designed to bring extra value and skill-building instructions to the reader. Our books are written by experts who understand and care about our readers. The knowledge base of our editorial staff comes from years of experience in publishing, education, and journalism — experience we use to produce books to carry us into the new millennium. In short, we care about books, so we attract the best people. We devote special attention to details such as audience, interior design, use of icons, and illustrations. And because we use an efficient process of authoring, editing, and desktop publishing our books electronically, we can spend more time ensuring superior content and less time on the technicalities of making books.

You can count on our commitment to deliver high-quality books at competitive prices on topics you want to read about. At IDG Books Worldwide, we continue in the IDG tradition of delivering quality for more than 30 years. You'll find no better book on a subject than one from IDG Books Worldwide.

John Kilcullen
Chairman and CEO
IDG Books Worldwide, Inc.

Steven Berkowitz
President and Publisher
IDG Books Worldwide, Inc.

*Eighth Annual
Computer Press
Awards ≥1992*

*Ninth Annual
Computer Press
Awards ≥1993*

WINNER

*Tenth Annual
Computer Press
Awards ≥1994*

WINNER

*Eleventh Annual
Computer Press
Awards ≥1995*

IDG is the world's leading IT media, research and exposition company. Founded in 1964, IDG had 1997 revenues of $2.05 billion and has more than 9,000 employees worldwide. IDG offers the widest range of media options that reach IT buyers in 75 countries representing 95% of worldwide IT spending. IDG's diverse product and services portfolio spans six key areas including print publishing, online publishing, expositions and conferences, market research, education and training, and global marketing services. More than 90 million people read one or more of IDG's 290 magazines and newspapers, including IDG's leading global brands — Computerworld, PC World, Network World, Macworld and the Channel World family of publications. IDG Books Worldwide is one of the fastest-growing computer book publishers in the world, with more than 700 titles in 36 languages. The "...For Dummies®" series alone has more than 50 million copies in print. IDG offers online users the largest network of technology-specific Web sites around the world through IDG.net (http://www.idg.net), which comprises more than 225 targeted Web sites in 55 countries worldwide. International Data Corporation (IDC) is the world's largest provider of information technology data, analysis and consulting, with research centers in over 41 countries and more than 400 research analysts worldwide. IDG World Expo is a leading producer of more than 168 globally branded conferences and expositions in 35 countries including E3 (Electronic Entertainment Expo), Macworld Expo, ComNet, Windows World Expo, ICE (Internet Commerce Expo), Agenda, DEMO, and Spotlight. IDG's training subsidiary, ExecuTrain, is the world's largest computer training company, with more than 230 locations worldwide and 785 training courses. IDG Marketing Services helps industry-leading IT companies build international brand recognition by developing global integrated marketing programs via IDG's print, online and exposition products worldwide. Further information about the company can be found at www.idg.com. 1/24/99

Dedication

To Mary, Sara, and Matt — the greatest possible family!

Author's Acknowledgments

I'd like to thank all the many dummies who helped make this book possible. Just kidding. They are all wise people. I'm especially thankful to Tami Booth, who suggested it and Kelly Ewing, who edited it. Reid Boates, my literary agent, encouraged me regularly to write at blinding speed and helped me to get flowers to my acquiring editor when I was late on a deadline.

I thank the thousands of Notre Dame undergraduates who helped me think through all these topics over a period of 15 years with their questions, comments, and loud laughter, as well as their occasional looks of utter perplexity. I'm also grateful to the many people in my business audiences around the country who have told me that they were thrilled that I was writing a book with this title — I think they typically wanted it as a present for their bosses.

I want to give the greatest thanks possible to my family, who supported me every day in a very intensive time of writing. But not even my tight deadlines put a stop to our beach walks, trips to guitar stores, and family snack times. My wife Mary, my daughter Sara, and my son Matt make me glad that I'm a philosopher, with no real schedule whatsoever. They offer me all sorts of fun and make wise comments on whatever subject I bring up. To all of them it is dedicated.

Publisher's Acknowledgments

We're proud of this book; please register your comments through our IDG Books Worldwide Online Registration Form located at http://my2cents.dummies.com.

Some of the people who helped bring this book to market include the following:

Acquisitions, Editorial, and Media Development

Project Editor: Kelly Ewing

Executive Editor: Tammerly Booth

General Reviewer: Michael Murray

Editorial Coordinator: Maureen Kelly

Editorial Director: Kristin Cocks

Acquisitions Coordinator: Karen S. Young

Production

Project Coordinator: E. Shawn Aylsworth

Layout and Graphics: Karl Brandt, Brian Drumm, Angela F. Hunckler, Oliver Jackson, Kate Jenkins, Clint Lahnen, Shelly Norris, Tracy Oliver, Brent Savage, Jacque Schneider, Janet Seib, Michael A. Sullivan, Brian Torwelle, Mary Jo Weis, Erin Zeltner

Proofreaders: Christine Berman, Laura L. Bowman, Nancy Price, Marianne Santy

Indexer: Sharon Hilgenberg

General and Administrative

IDG Books Worldwide, Inc.: John Kilcullen, CEO; Steven Berkowitz, President and Publisher

IDG Books Technology Publishing Group: Richard Swadley, Senior Vice President and Publisher; Walter Bruce III, Vice President and Associate Publisher; Steven Sayre, Associate Publisher; Joseph Wikert, Associate Publisher; Mary Bednarek, Branded Product Development Director; Mary Corder, Editorial Director

IDG Books Consumer Publishing Group: Roland Elgey, Senior Vice President and Publisher; Kathleen A. Welton, Vice President and Publisher; Kevin Thornton, Acquisitions Manager; Kristin A. Cocks, Editorial Director

IDG Books Internet Publishing Group: Brenda McLaughlin, Senior Vice President and Publisher; Diane Graves Steele, Vice President and Associate Publisher; Sofia Marchant, Online Marketing Manager

IDG Books Production for Dummies Press: Michael R. Britton, Vice President of Production; Debbie Stailey, Associate Director of Production; Cindy L. Phipps, Manager of Project Coordination, Production Proofreading, and Indexing; Tony Augsburger, Manager of Prepress, Reprints, and Systems; Laura Carpenter, Production Control Manager; Shelley Lea, Supervisor of Graphics and Design; Debbie J. Gates, Production Systems Specialist; Robert Springer, Supervisor of Proofreading; Kathie Schutte, Production Supervisor

Dummies Packaging and Book Design: Patty Page, Manager, Promotions Marketing

◆

The publisher would like to give special thanks to Patrick J. McGovern, without whom this book would not have been possible.

◆

Contents at a Glance

Cartoons at a Glance

By Rich Tennant

page 185

page 11

page 39

page 323

page 279

page 231

page 149

page 123

page 81

Fax: 978-546-7747 • E-mail: the5wave@tiac.net

Table of Contents

Introduction

* *

I only wish that philosophy might come before our eyes in all her unity, just as the whole expanse of the firmament is spread out for us to gaze upon! It would be a sight closely resembling that of the firmament. For then surely philosophy would ravish all mortals with love for her; we should abandon all those things which, in our ignorance of what is great, we believe to be great.

— Seneca (First century Stoic philosopher)

*P*hilosophy For Dummies? What a concept! Is this the ultimate oxymoron, a contradiction in terms, or at least an impossibility in the making, an exercise in futility, on a par with *Advanced Calculus For Toddlers,* or *Neurosurgery For Nit Wits?*

No. Not at all. The ancient philosopher Socrates (fifth century, B.C.) thought that, when it comes to the Ultimate Questions, we all start off as dummies. But if we are humbly aware of how little we actually know, then we can really begin to learn.

In fact, Plato (circa 428–347 B.C.), the close student of Socrates, passed on an interesting story about this. He tells us Socrates had learned that the Oracle at Delphi had proclaimed him to be the wisest man in Athens. Shocked at this announcement, he began to search out the men of Athens known for their wisdom and began to question them closely. He found out very quickly that, on truly important and basic issues, they didn't really know very much of what they were thought to know, and what they themselves believed that they knew. On the basis of this experience, he slowly came to understand that his own wisdom must consist in realizing how little he really knew about the things that matter most, and how important it was to find out whatever we can about these issues. It's not the complacent and self-assured intellectual who exemplifies wisdom, but the genuinely curious, open-minded seeker of truth.

Bill, reading aloud about Socrates:

"The only true knowledge is knowing that you know nothing."

Ted, stunned:

"Dude — That's US!"

— Bill and Ted's Excellent Adventure

The word *philosophy* just means "love of wisdom." This is easy to understand when you realize that love is a commitment, and wisdom is just insight about living. Philosophy is, at its best, a passionate commitment to pursuing and embracing the most fundamental truths and insightful perspectives about life.

Aristotle (384–322 B.C.) also had an insight we can use here. This great thinker, Plato's long time student, and tutor to Alexander the Great (way back at a tender young age, when he was still just Alexander the Average) once said "Philosophy begins in wonder." And he was right. If we allow ourselves to really wonder about our lives, about those things that we take for granted, and about those big questions that we usually manage to ignore during the busyness of our daily schedules, we are beginning to act as true philosophers. If we think hard about these things, and discipline our reasoning in such a way as to make real progress, we are beginning to act as good philosophers. But we can't really live philosophically without acting in accordance with our insights. To be philosophers in the deepest sense, we must put our wisdom to work.

> *He is not wise to me who is wise in words only, but he who is wise in deeds.*
>
> — St. Gregory

About This Book

I've spent a good number of my years on earth wrestling with the questions that I will raise in this book. At the University of North Carolina, as an undergraduate, I majored in religion but took the equivalent of a double major in philosophy, turning my senior honors thesis in the philosophy of religion into my first published book. At Yale, I spent six years becoming only the second person ever to earn two master's degrees and a joint Ph.D. between the two departments of Philosophy and Religious Studies. I wanted to leave no ultimate intellectual stone unturned. My doctoral dissertation formed the basis of what would become my next two books and launched me into an international adventure of questioning and understanding that form the deep background of what I intend to cover with you in this book.

The 15 philosophical books that I've written before this one provide the scholarly side of my preparation for this book. But the intellectual action in the lecture halls and seminar rooms of the University of Notre Dame, where I taught for 15 years, is what really began to rev my philosophical engine and show me the practical effect of great ideas in launching a good life.

In that time as a professor of philosophy at Notre Dame, I sometimes taught as much as an eighth of the student body in a given year. My most popular course was my freshman Philosophy 101, Introduction to Philosophy. It was anything but a death march through the history of philosophy — no plugging along, putting one footnote in front of another, dragging my charges through names and theories, dates, and titles regardless of their relevance or interest to modern life. My students and I took, by contrast, a lively, energetic look, filled with all appropriate drama and humor, at the fundamental issues that pose the ultimate context for the most basic understandings of life.

Philosophical questions often deal with serious issues, but we don't need to be particularly somber in our approach to them. We can actually have fun thinking about things that matter. In my Notre Dame course, for example, I'd tell as many stories derived from the wild and weird events of everyday life at the end of the century as I'd take from the lives of the great philosophers throughout previous centuries. Personal tales from my own wild trajectory through this world often provided just the right imaginative boost necessary to help first-time philosophers see the importance of a particular philosophical question about life — and even glimpse the best path toward its resolution.

> *Philosophy is so awesome. Who would have guessed?*
>
> — A Notre Dame undergraduate

Since those days in the classroom, I've been living an incredible adventure as a public philosopher, engaged in soul searching and world-view building with people from all around the world and in nearly every walk of life. I've spoken to thousands of company presidents, military officers, and educators, as well as tens of thousands of managers, small-business owners, and front-line workers. And I've gleaned much more from them all than I ever imagined.

Extensive work in the world of business has shown me especially how many extremely smart people live in our time — those who regularly show great intelligence and even brilliance in their professional activities and who don't want to feel like dummies in dealing with the ultimate issues of life, even though they may never get to think about such concepts in any extended or disciplined way. In these pages, I intend to use everything that I've learned to help you bridge some of those huge gaps that too often exist between academic philosophy and the practical concerns of real life that everyone faces daily.

The greatest philosophers always seek to understand life. They want to attain the deepest perspective they can about this world and about any other world that may exist. They take nothing for granted but question and probe in search of illumination, insight, and what some call "enlightenment." We all want to understand the context within which we live and move and exist. And getting at least a good start on that task is the humble purpose of this book.

> *In the country of the blind, the one eyed man is king.*
>
> — Michael Apostolius

You don't need to be a world-class visionary to benefit from looking more closely at the fundamental issues of your life. Any new measure of understanding is a move in the right direction.

In our look at the great philosophical questions, we will allow ourselves to ask basic and probing questions about what it is to be a human being in this world, what life is all about, and how we can live in the most satisfying ways. We ponder the most important things in life. We tackle head on some of those most fundamental issues that we too often dance around and never really address.

I love being a philosopher full time. People come up to me and ask me the most amazing questions. Sometimes they tell me the most incredible stories. It is such questions and such stories that will help us make our way forward, as I share them with you throughout this book for both intellectual and emotional leverage on the Big Issues.

Philosophical issues are all connected with each other in interesting ways. But I've written this book so that you can start anywhere or read different chapters independently of each other. Of course, if you start here and read on you'll be following the order of my own thinking. But the point is that you need not. This is a reference guide that is for your convenience and is intended to answer at least many of the questions you might have about philosophy and philosophical thought.

Conventions Used in This Book

I've put quotes from great philosophers and other insightful thinkers throughout the text as a spice to our stew. You don't have to read them to get what is going on in the body of the book, but, boy, you'd miss some great wisdom nuggets if you didn't. You can turn this book open to almost any page and get wisdom that doesn't come from me, but that I'm happy to bring you. You can also skip the boxed inserts that are shaded, if you want. They add subsidiary information or perspective on what I'm presenting, and are often lots of fun, but they are not absolutely necessary either. Also, be on the lookout for icons that will guide you to stories, great ideas, and things you might particularly want to think about.

I use the word "we" a lot in this book, and that's not often done in the other ...For Dummies books. It's for a special reason. In philosophy, ultimately, there are no authoritative experts. We are all in this together. I often ask you to consult your intuitions about something, and I sometimes suggest what we human beings usually arrive at when we do so. I sketch out the deep contours of experiences we all have. And I ask you to think through many issues for yourself. We are on a journey of understanding together. So feel free to talk back to me if you ever think I'm getting something wrong.

What You're Not to Read

Sidebars, summaries, and bullet points are all for your convenience. They are not essential parts of what we have here, but are just helpful extras. Read them as you choose. And feel free to skip over them if time demands. You'll still get the main ideas, but you'll miss a lot of good stuff if you don't check in to them at some point.

Also, catch yourself if you spend too much time staring blankly at a page, mesmerized. Philosophy can sometimes have that effect. And, please, try not to ever fall asleep with this book in your hands. It might give other people the wrong idea about the exciting, rousing, exhilarating enterprise of philosophy.

Foolish Assumptions

I am assuming that you are new to philosophy. You're not new to all the questions of philosophy — you've been asking some of them since you were little. But I'm assuming that you are new to the discipline of philosophical thinking. I don't take for granted that you've ever sat in a philosophy classroom, or even that you've ever donned a toga. I assume only that you sometimes wonder about life and this world, and want to get your bearings a little better.

In philosophy, it's dangerous to make any foolish assumptions, so play along with me here. Hold on to your questions, use them to challenge this text, and be prepared to employ your own insights about life to evaluate what I say. If you are that rare reader who already has had a philosophy course, or proudly hold a (non-income generating) degree in philosophy, temporarily suspend everything you thought you knew, and let's go at this afresh. If you did once have a philosophy course and have forgotten it all, it won't be too hard for us to start anew. Welcome to my world of philosophy.

How This Book Is Organized

This book is divided into eight parts. Each part introduces you to an important area of philosophical thinking.

Part I: What Is Philosophy, Anyway?

This part gives you a basic orientation to what philosophy is and what philosophers do. Who were the great philosophers, and why have many of them been so controversial as well as influential?

We look at the importance of asking philosophical questions about your life, and see the role that beliefs can play in determining our experience of the world. This part launches us on the philosophical quest for wisdom.

Part II: How Do We Know Anything?

What is a belief? What is knowledge? How can we be sure that we get the real truth as we go through life? Our beliefs are the map by which we steer through life. It's very important that they be accurate and guide us well.

In this part, I introduce you to some of the most important questions in the area of philosophy known as *epistemology,* or theory of knowledge. We ask what the role of rationality is in life, and what it takes for a belief to be rational. We examine some of the strangest and deepest questions ever posed to human beings by the ancient skeptic philosophers. And, finally, we look at the nature of evidence and proof and ask whether it is ever rational to believe anything without good evidence.

In this part of the book, we develop some tools that it will be helpful to have as we tackle some of the most controversial big issues of philosophy.

Part III: What Is the Good?

What is the status of ethics in this world of ours? Are right and wrong just subjective, or are there objective standards for human conduct? In this part, we take a look at a few basic issues for understanding the role of ethics or morality in life.

If you aren't sure how ethical concerns relate to the rest of life, this is where I hope you'll be able to get your bearings. We look at what character is and see the role of the Golden Rule in a good life.

Part IV: Are We Ever Really Free?

Morality presupposes freedom. You can't be really praised or blamed for something that was not up to you. Many of our attitudes and emotions take it for granted that human beings have the freedom to chart their own way in life, or at least through the day. Do we? Or is free will an illusion?

In this part, we examine some of the most interesting challenges to the common belief that we are, at some fundamental level, free. We look at different philosophical views on freedom and try to work our way toward something that can make sense of our experience.

Part V: The Incredible, Invisible You

Are you just a complex organic body, or do you also have a nonphysical mind or soul? Is there more to human beings than meets the eye, even the eye aided by microscopes and MRI machines?

In this part, we address the age old question of whether there is a soul. We look at philosophical arguments on both sides of the question, and we try to evaluate what has been said. Am I a soul man or not? And what about you? This part can help you decide.

Part VI: What's the Deal with Death?

In this part, we confront one of the most difficult topics we ever have to think about. We examine the fear of death in its many forms and then look at what philosophers have had to say to help calm us down when we contemplate the ultimate off-ramp from life.

I introduce you in this part to the arguments for and against there being life after death. Do we survive bodily death, or is it an absolute end? We see what philosophers have said, and we try to get our own bearings on this crucial issue.

Part VII: Is There a God?

Some have called this the biggest issue of all. What is the most basic reality there is? Is it material, or could it be spiritual? We look at the great debate over this issue and examine the major arguments pro and con.

One thing that we begin to see in this part is how all the major issues of philosophy connect up with each other. We are each constructing a world view as we live our lives. Is it accurate and insightful or not? This part can help you contemplate what the cornerstone of your world view ought to be.

Part VIII: The Meaning of Life

See, we don't mess around in this book — we get straight to the big issues. I give you the major positions on the question of whether this life has a meaning, and then I give you answers. I actually say what I think the meaning of life is. Curious? You can skip straight to this, but I bet that, if you do, you'll backtrack to put it all in perspective.

In this part, we also look at one of the most fascinating and controversial arguments ever devised by a philosophical seeker, Pascal's Wager. Pascal claimed centuries ago that life is a wager. Are you making the right bet? Read this part to see.

Part IX: The Part of Tens

This is the part of the book that will put you on a fast track for impressing your friends with how much you know about philosophy. Are you in the need for weekend, party-size nuggets of wisdom and nibblets of historical insight about the great thinkers? Read this part. But after you've used what you discover here, be prepared to quickly go refresh your drink and reload your plate, leaving your conversation partners alone for a few moments to admire your unexpected erudition.

Icons Used in This Book

Throughout the book, I place icons to direct your attention to particular points of interest.

Next to this icon you can find information about some great philosopher.

This icon points the way to some great concept or brainstorm that can help you break through an issue or think about it differently.

A story from my life or reading accompanies this signpost. Expect vivid mental pictures. Or a concern over my sanity. Just remember, I am a philosopher.

This icon guides you to a piece of advice for thinking through a difficult issue.

This is our hazard sign. When you see it, beware of jumping to conclusions, or jumping off a bridge. This icon signals a philosophical fallacy or false step.

Where to Go from Here

This book is chock full of all those questions you may have long wanted to think about and talk with someone about, but have never had the time or opportunity to tackle head on. The best way to absorb all that I will be giving you is to share it with a friend or spouse. Talk about the issues you find here, share perspectives, compare thoughts and feelings with someone you respect. We all have to make our way in this world. And none of us is sure of all the answers. But if we can help each other think through the most funda-mental questions, we can make amazing progress in gaining clarity about our lives.

I am giving you the perfect excuse to bring up topics that you may never get to talk to anyone about, on a normal daily basis. Tell them you're reading a strange book on philosophy and that the philosopher has given you an assignment to ask someone else their opinion on any topic you feel the least bit puzzled about. And when they get intrigued by your newfound wisdom, and ask to borrow this book, just smile and tell them where to buy their own copy. You'll want it around to go back over.

And tell me what you think. E-mail me your philosophical reactions at my own philosophical website, www.MorrisInstitute.com, where I and my band of merry philosophers can be reached at any time. I want to know what you are thinking about these issues. We're all in this together!

Part I
What Is Philosophy, Anyway?

In this part . . .

In this part, we look at what philosophy is. What did all those bearded guys in togas actually start? And how should we view the philosophical search for wisdom now?

Chapter 1

Great Thinkers, Deep Thoughts

Conversation you're not likely to hear in the 20th century:

Him: "Hey, Honey, what do you want to do tonight?"

Her: "How about some philosophy?"

Him: "Sounds great!"

Her: "Invite the neighbors!"

Okay, let's face it. For at least a hundred years, philosophy hasn't exactly enjoyed the most appealing reputation in our culture. But that situation's about to change. This deepest, most exciting, and ultimately most practical activity of the mind has been misunderstood for long enough. We're going to do something about that. You and I. In this book.

A Few Nuts Spice the Cake

There may be no intellectual activity more misunderstood and wrongly maligned as philosophy. The great American historian Henry Adams once characterized the entire enterprise of philosophy as consisting of nothing more than "unintelligible answers to insoluble problems." As far back as the 16th century, the prominent French essayist Michael de Montaigne proclaimed that "philosophy is doubt." And, of course, who enjoys doubt? Doubt is often uncomfortable. Doubt can even be scary.

The 19th-century philosophical wild man, Friedrich Nietzsche, took it one more step and even went so far as to characterize philosophy as "an explosive, in the presence of which everything is in danger." So, then, it really comes as no surprise to see Nietzsche's predecessor, the English poet John Keats, asking, "Do not all charms fly at the mere touch of cold philosophy?"

In ancient times, the famous Roman statesman and author Cicero complained, "There is nothing so absurd that it hasn't been said by some philosopher." Of course, he, too, was "some philosopher." But what about the other human beings who bear that label? What's our view of them?

More fans of philosophy

The following quotes show what some prominent historical individuals have had to say about philosophy and philosophers:

Philosophy is such an impertinently litigious lady that a man had as good be engaged in lawsuits as have to do with her.
— Sir Isaac Newton

It has been said that metaphysics is the finding of bad reasons for what we believe on instinct.
— W. Somerset Maugham

Wonder is the foundation of all philosophy, inquiry the progress, ignorance the end.
— Montaigne

Philosophy will clip an angel's wings . . .
— John Keats

All philosophies, if you ride them home, are nonsense; but some are greater nonsense than others.
— Samuel Butler

Philosophy consists largely of one philosopher arguing that all the others are jackasses. He usually proves it, and I should add that he also usually proves that he is one himself.
— H.L. Mencken

If I wished to punish a province, I would have it governed by philosophers.
— Frederick the Great

There is only one thing that a philosopher can be relied on to do, and that is to contradict other philosophers.
— William James

When he who hears doesn't know what he who speaks means, and when he who speaks doesn't know what he himself means — that is philosophy.
— Voltaire

There is nothing so strange and so unbelievable that it has not been said by one philosopher or the other.
— Descartes (the Father of Modern Philosophy, strange and unbelievable as that may seem)

I have tried, too, in my time to be a philosopher but, I don't know how, cheerfulness was always breaking through.
— Oliver Edwards (18th century)

Philosophers? Crazy! Philosophers? Otherworldly! Philosophers? Gloomy! When we hear the word, we tend to have this modern image come to mind of badly groomed academics, carelessly dressed in tweed sport coats, wrinkled shirts, and rumpled pants, who go through life coated with chalk dust, stroking their beards, bearing scowls on their faces and arcane thoughts in their heads, all the while writing on blackboards in capital letters such weighty words as "DEATH," and "DESPAIR."

In 1707, Jonathan Swift wrote the following comment:

> *The various opinions of philosophers have scattered through the world as many plagues of the mind as Pandora's box did those of the body; only with this difference, that they have not left hope at the bottom.*

In our own era, the widely read American journalist and literary critic H.L. Mencken even once went so far as to announce, "There is no record in human history of a happy philosopher." (But, hey, remember that these guys never met *me!*)

So what's the deal here? Philosophy, done right, should be the *opposite* of all this gloom and doom stuff. It should be exciting, liberating, provocative, illuminating, helpful, *and fun.* Philosophers themselves should be great company, the life of any party, a hoot and a half. (Okay, so maybe I'm getting a little carried away here.)

> *If Wisdom be attainable, let us not only win but enjoy it.*
>
> — Cicero

I must admit that I know of at least a few great thinkers in human history I'm glad I don't have as neighbors. And some of their books can be . . . well, should I say, "less than scintillating"? And, all right, as long as I'm trying to be as candid here as possible, I should be willing to acknowledge — without naming any names, of course — that I have actually met a few exceedingly peculiar social misfits who seem to be fish out of water in ordinary life, and whose only discernible accomplishment appears to be an academic doctoral degree in philosophy from a major university. Along with, perhaps, a few unintelligible publications bearing their names. And, unfortunately, a teaching position that places them as ambassadors of philosophy in front of classrooms full of bewildered and yet sometimes bemused undergraduates. But things are not always what they seem.

> *There is often wisdom under a shabby cloak.*
>
> — Caecilius Statius

The enterprise of philosophy itself, philosophy as a genuine human activity, can and should be great. Not to mention the fact that philosophers can be our friends. On this topic, I should perhaps quote the great poet John Milton, who wrote:

How charming is divine philosophy!

Not harsh, and crabbed as dull fools suppose,

But musical as is Apollo's lute,

And a perpetual feast of nectar'd sweets,

Where no cruel surfeit reigns.

In other words, good stuff indeed.

The same Cicero who voiced his irritation at bad philosophers didn't shrink from praising a good one. He once described Socrates as "the first man to bring philosophy into the marketplace." In many ways, it is Socrates' example that we are following in this book. I want to bring philosophy back into the marketplace of ideas that are seriously contending for your attention. I plan to bring some pretty lofty ideas down to earth and examine their relevance for our day-to-day lives. My goal is to help you get clearer on some of the issues that matter the most, but that we ordinarily tend to think about the least. In this book, I hope that together we'll be explorers of the spirit, charting our way forward as we go. We'll take a close look at some exciting ideas, quite a few amazing questions, and several new perspectives for everything we do. We won't be able to nail down a definitive answer for every question that may arise, but if you stick with me, you're likely to find yourself making more progress in appreciating — and understanding — these topics than you may at first imagine. I might sometimes ask some nutty-sounding questions, but I promise you that, as you consider the answers, those queries are going to help you obtain some pretty amazing perspectives on this life that we're living. Our goal, throughout, is nothing less than the quest for wisdom itself.

Life is a festival only to the wise.

— Ralph Waldo Emerson

Socrates on the Examination that Counts

Socrates liked to walk the streets and go to parties, engaging anyone he could in philosophical dialogue. For him, philosophy was not a dry, intellectual subject, a game for pedants and scholars, but a requirement for living well. He even went so far as to famously proclaim the following axiom:

The unexamined life is not worth living.

But what in the world does this statement mean? Everyone knows what it means to say, "This car isn't worth $40,000," or "This shirt isn't worth $150," or "The tickets to this concert aren't worth $80 each." But what exactly does it mean to say about a certain form of life, a certain lifestyle — what Socrates is calling "the unexamined life" — that it's "not worth living"?

Essentially, an item is "worth" what it costs if the value or benefits that you derive from it are equal to or greater than the price you pay for it — which is ultimately the same value as the underlying effort or energy that you put into obtaining the resources you need to pay that price. Whenever I think about making a certain purchase, I always ask myself whether the item is truly worth the asking price: Is it worth that amount of money? Is it worth the work it took for me to earn that amount?

A pair of shoes that a wealthy person could see as a "good deal" might be perceived by a poorer individual as far too expensive. The less well-off shopper may need to work far too hard or too long to provide that same amount of money. He may then conclude that the shoes aren't worth the cost.

But how exactly does this commonplace sort of judgment relate to Socrates' famous claim? What is the cost — the worth — of the "unexamined life"? Well, first we need to understand what Socrates means by this phrase.

What *is* "the unexamined life"? Unfortunately, it's the form of life that far too many people live: Getting up, dressing, eating, going to work, breaking for lunch, working some more, going home, eating again, watching TV, leafing through magazines, exchanging a few words with fellow family members in the house or with friends on the phone, changing for bed, and falling to sleep — just to repeat the same routine all over, and over, and over, without ever thinking about what it all means or how life should be really lived.

We wake up already in motion in this life. The raft is already out on the river, and the current simply carries us forward.

When we're young, other people decide what we wear, what we eat, and when we can play. All too often, even after we're older, other people still decide what we do during the day. We make choices, lots of them, but often from a limited selection of options that our environment, our friends, families, and employers, and simple habit, present to us. Rarely, if ever, do we stop to reflect on what we truly want in life, on who we are and want to become, on what difference we want to make in the world, and thus on what's really right for *us.* And *that* is the unexamined life — the life that is lived at some level almost as a sleepwalker, somnambulating away the hours, days, and years. It's a life that is experienced on automatic pilot — a life based on values and beliefs that we've never really looked at, never really tested, never examined for ourselves.

Many people seem to fear self-examination, as if looking at and evaluating their most basic beliefs and values is somehow a threat. But a philosophically reflective examination of our most basic assumptions and commitments doesn't necessarily have a corrosive effect. It may, by contrast, have a *purifying* effect. The fundamental goal of philosophical examination isn't criticism in a negative sense, or any sort of rejection or abandonment. The true goal is *understanding.* And yet a greater level of understanding often results in a refocusing, a shedding of unnecessary or unimportant activities and an adopting of others — rebalancing and changing our lives in a positive way.

The unexamined life, on the other hand, isn't one of deep personal understanding. It's not a life of self-directed positive change.

And you pay a *big* price for living such a life. What's the price you pay? What's the cost? Socrates identifies it when he states that this form of life, the unexamined life, is not worth what you have to pay for it — when he, in fact, plainly says that this form of life simply is not worth *living.*

The price that you pay for an unexamined life, therefore, is precisely that — your *entire life.* And you can pay no greater price for anything. Notice, however, that Socrates didn't say that the unexamined life is not worth *anything.* He wisely left open the viewpoint that some positive value exists in any life, however unreflective that life may be. This great philosopher said only that the unexamined life isn't worth the high price that you must pay for it — the investment of all your energies in a direction that's not of your own choosing.

Philosophy, on the other hand, as an activity of reflection giving rise to a wiser way of life, involves investing your life energies in something that may prove worth the cost. Is the *examined* life, then, guaranteed to be worth living? Is such a life, alone, worth living? Well, Socrates never actually said so. His statement about the unexamined life does seem to imply, by contrast, such a conclusion. But the wise philosopher left us to draw that ultimate conclusion on our own, by examining ourselves and our own lives. And I hope that what you find in this book helps show you the way to such an examination.

> *Make it thy business to know thyself, which is the most difficult lesson in the world.*
>
> — Cervantes

The Questions We'll Ask

In this book, as in my Notre Dame philosophy course, we look at questions dealing with issues of belief, skepticism, and knowledge; good and evil; free will and determinism, death and life after death; the existence of God; and the meaning of life.

We touch on most of the main fields of philosophy — epistemology, ethics, metaphysics, and the philosophy of religion. And we consult many of the great thinkers of history. Throughout, I intend to keep the orientation of the discussion as practical as it is theoretical, because I believe that the best use of theory is in better practice. With each issue, we ask what difference it makes in our lives and how it helps us to chart our way forward in this world.

There is frequently more to be learned from the unexpected questions of a child than the discourses of men, who talk in a road, according to the notions they have borrowed and the prejudices of their education.

— John Locke

Here are some of the questions you can expect to find in these pages:

- ✔ How can we really know anything?
- ✔ What is the importance of rationality to a good life?
- ✔ What does the word *good* really mean?
- ✔ Is ethics just a matter of opinion, or do objective moral rules exist that are binding on every person?
- ✔ Why should we be moral?
- ✔ Why do people disagree so much on ethics?
- ✔ Are people really free, or are our actions all determined by genetics and environment?
- ✔ Can anyone predict the future, in principle, in every detail?
- ✔ What's the difference between a human being and a robot?
- ✔ Do people have souls, or are we just physically complex organisms?
- ✔ What is death?
- ✔ Why is death so feared by so many people?
- ✔ Do we somehow still exist after death?
- ✔ Where does the concept of God come from?
- ✔ Does God really exist?
- ✔ Why does the world contain so much evil?
- ✔ Can anyone prove what the truth is on such ultimate issues, or must we accept them just as matters of faith?
- ✔ What, for that matter, *is* faith?
- ✔ What is the meaning of life?
- ✔ How can people be happy?

These questions cover only a few of the basic concepts that I will consider with you throughout this book.

It is better to ask some of the questions than to know all of the answers.

— James Thurber

Chapter 2

Philosophy as an Activity

- -

In This Chapter

▶ Seeing what philosophy as an activity is

▶ Finding out how to do philosophy yourself

▶ Appreciating the power of belief

▶ Peering into Plato's Cave

- -

Philosophy is not a theory but an activity.

— Ludwig Wittgenstein (1889–1951)

*P*hilosophy at its best is an activity more than a body of knowledge. In an ancient sense, done right, it is a healing art. It's intellectual self-defense. It's a form of therapy. But it's also much more. Philosophy is map-making for the soul, cartography for the human journey. It's an important navigational tool for life that too many modern people try to do without.

In this chapter, we see exactly what that activity is, as well as how to do it well. I show you the power that belief can have in human life, and I bring you a distinction that Plato drew so vividly that it has echoed down the centuries, helping to free people from illusion and lead them into truth.

Outward Bound for the Mind

Philosophy can be a little like Outward Bound for the mind. Intellectual spelunking, mental rock climbing, cognitive rapelling, rafting, and reconnoitering. Sometimes it can seem like a conceptual version of Extreme Sports.

On those occasions when we push philosophical inquiry to the very limits of our world views, we find ourselves temporarily letting go of our customary assumptions, intellectually free falling and hoping the chute will open when we need it. When we do that, the point is to experience the outer boundaries of our ordinary beliefs, to come to understand the status of our most important presuppositions, those background convictions that support the perspectives and decisions governing our day-to-day actions, and that we normally just take for granted.

We question things as deeply as we can, in order to understand as deeply as possible. The ultimate goal is a firmer grip on who we are and what our place in the world really is.

But more often, philosophy can be thought of as a package of existential survival skills, along with the determined application of those skills in a sort of a search-and-rescue mission for the soul. Philosophy is not just a game. It's not just a mental sport. It is the most vital use of our minds for getting our bearings in life.

Mapping Our Way Forward

Consulting the great thinkers of the past, as we draw our own philosophical maps for the present and future, is like stopping to ask a cabbie or a cop for directions, rather than just wandering around lost. It's getting the advice of those who know, people who have been in the neighborhood before and can find their way around. We inevitably do a little exploring of your own, but any good advice and direction we get can help.

In any expedition into unfamiliar terrain, it pays to have a native guide to lead us, but ultimately we all have to pull ourselves up the side of the hill. We partner with the great thinkers who have gone before us and, with their help, try to see our own vistas and make our own way.

The popular American essayist and philosopher Ralph Waldo Emerson at one point wrote

> *Meek young men grow up in libraries, believing it their duties to accept the views which Cicero, which Locke, which Bacon, have given; forgetful that Cicero, Locke, and Bacon were only young men in libraries when they wrote these books.*

"Who am I to think about these things?" each of us is tempted to ask. Well, who did Socrates think he was to be tackling such ideas? Who was Plato? In the first century, Seneca wrote,

> *Philosophy did not find Plato already a nobleman; it made him one.*

It is every bit as much our business to ask about these things as it was theirs. But because they have already started the process, we can benefit from their thinking.

Who consorts with the wise will wise become.

— Menander

We consult the writings of the great dead philosophers not for any final word on the ultimate questions of philosophy, but rather to help get us started, using the insights and avoiding the pitfalls already discovered by those who have gone before us. Early in this century, William Ralph Inge explained,

The object of studying philosophy is to know one's own mind, not other people's.

So when we are doing philosophy, we go to the books of past thinkers not to take inventory of their thoughts, or to gather up from them all the answers we might want, but, rather, we go for the assistance and inspiration we need to do our own jobs as thinkers.

Emerson comments,

Books are the best of things, well used; abused, among the worst. What is the right use? What is the one end which all means go to effect? They are for nothing but to inspire.

I hope in this book to begin to inspire you as I have been inspired by the books of others to look into these matters for yourself and fight to attain a bit of your own wisdom for life. Likewise, I'll be your guide, as I use many guides myself, to make our way forward together.

The Extreme Power of Belief

Right up front, let me pass on an important lesson I've learned about the role of assumption and belief in our lives. It demonstrates our need for the discipline of philosophy, in an unusual way.

For a long time, my family had wanted to own a gas grill, the kind that has a fat tank of propane under it. But people had warned me about the dangers of propane gas. It's really combustible. And, breathed, they said, it's toxic. I seemed to remember that I had heard or read somewhere that in its natural state, propane gas is without odor, but that refiners added a smell so that any leaking gas could be detected immediately and avoided.

Socrates wasn't the only philosopher who enjoyed being involved in a good grilling (bad joke: his relentless questioning of people), so when my family offered to get me the long-discussed gas grill for Father's Day, I agreed with enthusiasm to do my part in making all their charred dreams come true. My wife called Sears and ordered a deluxe model. She also offered to pay to have it assembled and delivered. Philosophers are often not the best at assembling anything other than ideas.

Some days later, we received a call from the store that the grill was in, assembled, and "ready to go." My wife bought the burgers and hot dogs, and all the other normal cookout stuff, and prepared for a feast. When the delivery guys arrived, they pointed out that I would have to hook up the gas tank to the grill itself when I was ready to use it. They explained that they were required to deliver it unattached. I assumed it was dangerous to transport the tank hooked up. Poisonous gas might take out the delivery guys.

They drove away, and with the assistance of written instructions and diagrams, I went to work trying to hook up the tank. I fumbled with the hose and connectors, and kept getting it wrong, and I felt myself getting short of breath. I was doing all this outside so that any leaking propane would dissipate quickly, but obviously there wasn't enough breeze and I was getting too much of it into my lungs. My family watched as I adopted a new rhythm of action. I'd take a deep breath, run up to the grill, feverishly bolt and twist and hammer, and dash back to a chair 20 feet away, gasping for fresh air. I did this quite a few times until I thought the connection was complete. But when I tried to light the grill, there was no fire. As I hung over it inspecting all the connections, I could feel myself getting light-headed and nauseous from the gas.

We decided to call Sears. I explained what I had done, and that I was obviously breathing too much propane at this point, I was so sick. Mental confusion was starting to set in. As a philosopher, I feared I was losing precious brain cells. My lungs ached. In my mental fog, I could hear the Sears guy asking me a question.

"Where did you take the tank to get your propane?"

"What do you mean? The grill was just delivered this afternoon, and the guy said it was ready to go."

"Oh, it was, except for the gas. We sell only new tanks with our grills, and they come empty. You have to go to a gas station or mini-mart to get gas for it. That's why it won't light. You got an empty tank."

Oh. Well. Boy, did I feel silly. I was being asphyxiated by a false belief. I was having physical symptoms from something that wasn't there. I smelled it. It made me dizzy. I felt sick. But a breath of fresh information was all it took, and I was fine. Physically, at least. Mentally, I was a bit mortified. My wife and kids laughed and laughed. And went to get some take-out food.

People can die of mere imagination.

— Chaucer

In a way, it's really good that this happened to me. As a philosopher, I learned something important about the power of our beliefs, and our imaginations, as well as about the hidden assumptions that can govern our thinking, acting, and feeling. The mind is indeed a powerful thing. And false beliefs can have a big impact on us.

The image of Plato's Cave

Plato had a memorable image for the false beliefs and illusions we too often suffer. He wrote that we are all like people living in a cave, chained down to the floor, our gazes fixed on shadows flitting across a wall, shadows we mistake for realities.

Plato's image of the cave was actually quite elaborate. Imagine that behind us in this cavern, he went on, there is a fire burning that casts shadows on the walls that are all we ever see, until the day someone breaks free of his chains, sees our situation as it truly is, and escapes the cave altogether, emerging into real daylight. At first, he would be blinded by the glare of the sun, that object of which the cavern fire was but a poor copy. But then his eyes would begin to adjust and make out real objects, animals, rocks, and trees. Seeing the difference between the outside world and the poor dim shadow world in which he had been imprisoned, he returns back into the cave to convince his fellows to break their chains as well and ascend into the light of reality.

The philosophical Houdini

The man who first escapes the cave of illusion that Plato thinks we live in is the philosopher, the one among us who comes to realize that we are all in some way living lives of illusion, held captive by shadows and chains not of our own making. When he brings back into the cave his strange tale of other realities, he will be cheered by some, jeered by others. We have a way of becoming comfortable with our illusions. And so we are easily threatened by any strange reports of greater realities. But the true philosopher tries to free as many of his fellow captives as possible, liberating them to live in the broader, brighter realities that lie beyond the narrow confines of their customary perceptions.

That is a vivid image of the ultimate task of philosophy. Its goal is to free us from illusion and to help us get a grip on the most fundamental realities.

What illusions are you living under right now? What things do you value that really lack the importance you attribute to them? What could you be ignoring that is really of true value? What assumptions are you making about your life that may be based on appearances and not realities? Most people are chained down by all sorts of illusions. It is the goal of philosophy, well done, to help us all break those chains.

We actually have no choice of whether to have a philosophy or not, of whether to be philosophers or not. We inevitably operate out of some philosophical world view, however well formed or incomplete it might be. Our choice is between bad philosophy unreflectively absorbed from the culture around us and the prejudices of our time, or good philosophy built on critical questioning and sustained thought.

We can be poor thinkers or good philosophers. But quality comes only with care. So, careful thinking makes for the best philosophy. Does your philosophy of life imprison you or liberate you? In this book, I try to dispel some of the myths and platitudes of our own age and get out of the cave of our false assumptions. We seek philosophical enlightenment, philosophical liberation.

The first day of the rest of your life need not begin and end in Plato's Cave.

Plato as the source

Plato is seen by many to be the ultimate fount of all western philosophy.

Out of Plato come all things that are still written and debated among men of thought.
— Ralph Waldo Emerson

The safest characterization of the European philosophical tradition is that it consists of a series of footnotes to Plato.
— Alfred North Whitehead

Chapter 3

The Love of Wisdom

Things have their seasons, and even certain kinds of eminence go in and out of style. But wisdom has an advantage: She is eternal.

— Balthasar Gracian

As you delve more deeply into the subject, you find many reasons to read, study, and practice philosophy in your life. Philosophy, as a way of thinking, for example, cultivates three intellectual skills that are very important for any of us to possess in the modern world. Philosophy also cultivates wisdom.

First, in this chapter, I look for a moment at those three skills. Then I say a bit more about wisdom — in particular, what it is and why it matters.

The Triple-A Skill Set of Philosophy

Philosophy is, simply put, a way of thinking. More accurately, however, it is a *bundle* of ways of thinking. It's a set of mental tools. And that fact is directly relevant to the question of why we study philosophy. It's not just to amaze our friends with our own profundity, perplex our colleagues with a newfound depth, or irritate family members with crazy-sounding questions (although first-year college students seem to value that last possibility the most in connection with their beginning philosophy courses). We study philosophy because of the mental skills it cultivates in our lives as well as for the new perspectives it gives us.

In my years at Notre Dame, every student was required to take two courses in philosophy. The fact that, long ago, Notre Dame required four courses in philosophy didn't assuage the students' initial complaints. Why should a pre-med or business major waste any time at all in a philosophy classroom? Wasn't this rule much like requiring that every student take a course in Ancient Babylonian entomology? Wasn't it just some esoteric relic of the humanities curriculum of the past, no longer relevant to modern life?

Why, for that matter, should any busy business executive take time out to read philosophy? Why should a parent at home engaged in the demanding tasks of raising children ever sneak away with a book of philosophy? What's its relevance? What could possibly be the payoff? The following sections may give you some answers.

Paralysis without analysis

Philosophy as a way of thinking cultivates our ability to *analyze* complicated problems. It helps us untie mental knots. It teaches us to get to the core of an issue. It shows us how to peel away peripheral issues and penetrate to the essence of a matter: What's really important here? What's ultimately at issue? How can I break this problem down into more manageable questions?

Analysis is a skill that you need everywhere in life. Lawyers analyze complex claims and sort out the issues; physicians analyze symptoms; detectives look for patterns in the evidence; business people sort through the parts of an intricate deal; parents try to untangle and get a grip on the issues troubling a family. The skill of analysis is useful in every walk of life. Analysis is so prominent in philosophical ways of thinking that a major trend of 20th-century thought is even known as *analytic philosophy* because of its emphasis on the centrality of this skill. But all good philosophy involves close analysis.

Ultimately, philosophy teaches us how to analyze our lives: Who am I? What do I really want? What is this life all about? What can make me happy? How can I make my greatest contribution to the world? What are my highest talents? How can I best make use of my time?

In following a philosophical analysis of a major human question and learning from some of the greatest thinkers in history how to tackle a complicated issue, we can learn to be better analysts ourselves and more analytical in other aspects of our lives. Now, I don't mean this statement as an endorsement of analysis as the most important mental skill or as a claim that a practice of philosophical analysis is somehow paramount in human life. It's not. It is, however, important. We are genuinely paralyzed in many ways in life if we are unable to analyze properly the circumstances that we are in, and the opportunites that we face.

Man is but a reed, the weakest thing in nature, but he is a thinking reed.

— Blaise Pascal

Analysis is a vital mental skill. It must, however, be used appropriately. There is a well-known phenomenon, commonly called *analysis paralysis,* which results when too much thinking actually gets in the way of action — or in the way of feeling. A person can analyze a relationship to death. The unexamined life may not be worth living, as Chapter 1 explains, but the *unlived* life is definitely not worth examining. Thinking should never replace taking action; thinking should merely guide what we do. All good things can be misused. And certainly, logical, analytic thinking can be misused. It is up to each of us to use it well.

My point here is that the better you become at analyzing complex problems, the better off you are for solving them. Analysis is a skill that philosophy cultivates. And it's a skill for all of life. The real truth about thinking and action is that, if you don't possess analysis as a life skill, you're much more likely to experience fruitless paralysis in the face of difficulty. Analytical acumen, at its best, truly liberates.

The skill of assessment

Philosophy trains us to analyze. It also trains us to *assess* competing claims. Do people have free will, or are all our actions determined by heredity and environment? Does God exist . . . or not? Do humans survive physical death, or is everyone destined for personal extinction on the cessation of bodily functions? Does life truly have meaning, or is everything we do ultimately without any real sense and purpose? Is rollerblading great exercise, or is it the fastest route to the emergency room? (Okay, so not all questions are cosmic in proportion.)

We are often confronted in everyday life by competing claims and alternative proposals that we must assess: Should we appropriate more funds to increase the quality of our product, or should we concentrate instead on beefing up our advertising? One group claims that we need more research and development; another declares that only more marketing is necessary. One group of experts says that children need more freedom. Another group claims that they require more clearly defined limits and discipline. How do you evaluate and assess such competing claims? Philosophy trains the mind in the fine art of *assessment.*

All that glitters is not gold. Appearances and realities can diverge. We live today in a world of hype, exaggeration, and hyperbole. Plato's Cave is bigger and deeper than ever before (see Chapter 2). Illusions rule the world. Everyone has something to sell, and we're bombarded every day by claims that we must be able to evaluate. In a world of conflicting views vying for acceptance, how do we separate the wheat from the chaff, the sheep from the goats, the collectibles from the trash? Caution is necessary. We need discernment. And discernment — assessment — also is a skill that philosophy can nurture.

The judgment of man is fallible.

— Ovid

In philosophy, we assess a view by asking for evidence and reasons to think that it's true. We evaluate how one proposal for our acceptance may fit or fail to fit with other things that we already have strong reason to believe or even know to be true.

In assessing a world-view or major philosophical position, just as in evaluating a business proposal, we must ask the following three basic sorts of questions, which we can call the *3 Cs:*

✔ **(C1) Is it coherent?** Do the various components of the view or position hang together logically? Does it make sense? Is it internally consistent? Is it inwardly congruent?

✔ **(C2) Is it complete?** Does it touch on and deal with all the relevant issues that it ought to take in, or does it contain gaps and blind spots? Are any concerns swept under the rug? Is it comprehensive enough?

✔ **(C3) Is it correct?** For a position to merely be coherent and complete isn't enough; the available evidence must point in its direction as the correct contender for truth. Coherence is necessary; completeness is important; but only correctness, in addition, gives you what you fully need. An internally consistent viewpoint that's comprehensive in its sweep but at odds with the facts doesn't do you much good in a practical way.

These, therefore, are the 3 Cs of assessment: coherence, completeness, and correctness. A philosophical position, similar to a business plan, may be correct as far as it goes without going nearly far enough. A viewpoint may be correct, within limits, without being complete enough. Such an assessment tells you that the view needs more development. It may be correct in its main principles but incoherent in some of its less vital components — in which case, it needs some logical retooling before we can accept it as a whole. We must check for and identify all three qualities in a position to evaluate it decisively. Keeping this concept in mind, we can greatly enhance our skills of assessment through our philosophical examinations of any position.

The use of argument

Philosophy cultivates our skills of analysis and assessment. It also schools us on the correct use of *argument*.

Arguments are not, in philosophical terms, shouting matches, verbal tug-o-wars, or altercations. When I was in graduate school in the late '70s, I often started my day by watching a talk show on television. Even in those early days of audience participation and debate-oriented talk shows, I was amazed at what people seemed to think constituted a reasonable exchange of differing ideas. The squared jaws, red faces, and bulging veins that accompanied such rejoinders as "Oh *yeah?*", "Who *says?*", and "That's just *your* opinion!" seemed impervious to the call of real argument. This was, of course, long before chair-throwing, kicking, spitting, and hair pulling began to serve as the vehicles of televised argument. And I'm not just referring metaphorically to the syndicated talk shows of political pundits here. As a culture, Americans these days seem to misunderstand what argument at its best really is.

Reason

Analysis involves the use of *reason*. So does assessment. As does argument. But what exactly *is* reason? The philosophers all use it and urge the rest of us to use it, even as they point out its limits as well as its strengths.

We can think of reason clearly as one of the powers of the mind, as is perception or imagination. It is the power of moving logically from one idea to another, of seeing connections of logic or cause and effect, and of inferring conclusions from given premises. By the power of reason, we can see where truth is to be found.

"Use your head!" we may urge a friend, meaning to advise the use of reason. ("Use the common sense God gave a squirrel!" is sometimes a less complimentary version of the same advice.)

In the history of philosophy, some philosophers have thought that reason could do everything — from discerning the truth of "First Principles" to deducing all less fundamental truths from those same principles. Others have insisted that experience of the empirical world — seeing, hearing, and so on — is necessary for discerning substantive truth about life. Swinging from one extreme to the other characterizes a good deal of the history of philosophy, as it does most of life, for that matter. We often call a person a "rationalist" who views reason as very powerful and who wants an argument for the proof of almost anything he believes. We sometimes call a person an "empiricist" who, by contrast, just keeps hammering away on the importance of sense experience for confirming anything that we believe. "I'll believe it when I see it" is a typical empiricist sentiment. But even the most experientially oriented philosophers value the role of reason in analysis, discernment, evaluation, and inference or logical argument.

In philosophy, an argument is a reasoned presentation of ideas, where you marshal evidence in favor of the truth of a conclusion. Arguments, in their essence, aren't something that you direct at people as you would a gun that you're aiming at a target. You don't primarily argue *with* someone or *at* someone; you present an argument for a conclusion, which you often intend as a means to persuade someone else, but sometimes employ just as a means of discovering for yourself where the truth lies.

> *The aim of argument, or of discussion, should not be victory, but progress.*
>
> — Joseph Joubert

So, in philosophy, arguments aren't the sorts of things that you win or lose. They're not like games or athletic contests of the mind. Even if you engage in an argument with another person in the colloquial sense over a substantive issue — and you truly want to convince your interlocutor of the persuasiveness of your viewpoint — you'd better be able to construct a good argument in the philosophical sense as well. And studying some philosophy helps you know how to do so better than you may already.

In every walk of life, we need to be able to give a reasoned presentation of our beliefs in such a way as to persuade other people. Lawyers aren't the only ones who must worry about convincing others to accept a particular point of view. Persuasive argument is an important part of every management job, is a requirement in the arsenal of any challenged parent, and is as important to preachers and teachers as to practicing scientists. A good argument helps us to intellectually "see" where the truth lies.

In my first year at college, I discovered an important truth about the limitations of argument. For some reason, hair had always been an issue in my family — head hair *and* facial hair. Until I went away to college, my parents had insisted that I shave daily and keep the hair on my head cut fairly short. Off on my own, I let my hair get long and began to grow a Fu Manchu mustache. This bit of rebellion occurred during the early '70s, when a good deal of "the '60s" actually took place. Bell-bottomed pants, ridiculous shirts, and long hair ruled. I shudder now to think what I looked like, but I was exercising my newfound freedom and experimenting with my appearance. A few months later, I saw my mother for the first time since the inception of my new, hirsute look. She offered me a hundred dollars on the spot to shave off my mustache and refused to go to any public place with me until I did. I wish I hadn't taken a stand on principle. Two weeks later, my 'stache itched me half to death, and I shaved with no reward. But that day, mother was adamant and trying any strategy she could. She even went so far as to say to me, point blank, "Something's psychologically *wrong* with anyone who has a beard or mustache!"

I was in my first philosophy course at the time, and was learning how to argue a point, so I wasn't about to let this one pass. I suddenly remembered what philosophers call "argument by counterexample" — that is, you can refute any general claim of the form *All As are Bs* by producing one example of a *B* that's not an *A*. Employing the standard "But, *Mother* . . ." opening of any frustrated adolescent bent on proving a point, I started enumerating aloud all the great personages of history I could think of who had mustaches or beards and yet who were, by any fair estimation, paragons of psychological health and worldly success. Working my way from ancient Greece through the American Civil War, and not forgetting Southern paradigms such as Robert E. Lee, I was taken up short and momentarily struck mute by a sudden realization.

"Mother," I said with all the conviction I could muster, suddenly certain that I had unassailable proof of my own conviction that facial hair and sound psychological health can go quite well together, "Dad has *always* had a mustache!"

"You see what I'm saying?" she instantly replied.

An old country-music lyric says, "One man's ceiling is another man's floor." Sometimes traffic can flow both ways in the analysis or assessment of an argument. What I'd thought was the most decisive possible refutation by counterexample of a general claim that I knew to be false was taken by my dialogue partner as a particularly clear confirmation of her own emphatic view to the contrary.

> *There are two sides to every question.*
>
> — Protagorus

Of course, people can sometimes reasonably differ on the obviousness of a piece of evidence cited in an argument, or they can blind themselves to the truth and can even refuse to listen to rational argument at all. The best intellectual reasoning can fail completely to overrule strongly opposed passions.

Emotion and logic are sometimes at odds. But I intend to discuss such profound matters later in various parts of this book. My point now is simple.

In the right context, the ability to argue cogently can prove of great importance for seeing where truth lies and for convincing others to join us in its pursuit. Good argument isn't always guaranteed to produce the good result you may desire, but good argument is better than bad argument any day of the week. And argument, along with imagination and emotion, can provide part of a total case for enlisting the whole person in believing or acting on an important truth. Rational argument is one of the most distinctive of genuinely human abilities and one strongly cultivated by philosophy.

The dangers of argument: A short survival guide

How can you actually use argument well and maybe even make progress in an argument with another person — or at least not get your shorts all twisted and wind up with an intellectual wedgie? You can find all sorts of advice on this subject from throughout the centuries. A bit of this advice is philosophical, some of it is psychological, and part of it is just plain pragmatic.

First is the pragmatic advice, such as, "In arguing, answer your opponent's earnest with a jest and his jest with earnest" — Leontinus Gorgias (as quoted in Aristotle's *Rhetoric*). In other words, keep the person with whom you're arguing off balance. But this practice is indeed a subset of rhetoric, which is the art of persuasion, and not of philosophy, which is a search for the truth. Most of the pragmatic advice available about argument presupposes precisely that you're after a win and not after the truth.

The psychological advice warns us most often about the limits of argumentation in dealing with another person and the truth at the same time. Sir Thomas Browne, for example, warned, "In all disputes, so much as there is of passion, so much there is of nothing to the purpose." Debate, you often hear, typically generates more heat than light. Know that likelihood going in. Passion clouds reason. And in the context of an interpersonal argument, or debate, people sometimes are willing to do anything to save face. Joseph Addison once observed, "Our disputants put me in mind of the scuttlefish, that when he is unable to extricate himself, blackens the water about him till he becomes invisible." So, as Publilius Syrus concluded long ago, "In a heated argument, we are apt to lose sight of the truth."

Finally, some modest philosophical advice of a practical bent: Protagorus did affirm that every question has two sides. And Henry Fielding added in the 18th century that "Much can be said on both sides." Whenever you see sincere, intelligent people supporting a cause or arguing a point of view, you can expect as a maxim of common sense to find more than sheer foolishness in that position or cause. By extrapolation, I think I can say that, in all the history of philosophy, with all the competing schools of thought and opposed points of view, you're never going to come across large numbers of sincere, intelligent, and relatively well-informed people who are just completely wrong in every way. So always try to remain open-minded and look for the truth that any opposing view may capture. On the other hand, Oscar Wilde warned us, with more than a bit of hyperbole, that "The man who sees both sides of a question is a man who sees absolutely nothing at all." Neither reason nor common sense dictate or even advise that we aspire to balanced indecision anywhere in life.

And, of course, life consists of much more than argument. Socrates once remarked, "You are fond of argument, and now you fancy that I am a bag of arguments." You don't want to avoid argument, and yet neither do you want to constantly seek it out as the only thing in life worth your time. Tell your undergraduate philosophy-major friends: Not even Socrates was a bag of arguments.

Wisdom Rules

To praise and recommend philosophy as an activity worthy of human attention just for its ability to enhance our skills of analysis, assessment, and argument is a bit like praising brain surgery by saying that it's a good thing because it cultivates the hand-eye coordination of the surgeon. Philosophy can seem like aerobics for the intellect and weight-training for the soul. But its most important feature is the one built into its name.

> *Wisdom is the perfect good of the human mind; philosophy is the love of wisdom and the endeavor to attain it.*

> — Seneca

Philosophy is one of the noblest activities in which we can engage because it promotes *wisdom* in our lives. And wisdom brings with it two benefits: Depth and practicality.

Wisdom is first and foremost simply insight about living. Insight itself is a sort of perceptiveness or perspicacity of judgment that penetrates beneath appearances and latches onto realities. Wisdom cuts to the core.

In the ancient world, Seneca referred to wisdom as "the only liberty." Juvenal called wisdom "the conqueror of fortune." In the pages of the New Testament, Jesus once remarked, "You shall know the truth, and the truth shall set you free." Wisdom is knowing the truth about what really matters in life. It is glimpsing the foundations and comprehending at least some of the significance of all that's around us.

A wise person does not readily fall prey to false appearances. Wisdom isn't easily spooked or unhinged. Wisdom sees the hidden side of any situation. It is patient and measured in its responses.

Wisdom is neither rushed nor stampeded into foolish action.

A wise person has *depth*. In his 17th-century manual on success, *The Art of Worldly Wisdom*, Balthasar Gracian wrote the following concerning depth:

> *You are as much a real person as you are deep. As with the depths of a diamond, the interior is twice as important as the surface. There are people who are all facade, like a house left unfinished when the funds run out. They have the entrance of a palace but the inner rooms of a cottage.*

A wise person is never all ornament and no substance. Any veneer is backed by a strong reality. A wise person sees everything in its ultimate context and so does not easily mistake value.

Superficial living has too often become the way of the world. People suck the foam off the beer of life and never drink deeply of the real brew. Philosophers, on the other hand, insist on depth.

> *Wisdom is to the soul what health is to the body.*

> — La Rouchefoucauld

Wisdom is, above all, practical. It gives us guidance for living well. That's why its pursuit is worth our time and effort. The great philosophers are just people who've sometimes done extraordinary things in this pursuit. Some of them got some things wrong. But others found truth. Even those philosophers who erred deeply in their own conclusions often bring us into the neighborhood of great truth by showing us how to find paths of discovery concerning important issues.

Don't get me wrong here. I don't mean to say that all philosophers pursue practical questions and create points of view that can help us with our day-to-day lives. The Greek philosophers who lived before Socrates most often pursued questions of cosmic import not directly related to daily life. The Presocratics asked mostly about the nature of the universe in which we live and not about how best to live in it. And they came up with some pretty wild answers, as the following samples indicate:

> Thales: *Everything is made out of water.*
>
> Anaximander: *Everything is made out of The Boundless.*
>
> Anaximenes: *Everything is made out of air.*
>
> Heraclitus: *Everything is always changing.*
>
> Pythagorus: *Everything is made of numbers, and don't eat beans because they'll do a number on you.*
>
> Parmenides: *Nothing ever really changes, and appearance in the physical world is always illusion.*

The Presocratics sought an understanding of the universe. And they engaged in remarkable feats of intellectual discovery, not always involving such strange-sounding conclusions. In a sense, they were doing scientific cosmology without having yet developed the scientific equipment and method necessary to explore and uncover the secrets of the natural world. And yet much of what they did launched the process of intellectual inquiry that led eventually to the rise of modern science.

For many centuries, philosophy was not sharply distinguished from what people now think of as many other domains of human thought and knowledge. The early philosophers were protoscientists, and they were mathematicians and psychologists before separate disciplines of biology, chemistry, zoology, physics, math, and psychology existed. Even now, some of the academic professorships of science in England and Europe are still called "Chairs of Natural Philosophy." Philosophy's domain was for a long time limitless.

But the philosophy that began in earnest in ancient Greece with Socrates and Plato and Aristotle — the focus on wisdom that you can also find in the writings of Confucius and Lao Tsu and many other ancient Oriental thinkers —

resulted in the tradition of philosophical inquiry that people follow today, a tradition that seeks, at its best, both depth and usefulness in matters concerning human life.

The Socratic Quest for Wisdom

Socrates was a pretty amazing example of a person living the search for wisdom. He himself did not leave any writings. He did his philosophizing orally, in the company of other people — and not always in the company of people who were enjoying the journey with him. As he went about Athens questioning reputedly wise people on topics of importance and finding them not so wise after all, he insisted on pointing this fact out to them. And this proclivity, as you can well imagine, did not lead to widespread popularity.

Many of the young people in Athens were impressed with Socrates' razor-sharp intellect and often followed him about, imitating his probing style of conversation and offending even more people. In fact, by the age of 70, Socrates and his followers had angered so many prominent citizens in Athens that he was accused and tried on the two trumped-up charges of corrupting the youth and of not believing in the gods of the city but following other gods instead.

Plato provides a riveting account of the trial of Socrates. His fate was in the hands of a crowd of 501 citizen-jurists, who were to weigh the evidence and decide his fate by vote. The evidence seems clear that, if Socrates had just promised to stop philosophizing in public and stirring up trouble, he'd most likely have been freed. In his speech to the jurists, he considered this possibility and said that, if the offer were made, his response would be simple. His words ring through the centuries. He said that his reply would be as follows:

> *Gentlemen of the jury, I am grateful and I am your friend, but I will obey the god rather than you, and as long as I draw breath and am able, I shall never cease to practice philosophy, to exhort you and in my usual way to point out to any of you whom I happen to meet: Good Sir, you are an Athenian, a citizen of the greatest city with the greatest reputation for both wisdom and power; are you not ashamed of your eagerness to possess as much wealth, reputation, and honors as possible, while you do not care for nor give thought to wisdom or truth, or the best possible state of your soul?*

He went on to say:

> *Then, if one of you disputes and says he does care, I shall not let him go at once or leave him, but I shall question him, examine him and test him, and if I do not think he has attained the goodness that he says he has, I shall reproach him because he attaches little importance to the most important things and greater importance to inferior things. I shall treat in this way*

anyone I happen to meet, young and old, citizen and stranger, and more so the citizens because you are more kindred to me. Be sure that this is what the god orders me to do, and I think there is no greater blessing for the city than my service to the god. For I go around doing nothing but persuading both young and old among you not to care for your body or your wealth in preference to or as strongly as for the best possible state of your soul, but I say to you: "Wealth does not bring about excellence, but excellence brings about wealth and all other public and private blessings for men."

The verdict rendered after this speech was *guilty*. The penalty that the prosecutor proposed was an extreme one: Death. By trial procedures in that day, the accused could propose an alternative punishment. If it was reasonable at all, the jury would almost certainly have preferred it over this maximal sentence.

Asked what he thought he deserved for what he had done, Socrates pondered it a bit and replied that he deserved free housing and free food of the best kind, like what the Olympic athletes received, for life.

He was given poison instead.

> *Be wiser than other people if you can; but do not tell them so.*
>
> — Lord Chesterfield

Wisdom is worth the pursuit. Yet, despite its enormous relevance in helping us to live good lives, nothing may be as rare in the modern world as true wisdom.

Former U.S. president Calvin Coolidge once remarked that "Some people are suffering from lack of work, some from lack of water, many more from lack of wisdom." And one can make the same point even more strongly today.

Although it's sometimes considered nothing more than enhanced common sense, nothing may be less common in our time than real wisdom about living. We should seek as much as we can to enhance the wisdom we have, by exploring all the ultimate issues most fundamental to our understanding of life and our place in the world.

Is the search for wisdom worth your time? Socrates thought that it was worth his life.

As you launch into the series of philosophical questions that I ask throughout this book, you can expect to keep an eye on issues of depth and practicality at each turn. We want wisdom for the journey that we're now on. And we must never settle for less.

Part II

How Do We Know Anything?

The 5th Wave   By Rich Tennant

3 VIEWS OF FREEDOM AND THEIR ASSOCIATED PHILOSOPHER

©RICHTENNANT

Determinism — Pierre Simon de Laplace

Libertarianism-- Thomas Reid

Jerknism — Leroy Hoppenrath

Outta da way, squirt.

In this part . . .

1 n this part, we look at our beliefs about belief, the truth about truth, and our knowledge about knowledge. What is it to be a rational person? Whenever you have a belief, do you have to be able to prove that it's true? This part puts together some of the tools we need at various points throughout in the book. If you want to know how we can hold rational beliefs, then this part is for you.

Chapter 4

Belief, Truth, and Knowledge

· ·

In This Chapter

▶ Developing tools for the wisdom quest

▶ Exploring what beliefs are

▶ Analyzing knowledge

▶ Getting clear on truth and rationality

· ·

Man is what he believes.

— Anton Chekov

The philosopher Ludwig Feuerbach once said, "Man is what he eats." But I prefer the Chekov claim. I'd rather envision myself as the sum total of all my beliefs than as an enormous collection of various cheeseburgers, tacos, and chocolate chip cookies consumed throughout the years. Wouldn't you?

In this chapter, we ask some vital questions about belief, truth, and knowledge. We launch our philosophical quest together by getting clear on some of the basic building blocks of philosophical analysis. Finally, I introduce some fundamental concepts, and we start making some deep inquiries.

Our Beliefs about Belief

Your beliefs are your map of reality. They guide you through the day. They are the lenses through which you perceive the world. They are also the deep well from which your actions, attitudes, and feelings flow.

There is nothing more important about you than what you believe. What you value is equally important. But some philosophers think that this is just because a value is nothing more than a special sort of belief. When you value something, you just believe that it is important and worthy of honor.

Your feelings are certainly an important part of who you are. And so are your desires, hopes, and dreams. But they are all either results of your beliefs, or else are in some other way dependent on those beliefs. You desire what you believe to be good or pleasant. You hope for something because you believe it will contribute to your personal happiness, or your overall success. Again and again, belief is foundational to who you are.

Philosophy is the love and pursuit of wisdom. At some level, we all want wisdom for living. No one wants to wander this world as a fool, hobbled by false beliefs about important matters and misled by counterfeit values that can lead to nothing but misery. Because of this, philosophers have always suggested that it is important for us to examine our beliefs. Are those beliefs justified? Are they true? Are they capable of giving us good guidance in life? Do we have among our current beliefs real knowledge about the world in which we live, as well as about ourselves, or are we all just stuck with nothing better than mere opinion? These are questions we all need to ask, and answer.

> *Nothing is so firmly believed as that which we least know.*
>
> — Montaigne

How many beliefs do you have? Hundreds? Thousands? Millions? More than that? You have a great deal many more beliefs than you realize. If this comes as a surprise, the explanation may be quite simple. We sometimes use the word belief to refer to an important conviction, as in the sentences:

- They share the belief that stealing is wrong.
- She holds the belief that there is a God.
- It is his belief that democracy is the best form of government.

But we have also have trivial beliefs as well as important convictions. For example, I believe that 1 is less than 2, that 2 is less than 3, that 3 is less than 4, and so on. I believe that I am indoors now. I believe that *m, n, o,* and *p* are consecutive letters in the English alphabet. None of these beliefs are convictions crucial for the overall living of my life, but they are nonetheless beliefs. Of course, we also believe that we know these things. Some beliefs fall short of knowledge; others count as instances of knowledge. But for the relationship between belief and knowledge, wait until the section "The complete definition of knowledge," later in this chapter.

There are two sides to belief, a subjective side and an objective side. The subjective side is just the mental state of conviction. The objective side is the content of what is believed, a claim or representation about reality that philosophers refer to as a *proposition*. Throughout this book, when I speak of "the belief that there is a God," or "the belief in an objective moral order," or "the belief in life after death," I typically mean to speak of the proposition believed, the claim that there is a moral order or that there is life after death.

Our main focus is what some philosophers call *truth claims*. Occasionally, I find it important to comment on the subjective side of belief, on the mental states of people who typically accept certain propositions about the world, but for the most part, my concern is with the ultimate claims themselves. And this is true even though we will be vigilant throughout to keep in mind our own relations to these propositions — whether we ourselves believe them, disbelieve them, or maintain a suspended judgment concerning them, and whether we ought to have a very different relation to them instead.

The Importance of Belief

It's crucial at the outset to realize that we all have an enormous number of beliefs about all kinds of things, including things we've never even explicitly thought about. And if Chekov was right when he once said that we are what we believe, then we'd better be comfortable with what our most important beliefs are. We'd better examine them and make sure that we feel good about having them. Some of these beliefs are ones we are well aware of having. Others ordinarily may be hidden from view, but a little philosophical investigation will reveal what they are.

Our beliefs are important for a number of reasons Wars are fought over beliefs. Deals are made or broken because of beliefs. People gather together over beliefs they have in common. They also separate because of divergent beliefs. We chart out our lives in every way in accordance with our beliefs.

Many philosophers have analyzed human action as a natural consequence of our beliefs interacting with our desires:

Beliefs + Desires = Actions

What we do in this world is a result of what we believe and what we want. If what we want is a consequence of what we believe to be good or pleasurable, then belief is indeed the ultimate wellspring of action. Having the right beliefs is thus not just a matter of intellectual importance, but it is of the utmost practical importance.

But here's the problem. We have false beliefs. All of us. No one is completely infallible. Even a Catholic who thinks the Pope is infallible about matters of faith still realizes he could misplace his socks, believing they are in the dresser when they are not.

In my youth, I often saw my father running around the house, wearing a hat, looking for his hat. "Where's my hat? Has anyone seen my hat?" "It's on your head." "Oh." We can have false beliefs about obvious, easy to check things like that. Imagine how we can get it wrong about more subtle matters.

Superstition: A true story

False beliefs can creep into our minds in all sorts of ways. And they can affect our lives deeply. On September 13, 1996, I was flying across the country on a plane that was nearly empty. Shortly after take-off, I mentioned to the flight attendant how unusual it was to see all the unoccupied seats. She said, "Oh, that often happens on Friday the 13th. People are afraid to fly." My seatmate, a gentleman I had just met, laughed loudly and said, "What superstitious nonsense! Unbelievable! Ridiculous!" The left lens of his glasses promptly fell out onto the cabin floor. He looked shocked, and said, "Gee, I just lost a lens, and these glasses are less than a year old." Reaching down to pick up the loose piece of glass, he launched back into his tirade against superstition, saying. "I guess I'm supposed to think that *this* happened because it's Friday the 13th! Ha!" As he fumbled to insert the lens back into his frames, he looked up at me with astonishment on his face and said "I'll be damned. The frame just totally broke." Indeed. It might have been enough to make a less philosophical man . . . superstitious.

We're sometimes absentminded. We're often misinformed. Occasionally we seem to see what's really not there, or miss what is. At other times, we may draw false conclusions from what we do in fact know. We have prejudices. We have blind spots. And one of the strongest forces in human life is the power of self-deception — our ability to believe what we want to believe, and hide from ourselves what we'd rather not face, regardless of what the facts might indeed be.

How can we avoid the false beliefs that might steer us wrong and even derail our lives? How can we resist erroneous opinion? This is a question that philosophers have asked for millennia. For the answers, read on.

The Ideal of Knowledge

We want our beliefs to be true, to connect us to reality, to clue us in on what's really happening in our world, and in our own lives. We don't want our most important beliefs to be mere opinions; we want them to constitute real knowledge. But what is knowledge?

Our concept of *knowledge* is first of all *an attainment concept*. In basketball, we shoot in order to score. Shooting is the activity; scoring is the attainment intended. In the life of the mind, we believe in order to know. Believing is, in a sense, the activity; knowing is the intended attainment.

Philosophical analysis

Philosophers analyze ideas. We take them apart and then try to put them back together, to understand how they work. Like auto mechanics, we conceptual grease monkeys often aim to adjust and repair rough-running ideas.

The analysis of knowledge as properly justified true belief breaks it down into what are called necessary and sufficient conditions, or, to be more exact, into individually necessary and jointly sufficient conditions.

Maybe I should explain that. Take the concept or idea of bachelorhood. To analyze bachelorhood philosophically is to break it into necessary and sufficient conditions. We start with a definition: "A bachelor is an unmarried male human being of marriageable age." What are the components here? Male. Human being. Unmarried.

Of marriagable age. There are four conditions. Each of them is necessary for bachelorhood. You can't be a bachelor unless you're male. But this is not alone sufficient. My dog is male. You have to be human, too. But I'm a male human, and I'm not a bachelor. So we still don't have sufficiency. A guy has to be unmarried as well. But a little baby can be an unmarried male human without counting as a bachelor. So one more condition is necessary. An unmarried male human being has to be of marriageable age to count as a bachelor. Each of the four conditions is necessary, and all four together (jointly) are sufficient for bachelorhood. Philosophers use this same process of analysis to understand important concepts like our ideas of knowledge, freedom, or God.

Just as you can shoot a basketball and not score a basket, you can believe something and not thereby have knowledge. So knowing is not the same thing as believing. What then in fact is it?

Philosophers have a traditional analysis of knowledge that says,

Knowledge = Properly Justified True Belief

To break down this analysis of knowledge as properly justified true belief, part by part, we can start at the end of our definition and work forward. That way, we can come to understand it, and thus come to grasp more deeply what knowledge, as distinct from opinion, or conjecture, or prejudice, really is.

You can't know something unless you believe it. You can't know that philosophy is the love of wisdom unless you believe that it is. I can't know that there is a God unless I believe that God exists. Belief is necessary for knowledge. It is a part of the package deal.

But belief alone isn't sufficient for knowledge. You can believe something that is false. And you can think you know it. But you can't genuinely know something that is false. You can know *of* something false that it *is* false. But to know something is to know something to be true. And you can't know something to be true unless it is; which is to say, you can't know something unless it's *not* false. Got it?

What is truth?

— Pontius Pilate

Anyone who wants to know what truth itself actually is should be confronted with Aristotle's explanation, captured in these inimitable words: "To say of what is that it is not, or of what is not that it is, is false; while to say of what is that it is, and of what is not that it is not, is true." Clear enough? Try to say that real fast ten times in a row. Not even a philosophy graduate student can pull it off. And that's the truth.

When you know a thing, to hold that you know it, and when you do not know a thing, to allow that you do not know it, is knowledge.

— Confucius (Sixth century B.C.)

The truth about truth

But is there really any such thing as truth? The philosophy of *relativism* claims that all so-called truth is relative, that there really is no absolute truth, but that different things may be true for me and true for you. This is some-times also known as *perspectivalism*. Perspectives differ, this viewpoint alleges, and one is as good as another.

But notice a problem with the mere statement of relativism. There *really* is no such thing as absolute truth. Is relativism suggesting that this is the ultimate, absolute truth about truth? In that case, it actually asserts what it denies, and so it's self-defeating, simply logically incoherent as a philsophical position.

Why then are so many college students relativists? Why has relativism been so attractive to a number of intellectuals in the 20th century? I think the answers here are quite simple.

The mind is a dangerous weapon, even to the possessor, if he knows not discreetly how to use it.

— Michael de Montaigne

A little philosophy is a dangerous thing. Too many undergraduates are exposed to relativism in a way that they tend to misunderstand. The philoso-phy professor often raises the specter of relativism, or perspectivalism, just to jolt his students into a deeper grasp of what is at stake in making truth claims. It is meant to be a rhetorical challenge to natural childhood feelings they've long had that what we believe is typically the absolute truth. In phi-losophy, everything can be challenged. But some views can meet the challenge and stand firm. The professor may actually want his students to see through or refute the relativist challenge and thus understand truth more deeply. But too many students come away grasping just enough of the challenge, while failing to see its fatal flaws, that they themselves begin espousing relativism-with-an-attitude back in the dorm, or back at home with the family. Relativism too often is nothing more than a fancy last gasp of adolescent rebellion.

There is no worse lie than a truth misunderstood by those who hear it.

— William James (1842–1910)

But some serious adults have fallen into relativism, too, and a number of otherwise very smart people have found it tempting. What could possibly attract them to a logically inconsistent position? First, relativism can serve as a very persuasive intellectual excuse for very bad behavior. If there is no absolute truth, there is no absolute moral truth, and we can get away with anything we want. Some people are relativists because it's a wonderful form of self-deception, licensing anything they want to do. And it's a view they can use speciously to attempt to convince otherwise good and sensible people to join them in their shenanigans.

There is a second path to adult relativism that is certainly more respectable, however wrong it nonetheless also is. Many academics have wanted to promote the virtue of tolerance in our pluralistic world, and have wrongly thought that relativism is the royal road to cultivating a firm and resilient openness to other people's beliefs. But the sort of tolerance that is indeed a virtue is best grounded in respect, and it's not showing respect for any point of view to say that no points of view can possibly capture reality the way that it is.

My remarks here are meant to apply to any utterly general relativism. That is what is self-defeating. There are, certainly, small areas regarding issues of personal taste and comfort where a very limited perspectivalism seems appropriate. The statement "This ice cream tastes good!" might be an appropriate example. It could be true for you — from your perspective, given your tastes — but not for me. But that is very different from the statement, "This ice cream is three years old!" which is a standard truth claim and is not subject to relativistic restriction. Compare the difference between "It's too hot in here" and "It's over 90 degrees." It is the latter statement that is a better example of standard claims about reality. And it is either true or false. No relativity muddies the water.

Truth is our tie to the world. Believing a truth, or stating a truth, is like hitting a target. Falsehood misses the mark. Truth anchors us to reality. Falsehood cuts our connection to the way things really are. We need truth like we need air, or food, or water. Falsehood, by contrast, kills.

The complete definition of knowledge

One necessary condition for knowledge is belief. (See the earlier section "Our Beliefs about Belief.") A second is truth. (Laid out in the preceding section.) Knowledge is built on true belief. But these two conditions are not alone sufficient for knowledge. I can believe something, and my belief can be true without my actually knowing the thing believed. How so?

Suppose that I somehow conjure up for myself right now the belief that, at this very moment, Fidel Castro is brushing his teeth. Imagine that I actually make myself believe this, by sheer force of will. And suppose further that, by extraordinary coincidence alone, he happens at this very moment to be polishing those communist molars, nearly ready to rinse and spit. I have the belief. And the belief happens to be true. But I had no evidence that it was true. I had no intuition that it was true. No physical or psychic connections conveyed the truth to me. I just got lucky and happened to form the belief at a rare moment when something was going on that made it true. Philosophers deny that I had therein real knowledge. I did not know that Castro was brushing. A wildly lucky correspondence is not an attainment. An amazing coincidence is not a connection sufficient to create something as solid as knowledge.

> *Luck never made a man wise.*
>
> — Seneca

Philosophers insist that, in order for a state of belief to qualify as knowledge, there must be a link, a connection, a tie between the mental state of affirmation and the state of reality, which makes that affirmation true. Furthermore, this link must be of the right sort to properly justify my having that belief.

Famous last words: A random sample

The difference between truth and falsehood can indeed be the difference between life and death. Consider the following statements, which, if false, in the right (or wrong) circumstances could be your last:

"This is not as dangerous as it looks."

"He does it all the time; he knows what he's doing."

"We're not that close."

"I'm sober enough."

"We'll be perfectly safe under here."

"No, this is how you connect the wires."

"If it wasn't safe, they wouldn't let us do it."

My point? There is an absolute difference between truth and falsehood. And it matters!

Knowledge is properly justified true belief. If I was looking at a live broadcast on CNN of Fidel Castro over his bathroom sink, brushing away, my true belief would then have been properly justified and could thus have counted as real knowledge. I could also use that link to defend my claim to know that Castro was brushing. The question "How do you know?" would then be answered by "I'm seeing it right now live on CNN."

What exactly is proper justification? What counts as sufficient reason, or sufficient grounds, for a belief to be held, and to count as knowledge? That is a question we answer in the rest of Part II.

Truth and rationality

Do not believe hastily.

— Ovid

We live in a world of irrational beliefs. People believe all sorts of crazy things. Have you ever bought a tabloid newspaper at the checkout lane in a grocery store, and actually read the articles? Okay, you don't have to answer that. But have you watched other people buy these papers? They don't always seem to be doing it as a joke. There seems to be no limit to what some people can believe. In fact, it has often been observed that there is a strong tendency in human life for people to believe what they want to believe, whether those beliefs are even remotely rational or not.

Here is the problem. Irrational belief is belief without a reliable tie to truth. Therefore, irrational belief can be dangerous belief. Our natural tendency to believe is like our natural tendency to eat or drink. Not everything you come across is safe to eat. Not every liquid you find is safe to drink. Likewise, not every proposition that comes your way is safe to believe. Our eating and drinking should be subject to the guidance of our beliefs. And that is even more reason for our beliefs to be subject to reason.

We want to be reasonable people because reason can connect us to truth. We value rationality as a reliable road to truth, and thus to knowledge. But what is reason? What is rationality? And why exactly should we think it's important in our ongoing quest for truth in this world?

Human reason is just the power we have to organize and interpret our experience of the world (what we see, hear, touch, taste, smell, or sense in any other way), as well as the ability to draw reliable conclusions that move beyond the confines of immediate experience. It is also the power to govern our actions and expectations in such a way that they make sense, given all the realities with which we have to do.

The mind is a strange machine which can combine the materials offered it in the most astonishing ways.

— Bertrand Russell

"Please be reasonable" is something we say to a person whose actions, attitudes, expectations, or beliefs are out of line with what we think the realities of their situation manifestly are. When we say this, we typically want the unreasonable person to bring himself into line with whatever the evidence is that would indicate the preferability of a course of action or thought other than what he has chosen. Reason is supposed to better connect us with reality, and thus better guide us into the future.

Be led by reason.

— Solon

Reason is of great importance in human life. But it is neither as extensive nor as pure as some philosophers of the past have given us to believe. What we are able to perceive, how we organize our perceptions, and what we conclude from our experience, is often as much a result of our feelings and attitudes as it is of rational rules and constraints.

The great thinkers on our tendencies to believe

Great minds have always commented on the human tendency to form beliefs even when there is no good evidence to think they are true.

It is natural for the mind to believe, and for the will to love; so that, for want of true objects, they must attach themselves to false.

— Blaise Pascal (1663–1662)

Men freely believe that which they desire.
— Julius Caesar

Man prefers to believe what he prefers to be true.

— Francis Bacon

We are born believing. A man bears beliefs as a tree bears apples.
— Ralph Waldo Emerson

Every man, wherever he goes, is encompassed by a cloud of comforting convictions, which move with him like flies on a summer day.

— Bertrand Russell

Each man's belief is right in his own eyes.
— Cowper

The greatest part of mankind have no other reason for their opinions than that they are in fashion.

— Samuel Johnson (1709–1784)

Logic cannot lead us all the way in life. But logic, or the laws of reliable thought, can indeed keep us more closely aligned with reality if our perceptions themselves are in tune with the way the world really is. Logic alone can't turn a dead fish into a diamond. But it can take us from diamonds to diamonds.

> *Logic is the art of making truth prevail.*
>
> — La Bruyère (1688)

The standard philosophical analysis of knowledge presents it as nothing more, or less, than properly justified true belief. The concept of justification here is that of rational justification. So philosophers have asked throughout the centuries, "What is required for rational justification?" What is needed to support a belief if that belief is to have a chance of qualifying as knowledge? What makes a belief rational or reasonable to hold? What indicators of truth does rationality demand?

Some people think that something like logical proof is required for rationality. Their mantra is "Prove it." An old friend of mine, a former professor of philosophical theology at Yale, told me that he once received an unexpected phone call from his little son's Sunday School teacher. The teacher said, "Professor, everytime I say anything new in Sunday School class, your little boy blurts out, 'Prove it!' Could you please have a talk with him and explain that no one can prove everything?"

> *He that, in the ordinary affairs of life, would admit of nothing but direct plain demonstration would be sure of nothing in this world but of perishing quickly.*
>
> — John Locke

It seems clearly excessive to think that no belief is rational to hold unless the believer is in possession of some decisive proof that it is true. I have beliefs about the galaxy, nuclear energy, my computer, and even about my own body that I cannot prove in any decisive sense. I can most often produce evidence, or the reported testimony of some expert, or at least a vague memory of having once had either evidence or testimony to the truth of what I believe, but I am rarely in possession of a knock-down, air-tight proof. Life just doesn't work like that.

Well, some philosophers have suggested, perhaps it is excessive to require proof for rationality, but it may indeed be necessary to have sufficient evidence in order to be justified in believing anything.

On this philosophy, which is widely known as *evidentialism,* it is irrational ever to believe anything without sufficient evidence that it is true. Heresay is not enough, faith is not to be trusted, and intuition is not admissable at all. Hard evidence or nothing is the demand. Is it a reasonable demand? Is rational belief dependent on evidence?

Logic 101

Simply put, logic is the study of human reasoning. The laws of logic are those patterns of reasoning that will allow you reliably to stick to the truth if you've started with the truth. In other words, logic itself is not a source of substantive truth of any sort at all, but it is like a mechanism, or set of rules, or procedures, for moving from known truths to previously undetected truths.

The subject matter of logic is arguments. Not altercations, or shouting matches, but something very different from these displays of human disagreement. In a philosophical argument, no one actually needs to be disagreeing with anyone. An argument can be a search for truth.

In logic, an argument is a series of propositions, or statements about reality, one of which is a conclusion drawn from the others, the latter thereby serving in that context as premises for that conclusion.

Here's a little lingo to impress your friends. In *deductive logic,* a *valid* argument is an argument of such a form or nature that, if all its premises are true, then we have an absolute 100 percent guarantee that its conclusion is, too. Here is an example of a valid argument, based on a simple, valid form of deductive reasoning, or inference, called by logicians *modus ponens:*

(1) If A, then B

(2) A

Therefore

(3) B

Suppose it's true that (1) If it's raining, then my car is getting wet (because I parked outside). If it's also true that (2) It is raining, then the conclusion follows logically from (1) and (2) that (3) My car is getting wet.

A valid argument with all true premises is called a *sound* argument. Simply put, in arguments, soundness = validity plus truth. Only a sound argument gurantees the truth of its conclusion. An argument can be unsound in either of two ways. It can have a false premise. Or it can be invalid, such that even if all its premises were true, its conclusion could still be false.

In *inductive logic,* the truth of the premises just raises the probability of, or renders more likely, or gives evidential support to, the conclusion, without giving a 100 percent guarantee that it is true. Here is an example of inductive reasoning:

(1) All objects of type A that we have seen have had property B.

(2) There is likely nothing atypical about these A-type objects.

Therefore, probably,

(3) The next A that we see will have property B.

Inductive logic is not as iron clad as deductive reasoning, but it is the basis of science and technology and thus has achieved tremendous results.

It will take us on one of the most unusual intellectual journeys of our lives to answer that question, a journey we can undertake in the next two chapters. So, if you're up to it, buckle up your mental seat belt, keep reading, and prepare for the philosophical ride of your life.

Chapter 5

The Challenge of Skepticism

• •

In This Chapter

▶ Looking at the ancient challenge of skepticism

▶ Asking some of the deepest questions ever

▶ Understanding when to doubt, and when to doubt our doubts

▶ Discovering one of the most important principles of rationality

• •

Doubt is the vestibule which all must pass, before they can enter into the temple of truth.

— Charles Caleb Colton (1825)

*W*e live in a culture awash in information. We're drowning in data each day. The media trumpet that, with the advent of modern communications and computer technology, human knowledge is expanding geometrically faster than at any other period in history. Our knowledge, we are told, at least doubles every four years now.

But do we really know all that we think we know? Is it precisely knowledge that is expanding, or just belief, or perhaps mere opinion? Does the constant and rapid flow of apparent information into our lives lull us into thinking we have increasingly more knowledge, when actually we may have nothing of the kind? Do we know even a fraction of what we think we know?

Since the ancient world, a series of philosophers have cautioned us about our natural tendency to claim knowledge where knowledge, in fact, may not exist. The ancient philosophy of *skepticism* helps us to understand more deeply what exactly knowledge is, and where it comes from, as well as to answer the open question philosophers have often asked of whether evidence is always required for rational belief, and thus for knowledge.

In this chapter, we see how the most basic form of skeptical inquiry can give us a fresh perspective on the foundations of all human knowledge. We ask some amazing questions, and in the process of trying to answer them, we discover an often overlooked principle of rationality. This just may be the most philosophically challenging chapter in the whole book, but if you can grasp its reasoning and its implications, you'll see all the other issues of philosophy in a new light. The questions that are raised by skepticism can put everything in a new light, and, I think, can inspire us with a new and needed humility concerning all our claims to knowledge.

The Ancient Art of Doubt

The words *skeptic* and *skepticism* come from an ancient Greek verb that meant "to inquire." Etymologically, then, a skeptic is an inquirer. This should form important background for our understanding of skeptical doubt. Skepticism at its best is not a matter of denial, but of inquiring, seeking, questioning doubt.

> *How prone to doubt, how cautious are the wise!*
>
> — Homer *(Odyssey)*

The first great skeptical philosopher of the ancient world was Pyrrho of Elis (circa 310–270 B.C.). After traveling with Alexander the Great as a court philosopher, he returned home to teach, we are told, great crowds of admirers and seekers. Pyrrho was known for presenting philosophy as a way of life that aims at a calmness of the spirit and happiness of the heart.

Pyrrho believed that we should always be quick to question, and slow to believe. He seemed to think that we too easily become convinced of things that trouble our minds and disturb our souls. So he practiced, and preached, withholding judgment as much as possible.

Some stories from the ancient world portray Pyrrho as far too calm, and even indifferent, concerning dangers in his daily environment. We are told that his friends were constantly saving his life, pulling him from the paths of speeding carts, from the edges of cliffs, and from other dangers. Commentators ascribe this to Pyrrho's skeptical disinclination to trust appearances, and thus to a philosophical disinclination actually to believe anything that appeared to be going on around him. But I doubt this, appropriately enough. In graduate school, my best friend and I frequently saved each other's lives, alternately pulling each other back from the paths of oncoming cars, as we walked the streets of New Haven, Connecticut, deep in thought. Our apparent indifference to the dangers around us came about just because we were lost in the intricacies of philosophical reasoning, constructing an argument concerning some abstract issue, and had nothing to do with the peculiarities of skeptical doubt. Philosophers just tend to get lost in thought. And in cities the size of New Haven. Or even Elis.

Other stories about Pyrrho seem more credible, and more likely attributable to his skepticism. We are told that he was once attacked by a fierce dog, that he reacted with fear, and that he later apologized to his friends for not acting consistently with his own philosophy. Another story does have him attaining this consistency of withholding judgment and experiencing inner calm as a result. He was on board a ship during a violent storm, but showed no fear. His terrified fellow passengers asked how he remained calm. We are told that, in the midst of the storm, he pointed to a little pig on deck calmly eating his food, and said that this is the unperturbed way a wise man should live in all situations.

The city of Elis exempted all philosophers from taxes in honor of Pyrrho, because of his example and his service to the community. And they would all have been thrilled at this great news, if they just could have brought themselves to actually believe it.

I should mention one other ancient skeptic by name, the physician Sextus Empiricus. We are uncertain of his birth, the date of his death, and of where he lived, appropriately enough. He seems to have lived in the second half of the second century A.D., and into the first quarter of the third century. We think he was Greek, because of his facility with the Greek language, and apparent knowledge of places in the Greek world. His works have been very influential and are our best sources for the arguments and positions of classic Greek skepticism.

The dogmatic naysayers

Some curmudgeonly ancient thinkers, like Carneades, boldly declared that "Knowledge is impossible." Others averred, a tad bit more humbly, merely that "Nothing is known." But what's the most obvious, embarrassing question you could ask such a person? Right: "How do you know?" Another related negative position might maintain only that "No beliefs are rational." But all these claims are examples of propositions that, in one way or another, are self-defeating or self-undermining. Consider

✔ No propositions are true.

✔ This sentence is not in English.

✔ No, I don't speak any known language.

All these are self-undermining as well. Self-undermining statements fall into these categories: Those that can't possibly be true; those that can't be rational to hold; and those that defeat themselves when expressed. They are linguistic curiosities, but not much else.

The skepticism that we are examining is not self-defeating like any form of dogmatic naysaying. Proper skeptics do not deny. They just hesitate to affirm, and question the affirmations that the rest of us naturally make.

Like Pyrrho, Sextus was no dogmatic naysayer about human knowledge. He didn't deny its possibility, or actual occurrence. He was just extremely careful about committing belief to anything that went beyond immediate appearances and urged us on to similar caution.

The skeptic like Pyrrho and Sextus thought that we should live our daily lives in accordance with appearances, but that we should refrain from drawing any conclusions from those appearances as well as from holding any firm beliefs based on those appearances. The point of this caution was always the goal of unperturbedness of spirit, and ultimately a sort of peaceful happiness of life.

This is the ancient heritage of skepticism. But our use of skeptical questioning in this chapter is a bit different. We do not aim at the attainment of spiritual calmness here but rather at intellectual enlightenment. Later in the book, we can put this to the service of matters of the spirit. But for now, we want merely to probe into the foundations of what we normally consider human knowledge.

> *By doubting we come at the truth.*
>
> — Cicero

Incredible Questions We Cannot Answer

The skeptic asks us some deep and challenging questions to which there are no quick and easy answers. As a result of studying these questions, we can come to a much deeper understanding of things we've long taken for granted.

To put it as simply as possible, the skeptic wants to ask us why we have any of the beliefs that we hold. He wants to know why we think we know the things we claim to know. He asks us how we can have the knowledge we claim. And his questions shed light on the foundations for all our beliefs.

In order to introduce the questions the skeptic wants us to ask, I want to start off by making some simple distinctions. We can divide all the beliefs we have into three categories. I list here those three simple categories and then give examples in Table 5-1:

- ✔ **Past Oriented:** Beliefs about the past
- ✔ **Present Oriented:** Beliefs about the present
- ✔ **Future Oriented:** Beliefs about the future

Table 5-1	Examples of Three Belief Categories	
Past Oriented	*Present Oriented*	*Future Oriented*
I believe that Plato taught Aristotle.	I believe that Russia is experiencing economic trouble.	I believe that global warming will raise ocean levels.
I believe that America asserted its independence in 1776.	I believe that my investments are doing well.	I believe that America will remain a democracy.
I believe that my father fought in World War II.	I believe that my wife is gardening.	I believe that my daughter will finish college near home.
I believe that I had toast and jam for breakfast today.	I believe that it's a sunny day outside.	I believe that you'll eventually finish reading this book.

Now, the skeptic has some simple questions to ask us, in two categories. First, the skeptic questions the reliability of the sources of our beliefs concerning things past, present, and future. Then the skeptic raises even more radical questions about each of these categories of belief. I call these two types of questions, or inquiries, *source skepticism,* and *radical skepticism,* which I cover in the following sections.

The questions of source skepticism

What are the distinctive sources for our beliefs about the past? Most of the beliefs we have about the past come to us by the testimony of other people. I wasn't present at the signing of the Declaration of Independence. I didn't see my father fight in the second world war. I have been told about these events by sources that I take to be reliable.

The testimony of others is generally the main source of our beliefs about the past. But sometimes we were there. Things we have experienced directly, we have access to through the means of memory. The second distinctive source of our beliefs about the past is then memory.

Good mind, bad memory

Even very smart people often have terrible memories. I once walked across campus at the University of Notre Dame with a visiting philosopher from Oxford, a notoriously eccentric individual who had the strangest walk I had ever seen. He bobbed up and down as he strode full stretch, and yet, when he came to a crossing of sidewalks, he switched instantly to a tiny stepping run, knees high and arms tight to his sides. In the midst of our animated philosophical conversation, I suddenly realized that I was face to face with something out of Monty Python's *Ministry of Silly Walks.* I was utterly astonished at the sight, as I nearly breathlessly tried to keep up with this gymnastic, fast-paced dance of jog and bob, while thinking logically about arguments for the existence of God.

After ten minutes of this odd and aerobic theorizing, the imminent professor tried mightily to remember the name of one of his best friends and closest colleagues at Oxford, a don known as even more eccentric, with whom he had worked for many years. He wanted to recommend the man's book to me, but for the life of him could not recall the man's name. Finally he sputtered, "You know, you know, the chap who walks so funny." True story.

The memory represents to us not what we choose but what it pleases.

— Montaigne

If you doubt my veracity here, go to any major college or university, and venture into the parking lot where the mathematics faculty park their cars. Arrive at about five o'clock in the afternoon, at the end of the day, and watch them look for their automobiles. Quite a sight.

Genius is more often found in a cracked pot than in a whole one.

— E.B. White

Some people think that physical evidence is an independent third source for beliefs about the past. But whether it consists of fossilized footprints in stone, or a videotape of an event, it is always presented to us now by either the testimony or memory first, that it is authentic and not faked, and secondly concerning what it means. So because of its dependence on the reliability of these other two sources, we don't have to treat it as a third source category for our purposes here.

So all our beliefs about the past depend on testimony, or memory, or both. The skeptic wants to ask us a simple and yet penetrating question. "How do we know that any of the sources of our beliefs are ever reliable?" But take it a step at a time. We begin with our beliefs about the past. The skeptic asks, "How do we know that memory or testimony are ever reliable?"

Memory

How do I know that the mental function of memory is ever reliable? How do I know that it ever gives us true beliefs? Notice that the question here is not whether human memory is always reliable, or even trustworthy most of the time. Most of us will admit that memory is not the dependable thing it purports sometimes to be.

> *Memory is the thing you forget with.*
>
> — Alexander Chase

But our question is not whether memory is infallible or even mostly reliable. The skeptic wants to know whether human memory is *ever* reliable at all. This may seem like a silly question to ask. But watch what happens when we try to answer.

How do I know that memory is ever reliable? Well, I might answer that at least I know that my memory is often reliable. How do I know that? Simple. I can recall many times in the past when I seem to remember parking in a particular place and there the car in fact was. I recall many times remembering where I put my watch, and I was right.

But wait a second. If that is how I justify ever relying on memory, by appealing to my memory that it has sometimes been reliable in the past, I am relying on memory to justify memory, and so I am engaging in *circular reasoning,* reasoning which just assumes the truth of the thing we are trying to prove. That is to say, I have not yet produced a single shred of untainted evidence for what needed evidence.

But another tack is possible. In the third grade, my teacher once told me that I had a photographic memory. And I still may; I just don't have same-day service any more. Actually, I think the film was exposed somewhere along the way. But, surprisingly often, other people still praise my memory. If that's my answer to the question of how I know memory ever to be reliable, I have a double problem. First, I am still relying on my memory of what people have said about my memory. And second, this will be a good argument only if I have reason to believe that the testimony of other people is sometimes reliable, and that needs to be established on its own merits. In the next section, we see the problem we run into when we try to justify ever relying on testimony.

Testimony

Testimony is our main source of belief about the past. Skepticism asks a simple question: How do I know that testimony is ever reliable? How do I know that what other people tell me is ever the truth? I get nowhere if I reason in a circle and say, "Well, when I was growing up, my parents told me that other people can usually be trusted, except where money and real estate are involved." I can't appeal to a piece of testimony to justify ever believing testimony, or I have reasoned in a tight circle, assuming precisely what is to be proved.

Let the greatest part of the news thou hearest be the least part of what thou believest, lest the greater part of what thou believest be the least part of what is true.

— Francis Quarles

But suppose that in response to the skeptic's question I say, "I just recall that many times in the past, what other people have told me has turned out to be true; therefore testimony is sometimes reliable." If I reason like that, I am depending on my memory of past reliability for the testimony of others, and the only noncircular argument that we are able to give for the reliability of memory appeals to testimony. But if I can know that memory is sometimes reliable only if I can reasonably believe that testimony is, and I can know that testimony is reliable only if I can reasonably believe that memory is, we just have on our hands a bigger circle of reasoning, and thus have gotten nowhere at all. We have not been able to produce a single piece of untainted, pure evidence that either of our distinctive sources of beliefs about the past is ever reliable.

Surely, we might think, we are on better footing when we examine our beliefs about the present. We can be vague about the past. It can be shrouded in the mists of time. But the present stares us in the face.

What are our distinctive sources for our beliefs about the present? Well, hmm. Gee, when you think about it, it seems that most of our beliefs about the present moment, about things going on beyond the purview of our own perception, are based on the testimony of other people. That's how I know about current events around the world. Testimony. And we have just seen the wall we run into when we try to produce a single shred of evidence that testimony is ever reliable.

But we can get much more immediate. Even testimony comes to us through the medium of sense experience. And many things that we know about the present we know just from our current sense experience. Perhaps sense experience can give us the direct, provable tie to reality that the skeptic seems to be seeking. In the next section, we need to ask the skeptic's questions about sense experience.

Sense experience

I don't need the testimony of others to tell me what's going on in this room right now. I know by sight that my computer monitor is on. I know by sight and touch that the keyboard is working. I can smell the British aftershave that I just splashed on. I can hear the unmistakable hum of my printer. A great number of present moment beliefs are just rooted in the immediacy and intimacy of sense experience.

What can give us surer knowledge than our senses? With what else can we better distinguish the true and the false?

— Lucretius (First century B.C.)

The skeptic wants to ask, "How do we know that sense experience is ever reliable?" I bet you could see that one coming. And what can we answer? I am tempted to say, "Look, I recall many times in the past seeming to see something, like a penny on the street, and when I got closer, there it was, just as it had appeared to be. So sense experience is sometimes reliable."

This is almost embarrassing. First, I just made use of my memory of a past experience. But, as we see in the preceding section on memory, we can't come up with any good evidence that memory is ever reliable. Forget that for a moment, though, for the sake of argument. My little story just recounted one sense experience later confirmed by what? Another sense experience. Circular reasoning again. If all sense experience has been called into question by the skeptic, it is not sufficient for me to answer the challenge by appealing to a particular piece of sense experience.

Things are looking bad, so to speak. But that appearance might itself be deceiving, so hang in there. If you read on, I promise that it's going to seem to get much worse for a few minutes, and then you'll be truly amazed at what happens. Trust me. Aren't you almost afraid to peek at our beliefs about the future?

We don't have to, because the same reasoning will apply. We form beliefs about the future based on the past and present. And since we can't come up with any good reason for trusting the sources for beliefs about the past and present, that just transfers over to an equal lack of justification for trusting our formation of beliefs about the future. I leave it to you to think this through thoroughly.

> *No man can tell what the future may bring forth.*
>
> — Demosthenes

Conclusions about source skepticism

Notice that the skeptic's questions don't just show that we can't prove the reliability of our sources for belief. The point is much deeper. We can't provide one single, pure piece of evidence for this assumption that we all share, and on which the credibility of all our other beliefs depends:

> The sources of our beliefs are sometimes reliable.

And this fact is certainly perplexing, if not deeply troubling. Where is our anchor to reality? What ties our belief-forming mechanisms to the way things really are? The skeptic has questions. We seem to have no answers. But, as I warned, it gets worse. Or, at least, more interesting. To find out, look at the next section, which covers a whole different type of skeptical questioning.

The questions of radical skepticism

The questions of source skepticism in the previous few sections direct our attention to the reliability of our most basic belief-forming mechanisms. How do we know that memory, testimony, sense experience, or any other possible source of our beliefs are ever reliable guides to realities outside ourselves? *Radical skepticism* proceeds differently. It suggests a radical hypothesis incompatible with a huge array of our typical beliefs, a hypothesis so opposed to what we ordinarily assume that if it were true, an enormous number of beliefs that we now have would be false. The radical skeptic points out that continuing to hold our normal beliefs requires denying this radical hypothesis, or believing it to be false. He then typically asks how we know that it is false.

Radical skepticism about the past

The 20th-century philosopher Bertrand Russell once posed a radical hypothesis concerning the past that we can call "The Five Minute Hypothesis." I have beliefs about breakfast this morning, about how I slept last night, about what time I went to bed, about my activities last evening as well as about what transpired throughout the entire day. I have beliefs about the day before yesterday, and the day before that. My memory reaches back to last week, and last month, and last year. I have a wealth of beliefs about the past, perhaps tens of thousands, or even millions of such beliefs. But consider this hypothesis:

The Five Minute Hypothesis: *The entire universe sprang into existence from nothing five minutes ago, exactly as it then was, apparent fossils in the ground, wrinkles on people's faces, and other signs of age all instantly formed and thoroughly deceptive.*

This hypothesis is incompatible with all my beliefs concerning anything five minutes or more in the past. If it is true, all those past-oriented beliefs of mine are false. If it is true, I have no natural parents, no natural children, I am not really married, I have never signed a contract of any kind, and so on. I have false memories about all these things, memories that sprang into existence along with me five minutes ago. But nothing existed before that cosmic appearance act five minutes past. Weird. Bizarre. Crazy.

"But," you might object right away, "how do we know the Five Minute Hypothesis is true?" If you react like this, your reaction is natural. The hypothesis is admittedly highly implausible sounding, to the greatest possible degree. But that is not the point. The skeptic doesn't believe The Five Minute Hypothesis to be true. And he is not trying to get us to believe it. He is just pointing out that the beliefs we now have commit us to being convinced that it is false, and he wants to ask us how in the world we know it, or even reasonably believe it, to be false.

On examination, it is easy to see that we cannot produce a single shred of good evidence that this crazy hypothesis is false. Anything we point to — hair that has been around enough time to grow long, scars from wounds long ago, age circles in tree trunks, and so on — all of this is compatible with the hypothesis, which alleges that all these things, with their deceptive appearances of age, just sprang into existence within the past few minutes, as part of an elaborate cosmic trick.

But if we needed some amount of good evidence in order to be rationally justified in believing anything, then we couldn't rationally believe this radical hypothesis to be false. That wouldn't mean that we had to believe it to be true. Not at all. It would just mean that we should withhold judgment on it, and become correspondingly uncertain about everything in the past, over five minutes ago. But that would mean giving up all the beliefs that we have concerning things actually having happened in the past. And that would be radical indeed.

Radical skepticism about the present

On to our beliefs about the present. The thinker often referred to as The Father of Modern Philosophy, René Descartes (Pronounced *"Renay Day-Cart"*) back in the 17th century offered a radical suggestion. How do we know that this is not all an extraordinarily elaborate dream? You could be dreaming that you are reading philosophy now. This skeptical reasoning could just be part of one big nightmare. Look at the room around you. It's a dream room, not a real one. Gaze down at your body and at what you're wearing. All a dream. Or, to put it in the skeptic's favored mode of suggestion: How do you know that it's not all just a dream?

Life and love are all a dream.

— Robert Burns

Descartes: Rebel without a pause

René Descartes, military man, mathematician, and philosophical whiz kid, was the ultimate intellectual rebel. He decided not to swallow anything that anyone had ever told him and not even to trust his own senses. In an attempt to determine whether there was anything utterly indubitable, he proposed to try to doubt everything. One thing he concluded that he could not deny — the fact that in his very act of doubting, he was thinking. And from this fact, he saw that it followed that he himself must actually exist. Thus he bequeathed to history the most famous piece of philosophical reasoning ever: "I think therefore I am" (in French, "Je pense donc je suis," or in the more famous Latin formulation, "Cogito ergo sum."). From this foundation, he then began to build up a body of knowledge that he believed he could trust absolutely.

Descartes also toyed with the idea that our present life could possibly all be one big delusion. Perhaps there is a very powerful evil demon who has us hypnotized to hold all the elaborate beliefs that we have, and to seem to see and hear all the things we think we are now experiencing. We don't for a second actually suspect that this might indeed be going on. But why not?

> *The privilege of absurdity; to which no living creature is subject but man only.*
>
> — Thomas Hobbes

We cannot refute The Dream Hypothesis, or The Demon Hypothesis, or any such wild, comprehensive scenario. We can't even come up with a single shred of positive, independent evidence that either of these radical alternatives is false. And yet we believe things that imply they have to be false. This, the skeptic suggests, is a problem.

Radical skepticism about the future

We should now take at least the briefest of glances at our beliefs about the future. The skeptic's radical hypothesis here is one invented by a philosopher friend I often saved from the bumpers of oncoming cars in New Haven, Connecticut, years ago (when he wasn't saving me, as we theorized our way down the sidewalks around Yale), contemporary philosopher J.L.A. Garcia. It's called Futuristic Nihilism and is very simple.

The futuristic nihilist points out that the future does not exist. In order for a belief to be true, the object about which it is true must be among the furniture of reality, and that object must have the property attributed to it in that belief. For it to be true that grass is green, there must be such a thing as grass, and it must have the property of being green. But the future is right now just one huge void. We pour into that void lots of beliefs, about what will happen later today, what will transpire tomorrow, and what will occur later this year. We hold beliefs about the next decade. We are deep into beliefs about the future, however tentative and cautious we might try to be with this territory.

The future oriented radical skeptic could buttress his argument even further by plugging in to some of the other forms of radical skepticism. Think about the radical hypotheses of the previous section. At any second, we could wake up from Descarte's Dream and find things in the immediate future to be very different from what we might have inductively inferred. Or Descartes' Demon could snap his fingers and wake us up to a radically divergent future from anything we had in mind. The deception could change radically. How do we know any of this won't happen and pull the rug out from under all our future oriented beliefs? To this question we have no good answer.

> *My mind is in a state of philosophical doubt.*
>
> — S. T. Coleridge

What the skeptics show us

The questions of source skepticism showed us that we can't come up with any good evidence that our most basic belief-forming mechanisms are ever reliable. The questions of radical skepticism then poured salt on the wound, showing us that we can't find any evidence to refute or even dislodge an array of crazy-sounding radical hypotheses that are logically incompatible with our current beliefs about vitally important things.

The skeptic's challenges show us that we can't prove some of the most basic and important, and otherwise uncontroversial, things that we all believe. We can't even marshal any good evidence that they are true. We just believe them. And the skeptic keeps asking why. One thing that skepticism shows us is that there is very little room in human life for cocky, arrogant dogmatism. We all need to be a little humble in our certainties. But the skeptics can help us to see even more than that. To see what that is, read on.

Doubting Your Doubts

Doubt is the beginning, not the end, of wisdom.

— George Iles

Skeptical inquiry can lead to a state of doubt. How do we know all that we think we know, or even any of it? How can we be rational in believing anything? Could it be that the ancient skeptics were right? Should we suspend belief about everything, or at least nearly everything? Sextus suggested that we just live in accordance with appearances, without ever concluding that appearances reliably indicate realities. Is this the reaction we should have to the skeptic's questions and our amazing inability to answer them?

No. Not at all. Skepticism can teach us an important lesson, but it can't shut us down as believers. Without believing that his words have certain meanings rather than others, the skeptic can't even formulate his questions and challenges. And neither can we. Belief is inevitable in human life. And it's rational.

Suspending all our beliefs as the classic skeptic suggests is literally impossible. And even if it weren't impossible, it would be impractical. And clearly dangerous. If there seems to be a truck bearing down on me as I cross the street, I'd better believe it and act accordingly. If the skeptic suggests that we always act in accordance with appearances while withholding mental assent, he is requiring an act of mental gymnastics of us for which he has given us no compelling reason. But isn't our inability to justify our beliefs in answer to his questions itself compelling enough? No, the skeptic's questions show only that the rationality of our most basic assumptions, and thus the rationality of all our beliefs, cannot consist, at base, in our having evidence independently available of their truth. This is the main lesson of skepticism.

Where Do We Go from Here?

So how do we in fact know that our basic belief-forming mechanisms like sense experience, memory, and testimony are ever reliable? How can it be rational to believe that the world has been around for more than five minutes? That life is not all one big dream? That there is no supernaturally powerful evil demon hypnotizing us all? And that there will be a future? These are among our most basic beliefs. Where do they come from, and what certifies them? If we can come to understand this, it will give us a crucially important perspective on all the Big Questions we are examining in this book. But for these answers, you need to read the next chapter.

Chapter 6

The Amazing Reality of Basic Beliefs

● ●

In This Chapter

▶ Examining the foundations of rationality

▶ Glancing at Empiricism and Rationalism

▶ Critiquing the universal demand for evidence and proof

▶ Discovering a surprising insight about basic belief

● ●

The skeptic does not mean him who doubts, but him who investigates or researches, as opposed to him who asserts and thinks he has found.

— Miguel de Unamumo

*O*ur look at skepticism in Chapter 5 shows something that is both interesting and important. Reason cannot certify with proof or even good evidence that our most basic beliefs about life are true, or even rational to hold. This chapter takes up the issue of how it can still be rational to hold these fundamental beliefs without proof or evidence. We also delve into the more general issue of whether it can be rational to hold any other sorts of beliefs without the supports of proof or compelling evidence.

If you haven't already, you may want to read and think through the reasoning in the preceding chapter. Chapters 5 and 6 together give us a vital new perspective on belief and knowledge that we can bring to bear on all the big issues of philosophy with which we need to grapple. We are setting ourselves up for important insights on issues concerning goodness, freedom, death, God, and meaning. There is a deep sense in which we are still stocking our tool kit with tools we can use to help us to answer the most pressing questions we can ever ask. But even finding these tools gives fresh new insight that we need for understanding life in this world.

The Foundations of Knowledge

The history of philosophy has seen many warring camps fighting battles over some major issue or other. One of the major battles historically has been over the foundations of all our knowledge. What is most basic in any human set of beliefs? What are our ultimate starting points for any world view? Where does human knowledge ultimately come from? Chapter 4 just lays out the basic concepts of belief, truth, and knowledge. Chapter 5 shows that we can't have evidence for all that we believe. In this chapter, we need to explore what the foundations might be for all our knowledge of reality.

Empiricism and rationalism

Empiricists have always claimed that sense experience is the ultimate starting point for all our knowledge. The senses, they maintain, give us all our raw data about the world, and without this raw material, there would be no knowledge at all. Perception starts a process, and from this process come all our beliefs. In its purest form, empiricism holds that sense experience alone gives birth to all our beliefs and all our knowledge. A classic example of an empiricist would be the British philosopher John Locke (1632–1704).

It's easy to see how empiricism has been able to win over many converts. Think about it for a second. It's interestingly difficult to identify a single belief that you have that didn't come your way by means of some sense experience — sight, hearing, touch, smell, or taste. It's natural, then, to come to believe that the senses are the sole source and ultimate grounding of belief.

John Locke

A scientist and physician as well as a political thinker and philosopher, John Locke maintained in his big book *An Essay Concerning Human Understanding* that every human mind comes into this world as a *tabula rosa,* or blank slate. But some surely seem blanker than others. Sense experience writes on this slate and is the sole source of our ideas and knowledge, the philosopher claimed.

Locke was an extremely influential thinker in the 17th century, and became known as "the philosopher of freedom" for his political thought.

Common Lockisms include

"No man's knowledge here can go beyond his experience."

"All men are liable to error; and most men are, in many points, by passion or interest, under temptation to it."

But not all philosophers have been convinced that the senses fly solo when it comes to producing belief. We seem to have some beliefs that cannot be read off sense experience, or proved from any perception that we might be able to have. Because of this, there has historically been a warring camp of philosophers who give a different answer to the question of where our beliefs ultimately do, or should, come from.

Rationalists have claimed that the ultimate starting point for all knowledge is not the senses but reason. They maintain that without prior categories and principles supplied by reason, we couldn't organize and interpret our sense experience in any way. We would be faced with just one huge, undifferentiated, kaleidoscopic whirl of sensation, signifying nothing. Rationalism in its purest form goes so far as to hold that all our rational beliefs, and the entirety of human knowledge, consists in first principles and innate concepts (concepts that we are just born having) that are somehow generated and certified by reason, along with anything logically deducible from these first principles.

How can reason supply any mental category or first principle at all? Some rationalists have claimed that we are born with several fundamental concepts or categories in our minds ready for use. These give us what the rationalists call "innate knowledge." Examples might be certain categories of space, of time, and of cause and effect.

We naturally think in terms of cause and effect. And this helps organize our experience of the world. We think of ourselves as seeing some things cause other things to happen, but in terms of our raw sense experience, we just see certain things happen before other things, and remember having seen such before-and-after sequences at earlier times. For example, a rock hits a window, and then the window breaks. We don't see a third thing called *causation.* But we believe it has happened. The rock hitting the window caused it to break. But this is not experienced like the flight of the rock or the shattering of the glass. Experience does not seem to force the concept of causation on us. We just use it to interpret what we experience. Cause and effect are categories that could never be read out of our experience and must therefore be brought to that experience by our prior mental disposition to attribute such a connection. This is the rationalist perspective.

The foundations of knowledge

Rationalist philosophers have claimed that at the foundations of our knowledge are propositions that are *self-evident,* or self-evidently true. A self-evident proposition has the strange property of being such that, on merely understanding what it says, and without any further checking or special evidence of any kind, we can just intellectually "see" that it is true. Examples might be such propositions as:

✔ Any surface that is red is colored.

✔ If *A* is greater than *B*, and *B* is greater than *C*, then *A* is greater than *C*.

The claim is that, once these statements are understood, it takes no further sense experience whatsoever to see that they are true.

Descartes was a thinker who used skeptical doubt as a prelude to constructing a rationalist philosophy. He was convinced that all our beliefs that are founded on the experience of the external senses could be called into doubt, but that with certain self-evident beliefs, like "I am thinking," there is no room for creating and sustaining a reasonable doubt. Descartes then tried to find enough other first principles utterly immune to rational doubt that he could provide an indubitable, rational basis for all other legitimate beliefs.

Philosophers do not believe that Descartes succeeded. But it was worth a try. Rationalism has remained a seductive idea for individuals attracted to mathematics and to the beauties of unified theory. But it has never been made to work as a practical matter.

Evidentialism

Empiricists and rationalists were concerned with the question of where our beliefs ultimately come from, and thus what the ultimate foundation for knowledge might be. *Evidentialists* are philosophers who are concerned with a related but somewhat different question. They want to know where rational beliefs come from. What does it take to produce a rational belief, or to make a belief that you already have rational to hold?

The quest for certainty

Human beings can be greedy for different things. Some are greedy for money. Others chase more and more power. For many people, it's a psychological sense of certainty that they crave endlessly. We want to know, and to know that we know. We want to be absolutely sure. There can't be any chance that we're wrong. We want it all nailed down.

Everyone has a natural psychological need to feel in control. And control is impossible without knowledge. So we crave a certainty of knowledge. And yet the world doesn't always provide what we crave. Rationalism is an expression of our greed for certainty that we may have to resist in order to live without undue frustration in the world in which we find ourselves.

Can't we find any certainty at all in life? I must admit, I'm not quite certain.

The only certainty is that nothing is certain.
— Pliny the Elder (I think)

Modern-day evidentialists hold that no proposition is rational to believe unless it is either self-evident, evident to the senses, or is sufficiently supported by evidence from propositions of either of these categories. An example of propositions evident to the senses might be

- I am experiencing a tingle now.
- The color white is in my field of vision.
- I hear a sound.

In a famous essay written at the end of the 19th century, the British mathematician W.K. Clifford maintained that it is objectively wrong for anyone, anywhere, to believe anything without sufficient evidence. Substituting the word *irrational* for *wrong*, we can discover here the main claim of traditional evidentialism:

The Evidentialist Principle: *It is irrational for anyone, anywhere, to believe anything without sufficient evidence.*

Interpreting the evidentialist principle as broadly as possible, we can understand both self-evidence and the evidence of the senses to be included among the allowable possible supports for a rational belief.

The evidentialist is always asking, concerning any claim or belief: "What's your evidence for that?" He believes that rationality always requires either proof or evidence. But it is interesting to ask the evidentialist's question about his own principle. If everything has to have proof or evidence, then what is the evidentialist's proof for the truth of the evidentialist principle itself — the principle that makes this demand? What is his evidence? Why should we accept it?

It is hard to see how these questions demanded by the evidentialist's principle could be answered by the evidentialist himself when they are directed at his own main claim. He could allege that his principle is self-evident, but many philosophers have denied that it's true at all, and they clearly understood it. So it's not such that merely understanding it is sufficient for seeing that it's true. And it's not the sort of proposition whose truth could possibly be evident to the senses. So why should we accept it to be true? If we did accept it, then it seems that we would have to reject it, which just means that it is a self-defeating recommendation.

As intellectually popular as evidentialism has been for a very long time, and as important as evidence admittedly is as a marker of truth, there are very important fundamental beliefs that we all hold, and surely hold rationally, since they are the foundations of any other beliefs we might hold to be rational, and yet these important, *basic beliefs* cannot be supported by either proof or evidence.

The importance of evidence

We live in a sophisticated, yet somehow at the same time, strangely gullible age. Think of all the times you've seen an amazing product on an infomercial late at night, and called the 800 number, eager to have your life changed. What arrived in the mail wasn't quite up to your expectations. Why were you such a schmuck? Okay, maybe you weren't, but I sure was. I've been hosed by flashy informercials, dazzled by pretty ads, and moved by slick con artists, and I'm supposed to be a wise man. We should be a little more demanding of evidence before rushing to form beliefs.

Think about all the diets that have come and gone, and all the claims that they have made. True story: During my first semester of graduate school at Yale, I invented my own diet. I ate two hot dogs in buns for each meal, three meals a day. Breakfast? Hot dogs. Lunch? Yum, hot dogs again. Dinner? Weenies à la Tom. The result was that I lost 30 pounds in three months. To be frank, maybe it was because I soon skipped meals regularly. Wouldn't you? Now, what if I had written a book, and launched an informercial campaign — The Yale Hot Dog Diet! Would you have gone tube steak crazy? You may not be that gullible, but if the bestseller lists are any indication, too many people are. We need to hear the demands of evidentialism, and heed the rigors of careful scrutiny before quickly giving our assent. Evidence matters in life, even if the evidentialist is excessive in his claim that it is literally always required.

If there is a single such belief that it is rational for us to hold without proof or evidence, then the demand of evidentialism is obviously inappropriate and rationally excessive. But evidence is obviously very important in life. So where do we draw the line?

The Principle of Belief Conservation

The proof of the pudding is in the eating.

— Cervantes

As we seek to understand more deeply our common conception of rationality, we can make some interesting observations. First, all our beliefs can't be irrational, or nonrational, or else the concept of rationality has no application at all. The concept of rationality derives its usefulness from its ability to demarcate some beliefs off from others, separating the sheep from the goats, or the wheat from the chaff. But how could any of our beliefs be rational unless it's rational for us to assume that the sources or mechanisms through which we received them are sometimes reliable? It must then be rational to hold that our basic belief-forming mechanisms — sense experience, memory, and the testimony of others, for example — are sometimes reliable. And if this rationality does not consist in our having a proof, or even any good evidence, for the truth of the proposition believed (the conclusion I establish in Chapter 5), then there must be some other road to rationality, other than proof and evidence.

I have come to believe that something like what I call *The Principle of Belief Conservation* gives us the proper, rational response to skepticism and shows how, by an independent rational principle, certain basic beliefs can be accepted rationally without evidence or proof. The principle goes as follows:

The Principle of Belief Conservation

For any proposition, *P:* If

1. Taking a certain cognitive stance toward *P* (for example, believing it, rejecting it, or withholding judgment) would require rejecting or doubting a vast number of your current beliefs,

2. You have no independent positive reason to reject or doubt all those other beliefs, and

3. You have no compelling reason to take up that cognitive stance toward *P,*

then it is more rational for you not to take that cognitive stance toward *P.*

This is a carefully and formally stated principle, but it captures a procedure of reasoning engaged in by all rational people. It is, in a sense, a principle of "least damage." In other words, it is most rational, as we modify our beliefs through life and learning, to do the least damage possible to our previous beliefs as we accommodate new discoveries that we are making along the way.

Your current beliefs are like a raft or boat on which you are floating, sailing across the seas of life. You need to make repairs and additions during your voyage. But it can never be rational to destroy the boat totally while out on the open sea, hoping somehow to be able to rebuild it from scratch, or else to swim without it.

> *Man's most valuable trait is a judicial sense of what not to believe.*
>
> — Euripides

Belief conservation and radical skepticism

To see how the Principle of Belief Conservation works, consider one of the wild ideas from Chapter 5, The Five Minute Hypothesis, Bertrand Russell's famous radical hypothesis that the entire universe sprang into existence five minutes ago, and so that all our beliefs about the past beyond that point are false. I show in Chapter 5 that we cannot refute or find any good evidence against this extraordinarily crazy claim, and yet in order to justify continuing to hold all our past oriented beliefs rationally, we have to find some rational principle by which to reject this incompatible hypothesis.

Let The Five Minute Hypothesis itself count as proposition *P* and let's apply the Principle of Belief Conservation to it. Is it rational to take the cognitive stance of belief toward this wild hypothesis? Doing so would require denying a great many of our previous beliefs. We have no independent positive reason to deny all those beliefs. And we have no compelling reason to respond to this absurd hypothesis itself with the affirmation of belief. Therefore, by the Principle of Belief Conservation, it is most rational not to believe The Five Minute Hypothesis.

But what about the alternative cognitive stance of suspension of belief? Remaining undecided about The Five Minute Hypothesis would require doubting, or remaining undecided about, a great number of our previous beliefs, all those beliefs that require its being false. We have no independent positive to become agnostic about all those other beliefs. And we have no compelling reason to take up the stance of suspension of judgment with respect to The Five Minute Hypothesis. So it is most rational not to take that stance.

But if it is most reasonable not to believe it or to withhold on it, the only cognitive stance left is disbelief. Thus in response to the skeptic's suggestion of The Five Minute Hypothesis, our most rational response is outright disbelief. Denial. Rejection. Just say no.

The very same reasoning will apply to the other radical hypotheses that skepticism confronts us with in Chapter 5: Descartes' Dream Hypothesis and The Demon Hypothesis both. The same applies to Futuristic Nihilism. The rational person rejects these wild stories as false.

Belief conservation and source skepticism

What about source skepticism, though? In response to the skeptic's fundamental questions of how we know that sense experience, memory, or testimony are ever reliable at all, we have no good answer (see, again, Chapter 5). We cannot come up with a single piece of untainted evidence for the deep conviction we all have that any of our basic sources of belief are ever reliable connections to reality.

Let the proposition under investigation be the claim that:

Our basic belief–forming mechanisms are sometimes reliable.

Applying The Principle of Belief Conservation to this proposition shows us that our most rational stance toward it is that of belief, just like we would have thought.

> *What has not been examined impartially has not been well examined. Skepticism is therefore the first step toward truth.*
>
> — Denis Diderot

Skepticism can't bully us away from our most basic beliefs. But it can show us that we hold them rationally without proof or evidence, which in itself is a startling revelation, for which we should be grateful. It should make us think. And it will.

The basic status of belief conservation

The Principle of Belief Conservation seems to capture a fundamental way in which all rational people think. And in it lies the basis on which we respond to the skeptic. But how do we know that the Principle of Belief Conservation itself is true? It passes its own test, unlike evidentialism, but there is still no independent proof of it.

We accept it without proof. We accept it without independent evidence that it is true. And we are rational in so doing. There is no independent standard of rationality that can condemn or call into question this principle. Nonetheless, we accept it without any independent support. It is just true. We just believe it. It is not based on any deeper beliefs. It is itself basic.

The Principle of Belief Conservation can be taken as what philosophers nowadays call a "basic belief." It can be used to justify other beliefs, but is itself without further independent justification. We find that we believe it, and that it would be impossible not to believe it. But that in itself is no proof that it is true. Yet it is true.

> *It is undesirable to believe a proposition when there is no ground whatever for supposing it true.*
>
> — Bertrand Russell (1872–1970)

The Principle of Belief Conservation indicates that it is rational to believe each of the following propositions, but it does not provide direct evidence or proof that any of them is true:

- ✔ Sense experience is sometimes reliable.
- ✔ Memory is sometimes reliable.
- ✔ Testimony is sometimes reliable.
- ✔ Our basic belief-forming mechanisms are sometimes reliable.

As a philosopher, I can't find any other certification of these beliefs that we all hold and that it is rational to hold. So I am reasonable in thinking the Principle of Belief Conservation to be true. But if it is true, then classic evidentialism is false (see the section "Evidentialism," earlier in this chapter). It can be reasonable to believe things that are neither self-evident, nor evident to the senses, nor evidentially supported or inferable from propositions that fall into those categories.

Evidentialism refuted and revised

The conclusion that evidentialism is false is an important one because so many intellectuals for at least the past century have tended to be evidentialists, demanding evidence or proof for everything. So I should say it again, loud and clear: Evidentialism is false. We have been able to see that its demands are impossible to satisfy, which disqualifies it from the category of philosophical principles that we ought to accept.

But let's be as fair as we can possibly be. The evidentialist could acknowledge what we have shown and still try to rescue his enterprise. He could say that in demanding evidence for anything that wasn't self-evident or evident to the senses, classic evidentialists were indeed being rash. We have shown that there is a third category of beliefs for which evidence is not needed — beliefs for which evidence is not even possible. But, he could continue, for any belief that is capable of being supported by evidence, we'd better not hold that belief unless we have good evidence for it. Anything else is irresponsible and irrational.

> *The cautious seldom err.*
>
> — Confucius

Let's make this valiant effort to save the general perspective of evidentialism a little clearer by defining a category of belief:

Evidence receptive belief = (by definition) A belief for which evidence is possible

Now we can modify the original evidentialist demand:

Modified Evidentialism: *It is irrational for anyone, anywhere, at any time, to hold any evidence receptive belief without sufficient evidence.*

In this version of the evidentialist principle, propositions like The Belief Conservation Principle, and "Our basic belief-forming mechanisms are sometimes reliable" are excluded from the otherwise universal demand for evidence. The evidentialist might think that by modifying his demand, he can accommodate the insights we derive from skepticism without giving up the spirit of his concerns.

But this will not work if there are any beliefs, for which evidence is possible, which can rationally be held without sufficient evidence to show that they are true, or probably true. And the great 19th-century Harvard philosopher and psychologist William James thought he had good examples of such beliefs. If he is right, then even modified evidentialism is false.

James thought that there is one kind of evidence receptive belief that it is rational to have in the absence of sufficient evidence. He thought that it can be held on the basis of a certain sort of rational faith. Is believing without proof or sufficient evidence the same thing as faith?

William James on Precursive Faith

William James wrote a famous essay entitled "The Will to Believe," where he explicitly criticized the evidentialist viewpoint of W.K. Clifford. Clifford had insisted that it was wrong ever to allow our beliefs to go beyond what evidence could demonstrate. James was convinced that Clifford was wrong.

James pointed out that there are two very different approaches to matters of life and belief, one negative, one positive. The negative approach is based on the fear of ever making a mistake. This approach always enjoins caution. Be careful. Never take risks. Take an umbrella. Wait for evidence. This is the evidentialist's perspective on life and conviction. It is miserly regarding belief.

The other, more positive, approach to life and belief is more concerned with embracing all the truth it can. Its primary interest is not avoiding error at all costs. It advises venturing forth, trying new things, having new experiences, and positioning yourself for great discoveries. This, James holds, is the better perspective. It is generous regarding belief.

James thought that we sometimes have to meet reality halfway. We can't just sit back and wait for the world to give us evidence of what is true. We need to move forward with an openness of mind, and even the first glimmerings of a positive conviction, in order to discover some truths.

He used as an example a common, normal social situation. Imagine that you are entering a room of people you've never met before. If you worry that they may not be nice people and may not like you, and you inwardly demand seeing evidence to the contrary before you form any positive beliefs whatsoever about them, you will probably not get into the position to have a positive experience of any good truths about them as people. If you take a very different approach, however, and enter the room prepared to think of these strangers as most likely fine people who will enjoy your company, and you act on this as a conviction, you will probably find your conduct reciprocated, and meet some friendly and interesting individuals there.

Sometimes something like the positive state of belief, however tentative, helps to create a situation in which evidence is more likely to be forthcoming. In such circumstances, it is not more rational to wait on the evidence before granting a measure of belief, but it is rational to launch out with what James called *precursive faith,* faith that, etymologically, "Runs ahead of the evidence."

Believe that life is worth living, and your belief will help create the fact.

— William James

James discovered that championship level endeavor in any sport was typically based on precursive faith. Champions are regularly challenged to do something they've never done before — climb a new mountain, wrestle a new opponent, break a new world's record. If they just look at the evidence they have concerning their past performances, it will never be sufficient to prove that they are up to the new challenge and will prevail. But James came to realize that what sets champions apart is their ability to engage in precursive faith and launch out with belief that runs ahead of the available evidence, believing in themselves up front.

William James didn't think it was always appropriate or rational to engage in precursive faith, or belief stretching beyond the available evidence. He said that this is only appropriate if the option to believe is a "genuine option" that could not be decided on the basis of evidence alone. After careful analysis, he became convinced that three conditions must be present in order for a possible belief to be a genuine option. The option to believe that is in question must be, he said, live, forced, and momentous. Let's see what he meant:

🗸 **William James:** It is rational to believe beyond the available evidence if the option so to believe is a genuine option.

🗸 **Genuine option (definition):** An option to believe is genuine if and only if it is

- *Live:* You can bring yourself to believe it.

- *Forced:* Not to choose has the same consequences of a negative choice.

- *Momentous:* Something of great importance is at stake.

An option to believe is *live* if it is within the bounds of believability. The option of believing that I could leap over my house in a single bound is not a live one for me. Thus, precursive faith is a nonstarter here. The option of believing that I can beat a tennis opponent who is generally a little better than me is a live one.

An option is *forced* if not choosing to believe is somehow equivalent in its consequences to choosing not to believe. I recently debated buying a particular car that had just arrived at a local dealership. I looked at it for two days and test drove it twice. I really liked it. It was an extraordinary deal, because of some rare circumstances. But, as much as I liked it, and as perfect a deal as it seemed, I couldn't manage to form the positive belief that I should go buy it. The situation was such that, unfortunately, this was equivalent to deciding not to buy it, as my hesitation allowed another interested party to snatch it away while I pondered the possibilities. If you are presented with a job offer and given 48 hours to respond, then not choosing is equivalent in its consequences to a negative choice. It is a forced option.

> *The difficulty in life is the choice.*

> — George Moore

An option to believe is *momentous* if something of great value is at stake and may be lost if you do not grant a measure of belief to the proposition in question. Imagine that you can't swim well and are on a boat dock completely alone when you see a sole swimmer out in the water get into trouble and begin to go under. The swimmer is too far out for you to make it there unassisted. And there is no one else around at all. The swimmer calls for help. You notice that an old, rickety rowboat is pulled up onto the shore right beside you. The evidence is not clear as to whether it will make it all the way out there to the drowning swimmer or not. But there are no evident holes. It just looks real bad. The option to believe that it will likely get you to the swimmer is a live one. It is believable. And it is what James calls a forced option. Not choosing to believe that the boat can help you will be equivalent in the circumstances to choosing to believe that it will not. Finally, the situation is a momentous one. A life is at stake. In these circumstances, James says, the rational and right thing to do is not to take an evidentialist stance and demand altogether sufficient evidence of the boat's seaworthiness before pushing it into the water and leaping into it, but it is rather to launch out in precursive faith in the effort to save the swimmer.

> *The great end of life is not knowledge but action.*

> — T. H. Huxley

If James is right, it can sometimes be rational to accept a proposition into a positive belief state, to affirm it as a choice of precursive faith, even if it is an evidence receptive proposition — it is such that evidence for or against it is in principle possible — and you have no sufficient evidence that it is true. And if this is right, then even modified evidentialism is false.

Leaps of Faith

It is sometimes rational to take a leap of faith. Now, whether this conclusion applies to controversial questions like those of religious belief and other deep philosophical issues is a matter yet to be determined. But our philosopher William James shows us something eye-opening and very interesting. Looking for, gathering, and following the evidence is generally very important in life, but sometimes rational belief can operate without a dose of evidence sufficient to show us where the truth lies.

We just believe. And we do it all the time. We believe that our senses are sometimes reliable. We believe that the world has been around more than five minutes. We believe that our memories sometimes get it right. We are not for a minute convinced that life is really all a dream or a mass hallucination. We reason from the past to the future. And all without proof or evidence. We also confront Jamesian situations (see the previous section) where belief properly outstrips evidence.

The human mind has its own basic grasp of reality that we don't fully understand. We seem to be made in such a way that our minds fit our most fundamental cognitive environment like a glove fits a hand. With the natural, unimpeded operation of our basic belief-forming abilities, along with enough care and attention in exercising them properly, we can get most basic things right. We can rationally believe. And we can know.

It is not enough to have a good mind. The main thing is to use it well.

— Descartes

What are you launching out to believe in your life? What are you seeking to know? How well are you using your mind in discovering the truth that you are here to know?

Part III
What Is the Good?

"Okay, let's get into something a little more theoretical."

In this part . . .

In this part, we look at the moral and ethical side of life. Goodness! Happiness! Character! Rules! Loopholes! You want wisdom and virtue? Then check out this part.

Chapter 7

What Is Good?

. . . .

In This Chapter

▶ Examining the nature of good

▶ Establishing the meaning of evaluative language

▶ Contrasting noncognitivism, subjectivism, and objectivism

. . . .

To be good is noble; but to show others how to be good is nobler and no trouble.

— Mark Twain

What is good? This is a question that philosophers have asked for centuries. And they are not asking the sort of question that can be answered by just a list of good things: Sunshine, chocolate, hot showers, cool drinks. They want to know about the nature of goodness. What is it? What does it consist in? How does it fit into life? And why isn't there more of it in human conduct?

In the past century, philosophers have come to appreciate the many ways in which language can be a clue to reality. It certainly is a doorway into how we think. So philosophers have often approached questions about goodness by asking: What exactly is the meaning of the word *good?* Maybe it's one that you've asked, too. And why? We don't go around puzzling about the meaning of the word *green*. It doesn't take a philosopher to explain the word *hairy*. What's so perplexing about *good?*

A green field seems to have something in common with a green football helmet — the color they share in common. A hairy dog seems to have something in common with the hairy guy on the beach — a certain sort of surface texture they share in common. But what does a good movie have in common with a good painting, a good meal, a good book, a good razor, or a good person? What in the world could they all share in common? Thus, the perplexity.

Goodness is easier to recognize than to define.

— W. H. Auden

In this chapter, we ask what good is. And we see how the answer applies to human life. The great thinkers have a lot to say about what goodness is. And they have a lot to teach us about what it is to be good. We begin our investigation by looking at language. But what we are hoping for is a deeper insight into reality.

A Basic Approach to Ethics and Morality

There are two things important for us to get straight on at the outset here. Many people use the terms *ethics* and *morality* differently. Roughly speaking, they use the term *ethics* when they're talking about professional obligations and rules of conduct — as in the phrases legal ethics and medical ethics — and restrict the term *morality* to refer to matters of private behavior. Some people even say, "Hey, I wear one hat at work, and another at home," implying that a person's professional ethics can diverge from her private commitments of morality. But I've always reminded people that they wear those hats on the same head. So I think of personal life and professional conduct as deeply continuous, rather than compartmentalized. Because of this, I often use the terms ethics and morality interchangeably.

> *There is only one ethics, one set of rules of morality, one code: That of individual behavior in which the same rules apply to everyone alike.*
>
> — Peter Drucker

A second point. Most philosophers approach the topics of ethics or morality by posing issues or reviewing history.

- **Issues-oriented approaches** start by asking the reader about abortion, euthanasia, capital punishment, gun control, pornography, or other hot topics, and present the arguments pro and con, helping the reader to discern the nature of rational argument over such issues.

- **Historical approaches** to ethics survey the varieties of questions philosophers have asked about moral matters and the array of fundamental options they have considered about where we get our standards. This approach acquaints the reader with the fundamental statements of such positions as eudaimonism, deontology, and utilitarianism. Aren't you glad this isn't my approach? I don't avoid the strange philosophical labels for historical positions altogether, but my look at ethics here is different.

I want to get right at the heart of what we're talking about when we bring up ethics or morality. What is good? And what is bad? How do we think of right and wrong, and how do these things weave themselves into the textures of our lives? My approach here gives us the biggest and most practical perspective for doing our own ethical reflection on any perplexing issue that crosses our path. But more than that, it will help us to appreciate that moral reasoning is not always a matter of problem solving. It is often a way of creating strength. But more on that in a bit.

Defining the Good in the Context of Life

I love being a public philosopher. I have conversations with people in every walk of life, and in every sort of job imaginable. They share with me their perplexities, their wonderment, and their questions about life. I don't have to buttonhole people like Socrates did, even before the advent of buttons (a man truly ahead of his time). They take the initiative to come up to me, and they say the most amazing things. They ask me about things that have never occurred to me before. Or they might make a comment that puts an old subject into an entirely new light. And I go away thinking about what I've just heard.

A few years ago, someone said to me, "Dr. Morris, I've been chasing the good life for 20 years, but I'm just now starting to wake up and ask myself, 'Am I living *a* good life?'" Interesting. What do you think that person had in mind? Look for a moment at these two phrases:

- The good life
- A good life

They differ in just one word, yet have very different connotations.

The good life. In talks around the country since that day, I've asked audiences what this phrase connotes, and they've answered comfort, luxury, and wealth. Lifestyles of the rich and famous. Indulgence. Security. Good schools, great houses, fine cars, exclusive country clubs, and wonderful vacations.

Some have backed out of these *Town And Country Magazine* answers and have stuck with *Good Housekeeping* — The good life? A loving spouse, fun, smart, kind children, a nice house on a quiet but friendly street, an obedient, loyal dog, an abundant supply of tasty, nutritious food, and comfortable, at least somewhat stylish, clothing that slenderizes. Maybe a couple of rounds of golf at a public course each month. A few close friends — maybe even one with a boat. A bank account with contents. Enough income to cover the outgo. Money for retirement. This is what comes to mind for many people when I ask about the phrase "the good life."

> *The good life, as I conceive it, is a happy life.*
>
> — Bertrand Russell

When I ask about the meaning and connotations of the slightly different phrase *"a good life,"* I get very different answers. The associations it has are felt to be more ethical, or moral, or spiritual in nature. A life worth living. An existence that helps others. True friendship. Love. Service. Fulfillment. Giving. Character. Dependability. Growth. Happiness.

Certainly the words *the* and *a* can't alone account for these tremendous differences. It's the whole phrases, and how they are differently used in our culture these days.

Is a life to be characterized as good if it's one of excellence and enjoyment? Or if it's one that embodies ethics and the spirit? What about the person whose life it is? What is it to be a good person? Can the word *good* just mean very different things?

A look at how the word *good* itself has been thought to function gives us a clue. But I want us to think together a bit more broadly first. In the following section, I want to approach a general question of what all broadly evaluative language means.

Three Views on Evaluative Language

I use the phrase *evaluative language* to refer to any uses of words like *good, bad, great, horrible, right,* and *wrong.* There are basically three different philosophical views about what evaluative language does. I want to briefly examine each one in the following sections.

The philosophy of noncognitivism: The boo/yay theory

Noncognitivism is a philosophical view whose name is derived from the word *cognition,* for knowing. The noncognitivist is a philosopher who is convinced that evaluative language does not convey any form of knowing at all. It is not fact stating, but is merely expressive in function. That is the noncognitivist claim.

Why would anyone say this? Primarily because of the phenomenon of evaluative disagreement. The noncognitivist typically argues that people differ too much over moral and ethical judgments for there to be any objective facts of the matter. If there were objective moral facts, they claim, we would not disagree so much over them. People disagree over the rightness or wrongness of abortion, capital punishment, gun control, premarital sex, pornography, solutions to problems of racial inequality, and much more. People also disagree over what movies are good or bad, what books, what restaurants. The noncognitivist believes that mere extent of evaluative disagreement, inside and outside of ethics, shows that evaluative language does not report objective facts, but rather serves some other function.

On the noncognitivist view, if I say,

"Honesty is the best policy,"

what I mean, or what I am really saying, is

"Honesty — Yaaaaay!!!!"

I am cheering honest behavior in general. I am giving it my endorsement. Two thumbs up. Correspondingly, when I say,

"Human sacrifice is wrong,"

I really just mean

"Human sacrifice — Boooooo!!!"

I am deriding or deploring human sacrifice. I am condemning or trashing it. Two thumbs down. Human sacrifice — yuck. Noncognitivism is, then, not surprisingly, sometimes referred to as the *Boo/Yay Theory of Evaluative Terms.*

> *Ethics is in origin the art of recommending to others the sacrifices required for cooperation with oneself.*
>
> — Bertrand Russell

The noncognitivist is right in thinking that there are uses of language that are not fact stating. We don't always use language to report; we often use it to exclaim, and sometimes to question. There are many functions of speaking other than the stating of fact. But I believe that noncognitivism is wrong to think that this category of the-non-fact-stating captures our typical usage of evaluative terms.

At least two philosophical problems with noncognitivism exist. First, ironically, the very phenomenon of apparent ethical disagreement that has moved some thinkers in the direction of this view really can't be accounted for by the view. People certainly do seem to disagree about moral matters. David believes all abortion is wrong. Susan disagrees. Katherine believes that all capital punishment is wrong. Bob disagrees. What exactly are they disagreeing about? Noncognitivism says that no moral fact is at issue. These different people are just reacting differently to the same things. One endorses capital punishment, while the other condemns it. One cheers, while the other boos. They don't really conflict cognitively over any such thing as an objective moral fact at all. That's what noncognitivism claims. But how plausible is this? If we asked Katherine and Dob, they would probably report that they are indeed disagreeing over objective facts, and that the noncognitivist is just wrong. Of course, they would likely say that this is an objective fact too.

We certainly seem to be able to disagree over right and wrong, good and evil. And if noncognitivism can't give a good account of this, I think that we are right in saying "Boo" to it.

Second, why do we cheer or jeer? We don't just randomly celebrate kindness and razz murder. We feel that our evaluative reactions are appropriate to the nature of the things evaluated. We condemn murder *because it is wrong*. We endorse kindness *because it is good*. Noncognitivism has no room in its world view for moral facts that might justify our moral reactions. And this just seems . . . wrong. Surely there is a Priority Problem here for noncognitivism. This philosophical view can't account for any prior facts that might make our reactions sensible or reasonable, rather than arbitrary or random. So, again, we say, "Boo."

> *The facts speak for themselves.*
>
> — Demosthenes (384–322 B.C.)

I think we should reject the philosophy of evaluative and ethical noncognitivism. It seems wrong — erroneous and philosophically inadequate. But what else is available as a philosophical account of moral and evaluative language?

Ethical subjectivism

A second view is also sometimes generated by reflection on the pervasiveness of moral disagreement in our world, and throughout the sweep of human history. Some philosophers have believed that, whenever we utter any sentence of the form "*x* is good," we are really not stating a fact about *x* at all (so far, agreeing with noncognitivism), but that we are stating a fact about our own subjective feelings toward *x* (here departing from the noncognitivist view).

On this view, the only fact that is conveyed by evaluative language is a fact about the subject speaking, not about the object on which he might otherwise seem to be commenting. Thus, subjectivism is a version of *cognitivism,* the view that evaluative and ethical claims do convey facts. It seems that most people are cognitivists deep down, but that subjectivism is a version of cognitivism that surprises them. It tends to surprise any of us with its claim about the sort of fact that is conveyed by this language.

The ethical subjectivist claims that whenever I utter any sentence like

"Vanilla ice cream is good,"

the sentence really means, or expresses the fact that,

"I like vanilla ice cream."

In other words, on the subjectivist account of evaluative terms like *good, bad, great, right, wrong,* and *evil,* these words never convey any property or quality of the apparent object they apply to, but instead are used only to express a fact about the inner, subjective psychological state of the person uttering them.

Likewise, on this view of evaluative discourse, if I say,

"Bob believes that charity is good,"

I am not ascribing to Bob a belief that the activity of human charity has a certain property — namely, goodness — but I am merely describing Bob as feeling favorably disposed towards charity. Likewise, if I say,

"Bob believes that human sacrifice is evil,"

all I am doing, according to the subjectivist, is saying that Bob feels a strong dislike for the ugly business of human sacrifice.

Why would anyone be an ethical subjectivist? Many philosophers who have adopted such a view point, like the noncognitivist, to the phenomenon of ethical disagreement. The argument, again, is this: If there were objective ethical facts in the world, then moral disagreement would not be so widespread. But moral disagreement is widespread. Therefore, there are no objective moral facts. Moral language does, however, seem to be fact stating. Thus, it must state facts about something other than objective moral properties. The most obvious candidate for the factual content of moral language is the psychological attitudes or feelings of the person speaking. Therefore all moral and evaluative language is subjective.

But if subjectivism were right, it would follow as a very strange implication that there is really after all no factual disagreement between Betty, who says, "Sex before marriage is wrong," and Charlie, who says, "Sex before marriage is perfectly all right." They are not disagreeing on a fact about sex before marriage; they are just reporting different mental states. Betty is reporting her disapproval of a certain activity, and Charlie is reporting his approval. Because Betty is not saying that Charlie, in his heart of hearts, really does censure sex before marriage, but won't admit it, and Charlie is not denying that Betty disapproves, they are not in any factual disagreement at all. This is the strange consequence of a subjectivist view.

And it's baloney. People like Betty and Charlie do disagree. And any philosophy that can't naturally accommodate this is wrong. Beware of hidden implications in a philosophical position. Always ask, in evaluating a philosophical view, how well it captures what seems to you naturally or intuitively right. Could you sometimes be wrong in your intuitions? Certainly, but you always need to be given good reason to think this. If you aren't, then hang on to your sense of what seems correct.

Sometimes we want to report on our inner attitudes, and sometimes we want to discuss the outer world. Why should we think of moral language as precluding the latter? Subjectivism ends up facing the same problems that plagued noncognitivism. It can't account for the undeniable reality of objective moral disagreement, and it can't explain why we feel justified in having the inner states we do have as attitudes toward moral issues. It faces The Priority Problem, too. So this, in my book, is good enough reason to move on.

A few words should be said about a cousin of straightforward subjectivism. We can call it *Cultural Subjectivism*. On this view, when Steve says that gun control is morally right, he is not stating an objective moral fact about gun control, but rather he is merely reporting a general cultural attitude. If Zelda says in response, "No, gun control is wrong," she can really be disagreeing with Steve. However, according to the cultural subjectivist, one of them can be right and the other wrong not because of what is objectively true of gun control, but rather because of what the general cultural attitude tends to be.

This version of subjectivism is just as problematic as the original. Disagreement is possible, but not the right sort of disagreement. And on cultural subjectivism, it is impossible to rise above the general beliefs and feelings of any culture and criticize it. But surely, we want to say that anyone living in a culture that condoned slavery could correctly rise up and denounce it as wrong. If cultural subjectivism were right, they would just be wrongly reporting the tendencies of their own culture and would therefore be wrong. But that is contrary to what any of us want to say. Therefore, this view also is unacceptable.

Moral objectivism

Killing an innocent person for sport is wrong. Infanticide is immoral. Political freedom is a good thing. Equal opportunity is preferable to arbitrary unfairness. Both justice and mercy can be very good things. People are born with a right to be treated with respect.

When we say such things, most of us believe we are doing more than cheering or condemning. And we are not just reporting on our inner psychological states autobiographically. Nor are we just registering cultural assumptions. We think of ourselves as stating facts about realities in our world. Torturing an innocent person is by nature, and as a matter of fact, wrong. There are moral facts regardless of what we think. And, just like in science, we can sometimes have trouble discovering what the objective moral status of a situation is, and thus we can reasonably disagree on it. These perspectives capture aspects of the most common and natural human stance on the nature of moral utterance and the ultimate status of moral matters. The philosophical position with respect to ethics and morals that is built on these convictions is called *moral objectivism*.

A more general philosophical position would be that of *evaluative objectivism*. Such a position would argue that all uses of evaluative language purport to be statements of fact about objective truths out in the world. But that is certainly too extreme. Sometimes when I say, "This ice cream is good," I do in fact mean to convey merely that I like it, along with my conviction that others probably would too. And yet with other ascriptions of goodness, as in "This is a good screwdriver," I do mean to convey something objective. Likewise with "Kindness is a good thing." And this is the domain of evaluative language that we need to concentrate on here, the moral or ethical domain.

The moral objectivist believes that at least a certain range of evaluative language — that range consisting in apparent statements of moral or ethical fact — is indeed fact stating, and that it can, and usually does, state facts about the objective world.

Objectivism and the moral skeptic

Of course, in response to moral objectivism, we can have moral skepticism. The moral skeptic would ask, "How do we know that any of our moral or ethical beliefs, taken as statements of fact about an objective moral reality, are true?" People do disagree. And it's hard to find anything much more compelling than intuition, or the judgments of conscience, to rely on in any attempt to settle a moral dispute or answer a moral question. The skeptic could be thought of as a cousin to the noncognitivist and the subjectivist in questioning how we could justify any claim to have objective knowledge of moral facts.

> *A sudden, bold and unexpected question doth many times surprise a man and lay him open.*
>
> — Francis Bacon

Moral skepticism can take many forms. The moral skeptic can ask how we know any of our moral belief-forming mechanisms, like conscience or intuition, are ever reliable. But the most basic skepticism here goes further and asks how we can possibly know that there are moral facts at all. Maybe conscience is just a widespread form of delusion. How could we answer this?

We can't prove that there are moral facts, starting from independent premises and using forms of inference we know to be valid. We can't even come up with compelling evidence that there are objective moral facts. Does this sound familiar? For anyone who read my earlier chapters on belief and skepticism, it should. Anyone who skipped that should go back right now and become the general expert on skepticism that you're capable of being. And then you'll see that there is one great way to answer the moral skeptic — The Principle of Belief Conservation. As a matter of fact, most human beings hold a great many moral beliefs, and a great many beliefs that imply that our moral judgments are representations of objective fact. The skeptic can call this realm of objective fact into question, just like he can call conscience and intuition into question. And we can't refute him on his own ground. What we can do though is point him to The Principle of Belief Conservation, which generates the conclusion that it is rational for those of us who incline to the position of moral objectivism to continue in that view undisturbed by the skeptic's inquiries. We just continue a little wiser.

Is morality then on shaky ground? Well, I'll answer a question with a question. Is our belief in an external world on shaky ground? Is our belief that sense experience, memory, and testimony are sometimes reliable on shaky ground? The inability to answer skeptical questions with proof itself proves nothing, except the limitations of proof. That is something we should keep firmly in mind. To be answered, the skeptic doesn't have to be refuted.

But we still have a nonskeptical question we need to address. If we are rational in thinking that there are moral facts, then what sort of factual property is moral goodness? Is it something you can see, hear, feel, or weigh? Is it a physical property? A spiritual attribute?

When we say of something that it is good, what sort of fact are we conveying? I want to ask this question in a general way first and then close in on the ethical implications of what we discover. The great philosophers since the time of Aristotle have had things to say that can help us here, which I cover in the next section.

Teleological Target Practice

When the great football quarterback Joe Montana scrambled away from tacklers and lofted a pass into the end zone for a touchdown, fans in the stadium would yell, "Good throw, Joe!" When I say that I have a good circular saw, a good fountain pen, and a good home security system, or when I praise a golfer for a good putt, what does all that have in common with the exclamation from the football fans? What job is *good* doing in all these contexts? What sort of fact is it being used to state?

According to Aristotle, something is good when it successfully hits the target for which it was intended. A good pass from Joe Montana made it into the receiver's hands. A good putt went into the hole. A good saw cuts wood efficiently. A good fountain pen puts ink onto paper where I want it to be. A good home security system warns of intruders in every possible way, and either frightens off those bold and crazy enough to persist, or else leads to their apprehension.

In every case, the good thing does successfully what it was intended to do. It hits the target, serves its purpose, fulfills its mission. It has a function, and carries it out well. Using the Greek term for an archery bullseye, *telos,* we can call this *The Teleological Conception of Good.*

The history of ethics is in many ways an attempt to answer the question "What makes a human being a good person? What makes a man a good man or a woman a good woman?" This is a question about moral goodness, or ethical goodness. In our effort to answer such questions, Aristotle would have us ask, "What is the target for human life? What is our proper function, our purpose, our mission?"

> *The great and glorious masterpiece of man is to know how to live to purpose.*
>
> — Montaigne

This question can arise in another, more oblique, way. Let's look for a moment at the strange behavior of evaluative and moral terms in contexts of simple logical reasoning. This shows us something very interesting, and something that can give us insight into ethical goodness.

We need to be careful about how we use evaluative terms in making inferences, or engaging in logical reasoning. To see this, compare a few simple cases of logical inference. First, we compare two that use nonevaluative language and succeed, and then several that use evaluative language and break down.

This is what philosophers call a valid argument:

1. (a) Bill is a swarthy hit man.

    (b) All hit men are human beings. Thus,

    (c) Bill is a swarthy human being.

In argument 1, line (c) follows logically from lines (a) and (b). If (a) and (b) are both true, the logical validity of the argument guarantees that (c) is true, too.

2. (a) Bill is a good hit man.

    (b) All hit men are human beings. Thus,

    (c) Bill is a good human being.

> *There are some jobs in which it is impossible for a man to be virtuous.*
>
> — Aristotle (384–322 B.C.)

It looks like we have a conclusion that could not possibly be true if the two premises from which it is derived logically are true.

Something clearly has gone wrong. 2(c) doesn't at all follow from its premises. A good hit man is in fact a bad person. Yet, the argument 2, which doesn't work, is completely parallel to argument 1, which did work. What has gone awry here?

It's easy to think that it's just because we are using a moral term.

It could be suggested that, perhaps moral terms are somehow uniquely unsuited for logical reasoning. But that would not be accurate. Consider

3. (a) Shorty is a tall jockey.

 (b) All jockeys are human beings. Thus,

 (c) Shorty is a tall human being.

Shorty can be tall for a jockey, in comparison to his fellow jockeys, and still be short compared to the general population.

Comparative and evaluative terms like tall and good are not logically like other modifying terms. Because of this, we have to be careful in reasoning with them. Consider

4. (a) Bob is a good father.

 (b) A father is a person. Thus,

 (c) Bob is a good person.

Maybe. Perhaps (a) gives us some evidence in favor of (c). But (c) is not guaranteed by (a) and (b). Some would suggest that Bob can be a good father to his children at home, and yet compartmentalize his life to such an extent that he cheats customers at work. Likewise if Bob is a good friend, a good uncle, or a good son. He could conceivably perform admirably in a number of roles in his life, and still fall short of overall, moral, or ethical goodness — goodness as a person — due to egregious violations in another part of his life. All these forms of goodness seem relevant contributors to overall moral goodness. That's why they are evidence for it. But if they don't fully prove it, then we can be left asking, "What is it?"

It is not always the same thing to be a good man and a good citizen.

— Aristotle

What is it to be a good man? A good woman? A good person? What is it to live a good life? Those are still the questions we have to answer. If you're interested in the answer, you can check out the next two chapters.

Chapter 8

Happiness, Excellence, and the Good Life

What is honored in a country will be cultivated there.

— Plato

*I*n this chapter, we look at what goodness is all about, and we explore the relationship between goodness and happiness, between ethics and human flourishing, and between morality and excellence.

Memo to the Modern World

Ethics is not primarily about staying out of trouble. Ethics is about creating strength. Inner strength. And interpersonal strength. Ethical living produces stronger people, stronger families, stronger communities, stronger organizations, stronger institutions of all kinds, and, ultimately, stronger nations.

Morality is not first and foremost about restriction and constraint. Morality is about human flourishing. It's about the deepest sort of happiness. And it's about living the best sort of life. It's all about what we honor, what we cultivate, and what we become.

We often think of rules and structures in a particular way. Imagine a spectrum representing an ideal continuum for human life. On one end of the spectrum is absolute order. On the other end is absolute freedom. When we think about life like this, we come to believe that we are faced with a dilemma. Do we want the predictability and security of order, or would we prefer the self-expressive options and creative possibilities of freedom? Do we want constraint or chaos? The streets of Singapore, or Downtown Detroit? (Just kidding, Detroiters! — sort of!)

Order————————————————————————— Freedom

Perhaps this is, to a certain extent, a false dilemma. Maybe morality offers, at least in principle, a structure, or form of order, that facilitates the most important, and most fulfilling sort of freedom. That's what I want to suggest.

This is the ancient perspective on goodness that we are in danger of losing as we enter a new millennium. We pursue excellence. We crave success. We want our organizations, and our country, to be great. But we are too often blind to the connections between these goals that we chase and the goodness that we need.

They are only truly great who are truly good.

— George Chapman

The Idea of Good: A Short Course in Options

Where do we get our idea of what is good in human life? Where does morality come from? Philosophers have suggested a number of different answers to such questions. Their most prominent theories deserve at least a brief mention.

Divine Command Theory

Many religious philosophers throughout the centuries have suggested that ethics originate in the commands of a creator God. These commands, or commandments, are then made known to human beings through either the normal operations of the faculty of reason with which He has endowed us, or else through the means of special divine revelation vouchsafed to a community of believers, and, through them, to the world.

On this view, goodness, or rightness, is established by divine commands and consists in conformity to divine decrees. The good and the right are whatever actions, attitudes, and attributes are in harmony with God's commands; the bad and the wrong are whatever happens to be contrary to those commands.

Okay, let's hold off on the issue of the existence of God. (See Part VII if you can't wait, though.) The main problem for this divine command theory is its implication that the decrees of God themselves could be called good only in the logically empty sense that they conform to themselves. And it seems that all traditional religions have wanted to say that God's commands are good in a more substantial sense than that. God's commands are thought to be what they are because of his love, or kindness, or benevolent concern for us as our creator. They are what they are because it is good for them to be precisely that. And no standard divine command theory can accommodate this intuition.

Perhaps ethics ultimately, at its best, reflects the eternal *nature* of a creator God. I call this approach *divine nature theory.* But this is a different position from the well-known divine command theory.

> *In nothing do humans approach so nearly to the gods as doing good to others.*
>
> — Cicero

One problem for either view is that, if it were true, people who do not believe that there is a God would lose all ground for holding to any sort of moral objectivism. Is this a decisive objection? No. But it has motivated even many religious believers to search further for a philosophical account of morality.

Social Contract Theory

Some philosophers have suggested that human beings long ago got together in social groups and then either implicitly or explicitly decided what rules of conduct would govern their personal behavior as well as their interactions toward each other. They saw rules as needed to avoid complete conflict and chaos. So they entered into a social contract, or agreement, to act in those ways, and that's the ultimate origin of morality, ethics, and law.

Good, on this view, would then be a matter of agreement with the social contract. Could it be good that there be such contracts? Or could a particular culture's contract be morally reprehensible? If so, then the basis for assigning that form of good or evil would seem to be independent of the alleged agreement, which means that, at its best, social contract theory is incomplete.

One major problem with the implications of social contract theory is that, in some societies, the most ethical individuals to be found have been those who explicitly took a stand against the prevailing norms of behavior in that society. They seem to stand in violation of that society's implicit social contract, and yet precisely because of that, they have merited attention as paradigms of moral heroism. But if their heroism consists in their being answerable to a higher standard than that of their society, social contract theory does not go deep enough, or high enough, to give us the ultimate answers we seek.

True morality consists not in following the beaten track, but in finding out the true path for ourselves and fearlessly following it.

— Mohandas Gandhi

Finally, social contract theory either hypothesizes a contractual moment in the remote past for which we have no hard historical evidence whatsoever, or else it just uses this as a convenient fiction, which leaves us with no real answers at all.

Utilitarianism

In the 19th century, a number of philosophers in England began to view goodness as tied to utility, or usefulness in producing pleasure, happiness, convenience, or other desirable human advantages. In any moral situation, the choice of action is right, they believed, which has the greatest utility, or produces the greatest quantity of positive states for people. Likewise, good human characteristics would be those personality and character traits that tend to lead to good actions.

Utilitarians divide into two camps:

✔ **Act-utilitarians** think that it's the business of morality to evaluate individual actions by asking how those actions themselves stack up when judged by the standard of utility. According to them, we should always perform the action that will, in its circumstances, produce the greatest good, defined as utility.

✔ **Rule-utilitarians** take it back a step deeper. An action is good, according to them, if it is performed in accordance with a rule which itself produces the greatest utility for the greatest numbers of people. On this view, an act can be right even if it fails to produce the most utility in its situation, but it has to be performed in accordance to a rule which, overall, produces the most utility in human society, relative to its relevant alternatives.

On standard utilitarian calculations, it could be right to execute an innocent person in order to prevent a riot. And that just seems wrong. Utilitarians insightfully see good and right as tied somehow to human flourishing. But I think that typically they just get it wrong in their attempt to spell out exactly what that tie is.

Deontological Theory

Deontologists believe that right and good consist in obedience to objective moral duties. Immanuel Kant (1724-1804) was the most famous and influential deontologist of all time. Kant believed that morality consisted in acting on the basis of duty alone. He went so far as to think that if you enjoy an action, and benefit from it, and that is even part of your motivation for doing it, then it can't count as a purely moral act. Baloney. Some of the best and most moral acts are performed by good people who take joy in doing the right thing, and that joy is a perfectly acceptable part of their motivation for so doing.

> *There is . . . only one categorical imperative. It is: Act only according to that maxim by which you can at the same time will that it should become a universal law.*
>
> — Immanuel Kant (in his typically lucid fashion)

Deontologists don't typically even address the question of what exactly duties are. Where do they come from? What do they consist in? If they aren't the result of divine commands, or social agreements, or utilitarian considerations of help and harm, then what exactly are they? All these things remain somewhat vague and mysterious in the writings of most deontologists.

Is duty important in human life? Certainly. But references to duties alone cannot give us a complete account of morality or ethics, or of what goodness most fundamentally is.

Sociobiological Theory

In the 19th and 20th centuries, a few prominent biologists, sociologists, and other scientifically oriented thinkers have suggested that it is the evolutionary survival value of behaviors for societies that have generated our known moral codes. Conduct that facilitated cohesion and survival was encouraged, and behavior that was judged detrimental to these ends was prohibited.

> *Failure or success in the struggle for existence is the sole moral standard. Good is what survives.*
>
> — W. Somerset Maugham

A good deal of sociobiology is suggestive and persuasive, even in the early forms we now have. But I can't see that it is comprehensive enough to give us what we are looking for.

The example of the moral hero may be relevant here just as it was in seeing a problem for social contract theory. The person who takes a moral stand in contradiction to the drift of his society may, short term, actually endanger the continued existence of that society as it is constituted. Anyone who does the morally heroic work of resisting and working to overthrow an immoral tyrant thereby threatens the social structure that his reign has established. And this runs against the grain of sociobiological explanation.

Worse yet for sociobiological theory, on its account of morality, it could be morally permissible, and even obligatory, for us to select a group of human beings, even involuntarily, for medical experimentation, however risky, painful, and degrading it might be, if that could enhance human survivability. And this is clearly wrong. Sociobiology does not seem to capture, or even accommodate, our deepest moral intuitions.

Virtue Theory

From the ancient world, there is another theory that not only deserves mentioning, but that I've come to think is not only insightful, but also true. Here's my version of virtue theory. There is such a thing as human nature. People are deep down alike in some fundamental ways. And there are things about human nature that make certain qualities or characteristics — the virtues — important to have if you're interested in happiness, fulfillment, and human flourishing. And who isn't?

Morality is that domain of human endeavor concerned with identifying, cultivating, and encouraging those qualities, or virtues, that facilitate ultimate human flourishing. Moral goodness is the quality of an action, attribute, or person that measures whether it accords with the virtues.

Virtue theorists can maintain that what sociobiologists discover to be true is in fact true because of that universal human nature we all share. They can also hold that social agreement on moral fundamentals typically arises as a reflection of our recognition of what the virtues are. Likewise, to the extent that we do consider questions of benefit and harm in ethical decision making, as utilitarians suggest, we can most deeply interpret what benefit and harm really are only if we do so in accordance with an account of human nature, and of the virtues. Fans of virtue can also hold that we have the nature we do because God has so endowed us. In addition, they can maintain that divine commands reflect that endowment and direct us as to how we should develop it.

> *Silver and gold are not the only coin; virtue too passes current all over the world.*
>
> — Euripides

To put it briefly, a virtue theory of goodness, properly developed, can incorporate the insights of all the other theories, while avoiding their distinctive problems. To find out how a virtue theory be developed, see the following section.

Four Dimensions of Human Experience

Our old friend Aristotle claimed that all human beings seek happiness, in everything they do. Human life is essentially teleological (see Chapter 7). We necessarily aim at targets in our day-to-day lives, trying to make things happen. And it's Aristotle's insight that underneath all that we do, happiness is our universal quarry. A real understanding of this claim will help us to appreciate the role of ethics in life.

If Aristotle was right that ascriptions of goodness are always teleological, then we may just have hit on what the goal, or intention, or purpose (*telos*) of human living is. It is happiness. Personal happiness? Sure. But also happiness for others. In fact, happiness and fulfillment for the greatest number possible.

But in order to understand what this means, we need to understand what happiness really is. Is it just sensual pleasure, as some philosophers have supposed? Aristotle himself thought that this is a view fit for grazing cattle, but not for human beings. Not that there is anything wrong with pleasure. It is impossible to imagine a happy life devoid of pleasure. But it's just a small part of a much bigger picture.

Is happiness the same thing as personal peace? This has been proposed by stoic thinkers. But, again, it alone is an inadequate view. Peacefulness is a passive state. And human beings are active, dynamic creatures. We need a view of happiness as dynamic as we are. Don't get me wrong. Personal peace, or tranquillity within, is an important part of the happy life, just like pleasure. But it also is just a small part of the picture.

Aristotelians think of happiness as more like an activity, or a process of participation in something that brings fulfillment. Genuine happiness is a byproduct of living in a way that is supportive of human flourishing. It is tied to excellence. Happiness comes from discovering who you are, developing your distinctive talents, and putting those talents to work for the overall benefit of others as well as yourself.

Moral goodness is then the quality of facilitating genuine happiness, fulfillment, and the deepest flourishing in human life. A good person is a person who shoots at the target of human happiness and flourishing for other people as well as himself. A good action is an action taken in this direction. A good quality, or personal characteristic, is an attribute that facilitates action toward this end.

In analyzing the insights of all the great philosophers concerning what it takes to attain real happiness, genuine fulfillment, and the deepest sort of human flourishing, I've come to believe that there are four fundamental and universal dimensions of human experience. These four dimensions of experience help us to understand the four corresponding targets we need to aim at if we ultimately are to attain and promote happiness in the lives of the people around us, as well as in our own lives. They are also the four foundations for creating and sustaining excellence in all that we do. And, as such, they are definitive of what it is to live a good life.

These dimensions of human experience, with their associated targets, are as follows (reading the arrows as meaning "aims at"):

- The Intellectual Dimension » Truth
- The Aesthetic Dimension » Beauty
- The Moral Dimension » Goodness
- The Spiritual Dimension » Unity

In the following section, I look briefly at each dimension. An understanding of them can promote a correspondingly deeper understanding of human happiness and of the relevance that ethics has to issues of human flourishing. For too long, we have thought of ethics in isolation from the other main concerns of life. Seeing how morality, with its target of goodness, fits within the sweep of human experience, helps us all to come to a deeper appreciation of the ethical domain.

Each dimension of experience that we need to look at has an associated target, which itself is to be viewed as a foundation for human excellence. Goodness is one of these targets and is tied to all the others.

The intellectual dimension

Every human being has a mind. We are all, to some extent, intellectual creatures. We need truth like we need air, or food, or water. We cannot flourish without ideas, and without truth we perish.

We all have an intellectual dimension to our experience of the world, and that dimension aims at the target of truth. In any relationship, in any situation, we need to be told the truth if we are to have a chance of being our best, and feeling our best, in that context. Likewise, we need to tell others the truth.

Truth is the foundation for trust, and without trust no human relationship can flourish. Without flourishing relationships, no human being can grow and experience a sense of deep personal fulfillment.

Knowledge is power.

— Francis Bacon

The British philosopher Francis Bacon (1561-1626) did say long ago that knowledge is power, and he has been quoted ever since. But what a shame it is how wrongly people have reacted to that insight. Too many in our time have reasoned: Without power, effective action is impossible in any domain. Therefore, power should be acquired and maintained; thus, as its basis, knowledge should be acquired and hoarded. This reasoning has led business people, politicians, and even physicians to withhold truth from people who desperately need it.

There is this fear that sharing knowledge is like sharing a piece of pie. When I share my dessert with you, I divide it down the middle, and subtract, or take away, a part that I otherwise could have enjoyed, and give it to you. The more I give you, the less I have left over. But sharing is a different phenomenon altogether in the realm of truth and knowledge. The more it's shared, the more it's added to, and even multiplied.

I learned this as a professor at Notre Dame. When I passed on new knowledge to my students, I ended up multiplying knowledge in a way that I had never fully anticipated. It's not just that what was in my head was now in 300 other heads. But the students heard what I shared from 300 different interpretive mind sets, and thus 300 different perspectives. This student grew up in Nebraska, next to him was a Floridian, and across the room a native German. Maybe in the back, someone from Brazil, or Mexico, and just seats away, a Japanese student. Some were from poor backgrounds; others had grown up in mansions. They heard my words from their differing perspectives, filtering my shared knowledge through so many different grids of belief, attitude, and emotion, and then they saw things that I might never have been able to see alone. Things they shared. And thus knowledge, in their minds, and in mine, was multiplied immensely, by my initial willingness to share.

The same thing can happen in any business, or in any family. Truth is the raw material for creativity. We need to respect it, live it, and nurture it. By sharing truth, we multiply knowledge and thus provide the basis for increasing the overall available power that comes from knowledge.

Truth is a foundation for human flourishing, fulfillment, and the deepest sort of happiness. Can't the truth sometimes hurt? Sure it can. But the deepest, most lasting forms of happiness can't be so fragile that they depend on keeping truth at arm's length. Illusion is never a necessary condition for ultimate fulfillment and human flourishing.

> *Nature has instilled in our minds an insatiable desire to see truth.*
>
> — Cicero

Is a person good? Does she respect and nurture truth? For herself as well as for others? Does she treat other people seriously, as having minds? Does she respect others by sharing with them any knowledge that might be relevant for who they are and what they are doing?

What are our relationships to truth? They can be thought of as falling into two categories, which we can label, for convenience, the passive and the active (see Table 8-1).

Table 8-1	Our Relationships to Truth
Passive	*Active*
Attentiveness	Honesty
Openness	Candor
Teachability	Forthrightness
We must be learners	We must be teachers

First, glance at what I'm calling the passive side of our relation to truth. Every major religion stresses the importance of what we pay attention to. We need to attend to the world around us in order to have any hope of grasping truth as we pass through life. We pay attention, which is actually an activity, in order to position ourselves to be proper passive recipients of what the world has to pass along to us. By the category of the passive, I don't mean to imply for a second that we are ever wholly passive in learning. We are not. But there is a side to our relationship with the truth where we are called upon to listen and take in. This is, relatively speaking, the passive side of our relationship to truth.

Secondly, we need to be open to new ideas and unexpected perspectives. Openness is a form of intellectual humility, and is an important human virtue. Paying attention won't pay dividends unless we are genuinely open to learn.

Thirdly, we need to be teachable by others. No one knows it all. And everyone we ever come into contact with has something to teach us. But we'll never fully access those truths available to us in the lives and experiences of other people unless we are teachable. Throughout our lives, we all need to be learners. This also, at its best, is a moral quality.

Now the active side of our chart. We need to be honest with ourselves and with others. Honesty is a way of respecting the truth. The honest person does not lie or deceive others. When asked, the honest person tells the truth.

But honesty can be a fairly minimal way of respecting truth. Candor goes a step farther and offers truth beyond what is requested, when it's needed. The candid person is inclined to deal in truth whether it's asked for or not, as long as it is helpful.

The way I understand forthrightness, it goes even farther. A forthright person hides nothing of his motives and withholds no truth that is relevant to the flourishing of other people around him. You don't have to second-guess forthrightness. What you see is what you get. The truth is laid out for all to take in. The forthright person is, in principle, the ultimate teacher. He embodies transparency to truth. We all need to be lifelong teachers. That is, in fact, one of the best ways to guarantee that we are also lifelong learners. We learn best what we attempt to teach.

To reach the target of human life, we have to aim in all ways at truth. We have to be open to it, and we need to make it available to others. It's one of the four foundations of human excellence and lasting happiness.

The aesthetic dimension

The second great dimension of human experience is the aesthetic dimension. I've come to believe that we need beauty in our lives just like we need truth. It is every bit as important. Without a regular experience of beauty, people cannot feel their best or be their best, in any activity, or in any relationship.

> *Beauty is the promise of happiness.*
>
> — Stendhal

One of the greatest errors of popular culture in the last 100 years is to encourage us to narrow our conception of what beauty is. A mountain range can be beautiful. So can flowers. And a beach. And a certain sort of face. Music can be beautiful. And dance. In the midst of a hotly contested game of basketball, a move to the basket can be a thing of beauty. And so can a mathematical theorem. And a philosophical argument. An act of love can be beautiful. And so can a joke.

The aesthetic encompasses all forms of delight. Beauty ranges over very different sorts of things and actions. But one aspect is constant. Beauty always inspires.

In a beautiful place, we are more open. In beautiful surroundings, we can be much more creative. Ugliness depresses the spirit. Beauty lifts our hearts and minds. It elevates the emotions and the attitudes.

But beauty does all this only if it's noticed, felt, and appreciated. Is beauty indeed in the eye of the beholder? To some extent. An experience of beauty involves an objective reality with the right qualities, but it also involves a subjective receptivity. The right sensibility can see beauty where others miss it. But beauty is not, at bottom, a relativistic phenomenon. It's truly amazing how universal the conditions for a perception of beauty happen to be. Whether this has to do with our evolutionary past or instead with divinely implanted sensibilities is a source of contention among philosophers. But the fact remains that an experience of beauty is universal, and that it's important for human flourishing.

The good is the beautiful.

— Plato

Philosophers haven't been of much help in recent decades in assisting us with our understanding of the importance of beauty. But that's no surprise, because philosophers have been singularly unhelpful in assisting us with our understanding of anything practical in this same period of time. Philosophy has been primarily an academic endeavor in the past century. And it has focused much of its attention on matters having to do with the extraordinary rise of science, technology, and mathematics in their impact on human life. It has in turn become itself more oriented toward theoretical topics and divorced from the practical flow of daily human experience. And one of the major topics that has been relatively ignored in recent philosophical activity has been the topic of beauty, or of the aesthetic, generally considered.

Again, we can say that there are two basic modes — passsive and active — of experiencing beauty in human life (see Table 8-2).

Table 8-2	Two Modes of Experiencing Beauty
Passive	*Active*
What we see	What we plan
What we hear	What we create
What we smell, touch, and taste	What we do

There are two kinds of beauty. Loveliness is dominant in the one and dignity in the other.

— Cicero

There is first what we might call the external beauty of the world and of things in the world that we passively take in and enjoy. But there is also what we might refer to as the internal beauty of what we ourselves do. There is such a thing as performance beauty, and each of us has a need to experience it. This is the form of beauty experienced by a ballet dancer, a jazz guitarist, a public speaker, a painter, or a basketball player in the process of creation and performance, as distinct from that form of beauty passively experienced by anyone else who just witnesses that performance. It's the form of beauty that, as a boy, I watched old men experience while they whittled away at hardwood sticks. It's the beauty the great auto mechanic feels as he solves a perplexing problem and coaxes an engine into running its best.

We are all by nature essentially creative beings, and we need to experience performance beauty every bit as much as we need to take in the more commonly acknowledged passive form of aesthetic experience. If we can provide others the opportunities for both passive and active enjoyment of the aesthetic dimension in our lives and work together, we provide the conditions under which they can flourish and sense fulfillment in what we are all doing.

Excellence in any activity directed toward human growth and flourishing is beautiful. We should never forget that.

> *Beauty is a form of genius — is higher, indeed, than genius, as it needs no explanation.*

> — Oscar Wilde

Respecting and nurturing the aesthetic dimension of our experience, aiming at the target of beauty in all that we do and in all that we are, makes it more likely that we'll hit the ultimate target of happiness in our activities and in our lives, the end we all seek.

The moral dimension

The dimension of human experience that we normally call the moral dimension is that domain of perception and judgment having to do with the good, the right, and the noble. It is the realm of kindness, fairness, sensitivity, justice, and self-giving.

What we normally call goodness in human life is all about inner peace and outer harmony. We have moral obligations to ourselves — to develop properly and take care of our own interests. And, in addition, we have moral obligations to others — to family, friends, and people who cross our paths in the normal course of daily life.

> *I expect to pass through life but once. If therefore, there be any kindness I can show, or any good thing I can do to any fellow being, let me do it now, and not defer or neglect it, as I shall not pass this way again.*

> — William Penn

It is impossible to find happy people performing, and experiencing, nothing but bad, wrong, and evil conduct. It is, admittedly, possible to find people undergoing pleasurable sensations amidst extensive wrongdoing. But genuine happiness cannot emerge outside the matrix of moral goodness.

> *Good, the more communicated, the more abundant grows.*

> — John Milton

We seem to be hardwired to attain the ultimate of human fulfillment and flourishing only in connection with an experience of moral goodness. People who depart from the path of kindness and treat others with disrespect find out sooner or later that crime does not pay. It has often been said that virtue is its own reward. It is just as true that vice is its own punishment. Plato wrote that to suffer evil is bad, but to do evil is much worse. Others can harm us on the outside. Only we can harm our own souls.

I say much more about this dimension in the next chapter. For now, it is most important to see just how it fits in with the other major dimensions of human experience. Morality is not something invented. It is ingredient in the nature of things. And it is crucial for the fullest and most satisfying experience of the world.

> *Everywhere in life, the true question is not what we* gain, *but what we* do.
>
> — Thomas Carlyle

The spiritual dimension

The fourth universal dimension of human experience is the spiritual dimension. Its target is connectedness, or unity — inner unity, unity between myself and others, between all human beings and the rest of nature, and, ultimately, between nature and nature's source.

When I say that all human beings have a spiritual dimension to their experience of the world, I don't for a moment mean to imply that everyone is, deep down, religious. I am not talking here about creedal affirmation or institutional affiliation. There are atheists in the world and agnostics. But even atheists have needs and aspirations deeper than those that we paradigmatically take to be psychological.

A paradigmatic psychological need would be our need to feel in control. This seems to be, to one degree or another, a universal psychological need. Yet it is one that we can put aside temporarily for the sake of some greater good, as when, for example, we get into a taxi or onto an airplane as a passenger. Spiritual needs are too deep for us to be able to temporarily put them aside for the sake of some greater good. They can be neglected or ignored, but always to our detriment.

These spiritual needs serve as something like intertwined strands of experiential cable, conveying to us distinctive band widths of our overall daily experience. I've come to believe that there are four such needs. When we aim to meet them, in the case of others as well as ourselves, we refine our aim at the ultimate target of happiness, fulfillment, or human flourishing.

In at least the briefest of ways, we need to look at each of these spiritual needs. We all have a deep need for a sense of:

- Uniqueness
- Union

- ✔ Usefulness
- ✔ Understanding

Everyone needs to feel special, distinctive, unique. The first great piece of philosophical advice was the command "Know Thyself." The endless quest for self-knowledge is the search for our own uniqueness. This need filters our experience of the world. If we can seek to make others feel distinctive, we enhance their chance at experiencing happiness.

Everyone needs a sense of union with something greater than the self. Whether it is something as exalted as a mystical sense of union with God, or a naturalistic sense of continuity with all the world, or it is as humble as a sense of family at home, or belonging at work, we all need to feel a sense of connectedness with something larger. This again affects our experience of the world and is crucial for our attainment of happiness. Any display of human kindness, however small, to another individual inevitably makes that individual feel less cut off, less alone, and just a bit closer to a sense of fulfillment in what they are doing.

> *Wherever there is a human being, there is the opportunity for a kindness.*
>
> — Seneca

We all need a sense of usefulness. That's why unemployment is never just an economic problem but always a spiritual issue as well. This is one of the deeper reasons that many welfare programs create problems. When people feel like beneficiaries but not contributors, they feel a deep malaise. We human beings are inherently creative, and we want to be useful in the world. That's why work is not an unfortunate necessity, but rather a life-giving force when engaged in properly.

> *I believe that any man's life will be filled with constant and unexpected encouragement, if he makes up his mind to do his level best each day, as nearly as possible reaching the high water mark of pure and useful living.*
>
> — Booker T. Washington

The fourth spiritual need is to feel a deep emotional understanding of our place in the world — in our families, our communities, our workplaces, and in our overall journeys through life. We filter our perceptions of the world around us through the lens of whatever understanding we've managed to acquire, and in turn, those perceptions alter that understanding, expanding it, or correcting it.

If we respect and nurture these four spiritual needs in our own lives, and in the lives of the people around us, we move in the direction of true fulfillment and human flourishing. If we neglect them, we founder.

Two sides of morality

There are two sides of moral goodness:

☞ Inner harmony

☞ Outer harmony

Ethics is all about spiritually healthy people in socially harmonious relationships. Inner health and harmony leads to outer health and harmony, which then in turn reinforces the inner states that created it. The proper starting point, in all ethical improvement, is always on the inside. But the best sign of moral goodness is always on the outside.

Together, these four needs help define the realm of the spiritual in our lives. But put in a nutshell, the spiritual is concerned with two things: Depth and connectedness. That is the essence of spirituality, and the core of the spiritual dimension of our experience.

The Ultimate Context of Good

Let's look back at where we've been and see where we have arrived. I've been suggesting that evaluative language, like the language of ethics and morality, is often used straightforwardly as fact stating language. I've reviewed most of the standard philosophical accounts concerning what those facts are and where they come from. And I've suggested where I think the truth is to be found — in a virtue theory approach that centers on Aristotle's insight that "good" always has to do with hitting a target. What then is the target in human life for evaluating whether an individual human being, an act, or a character trait is good? It is, as Aristotle suggested, happiness, understood as an activity structured around the four dimensions of human experience and coordinated by the four foundations of human excellence — intellectual truth, aesthetic beauty, moral goodness, and spiritual unity. This provides the ultimate context for talk of the good life for a person to live, as well as of the goodness we seek to find in a man or woman.

> *The good is, like nature, an immense landscape in which man advances through centuries of exploration.*
>
> — José Ortega Y Gassett

What does it take to be good in the moral sense? What does it take to satisfy the requirements of good living? That is the question we ask in the next chapter.

Chapter 9

Ethical Rules and Moral Character

● ●

In This Chapter

▶ Looking at the moral rules

▶ Appreciating the Golden Rule

▶ Investigating the role of wisdom and virtue

● ●

> *Seek not good from without; seek it within yourselves or you will never find it.*
>
> — Epictetus

Morality is connected to the deepest possibilities of personal fulfillment, individual happiness, and human flourishing in this life. Ethical conduct is behavior that respects and nurtures truth, beauty, goodness, and unity, in our own lives, and in the lives of people we deal with day to day. Good people live, and encourage others to live, as fully intellectual, aesthetic, moral, and spiritual creatures.

Every day, people treat others inappropriately. Millions of people lie. They cheat customers. They steal. They abuse. They manipulate. They act rudely. They inflict hurt. They treat other people as they would treat physical objects — mere means to their own selfish ends. More than a few even kill.

> *The good person loves people and uses things, while the bad person loves things and uses people.*
>
> — Sydney J. Harris (1917-1986)

Every day, good people struggle with how to live in a world where goodness cannot be taken for granted. They ask themselves how they can resist the pressures and temptations that would make them into something they would not be proud to have become. They want to know how to teach their children the right ways to live. They seek guidance for the gray areas of life, knowing that these places of moral ambiguity can easily lead into the dark areas.

What is morality, after all? I suggest that it's a fundamental foundation of human flourishing (see Chapter 8). But what exactly is this foundation of morality? And how can we use it as our map for living? How can morality guide us? In this chapter, we look at the two most prominent philosophical perspectives on these questions. In a world brimming over with good and evil, it's important to know how to think about these issues.

Commandments, Rules, and Loopholes

The best known philosophical view of what morality is holds that it consists first and foremost in rules — lots and lots of rules.

- ✔ Thou shalt not kill.

- ✔ Thou shalt not commit adultery.

- ✔ Thou shalt not steal.

- ✔ Thou shalt not bear false witness against thy neighbor.

- ✔ Thou shalt not covet thy neighbor's house . . . and all that other stuff that thy neighbor has and probably doesn't deserve but somehow lucked out and got anyway.

And these are just a few of the most famous to be found in the Bible. Look at the Old Testament book of Leviticus some time. It's truly amazing how many rules there can be.

And it's a strange thing about rules. There can never be enough, but it's easy to have too many.

There can never be enough in the sense that, no matter how many rules we have for acceptable conduct, there will inevitably still be some moral loopholes that the overachieving bad apples among us will just as surely find. In addition, there will always be some new innovations in human life for which we haven't yet figured out all the rules. Genetic engineering comes to mind at present. Remember that at one time no one knew what insider trading was. And the ethics of the Internet are still in the process of being formulated. New developments in human living call for new rules. So, in an ever-changing world, you can find at least two senses in which we can never have enough rules.

But we can easily have too many rules. What's the old saying? Too many cooks spoil the pot? Too many rules tie us in knots. Bad people will do what they want to do anyway. No proliferation of rules has ever made people better. And good people will waste a lot of time and energy just learning and worrying about all those rules — "I wonder if I'm still in compliance with Rule 357, Section 25, paragraph 12, item b, subsections i-iv? Will someone please get our ethics officer on the phone?" — whereas the people who are good would probably just do the right thing anyway, if utterly unfettered by all the codification. We even run the risk that good people will be tempted to work hard to become masters of the rules at the expense of losing sight of what they are really doing.

Centuries ago, the great Rabbi Hillel believed in simplifying the rules. He thought it all came down ultimately to just one thing. But we'll get to that in a bit (see the next section). Jesus said there was one more — so, two master rules, grand total. But we insist on making more.

> *When "Do no evil" has been understood, then learn the harder, braver rule, "Do good."*
>
> — Arthur Gutterman (1871-1943)

When we multiply rules, they tend to take on negative formulations. Have you ever noticed that? Consider a fairly random sample that goes beyond the biblical injunctions I mentioned at the beginning of this section:

- Don't cheat.
- Don't boast.
- Don't manipulate people for your own ends.
- Don't start fights.
- Don't be a user.
- Don't be a jerk.
- Don't be selfish.
- Don't be greedy.
- Don't break promises.
- Don't be insensitive.
- Don't deface other people's property.
- Don't violate people's privacy.
- Don't make people crazy.
- Don't just borrow *Philosophy For Dummies* — buy your own!

Okay, I added that last rule. But you get the picture. How many moral rules can there be? Lots. Rules for moral living have been promulgated in every culture. And they sometimes shade from clearly ethical enjoinders into the closely aligned realm of etiquette. It's not always possible to separate out the realm of manners from that of morals. Both involve what philosophers call *other-regarding behavior*, conduct that takes into consideration the needs and feelings of other people. Both provide for social harmony. And both affect how we ourselves develop.

> *Loving-kindness is the better part of goodness.*
>
> — W. Somerset Maugham

The Golden Rule: A few sample statements

The Golden Rule has been articulated in many different ways:

> *What you do not want done to yourself, do not do to others.*
> — Confucius (551-479 B.C.)

> *Try your best to treat others as you wish to be treated yourself, and you will find that this is the shortest way to benevolence.*
> — Mencius (c. 371-289 B.C.)

> *What is hateful to you don't do to another.*
> — Rabbi Hillel (c. 65 B.C.-9 A.D.)

> *Whatever you wish that men would do to you, do so to them; for this is the law and the prophets.*
> — Jesus

> *To do unto all men as you would wish to have done unto you, and to reject for others what you would reject for yourself.*
> — Muhammad (c. 570-632)

> *Do unto others as if you were the others.*
> — Elbert Hubbard (1856-1915)

The Golden Rule and what it means

The promulgation of moral rules has been a part of every major culture. But the universality of morality goes even farther than that. There is one rule that has been promulgated, in one form or another, across all major cultures. It is the moral command widely known as The Golden Rule:

> *Do unto others as you would have them do unto you. Treat others as you would want to be treated if you were in their place.*

I believe that The Golden Rule is at the heart of morality. It captures the main attitude of an ethical person regarding the impact of his actions on others. And it does so in such a way as to appeal to the greatest and most important natural power in human life — the power of the imagination. The Golden Rule calls on us to imagine what it would be like to be in the position of the other people who are affected by our actions, and on that basis to make our decisions as to how we will act.

Most of the real trouble in the world is due to someone's failure to live in accordance with The Golden Rule. But here is something interesting. Most people who fall short of this rule in their conduct tend instead to act in accordance with what philosophers call *The Rule of Reciprocity:* They treat others as they are treated — they merely mirror back the conduct that they believe themselves to be receiving. The good news here for Golden Rulers is that Reciprocators can often be fairly easily won over. If they are treated consistently in accordance with The Golden Rule, it becomes more difficult for them to act in any other way, mirrors that they are. Ultimately, though, The Golden Rule enjoins us to take the moral initiative in how we treat others. It urges us to take the high ground no matter what.

> *The meaning of good and bad, of better and worse, is simply helping or hurting.*

> — Emerson

The Golden Rule does not in the least purport to give us the whole of morality — just a thumbnail sketch, or essence, of the other-regarding side of the moral enterprise, that aspect of morality having to do with how we treat others. But it gives guidance to any normal human being endowed with a modicum of appropriate self-interest and acceptable self-love.

The precise role of The Golden Rule

The most common misreading of The Golden Rule thinks of it as pressing us to impose our own wishes and desires on other people. Why should we treat others as we would want to be treated, rather than treating them as they themselves actually want to be treated? That is the critic's most common question. But the answer is simple and is two-fold.

First, if I were in the other person's place, I would want to be treated in accordance with all my own legitimate desires and felt needs. So The Golden Rule enjoins me to treat him in accordance with all his legitimate desires and felt needs. Consequently, it does not after all, on closer inspection, require of me, or even suggest, the imposition of any of my more distinctive likes or dislikes on others at all.

Secondly, what if the other guy actually wants to be given unfairly preferential treatment? No moral rule should demand that I comply. But, the critic could retort, this objection can be easily avoided by saying only that we ought to treat others in accordance with all their legitimate desires and felt needs. Why should we bring any consideration of what we ourselves would want into the mix at all?

The Golden Rule is stated as it is in its classic formulations in order to give us not only guidance but also motivation. And each are equally important for moral behavior. The Golden Rule in all its traditional statements directs us into a mental exercise of imaginative projection. We must put ourselves into the place of the other people affected by our actions. That draws on all the emotions tied up with self-interest and uses them to move us in the direction of other-interest.

A man, to be greatly good, must imagine intensely and comprehensively; he must put himself in the place of another and of many others; the pleasures and pains of his species must become his own.

— Percy Bysshe Shelly (1792-1822)

Scottish philosopher David Hume (1711-1776) believed that morality is based in sentiment. It is precisely people devoid of natural sentiment, that affection of fellow feeling that is so natural to most of us, who commit the heinous crimes and immoral acts that we shudder to read about in the newspaper. The Golden Rule positions us to be sympathetic and empathetic with others. And it thus gives us an emotional push in the direction that we should travel. That is part of its genius.

But even The Golden Rule has its limitations. Like every other rule, it needs interpretation. And it can't alone turn a bad person into a good one.

Rules are important in the moral life of human beings. We begin to learn the moral life as children through an introduction to simple rules. Rules are thus important in early moral education. They are also crucial for establishing shared expectations in any joint human endeavor, such as a family, a business, or a profession.

But rules can't constitute the whole, or even the essence, of morality. Rules need interpretation. Rules can, in principle, conflict. And there could never be enough rules to cover every possible situation we might face, in all its complexity and distinctiveness.

Rules and precepts are of no value without natural capacity.

— Quintillian

Something more than rules is needed to capture the full essence of morality. And that something more is precisely what is highlighted by the second way of thinking about ethics to be found among philosophers, which I lay out in the next section.

Character, Wisdom, and Virtue

The second tradition of thinking about ethics sees character as at the center. The ancient Greek word *ethos,* from which we derive our term *ethics,* didn't mean *rules,* it meant, simply, character.

Character is just that settled set of dispositions or habits of thinking, feeling, and acting that make you who you are. It is determined by how much wisdom and virtue you have in your life. So, in order to fully understand what character is, we have to know what wisdom and virtue are.

Wisdom is a form of understanding, an understanding of how we ought to live. *Virtue* is just the habit or disposition of acting in accordance with wisdom. An ancient Japanese proverb says that wisdom and virtue are the two wheels of a cart.

The character tradition in ethics holds that the core of morality is not about good actions, but is rather about good people. It is not first and foremost about what we do, but is rather about who we are, as manifested in what we do. It is about settled habits of attitude and action. If we become wise and virtuous people, we perform wise and virtuous actions.

> *It is easy to perform a good action, but not easy to acquire a settled habit of performing such actions.*
>
> — Aristotle

This tradition of philosophical reflection on ethics sees both wisdom and virtue as central to moral goodness. Wisdom is the perspicacity to see what is right. It can never be totally codified in aphorisms, discourses, or rules. It is a skill of perception and judgment, as well as a set of insights, or beliefs, that come from applying that perception and judgment. And it is necessary for the deepest sort of moral living. But it is alone never sufficient. Wisdom must be joined to virtue. Insight must be linked to action.

> *The moral sense is as much a part of our constitution as that of feeling, seeing, or hearing.*
>
> — Thomas Jefferson

The universality of certain moral principles among human beings seems to testify to something like a moral sense, or a capacity for moral intuition, inherent in the makeup of a normal person. Perhaps this is very much like what we often call *conscience*. The voice of conscience informs us as to what is right — and as such it is a source of wisdom — and it does so in such a way as to move, or goad, or motivate us to comply with what we see to be right. Conscience is not a source of inert information, but is more like an inner guidance system.

Neither our insight nor our action has to be perfect in order to exemplify wisdom and virtue. There are glimmerings of wisdom available to us all. Full-fledged sagacity is not a requirement for the moral life. Likewise, there are many virtues, and saintly perfection in embodying them all is not a requirement for living a good and ethical life, a life of moral character.

If ethics is about insight and habit, wisdom and virtue, then we need to ask what the virtues for human life are. In order to do so, I start by going back to Aristotle, the first authoritative codifier of the virtues in the ancient world. Aristotle's list contains some items not usually thought of these days in connection with ethics at all. But is important to see that there is no isolated domain of the ethical which is out of touch with other aspects of our lives.

Some thoughts on character

A number of great thinkers have commented on the importance of character in human life.

Character is Destiny

— Heraclitus

Character is power.

— Booker T. Washington

Character is simply habit long continued.

— Plutarch

The one great requisite is character.

— Talmud

Following are the virtues according to Aristotle:

Courage	Friendliness	Temperance	Truthfulness
Liberality	Wittiness	Magnificence	Shame
Pride	Justice	Good temper	Honor

The world of ancient Greece viewed these human qualities as necessary for people to live well together. And they were seen by Aristotle as means between extremes. Consider, for example, the virtue of courage. It is a human quality having to do with how we respond to risk or danger. The vice of deficiency in this regard would be timidity, or fearfulness. The corresponding vice of excess would be rashness, or foolhardiness.

Cowardice ——————————**Courage** ——————————**Rashness**

(The Deficiency)   (The Virtue)   (The Excess)

Likewise, the virtue of pride that Aristotle refers to would be a midpoint between something like a deficiency of low self-regard and an excess of boastful arrogance.

Aristotle's enumeration of virtues has been of great historical importance. But other such lists have existed. For example, Christian theology counts humility as one of the central virtues. And this is a strength not appreciated in full by Greek thinkers, although it is by others in the ancient world, such as the Chinese Taoists.

It is always the secure who are humble.

— G. K. Chesterton

Our recognition of the virtues is due in part to our prevailing conceptions of excellence and human flourishing. The more broadly we see the truth about human possibility, the wider our conception of the virtues will be. A more modern listing of virtues might also contain, in addition to Aristotle's virtues, and in no particular order, many or all of the following:

Kindness	Decency	Consistency	Honesty
Modesty	Commitment	Loyalty	Humility
Integrity	Sincerity	Openness	Dignity
Reliability	Cheerfulness	Enthusiasm	Amiability
Humor	Trustworthiness	Benevolence	Tolerance
Insightfulness	Love	Perspicacity	Thoughtfulness
Sensitivity	Tactfulness	Steadfastness	Helpfulness
Gracefulness	Resiliency	Liveliness	Balance
Civility	Magnanimity	Harmony	Cooperativeness
Empathy	Persistence	Reasonableness	Prudence
Faithfulness	Resoucefulness	Boldness	Altruism
Warmth	Hospitality	Hopefulness	Coolheadedness
Politeness	Creativity	Truthfulness	Broadmindedness

You may think of other virtues not named here. A human being is a multifaceted creature with many possible virtues, or character strengths, personal properties that promote inner spiritual health and outer social harmony. The point is not so much to come up with an exhaustive inventory of the virtues as it is to understand the root nature of all these qualities. They are all meant to be characteristics that aid us in living well together, in making a positive difference in this life, and in becoming the best people that we can be. They are all attitudes, habits, or dispositions of character conducive to living a meaningful life in the best and deepest of ways. They are to be thought of as either causal contributors to, or else constituents of, genuine human happiness. They are part of a good life. And they are foundations of human flourishing.

A good person is an individual grounded in wisdom and virtue. Goodness can never be fully articulated, and can never be turned into a set of rules that can be mechanically applied. Morality is a skilled behavior, a bit more like an art than a science. But with that insight, a question can arise. Can morality be taught?

Can virtues conflict?

Suppose that you have the virtue of honesty. Surely this would rank near the top of any list of virtues. And you are also a loyal friend. Loyalty has been thought widely to be a virtue. Could you then find yourself in a position where you are asked a question about a particular good friend and (1) honesty requires that you answer truthfully, yet, (2) loyalty forbids you to do so? What would you do?

Some philosophers claim that faithfulness to one virtue can never force you to betray another. In the example given, perhaps all that honesty requires is for you to say truthfully and politely that you should not comment to a third party about the private affairs of a friend.

Can Goodness Be Taught?

Can moral goodness be taught? This question has been asked through the centuries. I believe that the answer is yes, but morality is more often caught than taught. We become like the people we are around. This is a universal human tendency. It is like imprinting in the animal world. The baby duck watches the mamma duck to see how to walk. The young lawyer watches his new associates, especially the senior partners, to see how he should walk, talk, and act. It's a sometimes sad truth in human life. We all tend to rise or fall to the level of the example set for us by the other people around us.

Ethical training is never just a matter of instruction. It involves guidance, encouragement, and motivation. But most of all, it involves modeling. We teach what we show with our own conduct.

Socrates taught Plato. Plato taught Aristotle. Aristotle taught Alexander the Great, way back when he was just Alexander the Average. But Alexander became great through association with the great man. This is how it works. We become like the people we are around. And not because of what they say. But because of what we see them do.

Character calls forth character.

— Goethe

Plato believed that in an ideal society, the poets, the artists whose works appeal so strongly to the popular imagination, should not be allowed to write or say just whatever they wanted. Any art with impact carries with it a social responsibility. The aesthetic dimension may be distinguishable from the moral, but it is never separable. In his time, Plato believed that poets were corrupting the youth by portraying the gods inappropriately as having such unvirtuous qualities as pettiness, carnality, and vengefulness. He was convinced that young people would tend to follow their imaginations and, whether consciously or not, emulate these portrayals in their own conduct.

The imagination engages the emotions, and the emotions move the will. It's the same now as it was in Plato's time. When vivid portrayals of the fictional gods of the modern world, those characters created in cinema and comics, on TV and the Internet, and in video games, engage the imaginations of children and adults, they inevitably affect the attitudes and conduct of their viewers. This is a reality of human psychology. It is up to all of us to ask what a particular form of art is teaching, and what the social responsibility of art in our time might be.

A culture concerned about human flourishing takes care how it allows the human imagination to be engaged. It encourages a proper development of moral imagination in many ways. Over the centuries, philosophers and practical thinkers have suggested a number of tests for moral matters that appeal to this faculty of the imagination. They fall into two categories, laid out in the following two sections.

What am I? — A test of character

This test of character dates from Plato. He represents Socrates as telling a story about a magic ring — the ring of Gyges. You put it on, and you become completely invisible. The test is this. If you could become invisible, or if in some other way your actions could remain absolutely secret, what would you do? How would you act? Would you behave any differently? Or would you be exactly the same?

By imagining your actions cut off from any possible punishment or censure, you get to know what it is that you value for its own sake. You get to know who you most deeply are. It can be an eye-opening exercise, if undertaken honestly.

What should I do? — A test of action

The tests of action are multiple and are meant to help with ethical decision making, using the power of the imagination.

- ✔ **The Publicity Test:** How would I feel if my contemplated actions were reported in the paper or broadcast on TV?
- ✔ **The Mentor Test:** How would I feel if my action were seen by my most revered mentor (old professor/father/mother/priest)?

- **The Role Model Test:** What would my greatest role model do here? (A common religious form is "What would Jesus do?")
- **The Mirror Test:** If I do this, can I look at myself in the mirror and feel a sense of pride and dignity?

As you can imagine, these tests of action presuppose a basically good character. People with bad character often do outrageously wrong things just for the publicity. They don't care what other people think or what any moral person would do. And some even take perverse pride in evil. So it's clear that these tests are useful tools for people who are already well-formed to some degree along the moral dimension of human life and are intended to help them in difficult decision making situations.

> *We are all in the gutter, but some of us are looking at the stars.*
>
> — Oscar Wilde (1854-1900)

These tests are also teaching devices. By conveying such bits of wisdom as we find in them, we attempt to pass on to others what we have found helpful as we seek to do the right thing. Sometimes what we need for ethical conduct is the right information. More often, it's the right guidance, which is as much motivational as it is informational, involving the imagination, heart, and mind.

The answer to our question

Goodness can be taught. And it can be conveyed. Any culture that wants to survive and thrive had better get the message.

Part IV
Are We Ever Really Free?

The 5th Wave   By Rich Tennant

@RICHTENNANT

"You know, Socrates said, 'The unexamined life is not worth living', however, in your case, Edwin, it might be a blessing."

In this part . . .

The best things in life are free. Are you? In this part, we look at the main challenges to our common belief that we are free to make our own way in the world. We look at some pretty wild and spooky stuff. And we also try to sketch out the best philosophical view of what sort of freedom we all might really have. Is there any such thing as a free lunch? To find out, check out this part.

Chapter 10

Fate, Destiny, and You

We have to believe in free will. We've got no choice.

— Isaac Bashevis Singer

*I*n this chapter, we look at the importance of free will and examine the three main philosophical challenges to its existence. We dig deep into the texture of decision making and human action, and we look at incidents of seeing into the future that belong in a *Believe It Or Not* file.

The Importance of Free Will

We make decisions every day. What do I want for breakfast? What should I wear today? Which tie goes best with this suit? Should I go shopping before dinner or after? Is today the day to have that difficult conversation with a coworker that I've been putting off?

The fact that we deliberate and think of ourselves as deciding what to do in many ways throughout the day demonstrates that we think of ourselves as having real options. We think of ourselves as having choices. We conceive of ourselves as being free.

A belief in free will is presupposed by all of traditional morality. We praise people for their good deeds and blame them for the bad that they do. But praise and blame make no sense unless people have real choices.

Without freedom there can be no morality.

— Carl Jung

Attitudes of regret and pride also presuppose free will. A feeling of regret is tied to the belief that I could have acted differently. Likewise, a sense of pride wells up from the realization that I could have settled for less, but didn't.

We all naturally believe that we are free. We naturally think that the future is open to our will, in large ways as well as in small things. And this is a crucial belief for most world-views.

A few decades ago, psychology was dominated by academics who had come to believe that free will is an illusion. Followers of Freud thought of us all as captives of early childhood experiences and unconscious drives. Supporters of Binet saw us all as prisoners of IQ. Professors and practitioners trained in the thought of B.F. Skinner modeled human behavior on that of rats who could be manipulated through physical mechanisms of positive and negative reinforcement. ("Feed me, shock me, I'll do whatever you say!") There was no room in the academic psychology of the time for true freedom. That's one of the reasons why, after one undergraduate psychology course, I decided (freely) to get out of the lab for good and turn my attention to what the philosophers had to say.

It turns out that one of the great 19th-century psychologists and philosophers, William James, like a multitude of great thinkers before him, was a firm believer in free will. He was convinced that we can all change our lives by changing our thoughts. Disciples of Freud, Binet, and Skinner no doubt can identify and offer diagnoses of human behavioral and personality problems. But they have a notoriously dismal track record for actually helping people. A follower of James, by contrast, can make a difference in the lives of real human beings.

Our belief in free will is important. And it's powerful. We all deep down want to believe that we can make a difference in this life, that we can overcome obstacles and creatively make our mark on this world. And we can't believe in either creativity or responsibility unless we presuppose freedom.

> *When you want to believe in something you also have to believe in everything that's necessary for believing in it.*
>
> — Ugo Betti

But the natural human belief in free will has been threatened throughout the centuries from at least three directions. In this chapter, we want to see what those challenges are. In the next two chapters, we ask whether they can be met and defeated.

Foreseeing the Future: The Theological Challenge to Freedom

If anyone can literally foresee the future, then it must already somehow be laid out in advance. It's already in the cards. And there's nothing we can do to change it. Notice that I'm not talking about someone merely envisioning a future possibility, but of someone literally seeing in advance what will in fact happen.

A teacher friend of mine was in an elevator in the Mayo clinic with her mother. The doors opened, and a man got on, joining them at first in silence. He then turned to them and said to the younger woman, "I'm sorry, I don't mean to disturb you, but your mother will be just fine. I thought you might like to hear that." The ladies were skeptical. The man wasn't dressed as a doctor. They didn't know who he was. But he knew them. He proceeded with a voice of kindness to tell them the names of the daughter's little children at home, and even the name of their family dog. He smiled and said that he had a psychic ability on occasion to just see these things about other people and liked to share good news when he could. Despite his gentle manner, the ladies were a little bit shaken by this stranger's apparent knowledge of their personal lives. And yet all that did serve as powerful confirmation for what he was saying. And he was right. My friend's mother was going to be just fine. It was good for them to hear that before even the doctors knew. It was a truly elevating experience. But how can something like that happen?

> *Your sons and daughters shall prophesy, your old men shall dream dreams, your young men shall see visions.*

> — Book of Joel, Old Testament

In graduate school at Yale, an old friend came up to New Haven to work on translating some of the Protestant theologian John Calvin's letters for publication. This man was one of the most educated individuals I had ever known. He read six languages well, held a Th.D. from The University of Edinburgh, had been honored in many ways with academic prizes and special scholarships, and in addition had always seemed to me wise beyond his years. One day that summer when we were sitting outside alone, he told me about a series of dreams he had experienced over a period of a year while living in Scotland. In each dream, a relative of his had an accident of some kind. One uncle fell off a ladder and broke his leg. Another more distant relative was in an automobile accident. In every case, within weeks of the dream, he received word from home, that the event he had dreamed had happened, in every detail. He had told no one about the dreams until that day of relating them to me.

> *The intimations of the night are divine, methinks.*

> — Henry David Thoreau

After two or three such amazing incidents, my friend began to wonder: Was he being shown what would happen unless he intervened? Or was he being shown what was going to happen no matter what he might do? What was going on? At the time, I had no answers. But I did have my own stories.

A dream is a prophecy in miniature.

— Talmud

At about the age of 17, one of my best friends invited me to drive with him from our hometown of Durham, North Carolina, to spend the weekend with his grandmother in Danville, Virginia, just to visit and play tennis. In the car, on the way there, Carter said that he needed to warn me about this wonderful relative of his. She was a little eccentric, he intimated, but in a good way. I asked what he meant. He explained that she often saw people after they were dead and caught glimpses of the future. He added that she was understandably reluctant to talk about such things, but that he would be able to get her to after dinner. He knew "how to push the right buttons."

When we arrived in Danville, we were met by an attractive, elegant Southern lady who welcomed us into her house with all the gracious hospitality for which the area is known. We sat and talked for a while, and then Carter and I went out for a little tennis. Back at the house, we had a very pleasant dinner, and near the end, Carter looked over at me with a grin on his face and then began to tell his grandmother of my interests in philosophy and religion. I would be fascinated by her unusual experiences. Would she tell me about some?

She demurred. He cajoled. And he succeeded in pushing all the right buttons. I was open-mouthed to hear of her conversations with her recently departed gardener. When he was supposed to be still in the hospital, he walked into her back yard uncharacteristically dressed up in a dark suit, calling out to her and asking for some water. She went to get him a glass, and on returning seconds later, was perplexed that he was gone. She later learned he had, at that very moment, died in the hospital. This little revelation brought about a good case of after dinner shivers. And that story was followed by others just as strange, from a very sensible seeming and highly intelligent lady. She said "Now, Tommy, don't go home telling your parents all these things; they'll think I'm a crazy old lady and won't let you visit again." I assured her I would not.

You ain't heard nothing yet, folks.

— Al Jolson

This psychic grandmother humbly explained to me that she believed it was God giving her special knowledge of things, sometimes things in the future. After dinner, we were in the kitchen, just the two of us, washing and drying dishes and talking away. Suddenly, she fell silent. I turned to look at her and found her eyes piercing right through mine. It was extremely eerie. She stared. And she said: "I see you when you're 35 years old." Oh man. I said,

"Really?" She continued, almost trancelike, "You're very successful in what you do. And very well known. Your work is known internationally." I said, "Is it business?" She shook her head and replied, "No, not business. It's like science, only spiritual."

I entered college a year and a half later as a business major. When I was 35 years old, I had switched into an area of scholarly pursuit known as analytic philosophy of religion and philosophical theology, which could best be described by a layman as a discipline "like science, only spiritual." I had had a very unusual number of books published by that age with the best academic publishers and had scores of articles in the professional journals that were being read and commented on by philosophers all over the world. I'd regularly get letters from such places as Israel, Norway, and Australia. Spooky.

This Grandmother From Beyond paused and said, "I see your wife. You're happily married and have children." I couldn't resist. I blurted out, "What's she look like?" "She has blonde hair, very blonde, very light."

> *We are never present with, but always beyond ourselves; fear, desire, hope, still push us on toward the future.*
>
> — Montaigne

Four years later, when I proposed to my very new girlfriend, as the light played off her shimmering blonde hair, I suddenly flashed back to that kitchen in Danville, Virginia. Twenty-five years later, I'm very happily married to this light-haired woman of prediction and have two wonderful children.

I've always been open to life being much stranger than we typically give it credit for. Twentieth-century physics is portraying a more and more interesting universe than we ever had expected in our more pedestrian thoughts. We need the humility to recognize that our understanding of the world still goes no farther than scratching at its surface.

I come from a background that kept me open to this kind of strangeness, on one side of my family. My father left the farm as a teenager and moved to Baltimore, Maryland, where he went to work for Martin Aircraft, learning all facets of airplane design and construction. He worked strange hours and had the freedom to take a few days off whenever he had completed his week's or month's assignments. And so he made random trips back to North Carolina to see his parents. Each time he entered the house, the dinner table was set for three. "Your mother knew you were coming today," his father would explain, while adding that she was never wrong.

My father seemed to have some way of knowing what was different. In the second World War, on a ship in the South Pacific, he had once been in a game of dice where he said that he somehow knew what each throw would be, in advance. Each throw, he won. And he knew that he would. Throw after throw. For hours. Everyone on the ship who was not on duty gathered around to watch. They kept giving him new dice to use. He kept throwing winners. He won more money than he had ever seen, and that night lay awake trying to figure out what had happened. Had he just known what was going to happen? Or was he somehow making it happen? He had been in a psychological state that great athletes sometimes report as a "flow" experience, a somewhat altered state of consciousness that seems to operate above the ordinary theater of life, effortlessly seeing and doing with certainty and perfection. But all night Dad tried to analyze it. The wondering and analyzing soon became doubting. And the next day he lost all that he had won. He never felt that flow experience again and often wondered thereafter if he had closed himself off to it by all his intellectual curiosity, inquiry, and skepticism.

But in later years, a strange sense of things beyond our normal ken seemed to revisit my father at times. When he met my future wife on the campus of the University of North Carolina, when she and I were just apparently nothing more than merely casual social acquaintances, before we were even dating, he went home and told my mother, "I've just met the girl that Tom is going to marry." I didn't hear about that prognostication until after our wedding, over a year later.

> *And let in knowledge by another sense.*
>
> — Dryden

He once went to visit a friend he had been doing business with the day before, raised his hand to knock at the door of this gentleman's house, and "heard" the words "Don't disturb him, he's dead." He turned around and got back in his GMC Suburban and drove home. My mother said, "I thought you were going to see Reverend Harris today." Dad said, "He's dead," and told how he knew. My skeptical no-nonsense mother didn't believe a word of it. Until hours later when Reverend Harris' son called to say that his father had been found in the house, dead of a heart attack.

I could go on. But there is no need to. I'm as skeptical as anyone else of stories we hear about unusual events from people we barely know. Especially very strange stories like these. But when they have entered your own experience, and the experience of people you know well, love, and trust, it makes a difference.

> *How few things can a man measure with the tape of his understanding! How many greater things might he be seeing in the meanwhile!*
>
> — Thoreau

My point here is very simple. If there are ways of knowing that we don't fully understand, and if some of these put us in touch with details of a future yet to come, that can create a challenge for our belief in free will.

To make clear exactly how that challenge works, I'll use the example of God. Suppose that there is a perfect being who infallibly knows the future and can communicate aspects of that future to human beings for special purposes. And this is, by the way, a hypothesis that, as a matter of fact, was offered to me as an explanation for their experiences by the Virginia grandmother, the Edinburgh scholar, my father, and his mother. If an absolutely perfect God knows the future, presumably he knows it perfectly, and therefore completely. And a perfect God can't be wrong. So if he knows, for example, that you'll move across the country exactly one year from now, then no matter how much you desire to stay put, you'll be hitting the road. You have no choice. You can't prove him wrong. And, likewise, if he knows that you'll stay put in your current house and job for the next ten years, then you're stuck, like it or not. In either case, you don't have the options, or the freedom, that you otherwise typically assume you have. Nor do I.

Divine foreknowledge would then seem to be a serious challenge to human freedom. Even human foreknowledge, if it is truly knowledge. If the future is somehow already metaphysically "there" to be known, it is set, no matter what we think or try to do, and we have no freedom to make it otherwise. Can this challenge be answered? I say what I think in the next chapter, but read on here before you go there. I want to show you the whole big picture first.

What Will Be Will Be: The Logical Challenge to Freedom

The bitterest tragic element in life is the belief in a brute fate or destiny.

— Emerson

There is a famous law of logic called "The Law of Excluded Middle." Simply put, it says that, for every proposition *P*, Either *P* is true, or *Not P* is true. There is no middle ground. So either there is a God, or it is not the case that there is a God. Either it is possible to survive bodily death, or it is not possible to survive bodily death. This law of logic governs all propositions.

There is another famous law of logic called "The Law of Noncontradiction." It says that, for every proposition *P*, it is not the case that both *P* and not-*P* are true. It is not the case that there both is and isn't a moral order to the universe. Either there is or there isn't. You can't have it both ways.

It's fascinating, and a little troubling, to see what happens when we apply The Law of Excluded Middle, and then The Law of Noncontradiction, to a future tense proposition. Let *P* be the proposition:

You will eat an apple at lunch tomorrow.

According to The Law of Excluded Middle, either it is true that you will eat an apple at lunch tomorrow, or it is true that you will not eat an apple at lunch tomorrow. But then we can launch the following argument:

- ✔ Either you will eat an apple at lunch tomorrow, or you will not. (Excluded Middle)

- ✔ If you will eat an apple at lunch tomorrow, then nothing you do between now and then will stop you from having that apple at lunch. (Follows from Noncontradiction)

- ✔ If you will not eat an apple at lunch tomorrow, then any effort you make between now and then to eat such an apple will be, literally, fruitless. (From Noncontradiction) Therefore,

- ✔ You do not now have two equally available options to eat or not to eat that apple. (By definition of what an option is) Thus,

- ✔ You are not really free concerning whether you will or will not eat an apple at lunch tomorrow. (By the definition of freedom as requiring real options)

This same reasoning will apply to any future tense proposition whatsoever. Thus, it seems to follow that you are not free with respect to anything in the future at all. Ugh. This is what philosophers often call *The Problem of Logical Fatalism.*

> *Each of us suffers his own destiny.*
>
> — Vergil

But how do we know that the laws of logic really hold true? It is impossible, literally incoherent, to entertain the converse and suppose that they don't really hold. We cannot even think without presupposing the laws of logic. And they cannot be violated by a particularly tensed proposition. So it seems that, even for someone who does not believe in God or in human foreknowledge, there is a problem here for our common belief in human freedom. Can it be answered? Philosophers have asked this question for centuries. And we just may answer it.

Of course, either we will answer it, or we will not. Just kidding. Hold on a bit, and you will see a response in the next chapter.

Fate

Is the future all laid out in advance? Is there an ineluctable, necessary march of events that none of us can really control? The testimony of history is mixed. Let's sample it.

> Fate is the endless chain of causation, whereby things are; the reason or formula by which the world goes on.
> — Zeno

> All things are produced by fate.
> — Chrysippus

> Fate leads the willing, drags the unwilling.
> — Cleanthes

> I want to seize fate by the throat.
> — Ludwig von Beethoven (1770-1827)

> Men at some time are masters of their fates.
> — Shakespeare

> For man is man and master of his fate.
> — Tennyson

> As long as I am weak, I shall talk of fate; whenever God fills me with his fullness, I shall see the disappearance of fate.
> — Emerson

> Every human being is the artificer of his own fate. . . . Events, circumstances, etc., have their origin in ourselves. They spring from seeds which we have sown.
> — H. D. Thoreau

Robots and Cosmic Puppetry: The Scientific Challenge to Freedom

Since at least the time of Sir Isaac Newton, scientists and philosophers impressed by the march of science have offered a picture of human behavior that is not promising for a belief in freedom. All of nature is viewed by them as one huge mechanism, with human beings serving as just parts of that giant machine. On this view, we live and think in accordance with the same laws and causes that move all other physical components of the universal mechanism.

According to these thinkers, everything that happens in nature has a cause. Suppose then that an event occurs, which, in context, is clearly a human action of the sort that we would normally call free. As an occurrence in this universe, it has a cause. But then that cause, in turn, has a cause. And that cause in turn has a cause, and so on, and so on.

> Everything is determined, the beginning as well as the end, by forces over which we have no control. It is determined for the insect as well as for the star. Human beings, vegetables, or cosmic dust, we all dance to a mysterious tune, intoned in the distance by an invisible player.
>
> — Albert Einstein (1879-1955)

As a result of this scientific world view, we get the following picture:

Natural conditions outside our control
cause
Inner bodily and brain states,
which cause
Mental and physical actions

But if this is true, then you are, ultimately, just a conduit or pipeline for chains of natural causation that reach far back into the past before your birth and continue far forward into the future after your death. You are not an originating cause of anything. Nothing you ever do is due to your choices or thoughts alone. You are a puppet of nature. You are no more than a robot programmed by an unfeeling cosmos.

Psychologists talk about heredity and environment as responsible for everything you do. But then if they are, you aren't. Does it follow that you can then do as you please, irresponsibly? Not at all. It only follows that you will do as nature and nurture please. But then, nurture on this picture turns out to be just an illusory veil over a heartless, uncaring nature. You have what nature gives you. Nothing more, and nothing less.

Where is human freedom on this picture? It doesn't exist. It is one of our chief illusions. The natural belief in free will is just a monstrous falsehood. But we should not feel bad about holding on to this illusion until science corrects us. We can't have helped it.

This reasoning is called The Challenge of Scientific Determinism. According to determinists, we are determined in every respect to do everything that we ever do.

This again is a serious challenge to human freedom. It is the reason that the early modern scientist Pierre Laplace (1749-1827) once said that if you could give a super-genius a total description of the universe at any given point in time, that being would be able to predict with certainty everything that would ever happen in the future relative to that moment, and retrodict with certainty anything that had ever happened in any moment before that described state. Nature, he believed, was that perfect a machine. And we human beings were just cogs in the machine, deluded in our beliefs that we are free.

Is determinism right? Does science condemn us to a robotic status, regardless of our subjective feelings to the contrary? To find out the answer to this question, see Chapter 11.

Chapter 11

Standard Views of Freedom

• •

In This Chapter

▶ Examining the challenges to human freedom

▶ Turning back the arguments against free will

▶ Exploring differing views of what freedom is

• •

The glory of human nature lies in our seeming capacity to exercise conscious control of our own destiny.

— Winston Churchill

There are a number of serious challenges to the common belief that we human beings have free will, which I have laid out in Chapter 10. In our time, the single greatest threat to this traditional belief in free will has been the challenge of scientific determinism. And it has been the context within which two very different philosophical views of freedom have been developed. In this chapter, I want to show what those two views are.

God, Logic, and Free Will

Two challenges to the belief that we are free have been around for a long time. One is based in ideas from theology, the other from logic. I develop both in Chapter 10, but recap them now in order to indicate how philosophers have responded to them.

The Theological Challenge answered

Recall the theological challenge to free will in the previous chapter. If any future action of yours, say, ten years from now, is already somehow known, or 'seen,' in advance by anyone, then when the moment is about to occur during which you take that action — let's call it action *A* — it is not within the range of genuine choices that you then have for you to perform action *B* instead. Why? Because, if you did, you would be acting contrary to what is already the truth. *A* is already true. You would be making not-*A* also true. But the logical Law of Noncontradiction (see Chapter 10) makes it impossible for *A* and Not-*A* both to be true at the same time. Therefore, when the time for the action in question arrives, you do not have real choice with respect to that action, which means you are not free concerning it.

If there is a perfect God with perfect knowledge of the future, then by the reasoning we have already seen, absolutely generalized, you are not free with respect to any action you perform. And this means, you have no free will at all. This was The Challenge of Theological Determinism that I laid out at length in Chapter 10.

Can this challenge be answered? Yes, in a variety of ways.

First, some theologians have suggested that God knows the future in two ways only. First, he knows that some things will happen, by himself intending to do those things, and because his intentions can't be thwarted, he knows absolutely those things he intends. Second, he is a perfect diagnostician of present tendencies and dispositions, knowing all the probabilities of anything that we might freely do. But because he created us free, he himself has to wait, so to speak, just like we do to see what actually will happen. Nonetheless, he is prepared to deal with any eventuality, and like a Grand Master in chess, can flex around our choices to bring about the end game he desires.

> *We are responsible human beings, not blind automatons; persons, not puppets. By endowing us with freedom, God relinquished a measure of his own sovereignty and imposed certain limitations upon himself.*
>
> — Martin Luther King Jr. (1929-1968)

A second type of answer to our problem points out, from the start, that foreknowledge is not the same thing as predestination. Anyone who believes that there is a God who predetermines everything that ever happens does indeed have trouble making room in their world view for free will. Predestination is a causal notion. It is a conception of God's making things happen. But foreknowledge is, in principle, different. It follows from the nature of the concept of predestination that if God predestines *A*, then *A* happens because of God's predestining it. It does not follow from the concept of foreknowledge that if God foreknows *A*, then *A* happens because of God's foreknowing. Rather, God foreknows it because it happens. That leaves it open in principle that foreknowledge can be knowledge of actions freely caused by someone other than God, namely, by us.

God may know that you are going to do *A* just because you are freely going to choose *A*. The moment before you must act with respect to *A* is not then a moment that you must lack the power to do other than *A*, or a moment you must lack the opportunity or choice to do otherwise; it is just a moment that you will *in fact* use your free will to select action *A*. If the question is pressed "But how could you possibly have done otherwise, if a God who can't be wrong knew that you would in fact do *A*?", the answer might just be that if you were to chose to do otherwise than *A*, then God would correspondingly always have known something other than what he in fact knows, namely, that you do other than *A*.

> *Now, against the sacrilegious and impious darings of reason, we assert both that God knows all things before they come to pass and that we do by our free will whatsoever we know and feel to be done by us only because we will it.*

> — Saint Augustine

It is a typical scenario in philosophy that a problem is much easier to articulate than its solution. That's why so many people, upon first discovering or understanding a philosophical problem, give up on the possibility that there might be a solution. In philosophy, problems often fall into our laps, but we have to work hard to see their solutions.

Rather than foreknowledge undermining our freedom, it may be precisely as a result of knowing how that freedom will operate. And then, God could share with one of us creatures any bits and pieces of that foreknowledge without at all compromising the fact that what is known in advance nonetheless involves acts of free will.

The Logical Challenge answered

But what of The Logical Challenge to freedom that is also laid out in Chapter 10? Again, philosophers have taken a variety of strategies here. The most fundamental underlying strategy is this: If a piece of philosophical reasoning seems to call into question something that you naturally, strongly, and intuitively know to be true, then you are right, perhaps on the basis of The Principle of Belief Conservation (developed in Chapter 6), to call into question that reasoning itself.

> *As for the future, your task is not to foresee, but to enable it.*

> — Saint-Exupéry

What is the flaw in this case? Parallel reasoning can attempt to show that the future's being laid out somehow in advance need not preclude a role of freedom in laying it out. If it is already true that I will eat an apple for lunch tomorrow, it may be true because of the fact that I will, as an act of free choice, include that fruit in my meal about midday tomorrow.

Some logicians have gone farther though and have suggested that The Law of Excluded Middle (presented in Chapter 10), the logical law whose application to statements about the future creates the problem, can apply to future tense propositions only with a tentative truth assignment, representing present tendencies, but alterable by freely willed actions.

> *The future is endowed with* essential unpredictability, *and this is the only prediction we can make.*
>
> — Paul Valéry

Either of these routes can be thought successful. But our point here, if we want to avoid a stretch of mind-numbing reasoning, can be confined to the insight that the knot of logical fatalism can be slipped in reasonable ways. So if there is a decisive argument against human freedom, it will have to come from somewhere else.

The Modern Scientific Challenge

As a matter of fact, in the 20th century, most philosophers, psychologists, and commentators on human nature have found their views on human action most affected by the scientific challenge to human freedom (see the end of Chapter 10). This challenge is based on a principle that we can call The Principle of Universal Causality (UC). This principle states,

Every event (a) has a cause, and (b) thereby stands in a causal chain with a very long history.

Consider any act I perform, such as the simple action of raising my arm to stretch. I've been sitting typing and feel a bit cramped. I decide that I'd feel better if I took a second to stretch. So I raise my right arm and then my left arm, stretching out and relaxing. In my own mind, I think that I could have continued typing instead of taking that little stretch break, had I so chosen. But the scientific determinist tells me a different story. He says that my stretching when I did had a physical cause, like everything else that happens in the world, and that the event that caused my stretching itself had a cause, and that this cause in turn had a cause, and so on, and so on, back and back and back into the past history of my little part of the universe. The simple act of raising my arm to stretch was, on the scientific determinist picture of the world, set in the cards long ago. Universal Causality demands it.

In the following sections, I want to show you how three different groups of philosophers have reacted to The Principle of Universal Causality. One group has let it convince them that there really is no freedom in the world, despite all feelings and appearances to the contrary. The other two groups have offered definitions of freedom that have caused them to view Universal Causality differently, and they have arrived at two different views of human freedom.

Scientific Determinists

Scientific determinists define a free action as an event having to do with a person's intentions that is without a cause. Because of The Principle of Universal Causality, they deny that there can be any such events. Therefore, they deny that human beings are ever really free.

> *The implacable destiny of which we are the victims — and the tools.*
>
> — Joseph Conrad (1857-1924)

Libertarians

Philosophers known as *libertarians* believe that we are in fact free. One version of libertarianism is called simple indeterminism. Simple indeterminists define freedom the very same way that scientific determinists do. They think of a free act as an event involving the body or mind of a human being, which corresponds to that person's intentions and yet happens without a cause. They insist that we are indeed free. And so they deny the truth of Universal Causality. They believe that there are uncaused free actions.

Why do these libertarians deny Universal Causality? First, they believe that our freedom is so obvious that no tricky scientific or philosophical argument to the contrary should be trusted. Secondly, these simple indeterminists maintain that The Principle of Universal Causality is not really a scientific principle at all, in the sense that it is not a principle that any scientific work has ever established as true. It is an assumption that many scientists in fact make, but that doesn't prove anything. Its truth is not strictly necessary for the work they do, and their work does not demonstrate its truth.

> *We are not launched into existence like a shot from a gun, with its trajectory absolutely predetermined.*
>
> — Jose Ortega y Gasset

But this version of libertarianism has had plenty of critics. Most critics will acknowledge, however reluctantly, that no one has demonstrated Universal Causality. But they think it is extreme to just deny its truth, like simple indeterminists do. The critics of indeterminism often agree that we should take seriously our natural feeling of freedom, but think that we can accommodate that feeling without trashing The Principle of Universal Causality.

Critics also claim that the definition of free action offered by indeterminists is inadequate. A free action, they say, should not at all be understood as an action without any cause whatsoever. Imagine that my arm shoots up without any cause whatsoever, as a cosmically random event. I have intended to stretch at some point, but at the precise moment it rises, I am astonished to see it moving quickly from the computer keyboard, and have no idea why it's happening now. This is not a paradigm instance of my freely doing anything. It is a freak occurrence. We need a better definition of what a free act is.

Compatibilism

Compatibilists are philosophers who have tried to supply a better definition of freedom, one that will show it to be compatible with scientific causation. They define a free act like this: A *free act* is any event, involving the body or mind of a person, that is caused by an inner state of that person, such as a desire, or intention, or decision to so act.

Compatibilists got their name by holding that free will is compatible with Universal Causality. Every event does have a cause, they maintain, but if the cause of your action is an appropriate inner state of your own mind, then your act is free. Free actions arise out of inner choices. It's just that simple.

Compatibilism is a philosophical position that has gained a lot of ground in the past 50 years. It seems to have two strengths. First, it acknowledges that there is a sense in which we are free, while yet at the same time acknowledging The Principle of Universal Causality so widely assumed by scientists. And second, it provides a definition of free action that is not vulnerable to the criticisms leveled against the simple indeterminist definition.

Is Compatibilism true? Critics reason like this. If compatibilism assumes Universal Causality, it assumes that all our actions are caused, and that their causes are caused, and so on. Tracing any causal chain back far enough, you eventually get to initial conditions clearly beyond our control. It follows, then, that these conditions beyond our own inner states, far back in the causal chain, actually end up bringing about our actions. If that is so, then they also prevent our actions from being any different than what they are. But if at the time of performing any action, we can never do otherwise than as we in fact do, it seems like we lack the options of choice that are intuitively definitive of freedom. So perhaps the compatibilist definition of free action is inadequate in its own way.

To understand this problem, let's tell a story.

The story of Dr. Delusion

Imagine that a master hypnotist, Dr. Delusion, has such powers of mystical persuasion that he can put anyone under a spell and cause them to do whatever he says. His victims are utterly helpless to refuse. Imagine then that Dr. Delusion hypnotizes a man, Jones, and tells him that when he first snaps his fingers, Jones will forget the hypnotism altogether and will turn and walk down the hall to enter a large room and close the door behind him. He will see in the room an old friend, Smith, sitting reading a paper, and will walk over to join him in some conversation. He will look at his watch every 30 minutes and say something about leaving. But he will stay exactly two hours and then suddenly leave. Dr. Delusion snaps his fingers, and the sequence of events transpires exactly as he has directed.

While in the room during the next two hours of lively talk with Smith, Jones often thinks of leaving to run errands, and each time decides to stay just a bit longer to talk with Smith. He looks at his watch every half hour. At exactly the two-hour mark, he finally decides he must go, says good-bye, walks across the room, opens the door, and leaves.

Question: During those two hours, did Jones freely stay in the room?

Pro: Jones stayed because he wanted to. It was his desire to stay, an inner state, that most immediately caused him to stay. Therefore, he stayed freely. This is the compatibilist answer.

Con: During those two hours, he stayed because he was programmed to stay. His inner states that caused him to stay were forced on him by a power outside his control. He was Dr. Delusion's puppet. So he did not stay freely.

The moral of the story

The compatibilist wants to present us with a picture of freedom that allows our actions to be caused and constrained by natural laws and natural conditions outside our control and defines freedom in such a way that acting freely does not imply having been able to do otherwise. The compatibilist wants to say that being unable to do otherwise than as we do does not rob us of our freedom.

But the story of Dr. Delusion seems to elicit an intuitive judgment that this cannot be. In this story, poor Jones was clearly not free. And yet this story models the world of the compatibilist. From this, I think we should draw the conclusion that compatibilist freedom is not the freedom of intuitive common sense and is really no freedom at all. Thus, the compatibilist gives us an inadequate definition of free action and cannot be seen as providing us with the philosophical view of freedom we need after all.

Some contemporary compatibilists object to this simple dismissal. They claim that if our actions are caused by our desires, and either we desire to have those desires, or else don't desire *not* to have those desires (in technical philosophical parlance, there is consistency between our first and second order desires), then that should be altogether sufficient for our actions to be free. They ask, rather rhetorically, what more we could want for freedom than that our actions take place in accordance with our wishes, and those wishes are in accordance with our desires. What more we want is that our whole set of desires not be forced on us by causes outside our control. We don't want to be even complex puppets of nature. We want to be freely who we are without having everything about our selves and our actions created in us by blind, impersonal forces. We want real options and real choices. We want to be really free.

Which approach is the right one?

Scientific determinism seems to run totally roughshod over all our natural intuitions concerning the nature of human action. The simple indeterminist version of libertarianism appears to equate freedom with randomness. And compatibilism claims a form of compatibility between natural causation and freedom that it can't plausibly deliver to satisfy the basic intuitions of most people.

Is there another alternative? To find out, see Chapter 12.

Chapter 12

Just Do It: Human Agency in the World

Destiny is not a matter of chance, it is a matter of choice; it is not a thing to be waited for, it is a thing to be achieved.

— William Jennings Bryan (1860-1925)

In this chapter, I lay out the big picture for the debate over free will. I marshal our intuitions and sketch out one of the most promising alternatives for capturing our deepest intuitions about freedom in a view that tries to make sense of human agency.

Some Wisdom about Freedom

Most of us feel that we have options for our action throughout the day, in big ways and in small ways. We have alternative courses of activity available to us, and it's ultimately up to us which one we take. We are not like monorail trains running along the iron track of fixed destiny that is already laid out for us. We are more like off-road vehicles, capable of making our own paths through life.

Even a prisoner in jail has this metaphysical form of freedom. He can decide what to think about and how to feel. He can typically move his body as he wants, within the confines of his imprisonment. Even those of us who have never been imprisoned live within limits of some sort. But we typically assume that our freedom within those limits is incredibly vast. People can pressure us to conform, circumstances can make some options more difficult than others, but it is truly our responsibility how we live and what we do. Our freedom is that vast. And it's that important.

> *Outside, among your fellows, among strangers, you must preserve appearances, a hundred things you cannot do; but inside, the terrible freedom!*
>
> — Ralph Waldo Emerson (Journals, 1832)

How you use your freedom determines what sort of life you live. That's a maxim of the universe, and it governs all your days. Mine, too. If we choose to be passive, we eat the crumbs from the tables of those who choose to feast on the best this world has to offer. It is only those who use their freedom best who live the life we are here to live to the fullest.

This is some of the deepest wisdom about life that we have. And it presupposes that we are, in fact, metaphysically free. Are we?

The Big Picture

Chapters 10 and 11 look at the customary assumption that we have free will, lay out the standard traditional philosophical challenges to this assumption, and present the responses that can be given to the most traditional of those challenges. Yet, the scientific challenge lingers, dominating the philosophical articulations of views on freedom for the past century. We can understand the differences in the different philosophical views by seeing

- How they define the notion of a free action
- How they judge The Principle of Universal Causality (see Chapter 11).

Table 12-1 summarizes these views. The Principle of Universal Causality says that (UC) — Every event (a) has a cause, and (b) thereby stands in a causal chain with a very long history.

Table 12-1   Philosophical Views on the Question of Free Will

Philosophical Position	Definition of Free Action	Judgment on UC	Are We Really Free?
Scientific Determinism	"Event without a cause"	True	No
Indeterminism	"Event without a cause"	False	Yes
Compatibilism	"Event with an inner cause"	True	Yes

Each of these positions has been judged problematic. Is another possible?

A philosophical view developed anew in just the past few decades, but with a long history, called *agency theory,* says yes. It formulates a third definition of what a free act is and offers a split decision on universal causality.

According to the agency theorist, a free act is an act caused by an agent, where an agent is understood to be a person, or intelligent doer, possessing the capacity of volition. It isn't an event without a cause. And it isn't an event caused by an inner state. It is caused by an agent.

What does the agency theorist say about UC, The Principle of Universal Causality? He sees it as divided into two parts and divides his opinion into two parts as well. UC(a) is true, he asserts. But UC(b) is false. It is true that every event has a cause. But it is false that, in having a cause, every event stands in a causal chain with a very long history. This calls for some explanation.

Consider the following two propositions:

(1) Every event has a cause. UC(a)

(2) Every cause is an event.

Anyone who believes both these things is logically committed to believing that every event that happens, even the most trivial, has infinitely many past causes. Such a person cannot believe that the universe ever sprang into existence from nothing, or was ever created, because it follows from UC(a), and (2) together that the causal chain bringing things about in the world now could never have begun. Never. So UC(b) is a gross understatement. The universe is thus, not just very, very old, or even 18 billion years old; it is infinitely old.

But this seems wild. What has gone wrong here?

> *The mind is a dangerous weapon, even to the possessor, if he knows not discreetly how to use it.*
>
> — Montaigne

Agency theorists would suggest that proposition (2) is just false. It has counterintuitive implications, and so must be rejected. It is not true that the only form of causation is event-causation. But what other kind of causation can there be? Event-causation is the paradigm we usually have in mind when we talk about anything *A* causing anything else *B*. In bowling, the rolling of the ball — an event — causes the striking of the pins, another event, which in turn causes the tumbling over of the pins, yet another event. Things happening make other things happen.

But, the agency theorist insists, there is another form of causation even more intimately known to us. We make things happen. We cause things. We set things into motion. From earliest infancy, we are fascinated with our own ability to cause things in the world around us to change. We knock over the milk. We pull the hair of the dog and set him into motion. We scream and set our parents into motion. We have power. We create our own activities. And we like doing it.

> *The quality of a life is determined by its activities.*
>
> — Aristotle

We initiate new causal chains for which we have responsibility. A tree branch falls and hits your new car. If lightning hit the tree branch and cracked it loose, then that was the cause of its falling on the car. But meteorologists assure us that the lightning itself had a cause, and so on. You can blame the lightning only in a metaphorical sense. But if there was really no storm at all and the tree limb fell because Bob sawed it off, then we have a very different sort of scenario on our hands. Bob is responsible in a unique way. He can be blamed in a literal sense. We assume that he initiated a new sequence of events that wasn't already in the cards, and the agency theorist tries to capture our assumptions here.

How to Be an Agent and Get More than 15 Percent

Agency theorists point out that even before we understand event-causation, we understand agent-causation. We know what it is for people to do things, however unable we might be to analyze that metaphysically (in terms of the underlying mechanisms of what philosophers call *being*). And here is a philosophical bonus: If not all causes are events — if some causes are people — then a commitment to UC(a) need not lead us to believing such things as that every little event that ever happens has infinitely many causes, or that the universe has been around for an infinitely long time. Agents can initiate new causal chains. We do it all the time. That means that some things happening now stand in causal chains with very short histories. And it even means that the chain of events in this universe could in principle have had an absolute beginning.

Agency theory proposes that agents can be causes. To see what difference this makes for free will, see Table 12-2.

Table 12-2	Philosophical Views on the Question of Free Will		
Philosophical Position	**Definition of Free Action**	**Judgment on UC**	**Are We Really Free?**
Scientific Determinism	"Event without a cause"	True	No
Indeterminism	"Event without a cause"	False	Yes
Compatibilism	"Event with an inner cause"	True	Yes
Agency Theory	"Event caused by an agent"	(a) True (b) False	Yes

This is a new theory of free will. It is considered by many philosophers to be a version of Libertarianism that is much more intuitively acceptable than the version of simple indeterminism. It accepts the assumption by science that, at least on a macrocosmic scale, things just don't happen uncaused. It defines free action in such a way as to avoid the problems plaguing the other views. It also side-steps altogether some bizarre implications of commitments that other views, which endorse only event-causation, find themselves saddled with. It is a view that can acknowledge what most of us believe intuitively, that we are in fact free.

> *I do not believe in a fate that falls on men however they act; but I do believe in a fate that falls on them unless they act.*
>
> — G.K. Chesterton

I won't pretend that agency theory doesn't have its critics. They ask two questions. First, what in the world is an agent? Secondly, what is the mechanism by which agents cause actions? In answer to the second question, there is a good deal of mystery yet to be resolved. In answer to the first, there is a whole tradition of reasoning, which I lay out in the next part of this book. Agency theory hooks in with some important views of human beings. My judgment is that, even if we can't explain all the mechanisms by which it works, it gives us more of what we intuitively judge true than any other view. And it helps provide an ennobling perspective on who we are and what we can do.

On this view of human freedom, our place in the universe is quite distinctive. We can, in fact, initiate wholly new chains of causal action. We can launch new things into the world. We can change things and really make a difference, by our creative action. We are not puppets of fate, or of logic, or of science. We can choose our own destinies.

This is big stuff, indeed. Stuff that follows from some fairly arcane philosophical reasoning. But is it true? Are we agents not wholly imprisoned in the nexus of physical causation? Can we somehow rise above the flow of natural causes and inject something of ourselves into the system?

Answers to these questions will turn, in part, on an answer to a more fundamental question. What, really, is an agent? What is the status of a human being in the world, such that this stuff can be possible? Are we more than complex physical links in the universal causal chain? Are we capable of real creativity?

Are human beings just bodies? Or do we have, not just brains, but minds?

> *Men are not prisoners of fate, but only prisoners of their own minds.*
>
> — Franklin D. Roosevelt

Who are you, really? Who am I? For the answers to those questions, refer to the discussions of the next part of this book.

Part V

The Incredible, Invisible You

The 5th Wave   By Rich Tennant

"All of our research seems to point to one irrefutable conclusion. There is a design to the universe, and it appears to be plaid with rounded gussets."

In this part . . .

Know thyself! What are you, anyway? What am I? Are we just complicated physical bodies, organic robots, or do we have souls? Are we composite beings, mind and body? This part is for you, soul brothers and soul sisters.

Chapter 13

What Is a Person?

The one thing in the world, of value, is the active soul.

— Emerson

In this chapter, we look at philosophical conceptions of what a person is. Are we just complex physical organisms? Or do we have souls as well as bodies? Are our minds just neural structures made of brain stuff, or do they partake of another domain? For what I have discovered, as well as what the great thinkers have said, read on.

Guitars, Ghosts, and People

When I was 12 years old, I had the fascinating experience of studying classical guitar for a short time with one of the world's best, and most eccentric, classical guitar teachers. A house painter by day, Mr. Flossie Moon was a musical virtuoso by night, sitting in a back room of his little white house by the railroad tracks in Durham, North Carolina, and coaxing unbelievable sounds from guitars custom made for him around the globe. He was a Michaelangelo of the fretboard. And I got to watch him create. Holding his guitar on his knee, his fingers would fly silently from string to string as glorious songs poured forth. Faster than I could think, the notes swirled and cascaded. Suddenly the sound of a snare drum was pulled from two strings effortlessly crossed with his left hand, while the fingers of his right raked and drummed on the sound box. Flamingo, classical, baroque. What a contrast I experienced when I returned home and tried to force my own fingers into position to press the right note and hit the same string for a simple rendition of my first lesson, the song *Little Brown Jug*.

But even more fascinating than the music were the stories. My teacher was a regular member of a psychic circle at Duke University, inspired by the work of J.B. Rhine, the early researcher into ESP, or *extrasensory perception*. I'd come in for my lesson on Thursday night, and before I could take my guitar out of the case, my master teacher was regaling me with tales from the circle meeting. I heard ghost stories, tales of auras and spirits, accounts of special photographs that captured fleeting images of souls leaving bodies at the moment of death. By the time the lesson began, my fingers were shaking so hard I could barely play. At least, that's the excuse I gave myself for my less than Segovian performances.

> *I'm inclined to think that we are all ghosts — every one of us.*
>
> — Henrik Ibsen

From an early age, I had become accustomed to occasionally hearing a story that intimated the supernatural, or at least the nonphysical. We human beings were more than our bodies. We could expect to survive bodily death, for better or worse. We had mental powers, if we could just tap into them. The realm of the mind was distinctive and strong.

Glimpses of the Mind

 In the near neighborhood of the famous Duke psychologist J.B. Rhine's influence, my family, like many Durham families, had a pack of cards that we occasionally used in a game to test for psychic abilities. One person would pick a card, look at the figure on its face, and try to mentally project the image to another family member, who would try to receive a psychic picture, and then draw or guess the image. We were given to believe that minds could touch minds without any physical means of communication at all.

> *Mind is ever the ruler of the universe.*
>
> — Plato

 Many years later, having forgotten about those family games, I was a young professor at The University of Notre Dame, and my daughter Sara was an elementary school student. One night before dinner, as we sat at the dining table, I noticed that Sara had a deck of cards, from the game Uno. The full deck was divided into cards with four different face colors, in equal numbers. It suddenly occurred to me to play a little game. I said, "Sara, let me look at a card without your seeing it, and I'll think real hard about the color I see. You make your mind a blank and try to pick up what color I'm seeing." She thought it would be fun. "Okay, Dad." I picked a card. I stared at it and said, "What color is it Sara?" She got it right. Another card. A second right answer. A third. Correct again. A fourth. She got it wrong. "Oops."

I said, "Sara, was that the very first color that came to mind?" She hesitated for a second and said, "No." I asked what came to mind first. She told me the right color. I advised her, "Always say what first comes to mind."

> *First thought, best thought.*
>
> — Jack Kerouac (1922-1969)

She got the next one right. And the next. And the next. When she had named 20 in a row, I decided to do something different. I said, "Sara, this time I'll pick a card and not look at it myself at all. I'll put it face down on the back of your neck. You say the color, and then I'll look." Even with this new procedure, she got the next one right. And the one after that. And on, and on. Thirty-eight in a row. Thirty-eight. I'll let you calculate the odds of that. And then we got called to dinner and stopped. We didn't realize until later that we had been engaged in an amazing experiment.

How long could she have gone on? And what in the world was going on? Does the mind have powers that we hardly suspect? Are there forms of mental access to information outside the normal realm of physical signs, signals, and channels of communication? And what does this imply about what a human being is?

Do you remember the first time that you consciously realized that you are a person distinct from other people, and that you have this incredible interior life that is fully accessible only to you? Okay, and maybe to my daughter Sara, too. Just kidding. I recall the first time I ever thought of myself as having a distinctive, separate, rich inner life and experience of the world. I was just two years old. It suddenly occurred to me one day that all this — all my experience of the world and the people in it — was something like The Tommy Morris Show. Starring Tommy.

> *Many of the brain's remaining mysteries need for solution mere wiring diagrams, yet a metaphysical halo lingers about the mystery of self-consciousness. A computer, after all, of sufficient complexity could handle all the stimuli and responses of living without any component that says "I." But within the human — and, dare we think, the cetacean and simian? — brain there is a watcher, who always recedes, and who answers every question with another question.*
>
> — John Updike

These were the early days of black and white television. But my show, somehow, was in color. I was always a bit ahead of my time. I suddenly wondered if all the other people around me, my neighbors, and my parents, realized that this is all my show, and that they are just extras. My supporting cast. It was almost dizzying when it immediately occurred to me that they might possibly have been under the misapprehension all along that this life drama thing was *their* show. And that I was an extra. Puzzling. And scary.

To ourselves, we all seem coeval with creation.

— Herman Melville

Childhood solipsism (the youthful version of the very strange philosophical view that "Only I really exist"). The utterly egocentric universe in which we start life, and too often stay in, unless we really absorb the inevitable discovery that, no, the world does not actually revolve around me. Yes, I am distinctive. I am unique. Just like everybody else. But these other people in my experiential landscape have inner lives, too. They are also distinctive. They have their own sense of "I." What a tremendous revelation.

Every man is more than just himself; he also represents the unique, the very special and always significant and remarkable point at which the world's phenomena intersect, only once in this way and never again.

— Herman Hesse

There is an interior theater of thoughts and feelings, sights, sounds, and ruminations that each of us experiences in a sort of solitude that can never be fully breached. But we can touch and be touched. In our souls. Not just in our bodies. We can reach out from this interiority and make things happen in our world. We can reconfigure nature. And we can inspire other people to join us in our endeavors. Other minds can be linked to ours. And incredible things can happen.

There is a continuum of cosmic consciousness, against which our individuality builds but accidental fences, and into which our several minds plunge as into a mother-sea or reservoir.

— William James (1842-1910)

What does all this say about me, and about you, as entities in the world? What are we? Are we minds? Are we bodies? Are we both? What is it to be a person? Philosophers have wrestled with such questions from the earliest days. And they have come up with a variety of answers.

Philosophical Views of the Person

Various philosophical views exist on what a person is. After years of teaching in the classroom, hundreds of students each semester, I came to realize that almost any of these philosophical views might be represented among the beliefs held by our neighbors in any larger city. In the thousands of years during which philosophers have been trying to analyze human nature, very few utterly different pictures have emerged. But those that have been articulated represent a widely divergent array of possibilities.

We can get our bearings initially by looking for a moment at general philosophical views about what exists. This preliminary examination of the most general set of options concerning what we believe most fundamentally exists can give us an overall context for understanding the different philosophical views of the person.

Monism

Monists are philosophers who believe that all of reality, everything that exists, falls into one and only one basic category of being. There is, according to every form of monism, only one fundamental sort of substance in existence. Everything is therefore somehow a configuration of this one substance. In contemporary physics, string theory can be thought of as just the most recent version of monism, proclaiming as it does that everything is ultimately composed of one-dimensional strings of energy — whatever exactly that means.

Historically, two main forms of monism exist: Materialism and idealism.

 ✔ **Materialism** is the view that all that exists is matter, configured into material objects. On the materialist view, there are no minds or souls or immaterial spirits. Physical matter, in all its permutations and combinations, is all that exists.

 ✔ **Idealism** is the view that all that exists are minds (immaterial thinking things) and ideas in minds. According to the idealist, nonmental matter is an illusion projected by our minds. All of the physical universe is just bundles of ideas, a virtual reality, perhaps produced by the mind of God. Bishop George Berkeley (1685-1753) was perhaps the greatest of the idealist philosophers. There are not many idealists, in the strict philosophical sense, around nowadays, although some developments in physics have caused a few contemporary philosophers to rethink this view.

Dualism

Dualists believe that there are two basic kinds of substance in existence. There are minds as well as bodies, mental properties as well as physical properties. There is spiritual stuff as well as material stuff. This viewpoint gets articulated in several different ways.

GREAT IDEA

Bishop Berkeley

Pronounced "Bar-clay," this Irishman, writing in the early 18th century, gave the world its most thoroughgoing introduction to idealist philosophy. According to the Bishop, all that exists are minds and their ideas. There is no such thing as matter. And there are no material objects apart from ideas of them. Famous quote: "To be is to be perceived." The chair on which you sit, as well as all the other seemingly solid physical objects around you are just bundles of perceptions in the mind. Whose mind? Well, yours, when you're in the room. But, according to the good bishop, when you shut the door to your room and no longer perceive its contents, they would all instantly cease to be were it not for God's ongoing perception of them, which keeps them in existence. Just as the visual images in your field of vision cease to be when you shut your eyes, all of reality would cease to be if God, so to speak, shut his.

Berkeley was an original philosopher and a man of practical ideas as well. He once planned an institution of higher education to be built at the beach in Bermuda. But, alas, the college never . . . materialized.

Physical substance, according to such dualist philosophers as Descartes, is characterized by such properties as extension and mass. Mental or spiritual substance is characterized very differently. Minds may be in time, but they are not, Descartes specified, in space. They do not have extension (length, height, breadth, or physical depth) or mass. They have no three-dimensional spread or solidity. They essentially think. That is their nature. And this is a very different sort of reality from any physical object.

Dualism as a view of human beings, the perspective that we are all composite beings, composed of mental and material stuff in intimate relation, logically implies a general metaphysical dualism. If we are two-fold, then reality is (at least) two-fold. But it is in principle possible for a philosopher to be a dualist about overall reality without being a dualist concerning human beings. Such a philosopher could believe that, in addition to the physical universe, there is a nonmaterial God, but that humans, as other creatures, are merely complex material things. Although this is a rare combination of views, I know at least one philosopher who seems to hold both. It is, however, more often to be found that a philosopher who is dualist about general reality is also dualist about human nature.

Materialism about human beings thus does not necessarily imply a general philosophical materialism. It's possible to believe that humans are just physical objects and nonetheless believe that there is at least one nonphysical entity, for example, a God. But, of course, a general monism of any sort implies the same monistic view of human beings. And the reason is quite simple. If you believe that all that exists is matter, then you'll naturally believe that we are nothing but matter. If you think that all is mental, you'll believe that we human beings are all fundamentally nonmaterial minds.

Typically, if a philosopher gives a monistic analysis of human life, he or she will do so because of a general uniformity to their world-view. And if a philosopher is a dualist with respect to general issues about reality, he or she most likely will be a dualist concerning human beings.

Contrary to what many people seem to assume, materialism is not a recent novelty. In the ancient world, there were materialists, like Lucretius and Democritus. But I think it's safe to say that until modern times, materialism has been a distinctly minority world view, even among philosophers. In the general population, dualism seems to be the philosophical view of human nature which is still just assumed to be true.

Why we are naturally dualists is simple to see. We obviously have bodies. Mine is over 6-feet tall and weighs in at a bit beyond the 200-pound mark. Thanks to Cybex weight machines, it's in much better shape than it used to be. It lies around when I want to rest and gets me where I want to go when I'm ready to move. It takes in food, and gets rid of what it doesn't need. It stores more than it should.

> *The abdomen is the reason why man does not easily take himself for a god.*
>
> — Friedrich Nietzsche (1844-1900)

I act by means of my body. I speak from the diaphragm, using my lungs, larynx, tongue, and lips. I gesture with my hands. I use arms, legs, and other body parts to work, to play, and to express myself. When my body is injured, I feel pain. When it's touched just right, I feel pleasure. A fever can make me miserable. Caffeine jolts me awake. And the older I get, the more attention I find myself having to pay to the care, feeding, and maintenance of the body I call mine.

I say that I have a body. But this body that I have is not something I own like a bicycle or car. It doesn't just serve me. To some extent, it is me, for better or worse. When you see it, you see me, not just my most prized, and trouble-some, possession.

We just as obviously have minds. Well, maybe not everyone I've had to deal with in recent years, but at least most of us. We do feel pain and pleasure. We experience delight and sadness. We think, ruminate, reflect, reason, dream, and hope for the future. We remember and we anticipate. We experience sensations of all sorts. The colors and smells and sounds that play across the screen of my consciousness can be amazing. I have secret thoughts. I have inklings. I have ideas constantly. I have a mind.

Whether or not the philosophers care to admit that we have a soul, it seems obvious that we are equipped with something or other which generates dreams and ideals, and which sets up values.

— John Erskine

When I say that I have a mind, I don't mean that I have it like I have an electric guitar — well, actually at least eight electric guitars, but don't tell my wife; she never sees more than three at any given time. I own the guitars. I own several pairs of shoes. I own a large number of fountain pens and computers. And a dog. I don't own a mind. I somehow am a mind. When you come into contact with my mind, you come into contact with me.

The spirit is the true self, not that physical figure which can be pointed out by your finger.

— Cicero

But wait a minute. If I am a mind, and my body is somehow me, and my mind is different from my body, how does all this go together? Dualists suggest that we are all composite beings. Part mind, part body. There is the physical component of Tom Morris and the mental entity that together make up me.

Plato thought that we are really minds who are for the moment imprisoned in bodies. We pre-existed our embodiment, and will continue to exist when this body is no more. In fact, he represents Socrates as looking forward to death as something like parole from this bodily incarceration.

It is true that paralyzed people can often feel imprisoned in their bodies. And as we age, we sometimes feel that the face staring back at us in the mirror is a stranger. In the last years of his life, my father used to say quite often that when he looked in the mirror he was most often perplexed by the contrast between what he saw and what he felt. He still felt 19. And yet the face that stared back at him looked 65. He felt trapped in a ship that was going down.

It is in moments of illness that we are compelled to recognize that we live not alone but chained to a creature of a different kingdom, whole worlds apart, who has no knowledge of us and by whom it is impossible to make ourselves understood: our body.

— Marcel Proust (1871-1922)

The great father of modern philosophy, Descartes, said that we must be related very differently to our bodies than a captain is to his ship. We do not just peer through our bodily portals and steer this vessel from one dock to another. There is an inwardness. There is an intimacy between mind and body that is very difficult to articulate. And yet we recognize it immediately.

How can our minds be related to our bodies? Are they indeed separate entities? Are they somehow dimensions of a deeply unified reality? Do they interact, or only seem to? Is the mind a greater reality than the body, or is it, in fact, an illusion cast by neural activity in a very material brain?

The Contenders

Idealism has fallen out of favor with most contemporary philosophers. There seem to be no compelling arguments for the conclusion that nothing really exists but minds and their ideas. And yet, the physics of the past 100 years has been moving more and more in the direction of postulating underlying entities and processes very unlike the standard physical objects we are accustomed to handling and bumping up against. There are even some indications that a materialism that becomes sophisticated enough may end up being indistinguishable in at least some respects from a new form of idealism. But I don't want to get too strange here. Yet.

Materialism, as a view of human beings, is just the claim that we are our bodies and nothing more. There are no nonmaterial minds, or souls, or thoughts, or sensations. Everything that exists in a human being is a material entity or material process involving only matter and its functions.

There are various versions of materialism that are of interest to academic philosophers. *Eliminative materialism* says that there are just no such things as thoughts and pains and itches. There are just brains and neural events. *Reductive materialism* allows that thoughts and sensations exist, but reduces them to, or identifies them with, neural events, states, and processes. There is also analytical behaviorism, central state identity theory, and other iterations of materialism that need not detain us. In our reflections, it is enough to grasp the fundamental materialist claim that we are all just hunks of meat. Interesting and complex meat, but meat only.

Dualism is a little different, in that the varieties in which it has come to us historically make a little more difference in how we think about the options. There are basically three historical versions of dualism that are worthy of our notice.

Interactionism

Interactionism is the most common version of mind-body dualism. It is the metaphysical view that most people take for granted before they've ever been introduced to philosophical reasoning and speculation. The interactionist holds that minds and bodies exist as separate sorts of entities, and that they both can and do causally interact with each other. Some bodily events cause mental events. And some mental events cause bodily events.

> *Man is to himself the most wonderful object in nature; for he cannot conceive what the body is, still less what the mind is, and least of all how a body should be related to a mind.*
>
> — Pascal

A mental event can result in a physical event, according to interactionism. You can decide to kick me in the shin, and that mental event — the decision — can cause a physical act, the kick. Likewise, the physical event consisting in the kick can, and most likely will, cause a mental event — of pain.

Epiphenomenalism

Another form of dualism is *epiphenomenalism*. On this philosophical view, the mind is an epiphenomenon, a byproduct of the body and its processes that itself plays no causal role in initiating any bodily events whatsoever. According to an epiphenomenalist, bodily events can indeed cause mental events, but the converse is never true. Mental events do not and cannot cause bodily events, all appearances to the contrary notwithstanding.

So, on the epiphenomenalist's picture, your kicking me can indeed produce pain as a mental effect of that physical cause. But it wasn't a mental decision or nonphysical intention that brought about your kick. It was certain neural events in your brain which brought about your inner feeling that you were deliberating or deciding to kick me. But that feeling of decision or intention is just a by-product of a wholly physical process consisting in one set of neural events producing another set, which in turn eventuate in your foot's making contact with my shin.

> *Never mind the mind, All that matters is matter.*
>
> — Famous Epiphenomenalist Ditty

Why would anyone be an epiphenomenalist? Isn't it just obvious that our thoughts, decisions, and intentions can cause bodily events? Even sensation can cause movement. A pain can make me jump. Why would any philosopher acknowledge the realm of the mind and then deny it any causal efficacy whatsoever?

It was once obvious to people that the world was flat. Apparent obviousness is not an inerrant guide to truth. It may seem obvious to us that mental events cause physical events, and yet not be true at all. There have been philosophers who could not in fact deny the undeniable reality of mental experience, and so were inclined to be dualists, but who at the same time believed, for reasons suggested by the physical sciences, that natural physical systems such as the material universe must be closed systems invulnerable to causal intrusion from outside. Wanting all physical events to have physical causes, and thus preserving all events in the material world as candidates for scientific explanation, these philosophers became epiphenomenalists. They felt forced into the view by other positions they held.

Parallelism

Some few dualists have cut the causal cord more completely. They have denied not just that mental events could cause physical events, but that physical events can cause mental effects. This highly unusual position maintains not only that no thoughts, decisions, or intentions cause bodily movements, but also that no physical injuries actually cause pain. Parallelists deny that light waves cause visual imagery and will not allow that sound waves cause sounds. They allow only that there is a harmony, pre-established by God, or concurrently maintained by a divine power, between the physical and the mental. The events involving these two different substances run in parallel, but never, on this view, interact.

Why? Again, wanting to see nature as a closed system, and wanting to respect principles concerning the conservation of energy in physical systems, parallelists choose to avoid postulating any causal energy or production from crossing the great divide. They claim that one advantage of this view is that we can avoid the postulation of mysterious causal connections that we don't understand at all. We can allow mental events causing other mental events, and bodily events causing other bodily events, but can avoid claiming that there is any intersection of causal propagation across the gap yawning between such different substances as bodies and minds.

Narrowing the Options

We want to know what the truth is about our most fundamental constitution. What are we? Chapter 14 covers the main arguments that can help us determine the answers. But in this section, we need to do a little elimination.

Most dualists are interactionists, believing that mind-body causation exists and goes both ways. Parallelism is just too odd a position. How two such different substances as mental and physical stuff could exist in perfect parallel with absolutely no interaction between them is just, in the end, unanswerable. Extraordinary coincidence and divine micromanagement just seem to be equally implausible hypotheses for the perfect parallelism of mental and physical episodes. In addition, parallelism cannot accommodate our deep feeling that we do cause physical things to happen by means of mental decisions and intentions. So in Chapter 14, we do not investigate parallelism as a lively contender for our belief.

Epiphenomenalism captures the obvious fact that bodily events can cause various sorts of experiences. But it fails just as badly as parallelism to capture the felt power we have to move from mental resolve to physical action. Most dualists would be prepared to acknowledge that their mental experience is utterly inert only as a last resort, if forced to such an opinion. But there are no compelling grounds to force such an option on the dualist. So, in Chapter 14, we ignore distinctively epiphenomenalist spins on the dualist world-view. When we ask about the truth of dualism, we are going to have in mind what is apparently the natural philosophy of the average man and woman, a full-blown interactionism, the metaphysical two-way street.

Likewise, when discussing the merits or demerits of materialism as a view of human beings, we don't have to be concerned with the variety of academic refinements possible. It just doesn't matter to most of us whether analytical behaviorism is right in its contention that all language about mental experience can be semantically analyzed in terms of language about behavior. We want to know if we have souls or not. We want to know whether we are just complicated lumps of flesh, or something more. Thus, even the differences between eliminative and reductive materialism are hardly at the center of our focus. Are we just matter? Or are we something more? That is the simple core question of our continued exploration into the problem of mind and body in Chapter 14.

Chapter 14

The Case for Materialism

There is one spectacle grander than the sea, that is the sky; there is one spectacle grander than the sky, that is the interior of the soul.

— Victor Hugo

The intellectual world these days is split between materialists and dualists. Some very smart specialists on human nature declare that we are just material organisms evolved from much more primitive forms of material life, and that the whole realm of mental experience is just a neural shadow cast by complex brain activity. Other profound observers of humankind disagree totally and insist that we are dualistic beings, with the material aspect of our existence embodying a very different sort of reality — the mental or spiritual aspect — which is, in the end, the most important dimension of our existence.

The mind-body debate has raged for millennia. And yet it's not the sort of topic over which we should just shrug our shoulders and say, "Oh, well, I give up. I'll leave it to the experts." This is a topic that relates to the core of who you are. Are you more than your body or not? Are you a free and creative person who can act into a world of matter, or are you just an intricate organic machine, totally programmed by your heredity and environment? Are there ways of knowing that go beyond physical signals, or are you confined to what your crude bodily senses can take in? Is there something about you that can and will survive bodily death? Or is death the total extinction of you as a person? Are these things worth our attention? You bet they are.

If you want a basic philosophical answer on this most important question of what human beings are, you can't just go to the experts. Every expert will give you a blend of reason and intuition, if you're lucky, or argument and prejudice if you're not. Highly intelligent, well-informed, and sincere people are on both sides of this issue, as is the case with so many interesting and important questions about life in this world, and beyond. So, what do we do? We have to figure it out for ourselves. But how can we hope to get it right, when Nobel Prize winners disagree? A Nobel Prize winner can have an intellectual blind spot. She can have a prejudice that gets in the way of philosophical wisdom. And you may not have that particular blockage in your life to seeing truth. How can you know? By giving it a shot. In this chapter, we look at the basic reasoning for the two main contenders on the mind-body problem, and I appeal to you to use your own mind to decide. Or brain. Depending on what you decide.

> *No one can be a great thinker who does not recognize that as a thinker it is his first duty to follow his intellect to whatever conclusion it may lead.*
>
> — John Stuart Mill (1806-1873)

The Positive Arguments

Materialists have both positive and negative arguments at their disposal. The positive arguments present a case for thinking that we're merely physical objects. The negative arguments are critiques of dualism, the liveliest alternative to materialism. To appreciate why people are materialists, and how they think they can win converts, we need to look at both sorts of considerations. I turn to the positive arguments first.

The man-is-an-animal argument

This argument, despite its name here, has nothing at all to do with beer, bachelor parties, belching, or boorish behavior (to stay just with the *B*s). It's a simple set of contentions that, first, we evolutionarily arose from animals, and therefore we are animals. Moreover, we arose ultimately from simple, organic entities like pools of pond slime that obviously do not embody spiritual, conscious souls, and so, again, we, as their offspring, are thus most likely not ourselves embodiments of spiritual, conscious souls. Matter gives rise to matter. Dust to dust. Ashes to ashes. If anything remotely like evolutionary biology is true, we are nothing more than highly evolved biological life forms. That is the claim.

Man the animal

Many great thinkers throughout the centuries have characterized human beings as animals. Here is a sampling.

Man ... is an animal, biped and reasoning.
— Boethius (c.475-524)

Man is a noble animal.
— Sir Thomas Browne (1605-1682)

Man is by his constitution a religious animal.
— Edmund Burke (1729-1797)

Man is by nature a political animal.
— Aristotle (384-322 B.C.)

Man is a custom-making animal.
— Walter Bagehot (1826-1877)

What is man? Shall I say a rational animal?
— René Descartes (1596-1650)

Man is a tool-making animal.
— Benjamin Franklin (1706-1790)

Man — a reasoning rather than a reasonable animal.
— Alexander Hamilton (1756-1804)

Man is an imitative animal.
— Thomas Jefferson (1743-1826)

Man is a moral animal.
— D. H. Lawrence (1885-1930)

Man is the animal who loves.
— Archibald MacLeish (1892-1982)

Man, I can assure you, is a nasty animal.
— Molière (1622-1673)

Man is first and foremost the self-fabricating animal.
— Lewis Mumford (1895-1990)

Man is a metaphysical animal.
— Arthur Schopenhauer (1788-1860)

Man is the only animal that laughs and weeps; for he is the only animal that is struck with the difference between what things are, and what they ought to be.
— William Hazlitt (1778-1830)

It bothers some dualists to note how much we have in common with nonhuman animals. Descartes thought that humans have souls, but that nonhuman animals do not. And this is certainly a big difference, if it's true. For Descartes, the soul or mind was the theater of conscious experience. But then, why is it that animals surely seem capable of experiencing pain and pleasure? Think of your dog's reaction when you scratch his tummy and of an animal's howls of pain when he is injured. If the soul is indeed the inner theater of conscious experience, it can look a lot like animals have souls. But if you argue the other way around, any reason to believe that an animal is just a physical organism is a reason to believe that human beings, despite the richness and complexity of their inner experience, are just no more than physical organisms either.

Well, what if something like an evolutionary account of the rise of human beings is in fact true? Can't we have qualities or characteristics that our forebears lacked? My son has curly hair. I don't. I have a head of hair, and my father didn't. But surely, it will be argued by the materialist, having a nonphysical mind is a much bigger deal than having curly hair and would signal the ascension to a different metaphysical plane altogether.

The materialist in this argument seems to have in mind (so to speak) something like a philosophical version of the homely principle that no stream can rise higher than its source. But neither hydrogen nor oxygen alone is wet. Yet put them together in the right combination and the right amount, and there emerges a property of wetness. Emergent properties are well known in the world. No pixel on a screen looks like my wife, but put enough together and you get a beautiful picture.

It could be that as organic life on earth grew more complex, certain forms of complexity were able to rise to experience, consciousness, and all the other attributes of mentality. Do I mean by this that natural neural events produce minds? No, not necessarily at all. It could be that when a physical system becomes complex enough in all the right ways, it is capable of embodying a mind. Lesser complexity, or complexity of the wrong sort, will just not do the job. But if emergent properties are possible, it may be possible that the conditions for embodying and exhibiting mentality are emergent from the process of natural evolution, a process what admittedly could have started at the most primitive level imaginable. And yet, it produces us. Amazing.

> *Man as we know him is a poor creature, but he is halfway between an ape and a god, and he is traveling in the right direction.*
>
> — Dean William Ralph Inge (1860-1954)

The artificial intelligence argument

A closely analogous argument to the man-is-an-animal reasoning goes as follows. We are building more and more complex computers, some of which are now capable of learning, changing their own programming in response to changing information. We can clearly imagine a super computer in the future, utilizing the ultimate in parallel processing, along with the right sorts of sensors, mimicking the human brain to such an extent that its behavior is indistinguishable from a highly intelligent human being with conscious experience. The computer will obviously be a merely physical entity. Therefore, because we exhibit all the same "mental" traits, we must be merely physical entities as well.

> *The Machine, the genie that man has thoughtlessly let out of its bottle and cannot put back again.*
>
> — George Orwell (1903-1950)

This argument falls short in the same way as the previous one. The dualist can suggest that it is something akin to racism to think that only carbon-based life forms of a certain sort are capable of embodying mentality. It could be that when any system is sufficiently complex in the right configurations, it

has become an appropriate host for a mind, whether that mentality is naturally emergent from the system, or is coupled with the system when its
emergent properties are appropriate bearers of conscious mentality. So the
materialist reasons,

1. The advanced supercomputer is behaviorally just like a human,

2. The supercomputer doesn't have a mind, so

3. We don't have minds either.

But the dualist can respond,

1. The advanced supercomputer is behaviorally just like a human,

2. We humans clearly embody minds, so

3. The supercomputer must embody a mind as well.

Of course, the dualist could also choose to argue that there is, if not some
behavioral difference, at least some remaining relevant metaphysical difference between the imagined ultimate product of artificial intelligence research
and us. Our point here is just that the materialist's argument does not work.

The brain chemistry argument

We perceive that the mind strengthens and decays with the body.

— Lucretius (Ancient materialist)

The brain chemistry argument for materialism contends that our increasing
knowledge of the brain and its functions leads us to treat mental conditions
that had once been viewed as purely psychological, as rather physiological,
states of the brain. We are making inroads year after year into the treatment
of formerly recalcitrant psychological conditions by means of drugs and
other physical therapies. If a person's mood, emotional disposition, and cognitive functions can be influenced by the amount of sleep they get, the food
they eat, and whether their bodies are producing just the right amounts of
various hormones and other chemicals, then, the materialist concludes, our
minds themselves must be nothing more than electrochemical systems.

The argument is that just as ascribing illnesses to curses and demons long
ago gave way to understanding them as due to viruses and bacteria, so likewise we are coming to understand the whole realm of mental activity as
biochemical and physical in nature.

*The body must be repaired and supported, if we would preserve the mind in
all its vigor.*

— Pliny the Younger

It's true that mental function seems to depend on the chemical state of the brain. But consider this analogy. If my car runs out of gas on the interstate, it will stop. So will I. But I am not the same thing as my car. I am not even made of the same stuff as my car. Yet I am affected by its various physical states, and by its proper functioning. When it goes fast, I am going fast; when it sits in traffic, I sit in traffic. When it has a problem, I have a problem. Yet I am obviously a different entity from it.

The mind is affected by the brain, and its states are affected by the brain's functioning. It doesn't follow that the mind is the same thing as the brain, or that it's made of the same stuff. The dualist can maintain that this just shows the undeniably close connection between the mind and the brain in this life, a connection of dependence much closer and more intimate than that between my car and me (and we are very close, indeed — it's a convertible). This argument from the materialist, like the others, is thus inconclusive and ultimately unconvincing to someone who is not already a believer.

The Negative Arguments

In the preceding sections, I set out the typical forms of positive argument for materialism. But, it's interesting to note, most of the argumentation brought forth by materialists for their world view usually consists in criticisms of dualism. I call this the negative argumentation. Let's see a sample.

The end of argument or discussion should be, not victory, but enlightenment.

— Joseph Joubert (1754-1824)

The superfluity argument

This argument alleges that dualism is "explanatorily superfluous," or unneeded for a full intellectual explanation and understanding of the behavior of human beings. The argument continues on with the contention that any explanatory theory that is superfluous, or unneeded, is to be rejected. It then concludes by rejecting dualism as false.

The assumptions of the argument are these: We accept the existence of unseen entities only if their *postulation* (the supposition that they exist) is necessary for explaining the existence or activities of entities that we do see. Various subatomic particles have come into our world views as theoretical postulates for explaining the behaviors of things we can see and measure. Also, various celestial objects have been identified by theoretical postulation before they were ever observed. A *perturbation,* or unexpected, uneven movement, in the behavior of another planet or a star we can observe is sometimes best understood by the postulation of a heretofore unobserved entity, and so we are rationally justified in accepting the existence of that new unseen thing as a necessary part of a best explanation.

The materialist goes on to claim that the postulation of nonmaterial minds as being among the inventory of reality is not necessary for a full scientific explanation of human behavior. And because it is not a necessary explanatory postulation, we cannot therefore be rational in accepting it. Thus, dualism must be rejected by any rational person, and materialism accepted instead.

There are at least two main problems with this argument. First, no materialist philosopher has ever demonstrated, or given compelling evidence for believing, that anything like a full scientific explanation making no reference to nonmaterial minds is in fact forthcoming for all of human behavior. No such full explanation now exists. And it's only a promissory extrapolation, or optimistic guess, on the part of the materialist philosopher that it ever will exist. What doesn't exist can't disprove what does. Thus, this argument is in trouble.

Secondly, and most importantly, even if dualism was superfluous as a scientific explanatory hypothesis, who cares? This is utterly irrelevant to the grounds on which is it standardly held. Do you think that I have a mind because that is the best scientific explanatory hypothesis for my intelligent behavior? Or, better yet, why do I think I have a mind? Why do you think you have one? Does either of us go around forming scientific explanatory accounts of our own behavior, just to discover, to our metaphysical surprise, that the postulation of a theoretical entity called "a mind" is needed? Do I look at myself in amazement and infer that I must have a mind?

> *Practice proves more than theory.*

> — Abraham Lincoln (1809-1865)

If my mind is anything like an unobserved entity, then I'm in serious trouble. I know I have a mind not by having to postulate the existence of a theoretical explanatory entity. I know I have a mind directly. By having it. I couldn't even begin an argument for its existence without using it. But this is all just nonsense. It doesn't matter that an appetizer is, by itself, a bad meal, if it was never intended to alone constitute a meal in the first place. It doesn't matter what kind of scientific explanatory hypothesis dualism would make if that's not what dualism is supposed to be in the first place. Dualism is a philosophical view. It is a metaphysical position meant to capture the realities of life and experience in this world, regardless of whether it can serve as a scientific explanation or not.

The mystery objection

The second negative argument presented by the materialist alleges that we cannot understand two things about dualism:

- The fundamental dualistic relation whereby one particular body and one particular mind together comprise one person

- Dualistic interactionist causation — how things so different as immaterial minds and material bodies could possibly interact: How mental things can cause physical effects, and physical things cause mental effects

And what cannot be understood cannot be believed. Therefore, at the heart of dualism is a stubborn chunk of mystery that renders it, ultimately, literally incredible. Therefore, it must be rejected. This is the contention.

> *There was the Door to which I found no Key: there was the Veil through which I might not see.*
>
> — Omar Khayyam

First, look at the claim that dualistic composition is too great a mystery. The question is asked how one mind can possibly be related to one body to form one human being. And the suggestion is made in response that no answer is possible, and that, therefore, dualistic composition is a mystery.

Is my body the physical object that my mind possesses? Is ownership or possession the relationship that we are looking for? No, because it's a social relationship, and we are looking for a deeper metaphysical tie. Well, what about the relationship of occupancy? My body is the physical object that my mind occupies. But occupancy is a physical concept and can't bridge the physical and the nonphysical. According to traditional dualistic descriptions of the mind or soul, it is not in space at all, and so can't be literally in my body.

Some dualists have tried a tool analogy. My body is the instrument my mind uses to express itself in the world. But could it use just any old physical object as an instrument? And do I view my body as no more than a tool? Isn't the true mind-body relationship much more intimate than this? If so, then what exactly is it? The materialist alleges that it is, necessarily, a mystery.

> *We employ the mind to rule, the body to serve.*
>
> — Sallust

What is to be made of this argument? Read first the next few paragraphs to see what we say concerning the other charge of mystery.

The second mystery is supposed to be that of interactionist causation, the perplexity as to how such different things as minds and bodies can causally interact. Why can't we understand dualistic causation, according to the materialist? The answer most commonly given is that minds and bodies are just too fundamentally different for there to be causal mechanisms allowing them to interact. Bodies are space-time entities with mass, position, and other physical traits that nonmaterial minds can't have. Neural events are biochemical processes that take time, that occur in particular locations in the cranium, and that stand in specific sorts of physical, causal relationships to other neural and bodily events that they could not stand in with respect to nonspatial, nonchemical, nonelectrical mental events. Materialists think the dualistic belief that mental decisions can cause neurons to fire, or bring it about that electrical impulses are redirected in the brain, is even more absurd than a belief would be that the musical note middle C can cause my soup to boil. The concept of equality, as an abstract linguistic or conceptual object, can't tie my shoes. Abstract objects and shoelaces are entities of such divergent metaphysical status that there could not be a causal connection between them. Likewise, the materialist urges, mental things, if they existed, could not cause physical things to happen, and vice versa.

All things and events are foreshown and brought into being by causes; but the causation is of two Kinds: there are results originating from the Soul and results due to . . . the environment.

— Plotinus (205-270)

Ultimately, this argument comes down to no more than the claim that, if dualism were true, then mind-body causation would be too mysterious, and therefore unlikely to occur. We can't understand it. Therefore it doesn't exist.

But there are at least two things wrong with this argument. First, what is it to understand any sort of causation at all? If we are told that A caused B, and we want to understand how that happened, there are only two sorts of explanation that can possibly be given:

(1) We can be assured that things like A typically bring about things like B, and reminded that here we just have a particular instance of that generality.

(2) We can be told that A caused B by bringing about C, which in turn resulted in B.

If the materialist, in claiming that dualistic causation can't be explained, means that no answer of type (1) can be given concerning any instance of mind-body causation, he is just, in principle, wrong. If I say that my decision to raise my arm caused it to go up, I can explain that instance of causation by referring to the general principle that decisions to lift arms, or move body parts, more generally, typically result in the bodily movement intended, unless something interferes. And if the materialist means that no explanation of type (2) can be given, he is also wrong. My decision to raise my arm caused my arm to rise. How? By causing certain neural events, N, which caused certain muscular events, M, which resulted in the arm's rising.

> *The more unintelligent a man is, the less mysterious existence seems to him.*
>
> — Arthur Schopenhauer (1788-1860)

But if the materialist insists that, in the last analysis, we can't explain how any mental event could cause any physical event to happen, a simple response is available to the dualist. In the last analysis, we can never explain what it is for any event of any sort to cause another event. It's a mystery. Are you surprised to hear that? The simple, and confounding, truth is that there is no generally accepted scientific or philosophical account of causation that allows us to ever really understand, in the deepest possible sense, the nature of causation. So we never really know, in the deepest sense, what it is for anything to cause anything else. Therefore, the dualist is in no worse position than anyone who believes in any sort of causation in this world.

The last flaw in this mystery objection — in both its forms, concerning composition and causation — is to think that a mystery is, in itself, inherently unbelievable. Anyone who pays any attention whatsoever to the discoveries of contemporary science in its most fundamental researches is confronted left and right by mystery. It is a mystery that this universe exists at all. It is a mystery that one and the same species can include Mother Theresa, Albert Einstein, and Adolph Hitler. It is a mystery that good people can do very bad things. It is a mystery that human mathematics can plumb the depths of physical reality. Rather than following the materialist in saying, "Mysterious, therefore false," I am inclined to go in the opposite direction and suspect that mystery can be a sign of reality.

> *Mystery is not the denial of reason, but its honest confirmation: reason, indeed leads inevitably to mystery. . ..: mystery and reality are two halves of the same sphere.*
>
> — Walt Whitman (1819-1892)

The problem of other minds

The last argument for materialism that I want to present briefly is known as The Problem of Other Minds. It goes like this. If minds are distinct from bodies, and all we ever have access to in the case of other people are their bodies and bodily behavior, then how do we know that there are any other minds distinct from our own? The people around us could be nothing more than just cleverly contrived robots programmed to mimic intelligent and sensate behavior. If dualism were true, there would be an unbridgeable gap between what we experience and what we believe, in the case of other people.

How DO we know that the people we meet are not computers programmed to simulate people?

— R. Buckminster Fuller (1895-1983)

As an argument against dualism, this is a bit silly, to say the least. The materialist believes that behind overt observable bodily behavior, there are complex inner neural processes going on that are responsible for what we see. But as the materialist interacts with colleagues in the coffee shop or with friends in the mall, how does he know that in their particular heads these complex neural events are transpiring? He has no more direct access to them than the dualist would to nonmaterial minds.

Secondly, the problem of other minds can be seen most insightfully, as just another form of overall skepticism concerning a range of ordinary belief. And as such, it deserves the same treatment. In Chapter 5, we saw that skeptics often have asked such things as: "How do we know that memory is ever reliable?" "How do we know that there really is an external world behind the veil of our sensations?" "How do we know that the universe has existed more than five minutes?"

How did we respond to the skeptic's questioning of our ordinary beliefs? With the use of The Principle of Belief Conservation, in Chapter 6. I claimed that this principle justifies our rational rejection of radical skeptical hypotheses and suggestions that would undermine wide ranges of our ordinary beliefs. The same response is appropriate here.

How do I know that anyone other than myself has a mind? I naturally believe that they do. Instinct and intuition guide me here. And I can rationally reject any suggestion to the contrary by invoking the same principle that I use to turn back any other form of skepticism. There is nothing here for the dualist to worry about.

A Verdict on the Materialist Case

When a debater's point is not impressive, he brings forth many arguments.

— Talmud

I judge the standard arguments for materialism and against dualism to be inconclusive. I admit that I am not naturally inclined to materialism, even though I am very empirically, or experientially, oriented in my own thinking. I am also careful not to be gullible. I would even say that I am by nature a Doubting Thomas. But, here, that just means I have my doubts about all the materialist bluster, despite its popularity in recent intellectual circles.

Argument seldom convinces anyone contrary to his inclinations.

— Thomas Fuller (1654-1734)

But you need to look at the other case to be made, for dualism. Our inclinations can be wrong. Or they can be subtle guides to truth. What are your inclinations on the mind-body problem? Are they leading you to truth? If you're interested to find out more about dualism, see Chapter 15.

Chapter 15

The Case for Dualism

We can only feel awe before a mystery that both is what we are and surpasses our understanding.

— Jonathan Schell

Human nature is in many ways a mystery, no matter how you cut it. Who are we? Where did we come from? How did we get here? Where are we going? We are the most inward of creatures, and yet the most social. We have great power for good and correspondingly enormous power for evil. We can change the world or sleep walk through the day. We are physical beings living in a material world. And we are, somehow, more. Or, are we?

Are we physical beings who have somehow developed a spiritual dimension? Or are we most fundamentally spiritual beings who have come to live a physical existence? Are we just brains that aspire to more, or rather immaterial souls attached to bodies?

In this chapter, we examine the distinctively philosophical grounds for thinking that mind-body dualism is true.

The Natural Belief in Dualism

The truth is always the strongest argument.

— Sophocles (c. 496–406 B.C.)

When we examine the problem of free will and determinism in Part III, we articulate a view of human beings as agents who can act creatively into the world from a vantage point somehow outside any deterministic causal nexus. But what is such an agent? What could make us so distinctive?

One of the most pervasive human beliefs since before recorded history is the conviction that we human beings are in some way radically different from at least most of the rest of nature. We are not just physical objects. We are not just complex organisms. We are, in some unique and distinctive sense, persons.

There is evidence that prehistoric humans buried their dead in distinctive ways, covering their graves with flower petals and viewing dead humans very differently from the ways in which they viewed dead animals. The death of a man or woman was presumably believed to be different as a reflection of the distinctiveness of the form of life, or existence, that had departed.

Consider for a moment the widespread belief in an after-life. When a physical object is destroyed, it no longer exists. Smash a vase into small pieces, and all you have are just shards of glass, or broken pieces of pottery. The vase is gone. When a truck hits a squirrel, that's it for the squirrel. All that's left are squirrel parts. But one of the most widespread and firmly held of human beliefs since ancient times is that we are importantly different, in such a way that we can survive the death of our bodies. Our existence is not as fragile as that of our bodies, or of any of the other physical objects in our environment, which resist nonexistence only by force — molecular cohesion, or the atomic force, and any of the other forces that metaphysically glue things together in the realm of matter.

In our regular behavior, we naturally treat humans as being importantly different from inanimate objects and nonhuman animals. We view other people as free moral agents who have responsibilities and rights. We hold people morally accountable for what they do. We think that spiritual development is possible. This is not an expectation that we have of iguanas or aardvarks.

This common view of human beings that has reigned supreme throughout the centuries and across many cultures, apart from small bands of naysayers in various places and times, is the philosophical view of dualism. This view that we have minds or souls as well as bodies is so pervasive, and yet we so rarely think about the possible reasons for believing it to be true.

> *I am positive I have a soul; nor can all the books with which materialists have pestered the world ever convince me of the contrary.*
>
> — Laurence Sterne (1713-1768)

I'm a Soul Man

Why are most people dualists? Ask a normal person (and by this, I mean of course, almost anyone other than a philosophy professor), and you'll often hear, "Because it's true." But why think it's true? The following sections look briefly at some of the main arguments in favor of the philosophy of dualism.

The introspection argument

We human beings have an unusual property — we are capable of looking within ourselves. We are capable of introspection. I can monitor my own inner states — look, as it were, and see what is going on in my mind. In addition to having sense experience, I can be reflectively aware of the nature and texture of that experience. I can ruminate on its significance. I can take it and perform various imaginative operations upon it.

The Scottish philosopher David Hume believed that when I try to locate my true self by introspection, I'll inevitably be disappointed. He thought that the most I could ever observationally capture was a specific experience — a thought or feeling or sensation — and that I'd never come into contact, in addition, with a core self. I believe that he was wrong.

By introspection, it can be argued, I am in contact with myself. I have direct acquaintance with my basic essence through the field of my conscious experience. I am aware, in that experience, of things not to be found in any neurological examination of my brain, by any means whatsoever. I know the feeling of being me. I have it available to me all the time. And it's nothing physical at all. It is a transcendent awareness mediated by the physical, but altogether distinct from any physical thing.

> *Whether or not the philosophers care to admit that we have a soul, it seems obvious that we are equipped with something or other which generates dreams and ideals, and which sets up values.*
>
> — John Erskine

Skeptics can claim that this is no argument at all, but rather is no more than a bald set of relatively unintelligible assertions masquerading as a logical inference. But there is nothing whatsoever unintelligible about it. And it is a feeling that most people have had. On the inside, I know myself in a way that no one else can know me. There is an essential interiority, an inner essence, to being me that is distinct from any physical property that I, or my brain, might have. The soul presents itself to itself, and any skeptical inability to see this is a philosophical malady, not a result of intellectual debunking and superior standards of credibility.

Divergent viewpoints: A random sample

Highly intelligent people have differed a great deal over the existence of a soul in human beings. Some of the great minds have been very outspoken on the topic. Two representative quotations can convey a sense of the debate.

If there is a soul, what is it, and where did it come from, and where does it go? Can anyone who is guided by his reason possibly imagine a soul independent of a body, or the place of its residence, or the character of it, or anything concerning it? If man is *justified in any belief or disbelief on any subject, he is warranted in disbelief in a soul. Not one scrap of evidence exists to prove any such impossible thing.*
— Clarence Darrow (1857-1938)

People will do anything, no matter how absurd, in order to avoid facing their own souls.

— Carl Jung (1875-1961)

There is another way to make this argument. We know certain things to be true of the mind and of mental experience "from the inside" that cannot be true of anything physical. Suppose that Susan is the world's top neuroscientist, and that she is a person who has been totally color blind from birth. We can even project into the future and imagine that Susan knows everything about the brain and its workings that there is to know. If mental items like color sensations were just brain events or brain structures, then, in virtue of her complete knowledge of the brain, Susan would know everything there is to know about color sensations, like the various appearances of red, green, blue, and yellow. But, surely, no amount of knowledge concerning the physical structures of neurons and their activities will make up for what Susan lacks in her personal sensory experience. There is something in the minds of color sensitive people that is just not to be found in their brains. Therefore, the mind is not the same thing as the brain.

The discernibility argument

Logic . . . lays down general principles and laws of the search after truth.

— John Stuart Mill

In logic, there is a law governing identity statements that says, for any object *A,* and any object *B, A=B* (*A* is identical with *B*) if and only if every property *A* has, *B* has, and vice versa. This would be too obvious to state if we weren't doing philosophy, because how could *A* be the same object as *B* unless there was just that one set of properties or characteristics had by this one thing, an object which we know by the two different names "*A*" and "*B*"? The fallout from this simple principle, though, is powerful. If anyone makes a claim that *A=B* and we can find one property that *A* has and yet *B* lacks, or one characteristic that *B* has that *A* is without, we have disproved the alleged identity.

Materialists claim that minds are just brains, or that mental events are just physical events. But brains have properties minds could not have. And minds have properties brains couldn't have. So they can't be identical.

Think for a moment about a distinctively mental property that it seems no physical object could have. I currently have in mind an intention to go exercise later tonight. I intend to take a walk, bike some, or lift weights. Actually I intend to do one or two of those three things. To that extent, my intention is a bit vague. Can a brain event be vague? What sense could that even make? My mental state under discussion has the property that philosophers call "intentionality." It is a thought *about* something. It is about something I intend to do. "Aboutness" is clearly a mental property. We think about all sorts of things. But what kind of physical property could "aboutness" be? There are no physical states or events among my neurons which have any physical property of "aboutness," or intentionality. Aboutness cannot be measured. It has no physical magnitude. It is at home in the mind but not in the physical brain.

My intention to exercise connects up with a future time period ("later tonight") and another place near where I live (where I would walk, or bike, or lift weights). But there is no physical way in which my neurons connect up with a future time, or another place outside my head and the current reach of my senses. Thus, mental events have properties none of my neural events can have. Therefore, those mental events cannot be identical to any neural events.

Mental states such as belief states stand in relations to each other, such as the logical relations of deducibility, implication, and contradiction, that no neural or any other type of physical states can stand in to each other. Therefore, by the law of discernibility, no physical states can be identical to those mental states.

A neural state can be roughly three inches across. It makes complete sense to ask whether my hopes and aspirations are reasonable, or are more than they ought to be, given my talents and commitments. But it makes absolutely no sense at all to ask whether my hopes and aspirations are more or less than roughly three inches across. Therefore, those hopes and aspirations cannot be identical to any neural state.

> *Man is something more than what he knows of himself. He is not what he is simply once for all, but is a process; he is not merely an extant life, but is, within that life, endowed with possibilities through the freedom he possesses to make of himself what he will by the activities on which he decides.*
>
> — Karl Jaspers (1883-1969)

A mind can transcend itself and freely determine to grow and develop in a new direction. A mind can adopt new aspirations and intentions. No physical stuff can do this. Therefore, no mind can be physical stuff.

We could go on. Discernibility equals nonidentity. In logic, and in metaphysics. The mental is discernible from the physical. Therefore materialism is false. The mind exists in its own domain. Dualism rules.

The materialist can claim that all these allegations about discernibility are themselves false. We may just be unaccustomed to speaking of mental states having physical dimension and measurement, but it doesn't follow that they don't have such qualities. We may be unaccustomed to thinking of logical relationships like implication holding between neural states, but it doesn't follow that they don't. In the end, the materialist will just claim that the dualist has faulty intuitions here. Some neural events and states both can and do have the same qualities as mental states, despite the admitted awkwardness of our language for recognizing that fact. The dualist, of course, will return the favor and declare the materialist's "intuitions" (read: "prejudices") to be completely off base. What do you think?

If I know your sect, I anticipate your argument.

— Emerson

The Cartesian argument

The great philosopher Descartes had a quick and simple argument for dualism. I can, in theory, doubt the real existence of my body. It is, so far as I know, logically possible that all the sensations I have of being embodied are delusory. But I cannot doubt the existence of my mind. In the very act of doubting, I realize that I am using my mind. It is not logically possible to entertain doubt without having a mind. Therefore, my body is not the same thing as my mind.

This is, in a sense, a historically notable version of a discernibility argument. My body (or physical brain) has the property of being such that it's possible for me to doubt its real existence. My mind lacks that property. Therefore, they are not identical. Dualism is true.

What can the materialist say here? Something like this: It's possible for me to doubt whether the celestial object traditionally referred to as "The Morning Star" ever appears in the evening. It's not possible for me to harbor that doubt about the celestial object traditionally called "The Evening Star." But if I hastily concluded that The Morning Star thus could not possibly be identical to The Evening Star, I would be wrong. They are both names for the planet Venus. It's doubtful whether much of interest can be established by doubt alone.

The Platonic argument

Plato, the first philosopher we know to have definitively distinguished the mental and the physical — the mind from the body — had another simple argument for dualism. It is possible for the mind or soul to pre-exist the body, and it's possible for it to survive bodily death, whether it in fact does so or not. We can describe disembodied existence without incurring the price of logical contradiction, and we can imagine it without incoherence. But if it is indeed possible for the mind to exist without the body, the mind cannot be identical with the body, or with any part of the body.

The other side of the argument is even easier. The materialist may refuse to admit even the possibility that my mind can survive the death of my body. And if he does so, this argument can't even get started. But the materialist will find it hard to deny that it's possible for my body to survive the death of my mind. Bodies seem to survive the death and disappearance of minds all the time. There may even be some examples in the office where you work. Just kidding. But if a body can survive the death and disappearance of a mind, how then could the body, or any of its parts, be the mind?

> *Put the argument into a concrete shape, into an image — some hard phrase, round and solid as a ball, which they can see and handle and carry home with them — and the cause is half won.*
>
> — Emerson (again)

The materialist will just say that it's not the body, or any part of the body, that is identical with the mind, but rather the well-functioning neural system. The death of the mind is the destruction of the well-functioning neural system. We may be confronted with a dead body without a mind, but we are not thereby in the presence of a well functioning neural system without a mind. And if we think that we can imagine a mind existing without the existence of a well-functioning physical system with which it is identical, we are just confusing ignorance with imagination, which is always a dangerous thing.

This response is a significant one. Arguments from what we can imagine to what is in fact true are tricky. And they are easy to resist.

The parapsychology argument

> *Ghosts remind me of men's smart crack about women, you can't live with them and can't live without them.*
>
> — Eugene O'Neal

At this point, it's easy to begin to doubt whether philosophical argument alone can ever establish the existence or non-existence of anything to everyone's satisfaction. We typically know that something exists by experiencing it. This is the assumption behind what we have called *The Introspection Argument*. But because that argument relied on experience that we ourselves have of ourselves, first hand, while embodied, it could be suggested that experience of non-embodied minds or souls would be the most powerful basis imaginable for rationally grounding the belief that souls or minds exist as objects distinct from any physical things.

If my friend's grandmother did indeed talk with someone after his death, after his brain had ceased functioning, and many miles from where his body lay dead (for this and the next two stories alluded to, see Chapter 13), then we could conclude that his mind did not depend for its existence and functioning on his brain or body, that it was an entity distinct. But did she really?

If my old guitar teacher once really saw a soul leaving a body (and how do you see a soul if it's not a material thing and thus can't reflect light?), then souls are not the same things as bodies or parts of bodies. But how can we know what the facts really were?

> *We ought in fairness to fight our case with no help beyond the bare facts: nothing, therefore should matter except the proof of these facts.*
>
> — Aristotle

If my father could know things that were going to happen in the future or grasp truths about persons not in any way physically available to him, then the mind does not depend on physical signals alone for knowledge. And in this case, it could perhaps be reasonable to suppose that the mind is itself not a physical organ of any kind. But how do we know what these cases of unusual knowledge really were?

If we could be sure that there are any real ghosts, "appearances" of non-embodied minds, perhaps consciously contrived for the sake of sensory contact with embodied beings such as ourselves, then we could conclude that minds are different from brains and can exist on their own. But most of the stories we hear about such things are fantastical. Are any believable at all?

> *Mind moves matter.*
>
> — Vergil

When I was in high school, I often read a bit in The J.B. Phillips New Testament at night, a contemporary paraphrase that was a lively rendering into modern English of the New Testament documents. The scholar, J. B. Phillips, who was an extremely well-educated, highly respected, and by all evidence, a perfectly sane individual, had recounted a personal story in print that had perplexed a great many of his readers and fans. It hit me deeply.

According to the account I heard, and since confirmed, Phillips had explained that he had been going through a personally difficult period in his life, and was in need of something. On Saturday, November 23, 1963, as the Rev. Phillips sat in his home watching television, the figure of C.S. Lewis, a famous literary scholar and writer of popular Christian essays, who had died just the day before, appeared suddenly in the room with him, seated in a chair, fully visible to Phillips. Phillips had only seen Lewis once during his life, but they had corresponded, and Lewis had encouraged him to seek publication for his paraphrases of the letters of Saint Paul. As he sat there, surprised at the figure suddenly appearing across from him, Phillips felt that Lewis was himself undeniably and yet inexplicably there, a few feet away, in three dimensions, with a healthy, ruddy complexion, looking real as life. The famous deceased scholar then spoke a few words to Phillips, told him just what he needed to hear, and then disappeared completely, as suddenly as he had arrived.

I had read some of the books written by C. S. Lewis. He had been a philosophy tutor and then a professor of medieval and renaissance literature. His writing was impressive, and personally helpful. I was benefiting daily from the translations and paraphrases composed by Phillips. This story had to have an impact. And it did.

> *In my youth, I regarded the universe as an open book, printed in the language of physical equations, whereas now it appears to me as a text written in invisible ink, of which in our rare moments of grace we are able to decipher a small fragment.*

> — Arthur Koestler (1905-1983)

But is this all hallucination? Well-meaning, well-informed, and sincere people claim occasionally to come into contact with human beings after they have died. Plenty of hucksters make those claims, too. But we can safely ignore them. What of the sane and sincere people? Can we take their experience to be evidence for the existence of souls distinct from the physical bodies we dwell in during this earthly life?

The materialist rejects all claims of the paranormal, all stories of ghosts, communications from disembodied human beings, and nonphysical forms of knowing. The materialist claim is that we are all naturally wonder-mongers, excited by wild stories of exotic things, and gullible to what we really want to believe. Ghosts do not walk among us publicly. Disembodied souls go to no trouble to manifest themselves clearly to CNN's cameras, or to regularly bring otherwise unknown information into the lives of public figures who desperately need it and can act on it either to do good, or else to avert ill that otherwise would most likely happen. The materialist is convinced that we have here as yet no hard evidence for the claims of dualism. He claims further that this is because dualism is false. But is it?

People everywhere enjoy believing things that they know are not true. It spares them the ordeal of thinking for themselves and taking responsibility for what they know.

— Brooks Atkinson (1894-1984)

Could there be more evidence relevant to our topic, evidence, or even argument that we have not yet consulted? I believe so.

The need for evidence

Men do not know what the nature of the soul is, whether it is engendered with us or whether it is infused into us at our birth; whether it perishes with us, dissolved by death, or whether it haunts the gloomy shade and bottomless pits of Orcus, or whether, by divine influence, it infuses itself into other animals.

— Lucretius

The philosophical argumentation examined in the previous sections can reasonably be judged to be inconclusive. It is not guaranteed to convince all fair-minded people. So, where else can we turn?

Is psychic experience an amalgam of fraud and fantasy, or is there a core of truthful and trustworthy evidence to be found there? Is death the end of life and conscious existence, or is it somehow a portal, not just into another dimension of existence, but into evidence within this world concerning who and what we are right now?

We need to cast our nets a bit wider. We need to look at some of the issues surrounding the phenomenon of human death. Perhaps then we will arrive at some evidence, or some solid philosophical reasoning, that will help us see where the truth lies.

These questions are so important, I devote the next few chapters to a topic that will help us ultimately deal with them. (See Chapters 16 through 18 if you're interested.)

Part VI
What's the Deal with Death?

The 5th Wave   By Rich Tennant

©RICHTENNANT

EXISTENTIAL PIZZA

"It's called that because we feel that people are entirely free and therefore responsible for what they make of themselves and for themselves. Now, do you still want the double anchovy with the fried mozzarella strips?"

In this part . . .

Death and taxes. You'll have to see an accountant for tax advice. But a friendly philosopher can help you understand the other unpleasant certainty in life. In this part, we look at human attitudes toward the end of life in this world. What is it? Should it be feared? Is it the end of all things for us, or is it rather the beginning of the greatest adventure? What should we believe?

Chapter 16

From Dust to Dust: Fear and the Void

. . . .

In This Chapter

▶ Getting a grip on the big picture for life and death
▶ Facing the phenomenon of death
▶ Examining four different fears that death inspires

. . . .

The end of all is death and man's life passeth away suddenly as a shadow.

— Thomas À Kempis

In this chapter, we begin to explore the subject of death. We face our mortality, and we look at four different fears that death inspires. But in philosophy, everything is connected with everything else. In looking at issues surrounding the phenomenon of human death, we will find ourselves touching on problems that come up in connection with other philosophical issues, and yet by looking at the questions distinctively raised by death, we can come to have a new perspective on all of the other concerns of philosophy.

I want to introduce the philosophical topic of death by first analyzing the concern it inspires within the human heart. We need to look first at the most common human reaction to the fact of death and explore its various manifestations.

Man is the only animal that contemplates death, and also the only animal that shows any sign of doubt of its finality.

— William Ernest Hocking

The Final Exit and the Four Fears

As a young boy, I heard about death only when my mother talked of her childhood. Her father, a strong gentleman farmer, had been crushed under a wagon wheel. He lingered for days. Mother was a small girl and didn't understand what was happening. Then, moments before he died, he spoke. "It's beautiful."

Those were his last words. And her culminating memory of his life.

Decades later, she thought of those enigmatic final words as his parting revelation concerning what was to come. He wouldn't be around to help her through life, but at that last moment, he could give her guidance into death that would fill her memory and heart for a lifetime of struggle and hope.

Caught between this world and the next, I was told, my grandfather had reported his first glimpse of the great beyond. More than that, he could not say. For he could see more only by leaving this earth forever.

My first real experience of death was when I was in the seventh grade. My best friend's wonderful mother suddenly discovered she had cancer, and was dead before I realized what was happening. I remember lying in my bed at night thinking about the fact that I would never see her again. Never. I was accustomed to going over to their house after school at least a couple of days a week. I had needed a bass player for my band, so I went over often and taught my friend how to play bass guitar. His mother brought us snacks and talked to me about school. She smiled a lot. And she was dead.

> *A death is the most terrible of facts.*
>
> — Iris Murdoch

There was suddenly a void in my life. An abyss. I couldn't imagine what it was like for my friend. My mind shut down when I tried to think about it from his point of view. It was all too sudden. Too final. And far too strange. Smiling one day, full of life and friendliness and hope. And gone the next. Totally. Permanently. Gone.

> *Death surprises us in the midst of our hopes.*
>
> — Thomas Fuller (18th century)

I lay awake at night filled with fear. An undefined fear, but a trembling over the power and speed of mortality. And the never-ending nature of that absence. That void.

Some famous last words

Some of the most active and creative human beings have left behind memorable last words.

I shall hear in heaven.
— Beethoven (referring to his deafness)

My desire is to make what haste I can to be gone.
— Oliver Cromwell

Give the boys a holiday.
— Anaxagorus the philosopher, who was a school teacher

I am going to see the sun for the last time.
— Jean-Jacques Rousseau

All my possessions for a moment of time.
— Queen Elizabeth of England

I am about to take my last voyage, a great leap in the dark.
— Thomas Hobbes

I see no reason why the existence of Harriet Martineau should be perpetuated.
— Harriet Martineau

The first step toward philosophy is incredulity.
— Denis Diderot

I am going to seek a grand perhaps; draw the curtain, the farce is played.
— Rabelais

So much to do, so little done!
— Cecil Rhodes

We fear death. And we all live in some measure of denial, pretending that it's a fiction. That it happens to other people. But that, somehow, I'll be the exception to the rule. First-semester logic students begin to master inference by seeing the classic argument:

All men are mortal.
Socrates is a man.
Therefore, Socrates is mortal.

And while we remember the conclusion, we forget the relevance of the first premise to us. Poor Socrates. But Socrates didn't have to drink the poison. He could have escaped. And maybe I can too.

I remember in college, in the 1970s, attending the meetings of a campus Christian organization, where there was good music, great fun, and a lot of hugging, I heard talks on the End Times. Extrapolations from the Book of Revelation suggested that the last generation would not have to die, but would be taken up bodily into heaven, to enter eternity with the returning Christ. It was hinted that this may be us. I always knew. Exceptional Tom. Poor Socrates.

All men think that all men are mortal but themselves.

— Edward Young (18th century)

As a young professor of philosophy, I was warned of the difficulty of talking to my students about death because, I was told, they wouldn't really believe that it applied in any way to them. The immortality of youth would not have worn thin, even by senior year. That's why they drank too much, and drove too fast, lay out in the midday sun to tan, and looked for a place where they could try bungee jumping.

But soon enough, after college, the youthful inability to take death seriously begins to wear off. Maybe a friend dies. That's a wakeup call for sure. Or a parent, or some close relative. Perhaps a bad accident illumines the mind and awakens the heart. Or sometimes all it takes is a very turbulent airline flight.

> *I will show you fear in a handful of dust.*
>
> — T.S. Eliot

For me, it was, oddly enough, a dentist's report that, for the first time in 25 years, I had a cavity. Suddenly I was awash in mortality. The decay of the body. The rebellion of the flesh. The inevitable, ineluctable march of death had begun to come within sight. Okay, it was an overreaction. But I have a creative disposition.

For some people, it can be nothing more than wrinkles. For others, lost hair. Or even new and unwanted hair in undesirable places. The illusion of eternal youth fades. And death looms ahead.

I went through a few years of young adulthood, in my early 30s, when I would wake up in the middle of the night suddenly convicted of the reality that I would one day die. That I could not avoid it. That it would really, truly, inevitably happen to me. I would envision myself dying. My heart rate would increase. There would be a heightened, crystalline focus of consciousness. I would have to leave behind everything that I love in this life and on this earth. I would lose the entirety of my earthly experience.

I have never been more awake. Or more alert. Or more frightened. Perhaps terrified is a better word.

> *It is torture to fear what you cannot overcome.*
>
> — Anacharsis

Why do we fear something that seems to be, as much as anything, a part of the cycles of nature? Why do we experience terror in anticipating death?

There are at least four different kinds of fear of death: Fear of the process of dying, fear of punishment after death, fear of the unknown, and fear of annihilation. The following sections look at each one.

Fear of the process of dying

It hath often been said, that it is not death, but dying, which is terrible.

— Henry Fielding

When some people say that they fear death, it's really not death itself as an end state that they fear, but rather the physical and psychological process of dying. They fear that they will suffer terribly. They fear pain and physical agony. They fear the psychological torment of letting go and leaving behind everyone and everything that they love. They even fear the utter solitude that is imposed by dying.

I saw my father die of lung cancer, way too young, at the age of 69. It had spread to his brain, and I watched at his bedside as he convulsed in apparent agony, suffering seizures that I could not imagine. We could do nothing to help. Death itself came as a release from it all. And as a relief to those of us who loved him. An hour after he died, I leaned over and kissed his still warm bald head and breathed a deep sigh of thankfulness that he was at last free of the terrible torment he had endured.

A fear of dying is natural in anyone who has witnessed a difficult death. Sometimes it comes so slowly as to be torture. And, other times, it comes too fast. My senior year at college, I read all the newspaper and magazine accounts of a commercial airplane crash at Boston's Logan International airport. If memory serves correctly, the plane was coming in for a normal landing. But it was too low on the approach, and landing gear caught on the sea wall at the end of the runway. It crashed. When the fire engines arrived at the scene, dozens, maybe even scores, of people were screaming in agony as they lay in the broken fuselage, engulfed in flames. By the time the firemen could reach them, they were all dead.

I remember dwelling a lot on this story. I tried to imagine what it was like to be reading *People Magazine* one minute, checking your watch and thinking about getting to the baggage claim area on time, then a minute later to be in flames, and then a minute afterwards, to be dead. It was all too unexpected. Too sudden. Too horrific.

This story kept me from flying. In the next six years, I flew only about four times. Then, for nine years, I refused to get on a plane. Did I fear flying? I feared dying like the people in Boston. Now I often fly over a 100,000 miles a year. I explain how I got over that fear in my book *True Success*. But my point here is only that it was a life-changing fear for many years.

Men fear death, as children fear to go in the dark; and as that natural fear in children is increased with tales, so is the other.

— Francis Bacon

A colleague's wife walked into a classroom to teach her class. She stood at the desk, looked at the room of students, and dropped dead. A brain aneurysm took that moment to take her away. A man sat in his car at the mall, waiting to pick up his teenage daughter after work. He was shot in the head. He didn't see death coming.

Whose death is more terrible, the person who knows he is dying and can attempt to prepare himself amidst terrible suffering, or the one who doesn't see it coming? Opinion is divided on this one. But most people seem to some extent to fear both ways of dying, yet for different reasons, and in different ways.

Fear of punishment

Some people who say that they fear death actually harbor anxieties about one particular possible set of events that they fear might happen after their bodily deaths. These are people who believe in an afterlife and fear an antici-pated divine moral day of judgment, along with its accompanying punishment for what they have done in this life. Often these are normal people who have not lived evil and criminal lives, but who have had a sensi-tivity instilled in them that renders them vulnerable to guilt and fear.

This fear most typically arises out of beliefs like the following. There is a morally perfect Creator God who brought about the existence of the universe and all its creatures under the governance of absolute moral laws that he will enforce. We human beings are not morally perfect, but often misuse our free-dom to do evil. Evil deserves, and under the demands of perfect justice, must receive, punishment. But just as good does not always flourish in this world, evil is not always punished here below. Therefore, after death, there must be a realm of existence in which justice prevails. This must involve an afterlife in which evil doers are punished for their sins and the good are rewarded for their virtuous choices. We are all to some extent doers of evil. Therefore, we shall all merit punishment by our perfect cosmic judge.

Throughout the centuries, many of the preachers, teachers, and artists of Christendom have excelled in portraying with great vividness the excruciat-ing pains and terrors of punishment to be faced in the afterlife. One of America's very best early philosophers, the Puritan minister Jonathan Edwards (1703-1758), is perhaps best known to subsequent generations for his fiery sermon "Sinners in the Hands of an Angry God." Speaking of sinners in the next world, he says:

> *The wrath of God burns against them, their damnation does not slumber; the pit is prepared, the fire is made ready, the furnace is now hot, ready to receive them; the flames do now rage and glow. The glittering sword is whet, and held over them, and the pit hath opened its mouth under them.*

There is no redemption from hell.

— Pope Paul III

The philosophical theologian confronts his congregation, and by implication the rest of us, saying:

> *The God that holds you over the pit of hell, much as one holds a spider, or some loathsome insect over the fire, abhors you, and is dreadfully provoked: his wrath towards you burns like fire; he looks upon you as worthy of nothing else, but to be cast into the fire; he is of purer eyes than to bear to have you in his sight; you are ten thousand times more abominable in his eyes, than the most hateful venomous serpent is in ours.*

Okay then. So much for pastoral cheerleading. Clearly this was before The Power of Positive Thinking hit the pulpit.

It's clear that devout religious believers might indeed be very concerned about their prospects after the grave. Even many believers who are convinced that their eternal destinies are protected from the endless torments portrayed by Edwards nonetheless fear a purging purgatorial intermediary state which alone might prepare them for entering the everlasting presence of a perfect God. And the prospect of any such suffering could assuredly arouse a sentiment of fear.

This is a particular kind of fear of death, of course, that is confined to those maintaining a certain specific sort of world view. Many contemporary Christian theologians abhor what they consider to be the fear-mongering of much past preaching on the afterlife. And yet, at the same time, in response to the 20th century's seemingly endless cycles of evil and horror, some contemporary philosophers have been revisiting the doctrine of hell and its implications for modern faith and morals.

Fear follows crime and is its punishment.

— Voltaire

It is often said that virtue is its own reward, and that evil is its own punishment. But there are still lingering suspicions on the part of many intelligent and sensitive people that more might be at stake in any universe ultimately governed by absolute justice. And that this more might appropriately ground a rational fear in its prospect.

Sinners in the hands of an angry philosopher: More from the Reverend Edwards

The philosophical pastor had no hesitation to give his congregation the most horrendous description of the punishment that evildoers would face:

O sinner! Consider the fearful danger you are in: it is a great furnace of wrath, a wide and bottomless pit, full of the fire of wrath, that you are held over in the hand of that God, whose wrath is provoked and incensed as much against you, as against many of the damned in hell. You hang by a slender thread, with the flames of divine wrath flashing about it, and ready every moment to singe it, and burn it asunder; and you have no interest in any Mediator, and nothing to lay hold of to save yourself, nothing to keep off the flames of wrath, nothing of your own, nothing that you ever have done, nothing that you can do, to induce God to spare you one moment.

It is everlasting wrath. It would be dreadful to suffer this fierceness and wrath of Almighty God one moment; but you must suffer it to all eternity. There will be no end to this exquisite horrible misery. When you look forward, you shall see a long forever, a boundless duration before you, which will swallow up your thoughts, and amaze your soul; and you will absolutely despair of ever having any deliverance, any end, any mitigation, any rest at all. You will know certainly that you must wear out long ages, millions of millions of ages, in wrestling and conflicting with this almighty merciless vengeance; and then when you have so done, when so many ages have actually been spent by you in this manner, you will know that all is but a point to what remains.

— Jonathan Edwards

Fear of the unknown

Up until now, my only surgery requiring general anesthetic was a tonsillectomy when I was ten years old. I remember vividly the nurse coming in to administer the first anesthesia, a shot in the rear. I was supposed to lie down on the gurney as they wheeled me out of my room, but I leaned up on one elbow, wanting to see everything that went on. I asked questions constantly. Was this the elevator to the operating room? What would it look like? Was I going to have to go to sleep? I was so eager to know, I refused to lie down flat, or to allow myself to get sleepy. Even when they were about to put on the mask to administer the ether, I was asking questions. They gave me an overdose. It took me ten hours to wake up, and when I was wheeled back into my room, still out, the odor of ether put my mother to sleep. Or, so she tells me.

I once asked a physician if an overdose of ether could kill brain cells. I said, "Could it be that I'd be a smarter person and a better philosopher if I hadn't been overdosed on anesthesia?" He answered, "I'm amazed that you're walking and talking." So no wonder I haven't solved all the mysteries of the universe yet.

Many psychologists would say that the curiosity that impelled me to ask and look and listen that day before surgery was the flip side of fear — fear of the unknown. In fact, some people think that it's fear of the unknown that is ultimately responsible for all human impulses toward exploration and discovery. It's the force underlying scientific research. And it's the goad to that most human of activities, asking questions.

One of the most common forms of human fear is fear of the unknown. This fear is related to our deep need to feel in control. When we know what's going on, we can feel some sense of control over our environment or our own fortunes, however accurate or delusory that sense might be. The unknown allows for no sure plans or reasonable expectations.

Man imagines that it is death he fears, but what he fears is the unknown. . . .

— Saint-Exupéry

Many people, in fearing death, fear precisely the unknowns associated with it. Will it be like sleep? Or like falling into a bottomless abyss? Will it be terrifying? Or will it be benign? Is death the end? Or is there afterlife? Even people who have well-formed beliefs concerning death and the question of its finality still wonder if they're right. And, in their heart of hearts, they are not sure. They could be wrong. They just don't know. And so they fear.

Fear of annihilation

Death . . . is simply the ultimate horror of life.

— Jean Giraudoux

Something happened once in college, unexpectedly, that I'll never forget. I had been playing tennis for four or five hours. I was back in the dorm, taking a shower. Half soaped up, I suddenly had the most vivid daydream. I saw myself lying in a bed, on white sheets, dying. It was my last minute of life. As the seconds elapsed and I came closer to the abyss, I grew more horrified of potentially losing consciousness for all eternity. I experienced those last few seconds of conscious existence on this earth as if my impending death would be a total extinction of my personhood, an annihilation of conscious existence forever.

Death has but one terror, that it has no tomorrow.

— Eric Hoffer

I did not at the time believe that death is annihilation, and I don't believe it now, but I experienced this daydream as if it were. The last second of life was agonizing, as I knew that this amazing, wonderful gift of experience would be taken from me forever. I clung to it, to the last remaining shreds of conscious experience, too terrified to even think. And I suddenly marshaled all the emotional energy in me to force the dream to end. I wrenched my mind away from that horrible scene and stood, staring at the shower wall, totally shaken within. After I got out of the shower and dried off, I sat for hours and reflected on the horror of what I had just imagined. It took me two weeks to recover fully from that awful and unanticipated experience that no one else ever knew I had.

This is the fear of death that gives many modern people night terrors. They find themselves suddenly aware that they will inevitably face death, and that what they will confront may in fact be the total cessation of conscious experience, the annihilation of the person they have been, forever. There is no abyss deep enough or sense of emptiness hollow enough to come even close to representing the utter void of extinction they feel. And it evokes a fear that can only be called horror. The fear of fears. The ultimate anticipatory agony of which a human being is capable.

> *Good-by world. . . . Good-by to clocks ticking . . . and Mama's sunflowers. And food and coffee. And new-ironed dresses and hot baths . . . and sleeping, and waking up. Oh, earth, you're too wonderful for anybody to realize you.*
>
> — Thornton Wilder

Do we survive bodily death, or is it the end of all ends? Anyone who suspects that it may be utterly terminal can be vulnerable to this fear of death as annihilation, a fear that is utterly distinctive. This is the materialist nightmare. The existentialist anguish without parallel. It is the promise of materialist philosophy and the threat to any dualism that cannot live up to its traditional assurances and deliver what it claims.

We need to examine the arguments and evidence that we have concerning the issue of life after death, and we will in Chapters 17 and 18.

Chapter 17

Philosophical Consolations on Death

. . . .

In This Chapter

▶ Looking at what philosophers have said to help us accept death

▶ Dealing with fears about mortality, no matter what death is

▶ Examining what some great thinkers have said about death

. . . .

> *The long habit of living indisposeth us for dying.*
>
> — Sir Thomas Browne (1605-1682)

*I*n this chapter, we see what counsel philosophy can offer any of us for dealing with the fear of death. We examine what can be said from several philosophical points of view to mitigate our deep worries about our own mortality. Some of the arguments that we look at will come from a materialist or agnostic point of view. Some can be used by dualists. But then, in Chapter 18, we look at the full array of dualistic arguments that death is not in any way an absolute end, and is not, in itself, to be feared.

My strategy here is simple. Some philosophical consolations concerning death can be offered to anyone. Philosophers have thought that we can begin to reconcile ourselves to the fact of our mortality by looking at some fundamental considerations plainly available to anyone, regardless of their position on the mind-body debate, and independently of any issues impinging on religious belief. I want to lay out and critically examine the various attempts that philosophers have made to do this.

For many people, the worst case scenario would be that death is annihilation. (See Chapter 16 for more on fears of dying.) Others worry that it's not extinction, but rather a state of conscious experience that is, let's say, less than pleasant. Considerations can be brought to bear to deal with both these concerns even before we address the issue head on of whether there is conscious experience after death.

Don't Worry, Be Happy

What, if anything, can philosophy itself do to mitigate, or assuage, these widespread forms of fear? Philosophers have provided at least four lines of thought in response to the fear of death (see Chapter 16 for more information on the fears involved). Two directly cover the fear aroused by anticipations of the process of dying. Two clearly address a fear of the state of death itself. And there is some overlap. First, we can look at some responses to our fear of dying.

The stoic response to fear of the process

It is not death or hardship that is a fearful thing, but the fear of hardship and death.

— Epictetus

The stoic philosophers, such thinkers as Seneca, Epictetus, and Marcus Aurelius, believed that life could never dish out to us, and make us endure, more than we were capable of taking. There are two versions of this assurance. One is based in the observation that, at a certain point of pain intensity, human beings tend to lapse into unconsciousness and no longer suffer. But obviously, this point does not come soon enough for many people, and it is no help in dealing with the sort of chronic pain experienced by some cancer patients, as well as many others who have to deal with lengthy, and extremely painful, fatal diseases.

The stoics believed, though, that whatever nature brought us without a cure, we could ourselves at some point reject by choosing to end our misery through ending our own lives. They clearly endorsed desperate measures for dealing with desperate situations. Stoic views on suicide are complex and nuanced, but the fact remains that the stoics believed that God has put in our hands the means for ending anything that we literally could not endure. An agonizing process of death can be brought to a prompt conclusion through human intervention.

Human life consists in mutual service. So grief, pain, misfortune, or 'broken heart' is no excuse for cutting off one's life while any power of service remains. But when all usefulness is over, when one is assured of an unavoidable and imminent death, it is the simplest of human rights to choose a quick and easy death in place of a slow and horrible one.

— Charlotte Perkins Gilman, Suicide Note

This is severe and austere counsel. And it has been rejected by a great many subsequent moralists and people of conscience, for a number of reasons. The fact remains, though, that it has nonetheless brought at least theoretical comfort to many, whether they ever anticipated actually using it or not. God, or nature, will never force us to bear on this earth what we cannot in fact endure. This may be the definition of "cold comfort," but it is a consideration that bears on one prominent fear of death.

The Natural Process Argument

It is as natural to die as to be born.

— Francis Bacon

Philosophers throughout the ages, and many other commentators on the human condition, often have attempted to convince us that death is a natural process, natural event, or natural reality, and as such is to be accepted, and is not to be feared.

This argument clearly could apply equally well to the process of dying, the fact that we face death, and even the state of death itself. Natural, therefore not to be feared.

Death as a natural part of life

All sorts of thinkers have argued the point that death is a natural part of the overall cycle of existence:

We begin to die as soon as we are born, and the end is linked to the beginning.
— Minilius Astonomica

For life is nearer every day to death.
— Phaedrus

Every moment of life is a step toward the grave.
— Crébillon

He that begins to live begins to die.
— Francis Quarles

In the midst of life, we are in death.
— The Book of Common Prayer

You will die not because you are ill, but because you are alive.
— Seneca

Dust thou art, and to dust shalt thou return.
— Genesis 3:19

All our life is but a going out to the place of execution, to death.
— John Donne

I, when I was born, was born to die.
— William Drummond (1656)

What new thing is it for a man to die, whose whole life is nothing but a journey to death?
— Seneca

But poisonous spiders, venomous snakes, incurable diseases, and destructive tornadoes are natural, too, and are just as natural to fear. I have never been comforted by this line of reasoning and honestly can't understand why so many people seem to be. I tend to suspect that they are just desperate for anything to cling to, for any line of thought that might possibly mitigate their fear, and so they allow this suggestion too easily to anesthetize them philosophically to the realities of their plight.

The Necessity Argument

Death takes away the commonplace of life.

— Alexander Smith (1863)

Closely akin to The Natural Process Argument is another line of reasoning that I call The Necessity Argument. It holds that we should be emotionally reconciled to the fact of death, rather than fearing it, once we understand that death is necessary for two important, and very positive, things. First, it's necessary for our appreciation of life. The more vivid our sense of the approach of death, the more we relish the small things in life. And secondly, death is necessary for the continued march of evolutionary improvement, an ongoing progress leading to more valuable states of good, to take place on earth.

For an example of this sort of thinking, we can look at a statement made by Charles Lindberg, in his *Autobiography of Values*:

> *Without death, there would be no awareness of life, and the recurring selection and renewal that has caused life's progress would be ended.*

Let's put this into commonplace terms, starting from the latter of the two different points made here. I know I'm going to get cut from the team, even though I'm working hard and seem to be playing well, and I'm supposed to feel good about the process because I'm assured that my departure will inevitably improve the team? I'm told also that I should even be prepared to stand on the sidelines, if I get the chance, and cheer the new and improved varsity on, because of what they can do without me pulling them down. But there is a small problem with the analogy. When I get cut by Coach Death, I don't obviously get to stand on the sidelines at all. I get buried under the field. This is hard to feel good about.

"But everybody gets cut at some point, or loses their eligibility, so none of us should feel bad about it." This might be okay if we were assured that there was some other team we could go to play on. But if this cut means being banned forever from the sport, I'm not sure how I'm supposed to feel so good about it.

Hardest of deaths to a mortal
Is the death he sees ahead.

— Bacchylides (Fifth century B.C.)

Look at the first point in Lindberg's remark. Is it true that without death there would be no awareness, or appreciation, of life? It is a sad truth about life that we often fail to appreciate what we have until its loss is threatened. That is a fact about human psychology. But it seems to be a weakness that can be overcome by sufficient reflection and training in sensitivity. People can learn to appreciate little things and live fully in the moment without being literally threatened with extinction. People sometimes just get tired of superficial living and voluntarily change their approach to life, learning new ways to love and savor what this world has to offer.

Often, it does seem to take the imminent threat of death to bring about such a change of perspective on life. But I see no reason to think that this is literally necessary. And the general fact of death is certainly, in itself, not enough, because we deceive ourselves about its inevitability when it's not in fact imminent, and regularly ignore its implications for the preciousness of the moments we do have. So, in the last analysis, it's hard to find this line of reasoning convincing.

The Agnostic Argument

Nobody knows, in fact, what death is, nor whether to man it is not perchance the greatest of all blessings; yet people fear it as if they knew it to be the worst of all evils.

— Socrates

The agnostic argument is better. But it's directed not at the process of dying. Its focus is the state of death. Plato represents Socrates as having reasoned something like this:

1. It is wrong (inappropriate or irrational) to fear something unless you know that it can hurt you.

2. You don't know that the state of death can hurt you.

3. It is therefore wrong to fear the state of death.

Again, it's important to keep in mind that this argument is just about the state of death (being dead) rather than about the process of dying. Clearly the process of dying can hurt you. And for this reason it can be rational to fear that process. But the end state of death itself is the main thing feared by most people. And rightly so. The process of dying is limited in duration, however long it seems to take in particularly unfortunate cases. But the state of death is eternal. So, the more reason we can be given not to fear it, the better.

Our final experience, like our first, is conjectural. We move between two darknesses.

— E. M. Forster

Socrates realized that we generally tend to think we know more than we do know about life. He came to realize also that we make the same mistake about death. We have all sorts of attitudes and emotions concerning death that imply knowledge that we do not in fact possess. Death is a great unknown in many ways. And in some of the most important ways. Thus, Socrates believes, we should calm down and not jump to conclusions. For all we know, death may be the greatest of things, not the worst. And our attitudes and emotions should reflect the slimness of our solid knowledge here.

The one permanent emotion of the inferior man is fear — fear of the unknown, the complex, the inexplicable. What he wants beyond everything else is safety.

— H. L. Mencken

The Two Eternities Argument

The two eternities argument depends on the presupposition that death is annihilation, or personal extinction. It can be used, though, by a person who is not convinced that this is the truth about death, but yet fears that it may possibly be.

The argument is constructed in connection with a thought experiment and is sometimes confused with a distinct line of reasoning that Epicurus invented, an argument that we examine in the next section. But this one stands or falls on its own.

There was a time when we were not: this gives us no concern — why then should it trouble us that a time will come when we shall cease to be?

— William Hazlitt

Imagine the mindset of a person who firmly believes that death is the absolute end. The person who is convinced that death is annihilation, the materialist, typically, believes thus that his own bodily death will be followed by an eternity of his subsequent nonexistence. He believes that his consciousness will be snuffed out forever, and he often fears this prospect with the greatest, deepest horror imaginable. But, looking backward, he typically believes that his birth was preceded by an unlimited past of his previous nonexistence, an abyss equal in duration to the one that will follow his death. And yet, he typically contemplates this prior stage of his nonexistence with utter equanimity, total unperterbedness, absolute calm.

But then, a philosopher can argue (and who but a philosopher would dare to?) that these are utterly equal eternities. One is as little to be feared as the other. During the previous eternity, the eternity past, nothing at all happened to harm or deprive the materialist contemplating his life and death. So also, the reasoning goes, during the upcoming eternity, the eternity future, nothing at all will happen to harm or deprive the man who so fears it. Thus the future is as little to be feared as the past.

But there is one big, crucial, dismal disanalogy between the future and the past, a difference that makes a difference. The past is always receding from us, and the future is, by contrast, continually bearing down on us. I can come to contemplate a past fact with equanimity now precisely because I do not have to deal with the prospect of facing and experiencing now anything that is truly past. I sometimes have to deal with repercussions of the past, but as to the past itself, it cannot harm me now. But as to things future, matters are quite different.

The attitudes and emotions, the beliefs and dispositions that are inspired in me by contemplating future possibilities, can indeed affect my imminent prospects of meeting those possibilities sooner or later. Fear can function in helping me to postpone a future state that I do not desire, by stimulating me to avoid any present states that might hasten its arrival. So the past and the future are not after all sufficiently parallel to allow this argument to go through. I'm not at all convinced, are you?

> *One life; a little gleam of Time between two Eternities; no second chance to us forever!*

> — Thomas Carlyle (1795-1881)

Epicurus' argument

The philosopher Epicurus (c.341-270 B.C.) constructed one of the cleverest, and most debated of arguments in all of human history, explicitly for the purpose of ridding us of our fear of death. It is sometimes connected to, or even confused with, The Two Eternities Argument in the preceding section, but is completely distinct from it and should be evaluated on its own merits.

> *Death, the most dreaded of evils, is therefore of no concern to us; for while we exist, death is not present, and when death is present, we no longer exist.*

> — Epictetus

Two philosophers speak their minds

It can be useful to see the exact thoughts of great minds who have reflected on this issue:

Death is non-existence, and I know already what that means. What was before me will happen again after me. If there is any suffering in this state, there must have been such suffering also in the past, before we entered the light of day. As a matter of fact, however, we felt no discomfort then. And I ask you, would you not say that one was the greatest of fools who believed that a lamp was worse off when it was extinguished than before it was lighted? We mortals are also lighted and extinguished; the period of suffering comes in between, but on either side there is a deep peace.
— Seneca, from "On Asthma and Death"

No one is so ignorant as not to know that we must at some time die; nevertheless, when one draws near death, one turns to flight, trembles, and laments. Would you not think him an utter fool who wept because he was not alive a thousand years ago? And is he not just as much of a fool who weeps because he will not be alive a thousand years from now? It is all the same; you will not be, and you were not. Neither of these periods of time belongs to you.
— Seneca, from "On Taking One's Own Life"

For look to the immensity of time behind you, and to the time which is yet to come, another boundless space. In this infinity, then what is the difference between him who lives three days and him who lives three generations?
— Marcus Aurelius, from his "Meditations"

Epicurus argued like this:

1. When you exist, your death does not, and what does not exist can't harm you.

2. When your death exists, you do not, and what does not exist cannot be harmed.

3. It is irrational to fear what can't harm you.

4. It is irrational to fear when you can't be harmed.

5. At any time, either you exist or your death exists.

6. Thus, for any time, either death can't harm you, or you can't be harmed by death.

   Therefore,

7. It is irrational at any time to fear death.

   Weep not for him who departs from life, for there is no suffering beyond death.

   — Palladas

Astonishing! Brilliant! And emotionally, absolutely unconvincing. Ever since Epicurus formulated his argument, philosophers have been trying to figure out what is wrong with it. The assumption has been that there has to be something wrong with it. After all, Epicurus is presupposing that death is personal annihilation, the extinction of consciousness forever. And this is, for many people, the most strongly feared possibility there is. No more sunshine, no more sights and sounds and feelings. No more love. No more thoughts. Forever. And it's this, of all things, that Epicurus is arguing that it makes no sense to fear?

Surely those who fear death as annihilation aren't fearing unpleasant experiences in the state of death. What they are fearing is an eternal deprivation of the most massive and complete sort. Lost goods. Missed opportunities. A vacuum of wonderful and pleasant experience. An absence of any experience whatsoever. And Epicurus alleges that this involves no harm, and bases on this his conclusion that it makes no sense at all to fear death.

> *"Where was it," thought Raskolnikov, "where was it I read about a man sentenced to death who, one hour before his execution, says or thinks that if he had to live on some high rock, on a cliff, on a ledge so narrow that there was only room enough for him to stand there, and if there were bottomless chasms all around, the ocean, eternal darkness, eternal solitude, and eternal gales, and if he had to spend all his life on that square yard of space — a thousand years, an eternity — he'd rather live like that than die at once! Oh, only to live, live, live! Live under any circumstances — only to live!"*
>
> — Fyodor Dostoyevski (1821-1881)

Despite the inability of philosophers to agree on what exactly is wrong with this intriguing argument, most people are not moved by it to cease fearing death. They are just perplexed. It is more like a conundrum than a rationally liberating line of thought.

Is this because people are not rational? Or is it because human emotion is not altogether rational? Is absolutely anything somehow better than nothing? And does the argument in some way miss this? What do you think?

Materialist Conceptions of "Immortality"

Philosophers who believe that death is the end, because they do not believe that there is any such thing as a soul or incorporeal mind to survive bodily death, have offered up their own conceptions of immortality to help reconcile us to our physical demise. These are not conceptions of the immortality of the soul, or of any continuation of personal experience beyond the grave, but they are projections into the future offered as something like consolations to which we can cling. The following sections look at the most standard.

Social immortality

When I was a junior in high school, I once went to Gatlinburg, Tennessee, on a ski weekend. Saturday morning, after a breakfast of pancakes in a restaurant a couple of blocks from the motel where I was staying, I started to walk back to my room. The main street was very busy with traffic whizzing by. I stopped at the corner, waiting for the light to change. A well-dressed man in his 40s or 50s walked up beside me, stopped, turned to me, and said, "When I die, I will live on in my children." Just that. No "Hello," or "Good Morning," or "Excuse me, I'd like to wax philosophical here on the street corner if you don't mind."

> *To live in hearts we leave*
> *Is not to die.*
>
> — Thomas Campbell

Imagine my reaction when I suddenly heard the words "When I die." There we were on a busy street. Cars were zooming by. Was I going to have to grab this guy before he dashed into traffic and sacrificed himself to an Oldsmobile? Why was he saying this to me at that very moment? Exceedingly strange. I guess from the earliest years, I was destined to be a philosopher. At the age of 17, it must have been written across my face.

What that stranger, that very strange man, was expressing is a widely held sentiment, a belief that somehow we can leave something of ourselves behind when we die, through our genetic offspring. For some, it is merely the genetics that counts. For others, it is the raising, the nurturing, the forming that matters most. It is very common for children to feel repressed and pressured by their parents to become appropriate vehicles for their immortality. A CEO, after all, can't live on appropriately in the person of a bum. Or, that's the attitude that many successful people tend to take. And they put pressure on their kids. Not just for their kids' own good. But for their legacy to the world.

> *He who has gone, so we but cherish his memory, abides with us, more potent, nay, more present, than the living man.*
>
> — Saint-Exupéry

Cultural immortality

One day during my graduate school years at Yale, I was visiting a friend in a Yale College undergraduate dormitory. A few students were sitting around talking. I asked one young woman what her major was. She said it was architecture. I asked if she had to learn all about materials and stress points and engineering. She told me no, they didn't do that at Yale. At Yale Architecture school, they were learning to be artists. They would one day go to work at a major firm and have some state university architectural graduates on staff to do the grunt work. They would know all that stuff. I said "But you don't have to know what materials will hold up the walls of a building?" She replied: "My job is to design the forms that will shape people's lives. You have to understand. We're artists. I plan to live on in the cityscapes of America."

> *All our efforts to attain immortality — by statesmanship, by conquest, by science or the arts — are equally vain in the long run, because the long run is longer than any of us imagine.*
>
> — Sydney J. Harris

Well, she won't live on for long in the buildings she designs if they all fall down. I have to say that this was a pretty amazing display of confidence. No, make that *hubris,* the Greek word for overreaching, overweening pridefulness. Arrogance. Presumptuousness. How many of us can reasonably expect to live on through our cultural creations? The young architectural student's artistic monuments will end up covered in soot and bird poop. If she's lucky. And the state university guys have done their job.

> *To occupy an inch of dusty shelf — to have the title of their works read now and then in a future age by some drowsy churchman or some casual straggler, and in another age to be lost, even to remembrance. Such is the amount of boasted immortality.*
>
> — Washington Irving

Even if it were reasonable to expect a form of cultural immortality, most of us would agree with Woody Allen when he said, "I don't want to achieve immortality through my work. I want to achieve immortality through not dying."

Cosmic immortality

I had a friend who once said to me, "When I die, I want to be buried in a pine box, or in no box at all. I want to rot fast, because then my molecules can enter the earth, and then enter plants and the animals who feed on those plants, and I will be disbursed, spread around to the point that, ultimately, I'll be blended in with the universe, and have a sort of cosmic immortality."

> *It cost me never a stab nor squirm*
> *To tread by chance upon a worm.*
> *'Aha, my little dear' I say,*
> *'Your clan will pay me back some day.'*
>
> — Dorothy Parker

This is certainly a more widely available form of "immortality" than that sought by writers, painters, politicians, and architects. But it's not much to aspire to attain. The more molecules I can spread around, the more cosmic immortality it seems I can have. So pass the double fudge nut ice cream and stand back.

I'm sorry, this doesn't inspire me with much comfort.

Scientific immortality

Scientific immortality is the last materialist conception of "immortality" I want to consider. It is certainly the most interesting, because it is the only one to address our desire to live on, not just in the memories of others, in the products of our work, or in our molecules, but with conscious experience. I want to live on as a person, not just as an influence. And you may, too. Materialists have one card up their sleeves that they are starting to play more readily.

Have you ever read about life expectancies 100 or 200 years ago? Even in technologically advanced countries, the average life expectancy was not even 50. Of course, this is skewed by infant mortality. But it is undeniable that modern medicine, as well as protective measures in all departments of life, an advanced understanding of nutrition, and a scientific approach toward exercise, have all combined to extend our expected longevity. And we look better (read: "younger") at 40 and 50 than people did in the past.

Surgery techniques and transplants have extended many people's lives far beyond what they would otherwise have been. The real news, though, is that with breakthroughs in our understanding of genetics and with an increasing technological ability to repair the human body with microsurgery techniques, we may be on the verge of a medical and longevity revolution qualitatively different from any such advances in the past. A few recent books even proclaim that some of us alive now will be the first generation that does not have to die.

> *Oh, what a valiant faculty is hope, that in a mortal subject, and in a moment, makes nothing of usurping infinity, immensity, eternity, and of supplying its master's indigence, at its pleasure, with all the things he can imagine or desire!*
>
> — Montana

The oddest repercussion of all this has been the rise of *cryonics* — the practice of freezing the dead in hopes that once medical science has come to understand how to reverse their condition, they can be thawed out to new and endless life. You may have read about cryonics in the newspapers in recent years. Not many people have yet had the procedure themselves, but several concerned individuals have provided it for loved ones, in some cases producing what you might call "mom and popsicles."

Okay, I shouldn't joke about it. But it's hard not to. The Alcor Life Extension Foundation advertised several years ago that they would freeze your entire body for $100,000. They would put into deep frozen storage a severed head for only $25,000. It was their "cut-rate deal." Clearly a business that knows what it takes to get ahead. I'll quit now.

Some few computer scientists even claim that an upcoming generation of computers will be able to support all the contents of our neural systems. You can upload your memories, personality traits, and state of consciousness into the software of an advanced multiparallel processing computer, for existence in that virtual format, or to be downloaded back into a carbon-based organic life form in the future. Pick a body of your choice and take it for a spin.

Is there any real hope in all this sci-fi sounding stuff? Will science and technology be able to progress to a point where they can actually allow us to live literally forever?

> *Time is that in which all things pass away.*
>
> — Schopenhauer

Not unless they can harness the large-scale processes of the universe and make some pretty radical changes. One day, our sun will burn out. Not any time soon, so don't be marking your calendar, but eventually. Physicist Freeman Dyson seems to think we can design spaceships to carry us, or at least a few of us, to other solar systems for ultimate survival.

But it's not just a problem with our sun. It's entropy. The disbursement and diffusion of usable energy in our universe. It's the consequences of the Big Bang some billions of years ago. There are only two acceptable scientific scenarios for the long-term picture of the cosmos. Under one, the universe keeps on its present course of expansion until all the stars burn out, and utter darkness prevails, with no life of any kind possible. The other happy scenario has the universe's expansion come to a halt and reverse itself, imploding upon itself into a future cataclysm impossible for any organized system to survive. So, have a nice day, but don't pin your hopes too much on science.

> *The longest-lived and the shortest-lived man, when they come to die, lose one and the same thing.*
>
> — Marcus Aurelius

Everlasting life is not within the prospects of human science to provide. Eternity is technologically out of the question. And that really is too bad, because I'm in the stock market for the long run, and I sometimes think it will take that long a run for some of my investments to pan out.

The bottom line is that there is no materialistic scenario under which immortality could ever be literally available. And so there is ultimately little that a materialist philosophy, or even a philosophy agnostic on the mind-body issue of dualism and materialism, can do to console those of us who aspire to an endless horizon of possibilities for living, experiencing, and creating. Because of that, we are forced to ask the question of whether any case can be made that we may in fact have the metaphysical wherewithal to survive bodily death in a form that can experience true eternity. Is there that kind of ultimate consolation for the fact that we must experience final limits in this world?

In Chapter 18, we ask that question and try to come up with an answer.

Chapter 18

Is There Life After Death?

. . . .

In This Chapter

▶ Considering the philosophical arguments about life after death

▶ Hearing the criticisms of belief

▶ Laying out the reasons for belief

. . . .

> *Death either destroys or unhusks us. If it means liberation, better things await us when our burden's gone: if destruction, nothing at all awaits us; blessings and curses are abolished.*
>
> — Seneca

C hapters 16 and 17 look at the various forms that the fear of death assumes in human life, and at the main philosophical attempts at consoling us in the face of the apparently inevitable that do not rely on a belief in afterlife. In this chapter, we tackle the issue of survival head on. Do we survive bodily death or not? Is there real life after death, or is death annihilation?

My strategy here is going to be to give the naysayers the floor first. Then we look at the positive arguments for survival.

Philosophical Doubts and Denials

From the ancient world to modern times, philosophers have constructed a number of arguments for thinking that we do not survive bodily death. In this section, we look at the five most common and forceful arguments.

The psychological origin argument

Men freely believe that which they desire.

— Caesar

The Psychological Origin Argument is a line of reasoning that is not directly geared toward the conclusion that we do not survive our bodily deaths, but rather is constructed just to cast doubt on the belief that we do.

The argument goes like this. People believe in life after death only because they want so badly to believe in it. A belief that is so obviously held on the basis of a deep need or desire is always, at least on the surface (or as lawyers say, *prima facie*), suspect. Wishes are not reliable guides to truths. Therefore, we should doubt the belief that there is life after death.

The reasoning behind this argument is straightforward. Just like water from a polluted well is dangerous to drink, a belief from an unreliable source is dangerous to have. Desire in general is an unreliable source for beliefs. Therefore, any belief that can be traced to a desire is dubious and is to be avoided.

> *We believe what we want to believe, what we like to believe, what suits our prejudices and fuels our passions.*
>
> — Sydney J. Harris

Wait a second. I have a deep desire to believe that I'm a nice and fun person to be around. Should everyone therefore be dubious concerning the claim that I'm a nice and fun person? Not at all! Why? Because I am in fact a jolly good fellow — that's why!

I think it's safe to say that many people believe the following proposition:

> *There is some good in most human beings.*

And I think it's safe to assume that at least most people who believe this proposition have a deep need or desire to believe it. Is it therefore a dubious belief? I don't think that follows at all. I think there is also ample evidence that it's true. And this supports believing in it, regardless of what sort of psychological needs or desires that most believers in it might have.

What reason do we have to think that people who believe in life after death do so only because they have a deep need or desire to believe in it? The mere existence of a deep need or desire to think that something is true does not imply that it is what in fact grounds the having of that belief. It could be that most human beings who believe in immortality do so because of reasons, evidence, or intuition, and that although their deep need to believe is thus satisfied, the need is not what produced the belief in them.

I recall hearing one philosopher actually say that he believed in life after death despite the fact that it irritated the life out of him. He was tired of living and wanted the prospect of extinction, but reason inclined to convince him otherwise, to his great dismay.

> *If you question any candid person who is no longer young, he is very likely to tell you that, having tasted life in this world, he has no wish to begin again as a "new boy" in another.*

— Bertrand Russell (in a fit of philosophic hyperbole)

Unless we can discover no reason or evidence at all for believing in life after death that might in principle be widely available to people who believe, we have no good reason to think that all, or most, who hold that belief do so solely only on the basis of a psychological need or desire.

But even if we granted most beliefs in afterlife are rooted in need and desire, a further argument can be constructed by believers to neutralize the inference from this source of the belief to its unreliability.

A religious person could argue that most of us have a deep need and desire to believe in life after death, because our creator, who has provided that future for us, has implanted in us that anticipation. And it could be argued that this is a better explanatory hypothesis for the existence of a psychological need to believe in an afterlife than any the materialist can come up with. It could be suggested by the materialist that this need and desire came about like all other naturally arising psychological mechanisms, through the operation of natural selection based on evolutionary survival value. But this seems unlikely. What could possibly be the survival value for the continuation of a life on this earth that would be delivered by a need and desire to believe in a life after death, which would be sufficiently strong as to produce that belief? Confident believers in an afterlife might be less likely to survive in this world, because they'd be more ready to sacrifice their lives for a worthy cause, and to take risks that nonbelievers would rationally avoid. A need and desire to believe in survival of a soul might thus act against the likelihood of physical survival in this world and so have what philosophers call evolutionary disvalue.

> *It seems to me that the most universal revolutionary wish now or ever is a wish for heaven, a wish by a human being to be honored by angels for something other than beauty or usefulness.*

— Kurt Vonnegut

This latter argument could, of course, be contested in various ways. But my point here is only to show that the materialist who seeks to throw into doubt the believer's conviction that there is life after death does not have at his disposal here the simple argument that he might have thought he could muster.

The original argument faces, then, two problems. First, it has not been shown that people who do believe in life after death actually do so because of a deep need and desire to believe it. And, secondly, even if this could be shown, the critic of the belief would have to show that this particular psychological mechanism has no reliable connection to the truth of the proposition believed, which has not been done. In addition, I think that a case can be made that there is a particular kind of desire for survival that may arguably be an instance of a generally very reliable belief forming mechanism (see the section entitled "The argument from desire," later in this chapter).

For these reasons, I find this argument unconvincing.

The silence argument

The silence argument is short, straightforward, and interesting. If millions, or even billions, of human beings have lived and died and survived their bodily deaths, then why don't we have a whole lot more evidence of this? Why don't all these people contact us and let us know? Or at least a significant percentage of them. Surely they would realize that the fact of their survival would be of crucial concern to those who remain behind and who love them. Surely they would realize that this is one of the most pressing mysteries in human life. Why, then, is there so much silence from beyond the grave?

> *Speech is of time, silence is of eternity.*
>
> — Thomas Carlyle

There are people on the bestseller lists, in carnival side shows, in Hollywood, and in quite a few roadside stands throughout the land, who claim that there is a lot more contact from beyond the grave than most of us would ever imagine. But most of their claims don't seem very credible, to say the least. Why isn't there a lot more obvious evidence of survival, and evidence of a very high quality?

The argument in a nutshell looks like this.

1. If human beings survived death, the many people who have already died would be communicating that fact to us clearly.

2. There is no such communication from beyond the grave.

   Therefore,

3. Human beings do not survive death.

The form of the argument is logically valid, which just means that if both premises are true, then so is the conclusion. But both premises are controversial. It's not just nuts who would dispute (2), although it unfortunately sometimes seems that way. But doubters about survival often use this argument to insist that if life after death were a reality, then there would surely be a great deal more, and more credible, evidence than there is.

But why accept premise (1)? Some believers in the afterlife have tried to claim that survivors have "more important things to do" in heaven, or elsewhere, than tapping on seance tables, helping to write bestselling books, or contacting CNN. Others speculate that the metaphysical divide between this world and the next just might not allow for communication from the other side to ours. In the end, we are just not in a position to judge (1) true or false. And thus the argument as a whole cannot convince. Yet, it has caused many to pause and ponder.

> *Silence is as full of potential wisdom and wit as the unhewn marble of great sculpture.*
>
> — Aldous Huxley

The trumpet analogy argument

Think for a moment about a musical note being sounded on a trumpet. As long as the trumpet is being blown, that particular musical sound exists, as a continually propagated note in the air. But suddenly smash the horn, destroying it, and the sound will cease. That particular sound's existence was dependent on the existence and proper functioning of the trumpet. Once the entity on which it was dependent was destroyed, it was extinguished as well.

The philosopher who denies life after death argues that this is an analogy for the mind-body relation. The mind, the consciousness with its thoughts, is like a note being blown on a trumpet. And it is dependent for its existence on the body that must be functioning properly for it to exist. Destroy the body, and the note will cease to be played. Death, in this analogy, robs the mind of its source and support, and thus it ceases to exist just as surely as the note ceases to be played. The conclusion drawn is that death is the end of conscious human life.

> *If there is a soul, what is it, and where did it come from, and where does it go? Can anyone who is guided by his reason possibly imagine a soul independent of a body, or the place of its residence, or the character of it, or anything concerning it? If man is justified in any belief or disbelief on any subject, he is warranted in disbelief in a soul. Not one scrap of evidence exists to prove any such impossible thing.*
>
> — Clarence Darrow (1857–1938)

A response to this argument can develop an interesting twist. A musical analogy for the mind-body relation, in order to be truly illuminating, may have to be a bit more complex than a simple trumpet analogy. The human body is a complex organization of distinct parts, on a macro and micro level. In the world of music, a symphonic orchestra is a complex organization of distinct parts, with all the different instruments and musicians involved. So let's pursue a Symphonic Analogy for the mind-body relation for a moment and see where it takes us.

We shed body parts constantly, on a small scale. Skin flakes shower down from our bodies daily. We lose hair. Fingernails and toenails are trimmed by the manicurist and pedicurist, or by clippers at home. These are just the obvious, manifest ways in which our human bodies are in flux, changing all the time. On a cellular level, change is just as ongoing. Some experts claim that, within a period of seven years, we have shed all the molecules and cells of our bodies, although we may look much the same. That means that your body of today is quite different in all its parts from, and in that sense non-identical with, your body of seven or ten years ago, viewed just as a physical object whose identity is dependent on the identity of its parts. In one sense it's the same body, and yet in another sense, it is a very different body. But it is definitely a body of the same person. You may have changed in personality, in wisdom, in financial status, and in many other ways, but it is you — one and the same person — who has undergone these changes. What is the relevance of all this for us?

The same person — you — has survived embodiment in very different collections of physical entities, considering how different your infant, toddler, teenage, and adult bodies have been. And yet it is still you. The person has survived embodiment in this complex series of physical states. This complex relationship of the mind and body over time can now be captured in an appropriately complex musical analogy.

You are, when all is done — just what you are.

— Goethe

Imagine a very strange symphony. It was composed to be performed like this. An orchestra enters the stage, the musicians all pick up their instruments, the conductor raises his baton, and the playing begins. A few minutes into the performance, while the percussion rests, all the percussionists get up, leave their instruments, and depart the stage, as another set of percussionist musicians enters from the other side, seat themselves, and, at just the appropriate time, take up the instruments and play their part. Imagine that this happens to the trumpet section, too. They walk off and are replaced by new musicians, who take up the score at just the right time. The trombones leave a bit later, immediately replaced in a seamless performance. The symphony continues, uninterrupted, as these players come and go across the stage.

Then imagine, at the halfway point in the symphony, just as individual sections have rested and have changed performers during those rests, there is an exactly 60 second rest of all the sections at once. The symphony has not ended. It was written to incorporate this overall rest. Imagine further that during these 60 seconds, all the musicians get up and leave the stage. A whole new group enters, sits down, and takes up the score at just the right moment. The original orchestra is gone. A new one sits in its place. And the symphony continues.

This is a better musical analogy for the mind-body relation. The cells of the body change just as the musicians come and go. And the person continues on in existence. Then, at death, the whole orchestra vacates the stage. There is a gap. But the symphony need not cease. What prevents a new orchestra from coming together to take up the beat and play the symphony on into the night? Christian theology talks of a resurrection body. Other dualists talk of a spirit body, or an astral body, a noncorporeal analogue of the physical body in which we are now ensconced.

> *All things change, but nothing dies.*
>
> — Ovid (43 B.C.–17 A.D.)

If the symphony of human personhood is composed in such a way as to allow for the death of the physical body and then a reimbodiment or new realization in some appropriate spiritual form, what is to prevent the continuity of the person's existence? I'm not sure the materialist critic has any compelling answer here at all. Our main point, though, at present, is that The Trumpet Analogy, which did seem to imply that death is extinction, is an inadequate analogy from the world of music, and that, when a more adequate analogy is formulated, the conclusion no longer seems to follow at all.

A further point, however, can and should be made. Many musicians claim that a symphony can exist in the mind of the composer before it is ever performed, and after its performance. It can have that form of existence even if it is never performed. But then the religious philosopher can claim that each person exists like a symphony in the mind of God. There is a form of existence dependent on the creative divine mind that does not require physical embodiment in any bodily analogue of an orchestral performance at all. This is an extension of the musical analogy that blocks even further the intended argument against survival of death.

The brain damage argument

The brain damage argument may be the most persuasive of all materialist arguments against life after death. It can also be put very simply.

Destroying a little brain tissue in a living subject can eliminate a whole range of mental function, including thought, emotion, and sensation. Therefore, it is a natural inference to conclude that the permanent death of all brain tissue amounts to the permanent cessation of all mental function, including thought, emotion, and sensation. But this just amounts to the annihilation of the conscious person, which means that none of us will survive bodily death.

Reflection on facts concerning brain damage and its implications for the integrity of personality and personal, conscious experience has caused many intelligent people to conclude, however reluctantly, that this argument is compelling. But a short thought experiment may show otherwise.

Imagine that you are locked in a small one-room building. You have contact with the outside world through only one window. You can see what's going on outside by looking out the window. It is open and also allows you both to hear passing street noises and to smell flowers right outside the building. You can also feel the cool breezes of the early morning air outdoors. Now imagine that someone comes along and closes the window, nailing it shut. Your ability to hear the sounds and smell the aromas in the outside world has suddenly been eliminated. You can no longer feel the cool breezes blowing outside. But you can still see out.

Now imagine that someone outside slathers black paint all over the window and nails boards tightly over its casing. Your ability to see outside has been eliminated. Each bit of change to the window has eliminated one or more ranges of your experience of the outside world. As long as you remain in that building, you will be unable to see, hear, smell, or feel what is going on out-side. But if the door is suddenly unlocked, and you can leave the building, you will no longer depend on that window for your access to the outside world. You will be able to perceive directly what is going on around you, with-out need of that now damaged and useless window.

This is an analogy for life and death. While we are "locked" in the body, we depend on the brain, and its connected sensory organs, as our window on the world. When this window is altered and damaged in various ways, our experience of the world is diminished and depleted in corresponding ways. But at death, the door is unlocked, and we leave the building. Then, we no longer depend on the state of the building, or its window, for our access to outside reality. The building at that point can be totally destroyed, and we are free of its constraints. How do we know that this is not an insightful analogy for the impact of death on human experience? It at least blocks the force of The Brain Damage Argument and depletes it of its otherwise straightfoward persuasiveness.

Some positive views of our prospects

There are many intelligent people who view death as the beginning of a great new journey:

To die would be an awfully big adventure.

— James M. Barrie (1860–1937)
Peter Pan Act III

Death, the last voyage, the longest, the best.

— Thomas Wolfe (1900–1938)

Death is a wild night, and a new road.

— Emily Dickenson (1830–1886)

Death is the supreme festival on the road to freedom.

— Dietrich Bonhoeffer (1906–1945)

To die is landing on some distant shore.

— John Dryden (1631–1700)

I shall see you in the next world.

— Plautus (c. 280–184 B.C.)

Arguments for Survival

The previous sections looked at the different arguments for doubting or denying the reality of life after death. I have found all unconvincing. But what is there to be said on the other side? Is positive argument in favor of our survival of death any more convincing?

Plato's indestructibility argument

Plato offered an argument for survival that has fascinated people ever since his time. Physical objects don't just cease to exist. Magicians and movies may make it look as if things can just pop out of existence without a trace, but that's not the way the real world works. In this world, Plato suggested, it seems that things are destroyed only by being dismantled into their constituent parts. A vase is smashed into tiny pieces and ceases to be. What remains are vase parts, shards of glass, and glass dust that formerly composed the vase. A book is burned. It is reduced to ashes. A nuclear weapon detonates. Anything at ground zero is reduced into very, very small pieces. This is the way destruction takes place in our world, and, Plato claims, it is the only way.

Here is Plato's news about the soul. The soul, he claims, has no parts. Therefore, it cannot be broken down into component parts. Therefore, it cannot be destroyed. It is immortal.

This is a very quick argument and is open to many lines of response. First, it is obvious that Plato is just assuming here that there is a soul. If what he is assuming is the existence of a nonmaterial entity, then that is something that cannot just be postulated, but is at the center of controversy, as we see in Chapters 13, 14, and 15. Many objectors will just deny what he assumes, and he needs to give us some reason for thinking that his view here is right.

Secondly, what exactly does Plato mean in claiming that the soul has no parts. Does he mean that it has no physical parts? If it is a nonphysical entity, that would be a safe claim, but the possibility is still open that it has nonphysical parts that it could be reduced to. We often speak of the soul or mind as encompassing intellect, emotion, and will. Are these parts? The claim is just too obscure to allow us any chance of a confident judgment that it is true.

Thirdly, even if the soul does not have the sort of parts that can come apart, how do we know for sure that dismantling is the only way something can cease to exist? Why can't something just fade away? Pluck a guitar string, and the sound that results will eventually fade away. Have your picture taken with a flash bulb, and there comes to be, in your field of vision, an afterimage, which finally just fades away. And if other forms of passing from existence to nonexistence other than dismantlement are possible, Plato has not given us any reason for thinking that the soul could not be subject to them, and thus suffer extinction.

Intriguing as it is, the argument is just not convincing. We are not in a position to know that its premises are all true. Thus, we are not in a position to see whether it really supports its conclusion.

> *Tis puzzling on the brink*
> *Of what is called Eternity to stare*
> *And know no more of what is* here *than* there.

> — Byron

Then nature analogy argument

> *Never does nature say one thing and wisdom another.*

> — Juvenal

Another common dualistic argument for survival is based on analogies throughout nature. When I was once in the Monteverde Cloud Forest in Costa Rica, I came to a new appreciation of this line of reasoning.

Walking along a trail amid the thick profusion of life deep in the rain forest, shaded by the high canopy above, I overheard a Costa Rican guide talking about the life cycle there. "In the rain forest, nothing just dies," he said. "Death is always the precursor to new life. Look at this tree," he said, pointing out the trunk of a huge fallen tree along the side of the trail. "It falls, and dies, and gives birth to new life, like everything else in this forest. Every ending is a new beginning." I looked carefully at the tree. New things, little shoots of life, sprouted out of its trunk all over. A variety of life forms were taking root in the dark, decayed wood, and forcing their way up into the filtered daylight.

The Nature Analogy Argument says that in this universe every ending is indeed a new beginning. Just as a caterpillar has to end one form of its existence in order to enter another, more beautiful form, as a butterfly, so also we have to end our physical, earthly forms of existence in order to enter into a new and better mode of existence after death.

This is a beautiful and poetically haunting sentiment. But how strong is the analogy? An argument from analogy always has the form:

1. All objects of type A have property B.

2. Objects of type C are analogous to objects of type A.

   Therefore,

3. Objects of type C likely have a property analogous to B.

All caterpillars have the property of surviving the cessation of one form of existence by being transformed into another state of being. Human lives in the flesh are analogous to caterpillar forms of existence. Therefore, it's likely that human beings have some property analogous to the property of surviving the cessation of one form of existence by being transformed into another state of being.

> *The mortal nature is seeking as far as possible to be everlasting and immortal: and this is only to be attained by generation, because the new is always left in the place of the old.*
>
> — Plato

But what does this say about life after death? Humans do survive the transformation from infancy to toddlerhood, from toddlerhood to rambunctious childhood, from that to adolescence, and then to young adulthood, to middle age — perhaps the most traumatic of all for some — and then to old age. That's a lot of caterpillar transformations. How do we know it goes one more, and one qualitatively different, stage into the future, with a transformation from physical life on earth to a very different state of being in some sort of afterlife?

Some versions of this line of reasoning attempt to do it all much more simply.

1. All endings are beginnings.

2. Human death is an ending.

   Therefore,

3. Human death is a beginning.

But again, what have we concluded with such an argument? The materialist will not dispute that human death is a beginning. With it, you begin to be a corpse. Or you begin to be history. No particular reason has been given for thinking that you begin a new form of conscious, personal existence in some new metaphysical realm. Human death may just be too disanalogous to, or different from, any clear cases of transformation within the continuity of ongoing individual existence that we can see elsewhere in life, for this argument to carry any weight at all.

> *In every empty corner, into all forgotten things and nooks, Nature struggles to pour life, pouring life into the dead, life into life itself.*
>
> — Henry Beston

Cosmic recycling there may be, but that is no guarantee at all that I'm going to be awake, alert, and enjoying myself in some new and improved form 10,000 years after my physical death here on this earth. Don't we have something better than this kind of argument to rely on?

The argument from desire

The argument from desire begins with a distinction between innate and artificial, or learned, desires. An *innate desire,* roughly, is a desire that we seem to be born with, or at least born with the natural tendency to develop. An innate desire spontaneously appears in a person without having to be suggested, planted, coached or acquired. Innate desires tend to be universal, unless their development has somehow been impeded. An *artificial,* or *learned, desire* is not one that is spontaneous, or even remotely universal. A desire for Tiffany jewelry would be a good example of a learned desire. A desire for air would be a paradigmatic case of an innate desire. Once this distinction is grasped, the argument can proceed.

Human beings have an innate desire for food. Food exists. We have an innate desire for water. Water exists. There is an innate desire for affection. Affection exists. There is also an innate desire to survive bodily death. Therefore, most likely, an afterlife exists.

> *Heaven always favors good desires.*
>
> — Cervantes (1547–1616)

The desire for an afterlife does seem to be amazingly widespread among human beings. It seems to be found in every culture and in every historical period, despite any official political or philosophical antagonism to religion or to beliefs in immortality, that might exist in a given culture. And this desire doesn't seem to be coached. People seem naturally to want to live. In fact, the desire for continued existence beyond death seems to be very strong in most people. There are exceptions, to be sure, but there are exceptions to most general rules, and exceptions are here explicitly allowed. So a case can be made for believing that the widespread human desire for a life after death is an innate desire. And this is all that is needed for the argument to go through.

There is no desire for what is unknown.

— Ovid

But is every innate desire satisfied? Sometimes we are hungry, and there is nothing to eat. Or we are thirsty with nothing to drink. Sometimes we want love, and it is not forthcoming. Yes, there is such a thing as food, water, and love. But particular desires for it are not always satisfied. Even if there is life after death, that does you and me no good unless we can expect to partake in it. And on this point, the argument is silent.

But, it could be argued that, if there is life after death, there is no particular reason why a particular person should worry about being excluded. This, however, might be nothing better than whistling in the graveyard. How would we know? The argument does nothing to establish a specific expectation, even if it is judged to have some merits in a general sense.

And yet, this is an argument that has had some significant weight for many people who have reflected deeply on it. Our innate physical desires seem to correspond to answering realities. But is the same true of any innate metaphysical desires we might have? Our innate desires for things in this world can be explained by an account of our physical, emotional, intellectual, and social needs, in an evolutionary framework. But desires for things beyond this world might be very different. And they might not find corresponding, answering realities.

So, what is the truth here? Are our deepest yearnings and desires a good guide to the deepest truths about existence? Or could some of them be, by contrast, totally out of joint with reality?

As we ponder this question, we can profitably move to the next form of argument that I want to consider for life after death. It will give us more to help us think on this question.

Moral arguments

Immanuel Kant (1724-1804) is known for, among many other things, popularizing a form of argument from morality to immortality. Actually, a moral argument for afterlife can take at least two forms, and both owe something to Kant.

First, Kant believed that the moral law demands that we pursue, and ultimately attain, moral perfection. But we can't reasonably expect to reach moral perfection in this life. Therefore, we must postulate, or suppose, that there is another life in which this demand of the moral law can be met.

Secondly, it can be argued that the dignity and integrity of the moral law demands that justice ultimately prevail. But justice does not always prevail within the bounds of this earthly life. Therefore, we must postulate, or suppose, that there is another life in which this demand for justice can be met.

> *Mortality has its compensations. One is that all evils are transitory, another that better times may come.*
>
> — George Santayana

Kant actually thought that something like this second argument can be marshaled in favor of the conclusion that we must postulate the existence of a morally perfect God who can see to it that justice ultimately prevails. But I cover that topic in the next few chapters, so I won't comment any more on it here.

Are moral arguments for an afterlife compelling? Many people would like to believe that moral perfection can at some point be reached. Even more of us would like to believe that justice will ultimately prevail. But what we'd like to believe is not always the best guide to what is true. And notice that the conclusion in these arguments is not in the first place that there is life after death. It's only that we should postulate that there is. What most people want, when confronting their own mortality, or the death of a loved one, is not the recommendation that they postulate something more, but the assurance that there is something more.

Another angle should be explored here, however. When I was in college, a wise physician friend told me that he believed in life after death because of the death of his mother. He said that he could not believe in the existence of a universe where such goodness as his mother exemplified could just be snuffed out forever. That great a form of love and goodness could not just be brought into existence merely for eternal annihilation. He felt a moral necessity in such a person's prevailing over death, in some way. He said that he had to believe in life after death, or this life made absolutely no sense at all.

This can be taken to be a version of the moral argument, which shows the force that such reasoning can sometimes have. And in this form, it is not an objective, abstract line of reasoning, but a vivid concrete response to a real situation. Sometimes, something in the world evokes such a strength of reaction, and an apparent forcefulness of responsive insight, that we find ourselves compelled to draw a conclusion beyond the direct evidence of what we've seen. And in a philosophical frame of mind, we need to take such inferences very seriously.

In a powerful passage, the prominent author C. S. Lewis once said about his dead wife:

> *If she is not now, then she never has been. I mistook a cloud of atoms for a person. There are not and never were any people. Death only reveals the vacuity that was always there. What we call the living are simply those who have not yet been unmasked.*

C. S. Lewis could not bring himself to think of his wife like that. Just as my medical friend could not possibly think of his mother like that. Lewis' remarks could be taken to launch a related form of moral argument. If no one survives bodily death, then there really are no people, as distinct from physical objects. But if that's true, then it's hard to make any sense at all of our moral sentiments. All of morality, after all, has been said to consist in this advice: "Love people and use things. Never love things or use people." If there is ultimately no fundamental difference between people and things, this otherwise sage sounding admonition completely collapses.

Did my friend, or C. S. Lewis, have a proof of immortality that would convince all nonbelievers? Of course not. But each of them did have a set of considerations capable of launching a line of reasoning that could be personally compelling. And there is no doubt about this.

But let's be really honest here. The arguments for and against life after death are likely to be, each and every one, unsettlingly uncompelling in the eyes of most cautious inquirers. They take too much for granted, or they move too quickly to be utterly convincing to just any serious, well-disposed person unsure of what to believe.

In most of the rest of life, the more that's at stake in a particular issue, the more solid evidence, good reasons, and compelling arguments we require before making a decision. How are we to decide what to think about life after death? The reasons given by most philosophers can seem so very unconvincing to anyone who is genuinely looking for the truth. Is there more? Is there any range of harder evidence that might be more vivid and more compelling?

Some people think so. If you're interested, make sure you look at the next section.

The Light at the End of the Tunnel

He who neglects to drink of the spring of experience is likely to die of thirst in the desert of ignorance.

— Lin Po

There are three types of claims concerning extraordinary experiences that, if true, seem to imply that there is survival of death. Each type of experience is controversial. But at this point along the road of examining ultimate questions, that should come as no surprise. In the following sections, we look briefly at two types, and more thoroughly at the third and, perhaps, most interesting.

Claims of former lives

Some people, either under hypnosis or spontaneously, claim to remember having lived before, long ago and far away. Some claim to recall numerous lifetimes. Now, most of these people just seem to be nuts. One woman I know of claims to have lived before as more famous historical personages than you could possibly imagine. She alleges that she formerly walked the earth as almost every epoch-making individual you can think of, male and female, except Jesus Christ. Her husband once before visited the earth as Jesus Christ. So, all around, it's a very impressive family.

But some serious cases are worth our reflection. One case on the record books is of an American woman named Lydia Johnson who claimed to have once lived before in a previous century as a Swedish farmer. She exhibited, under hypnosis, a phenomenon known as *xenoglossy:* in a trancelike state, she could speak Swedish, without there being any evidence that she learned that language in this lifetime.

Several researchers, including Ian Stevensen, have attempted to make careful investigations of particularly interesting sounding cases of claimed memories concerning past lives. Most have come out looking less than impressive. But a few shine through with just enough unlikely details as to give us all pause. If there is a single convincing case of reported memory of a past life, then it is possible for a person to survive bodily death, because this person did. Whether there is any case sufficiently convincing is not in itself a philosophical question, but one of empirical evidence. It's an intriguing question but one which, in my judgment, is at the present time an open issue.

Apparent contact with the dead

I mention in Chapter 10 and Chapter 15 the phenomenon of people claiming to communicate with others after their deaths. I also warn that there has been a long history of fraudulent claims made in this regard by people out to make a quick buck, or a quick few hundred thousand bucks, if best-selling books are to be counted. Despite all the con artists and crazy people making such claims, there are serious, intelligent, and apparently sincere people who insist that they really have somehow seen, heard, or in another way received convincing messages from other human beings who have previously died.

Everything that the modern mind cannot define it regards as insane.

— C.G. Jung (1875–1961)

Perhaps the most interesting case of this in history involves three British academics — F.W.H. Meyers, Henry Sidgwick, and Edmund Gurney — who often talked about the subject of life after death and agreed among themselves that whichever of them would be the first to die would, if he found himself surviving bodily death, do everything in his power to communicate that fact compellingly to the others. Meyers was the first to die. Shortly after his death, people in different countries began claiming to have had trancelike experiences in which they found themselves writing bits and pieces of ancient Greek poetry, which, when sent in to the Society for Psychic Research, turned out to be parts of some of Meyers' favorite ancient poetry.

Bizarre.

If there has been a single genuine incident of communication with or from a person after his or her death, in all of human history, then it is possible for human beings to survive bodily death. Are there any genuine incidents? I'm not altogether sure, but you may know of one.

Near-death experiences

Starting with Raymond Moody's book *Life After Life*, first published in 1975, and continuing with a torrent of volumes from him and other authors, there has been a modern resurgence of discussion concerning reports of what are now known as *near-death experiences*.

A near-death experience usually goes like this. Someone is involved in a traumatic accident, or in a surgical procedure, and loses vital signs. There is no heartbeat, respiration, or measured brain activity. This state continues for some minutes, during which time the victim is by all standard measures clinically dead. A resuscitation occurs, whether by means of medical procedures or spontaneously. Some time later, the individual who has undergone this sequence of events claims to have had a series of extraordinary experiences during that time when he was taken to be dead.

The reported experiences usually go something like this. The subject suddenly finds himself "out" of his body, looking down on the scene from a vantage point somewhere above his physical body. He sometimes sees details of the medical procedures being undertaken which he is later able to recount in detail. He feels movement away from his body and finds himself apparently rushing forward in a long dark tunnel. At the end of the tunnel, he emerges into a beautiful world of light where a pastoral setting greets him. There may be friends or relatives there, people who have previously died, apparently present for the purpose of welcoming him to a next world of existence. He encounters a Being of Light who exudes a sense of love and peace. This Being tells him that his time has not yet come and that he must return to the body. The next thing he knows, he is waking up in a hospital room after having been resuscitated. He is filled with a mixture of regret at having had to leave that world that he briefly had a glimpse of, with a new joy at the whole process of living. Typically, his life will then be changed forever. He will no longer fear death, despite any emotions he previously had concerning the prospects of his own mortality. And he will have a new attitude toward living.

Before I had read any of the literature on near-death experiences, I had a conversation with an uncle by marriage who told me confidentially of what I can only call a near-near-death experience. He said he hadn't even told his wife, because she was "too religious" and "would get all worked up about it." In a classic scenario, one Monday morning while shaving and preparing himself for what was to be a difficult and stressful meeting that he had been dreading, he had a heart attack. Pain and crushing pressure seized him. He knew instantly what was happening. As he dropped his razor and helplessly collapsed to the floor in total panic, he suddenly saw a large human-like figure standing above him, some feet off the floor in the upper corner of the bathroom. The figure spoke. "It's not yet your time. You will be fine." All his fear instantly left him. He was bathed in a calm and peace he had never before experienced. He told me that throughout his adult life, he had always had a tremendous fear of death, but that, since the moment of that experience, he had looked forward to the time that ultimately would be his earthly departure. "I know I won't be alone," he said.

> *We are told that when each person dies, the guardian spirit who was allotted to him in life proceeds to lead him to a certain place. . . .*

> — Socrates

Near-death experiences have been reported by people of many different ages and backgrounds. And the details of what they report can involve interesting differences, but what is most fascinating is the uncanny similarities in their basic reports. Have they survived bodily death to experience, however briefly, another world, or another dimension of human existence? Or have they merely undergone the last gasp hallucinations of a dying brain?

What has been most interesting to me about attempts to explain away these experiences is their apparent resiliency and resistance to any compelling alternative explanations. Some skeptics have posed the theory that it is drugs administered in surgery or in resuscitation procedures that have created hallucinations then mistaken for reliable experiences. But the drug theory has been found groundless. There have been many cases of near-death experience where any given drug suspected of hallucinogenic results was not administered and cases where no drugs at all were given.

> *Should this my firm persuasion of the soul's immortality prove to be a mere delusion, it is at least a pleasing delusion, and I will cherish it to my last breath.*

> — Cicero

Doubters have even claimed that after the attention that Moody's bestselling books and the general phenomenon of near-death experiences initially received in the press and on television, people have become suggestible to having such experiences or have become more prone to faking accounts of them. One of the most powerful responses to this suggestion has come from the reporting work of physician Melvin Morse, whose books, beginning with *Closer To the Light,* report near-death experiences among young children who had not been exposed to any media or cultural suggestions and had no need or desire to be booked on a talk show. Their accounts are sometimes even more persuasive than those of far more articulate adults.

But what is the evidential value of experiences whose claims we cannot independently check? First, there is the matter of their amazing uniformity in basic outline. Second, there are many such reports that do involve details of medical procedures, and the presence of people in the room, along with accounts of what they were wearing and what they said during the period of clinical death. Some people have even reported seeing individuals in the next life whom they had no natural way to know had already died in this life. The claims that can be checked out involve an astounding number of details that have been confirmed, and whose reporting no naturalistic explanation can plausibly accommodate. Third, these experiences change lives. They seem to alter permanently the way the people who have had them subsequently think about life and death. They don't fade like vivid dreams or unexpected hallucinations.

Are these reported experiences the evidence that we have been looking for? Here is an interesting thing that we come to realize in philosophy. World views are very resilient things. It's hard to disprove one. And so it's hard to eliminate one as a contender for your belief. Naturalistic, materialist explanations can always be offered for any near death experience, or any extraordinary human experience whatsoever that on its face seems to point toward other realms of existence. No single experience had by another person is guaranteed to change your mind, regardless of the effect it might have had on him. But in philosophy, openness of mind is usually, as Socrates saw, a virtue. If we remain open to the new, to possibly different insights, we may be able to expand our conception of what the world is all about.

Is there life after death? I think so, but what about you? Your answer to this question reflects what you think about ethics, freedom, the mind-body problem, and the biggest of all issues that we have yet to discuss. It ends up being part of your overall world view construction to answer this question. And some of the main challenges of that construction are covered in the next part of this book.

Part VII
Is There a God?

The 5th Wave   By Rich Tennant

"The ancient philosophy of skepticism is particularly helpful when confronted with bacon on sale."

In this part . . .

In this part, we take a look at the biggest and most ultimate question that human beings have ever asked. Is there a God or not? Do we live in a designer universe, or are we the hapless beneficiaries of a huge cosmic accident? Why is there evil in the world? If you want the biggest of all big picture perspectives on life, then read this part.

Chapter 19

Two World Views

If God did not exist, it would be necessary to invent him.

— Voltaire

Is there a God or not? This question defines two opposed world views. It is the task of this chapter to clarify what they are and to begin to introduce the things we need to think about in order to help us decide which is most adequate to our experience.

I want to set things up with a story.

The Lost Beach Ball

It was a sunny and unusually warm early spring day in the north Midwest. Desperate for some sun after a long gray and bitterly cold winter, I had taken my family to Warren Dunes State Park on Lake Michigan, to sit in beach chairs, enjoy the sunshine, and watch the waves roll in. I think my daughter Sara was about six years old, and Matt was only four. The very few other vacationers who were also silly enough to think that the lakefront itself would be sufficiently warm for a first day at the beach, or who were equally desperate to try to get a little early season sun, scattered along the shore, staying out of the frigid water, and trying to keep the wind from blowing their possessions away, because the lake breeze was a lot stronger than we all had anticipated.

Matt had brought a brand new little beach ball, a multicolored classic just a little bigger than a standard basketball. He was standing at the edge of the water tossing it just a few inches up in the air, and nearly losing control of it each time in the stiff wind. I said, "Matt, be careful with your ball. The wind is blowing toward the water, and if you're not careful, you'll lose it." He absentmindedly said, "Okay, Dad." I lay down in the beach chair and closed my eyes.

"Dad! Dad! The ball!" I opened my eyes just in time to see the beach ball 30 feet out in the water, being blown farther away every second. The wind was lifting it up and dropping it down. I jumped up off the chair and stood with Matt while we watched it literally disappear at what military people call one o'clock on the horizon, headed across the lake for Milwaukee. "Well, it's gone now," I announced with that sad I-told-you-so fatherly voice.

Matt looked up to me, and with the most angelic look on his face, said "Dad, if we pray to God, he'll give us our ball back."

The first reaction I had to Matt's remark was to say to myself, silently, in the most cynically sarcastic way possible, "Right." Out loud, I said, noncommittally, "Well, that's a thought." And I added, "Let's just be more careful with our stuff now." Inwardly I was thinking, "Poor Matt, he just doesn't understand yet the way the world really works."

> *A cynic is just a man who found out when he was ten that there wasn't any Santa Claus, and he's still upset.*
>
> — James Gould Cozzens (1903–1978)

As I walked back to my chair, Matt's words echoed in my head: "Dad, if we pray to God, he'll give us our ball back." The childlike innocence. Well, he was a child. The simple faith. I sighed deeply at the surprisingly hardened, worldly cynicism that had generated my inner reactions to his heartfelt assurance.

Now, let me put this in perspective. I was a philosopher, a specialist in matters of religion. I had at the time already written ten books focusing on the philosophical side of theological matters. Although a skeptic by personality, I was officially, by intellectual conviction, a believer. I had written subtle and, I thought, powerful defenses of classical religious beliefs. And here I was being inwardly dismissive about my son's simple faith. I was a little disgusted with myself. Was I writing my books like a religious believer and living day to day in a thoroughly secular way?

I lay down in the beach chair and closed my eyes. I felt a burning sensation in my face. A blush of embarrassment. An inward pressure. A sense of compulsion I could not resist. I said, silently, and with a complete focused sincerity, "Okay, God, give us our ball back." I thought to myself, this is a test. A perfect test. "God, I ask you to honor this little boy and give us that ball back." The pressure abated. I relaxed and nodded off.

There are few men who dare to publish to the world the prayers they make to Almighty God.

— Montaigne

Forty-five minutes later, I was eased into consciousness by the faint sound of a boat motor and opened my eyes to see on the horizon the small speck of a very large motorboat in the distance. It was the only boat we were to see all day. Something told me to stand up. I did. I suddenly had the thought that I should hold my arms in the shape of a huge circle and then point toward Milwaukee. I did. Twice. Then I said to myself, "That's enough." The boat was so far away that I could barely see a bright red cap on one of the boaters, but couldn't make out anything else. I sat back down. The boat turned and slowly disappeared from view across the horizon.

An hour passed. Again, I heard the faint distant sounds of a motor. I looked up, and there was another speck in the distance. It was coming in. Could it be the same boat that was by us before? As it came closer, I felt strange and stood up. It kept coming. It was a very big boat. When it was about 30 yards out, I found myself walking toward the water and then into the water. My skin is pretty sensitive to cold, and I promise you that this is not something that I would just do. I waded out in the freezing water until I was about waist deep, or at least *deep enough* (if you know what I mean). I was ten yards from the boat. There were two guys on it. One bent down into the boat and came up with the beach ball in his hand. "Is this yours?"

The Infinite Goodness has such wide arms that it takes whatever turns to it.

— Dante

I called out, "Yes, thanks a lot, how did you get it?" He yelled out that, earlier, they had pulled up even with where we were sitting and used binoculars to see if there were any girls on the beach. He saw me making a big circle with my arms and thought that was odd. Not seeing any likely prospects, they turned the boat and headed out. Half an hour later, way out in the lake, they happened to catch sight of a brightly colored beach ball bobbing on the water. Some way, they managed to get hold of it. They decided to turn around and scope out the beach one more time. The binocular check this time revealed some talent on the shore, not far from where we were sitting. So now, 30 minutes later, there they were. And seeing me approach the boat, one of them suddenly made the connection with the beach ball.

I asked them some more questions. They had not even been planning to be out on the water that day. It was too rough. No other boats were out. They had been cleaning their boat in its dock in New Buffalo, Michigan, and had just spontaneously had an uncontrollable urge to crank it up and head north, not really knowing why. They said to each other "Chick hunt" and thereby rationalized this unplanned excursion up the shore. It took them about half an hour to 45 minutes to get up even with us at Warren Dunes, when I made the arm signs.

Hmm. So they left the dock spontaneously at about the time that I offered my test prayer. Wow. I said to the guy, "This will be a story that my Notre Dame philosophy class will love." We were scheduled to talk about the topic of miracles the next day.

> *Chance is God's pseudonym when he doesn't want to sign.*
>
> — Anatole France (1844–1924)

I got back to the philosophy department and spun my tale for everyone who was sitting around in the mail room. Placing the ball down on the floor in front of me, I told the whole story. It had all the elements a philosopher would love: Childlike faith, worldly skepticism, prayer as an empirical test, apparently miraculous intervention, and the evidential confirmation of a world view.

One of my colleagues broke the silence that ensued and commented, "It would have been a lot better if the ball had floated back to you three feet above the water." I said, "Yeah, but that's not what I asked for."

> *The story of the whale swallowing Jonah, though a whale is large enough to do it, borders greatly on the marvelous; but it would have approached nearer to the idea of a miracle if Jonah had swallowed the whale.*
>
> — Thomas Paine (1737–1809)

Another professor shook his head and said, with a weariness bordering on disgust, "While the cancer wards and hospitals of the world are full of suffering and dying people, you get your beach ball back. Somewhere in the world, people were being murdered at that very moment, and yet you got your beach ball back." Everyone turned and looked at me. And then at the ball.

"Yes."

> *The gods give to mortals not everything at the same time.*
>
> — Homer (Ninth century B.C.)

The Great Divide

Two major world views are vying for our acceptance in the modern world. Each one certainly has many variations, but two main types define all the rationally persuasive possibilities. They are *theism* and *atheism,* or in other, broader, terms, *supernaturalism* and *naturalism.* In this chapter, we introduce the distinction that must be made between them, and then we set up the great debate that has raged for centuries over their truth.

Philosophers without beach balls speak out

There have been many reflective people who could not shake the sense that there is something more to reality than just this physical cosmos, some sort of divine being behind it all, but who have seemed unable to see any benevolent manifestations of divine action in the world assisting us creatures. Their remarks often express something like the viewpoint of philosophical deism:

> *I believe in the gods. Or rather I believe that I believe in the gods. But I don't believe that they are great brooding presences watching over us; I believe they are completely absent-minded.*
> — Jean Giraudoux (1937)

> *Is there no God, then, but at best an absentee God, sitting idle, ever since the first Sabbath, at the outside of his universe?*
> — Thomas Carlyle

God seems to have the receiver off the hook.
— Arthur Koestler

The gods are careful about great things and neglect small ones.
— Cicero

God is not a cosmic bellboy for whom we can press a button to get things done.
— Harry Emerson Fosdick

It is left only to God and to the angels to be lookers on.
— Frances Bacon

Father expected a great deal of God. He didn't actually accuse God of inefficiency, but when he prayed his tone was loud and angry, like that of a dissatisfied guest in a carelessly managed hotel.
— Clarence Day

First, I need to define some crucial terms:

- *Theism:* The belief that there is at least one God, or supreme being (from the Greek word for God, *theos*).

- *Polytheism:* The belief that there are many gods, or quasi-human yet very powerful beings who in some sense rule the natural world. Traditional Greek or Roman beliefs were polytheistic.

- *Monotheism:* The belief that there is exactly one God. Advanced Judaism is the original paradigmatic monotheism.

- *Henotheism:* No, not the belief that chickens are divine. This is the belief that there are many gods, combined with the conviction that we should worship only one.

- *Trinitarian monotheism:* The belief that there is exactly one God who exists somehow in three persons. This is the philosophically developed Christian belief.

- *Deism:* The belief that there is a God who created all else, but who stands apart and does not deign to intervene or interfere in any way with that creation. An absentee deity believed in by many scientifically minded yet theologically inclined people in the past few centuries.

- *Atheism:* The belief that there is no God. This is typically the conviction that there is no personal Creator of the universe, and no powerful, incorporeal, perfect being in heaven or anywhere else.

- *Agnosticism:* The state of not-knowing whether there is a God or not. The humble agnostic says that he doesn't know whether there is a God. The less humble agnostic says that you don't, either. The least humble agnostic thinks that we can't ever really know.

Theists believe in a supernatural realm of existence. Supernaturalism is a name often given any belief that there is more to reality than what is found in physical nature. Atheists believe that there is nothing above, or behind, or undergirding physical nature. *Naturalism* is thus another name for the atheistic view that nature is all there is.

Our main concern in this chapter, and in the rest of the book, is the contrast between the most philosophically developed form of theism endorsed to one degree or another by all Christians, Jews, Muslims, and philosophically sophisticated Hindus on the one hand, and simple atheism on the other.

> *God is to me that creative Force, behind and in the universe, who manifests Himself as energy, as life, as order, as beauty, as thought, as conscience, as love.*
>
> — Henry Sloan Coffin

Theism, as we investigate here, holds that there exists an absolutely perfect nonmaterial being who is the ultimate creator of all else.

Philosophically attuned theists have held that there is a God who has such astounding properties as the following:

- *Omnipotence:* God can do anything.

  > *If you know God, you know that everything is possible for God to do.*
  >
  > — Callimachus (Fourth century B.C.)

- *Omniscience:* God knows everything.

- *Omnibenevolence:* God is perfectly good.

- *Omnipresence:* God is present, in some sense, everywhere.

- *Incorporeality:* God is not a physical, bodily being.

- *Aseity:* God is not dependent for existence on anything else.

✔ *Eternity:* God is not bound by time, being either temporally everlasting or atemporally timeless.

The eternal Being is forever if he is at all.

— Pascal (1623–1662)

✔ *Ineffability:* God's nature can never fully be put into words.

✔ *Simplicity:* There is a unique internal unity to God, who is not composed of any parts whatsoever.

✔ *Perfection:* God is altogether without defects of any kind. This is a *summary property.* It is a higher order attribute generalizing over all the others. God is perfectly powerful, perfectly knowledgeable, perfectly good, and so on.

If God is truly god, he is perfect, lacking nothing.

— Euripides

Quite a list. And it could go on. Atheists deny that there is any being with all, or even most, of these properties.

Where does such a list of divine characteristics come from? Where does our idea of God come from? Some theists say that it comes mainly from God's own self-revelation. Others claim that it can be inferred from God's effects in the world. Still others say that it results from the idea of complete perfection. I've explored these sources in a book called *Our Idea of God* (University of Notre Dame Press) and won't repeat myself here. But I should say that, despite the many differences to be found in religious beliefs throughout the world, there is an amazing amount of agreement on the fundamental, and pivotal, idea of God.

The mainline theistic world view

The main form of philosophically developed theism believed in by most religious people in the modern world involves a God who not only created all of physical reality, but who also acts in the world miraculously. This is not the standoffish being imagined by deism, but an activist creator who cares for his creatures. This God is viewed as the ultimate governor of our universe and is thought of as being responsible for a moral order, as well as the physical structures, we see around us in the world.

According to this mainline theistic world view, we are created by God, and we all exist under the watchful intent of our maker. He who provides for us in this life also provides a life to come.

Skeptical warnings on making God in our image

A number of astute thinkers have cautioned us about our tendency to just define God in our own image, projecting on ultimate reality just those things that we happen to value:

> *Such as men themselves are, such will God himself seem to them to be.*
> — John Smith the Platonist (1618–1652)

> *Heaven always bears some proportion to earth. The god of the cannibal will be a cannibal, of the crusaders a crusader, and of the merchants a merchant.*
> — Emerson

> *If horses and cows could draw, they'd draw the gods looking like horses and cows.*
> — Xenophanes

> *If Triangles had a god, he would have three sides.*
> — Montesquieu

> *If God created us in his own image, we have more than reciprocated.*
> — Voltaire

On the theistic world view, human persons embody the image of God. Personhood is more similar to divinity than any form of physicality is. Personhood thus resonates with the deepest nature of reality. Persons can and will be given an eternal existence alongside God, whatever may happen to the physical universe in which we have come to be. We human beings are launched out on a great adventure. Half-animal, half-angel, we come onto the stage of reality from humble beginnings and with our feet of clay begin to walk a path that can take us into eternity.

> *Only God is permanently interesting. Other things we may fathom, but he out-tops our thought and can neither be demonstrated nor argued down.*
>
> — J. F. Newton

The naturalistic world view

A naturalistic world view thinks very differently about our life and place in the world. According to its tenets, reality is nothing more than matter and physical energy. Through a long series of highly improbable coincidences, this universe has developed in such a way as to allow the existence of large-scale structures and, ultimately, life to arise. Conscious life is just one more step in a blind, natural evolutionary process. We are organic structures programmed by the forces that impinge on us. We are born, we live, and then we die, departing the stage of reality forever with an extinguishing of conscious personhood on an individual level that mirrors the ultimate extinction destined to come about on a cosmic level.

How the two world views compare

Naturalism is ultimately a pessimistic world view. Theism tends to be optimistic concerning at least the long term. It is important to see that the world views we are confronting are, ultimately, package deals. The theist doesn't just think that the inventory of reality contains one additional being named God. The theist thinks differently about everything.

Your total career, according to standard naturalism:

Chance ⇨You are born. . . . You exist. . . . You die and disappear.

On the naturalistic world view, you are an almost unimaginably small and unimportant part of a huge, and mostly alien, physical universe. You're just a temporary blip on the screen of a totally impersonal reality, ruled by mindless forces. But, hey, have a nice day anyway.

Your total career, according to a theistic world view:

God ⇨You are born. . . . You exist. . . . You die and are transformed.

On a theistic, or supernaturalistic world view, you are an eternally intended and welcomed addition to a spiritually rich and ultimately fulfilling reality, meant to flourish forever. You are an almost unimaginably small part of the universe, which is itself unimaginably small compared to its Creator, and yet you are meant to be here. God created the universe so that you can exist, among other equally important reasons.

On the theistic picture, God has created us for a specific and everlasting purpose. On the naturalistic world view, blind chance has given us a brief opportunity to exist on this earth, with no meaning or purpose intended.

But which is true? Some people parse this as the question of whether the ultimate truth about reality is horrifying or comforting. But it could equally well be rendered as whether the final story about human existence is demanding as well as promising, or, on the contrary, uncaring and destructive.

Is there such a God or not? This is the great question debated throughout the centuries. Is personhood the deepest and most lasting truth about reality, or is the whole sphere of existence rather nothing more than atoms whizzing through the void?

The Great Debate

I was sitting one night in a restaurant in Nebraska at a table full of professional philosophers. I know, it sounds unlikely, but it happened. One of the philosophers pointed to a fellow thinker across the table, known for his outspoken religious belief, and said, "If someone asked you to prove that there is a God, what would you say?" The man being questioned took another bite of mashed potatoes, looked up, and replied, "I'd say, 'Come into my garden and look around.'" He took a long drink of iced tea and started cutting his steak. Everyone waited. He kept eating. "That's *all?*" his interlocutor responded, incredulous. "Yep," he said.

People at the table looked at each other. The questioner tried again. "But suppose I'm the one asking the question, and you say that, and I go into your garden and look around like you told me to, and I get no proof at all. What then?" The theistic gardener seemed puzzled at the other philosopher's confession of such possible obtuseness. He sighed aloud and then, with a world-weary professorial tone, slowly responded, "Well, I'd just say, 'Look closer!'"

> *People see God every day; they just don't recognize him.*
>
> — Pearl Bailey

We all chewed on that one for a minute. Was that all he could say? Did it all come down to just different strokes for different folks? Or, in this case, different cowpokes? Was not only beauty but even God just something "in the eye of the beholder"? Is this ultimate issue just finally a matter of whether you see with the eyes of faith or not?

Most of the people around that table would say no. There is a great deal that can be said in defense of either theism or atheism. And it's difficult to see how anyone can form a settled, philosophically adequate opinion without being aware of all the relevant issues. And yet, it may finally all come down to what happens to you in a garden. But we'll have to see about that.

> *Atheism is an urban phenomenon.*
>
> — Bernard Boyd

In Chapters 20 and 21, I lay out the main lines of argument put forth by theists and atheists for their positions. There is a great deal to think about in considering this issue that will color the way we think about everything else.

Chapter 20

Theistic Visions

· ·

· ·

It is incomprehensible that God should exist, and it is incomprehensible that He should not exist.

— Pascal

In this chapter, I want to present the main considerations theists bring forth to support belief in the existence of God. Chapter 21 allows the atheist his main response. I want to begin with what in many ways is the strangest argument for the existence of God and then sequentially move toward lines of thought that are more common. It's my hope to give a representation of the best theistic thinking and, by coming at it from different directions, to fill out a sense of the rationality behind the theistic vision of reality.

The Ontological Argument

The ontological argument is an argument for the existence of God that has impressed such diverse figures as Saint Anselm, Archbishop of Canterbury (c. 1033-1109) and René Descartes (1596-1650), as well as a good many philosophers in our own time. This argument is perhaps the most unusual line of reasoning ever offered for thinking that there is a divine being. Most arguments for the existence of God start from some fact about the world and reason that the best explanation for that fact would be the existence and activity of a being as different from anything in the physical universe as God is thought to be. The ontological argument starts from an idea alone and reasons its way to the existence of a being manifesting this idea.

The ontological argument gets its name from two Greek words, one for being, or existence *(ontos)* and one for rationality, or reasoning *(logos)*. It is an argument that is constructed on the assumption that human reason alone, operating without the aid of perception or evidence, can draw at least one important conclusion about what exists in reality.

This in itself is a fascinating concept. Usually, we think of the realm of ideas as one thing, and the realm of real existent beings as something else altogether.

The Realm of Thought and Ideas
_____
The Realm of Real Existent Things

We have many ideas of things that don't exist, like Martians, unicorns, and fairies. And presumably many things exist somewhere in the universe for which we now have no concepts at all, not having yet discovered anything like them.

Typically, when we have an idea of something that might exist, but that also might not, we have to somehow go look to see whether the ultimate inventory of reality includes any such thing or not. Anselm and Descartes seemed to think that, for at least one very special idea, you don't have to go look to see whether there is anything in reality corresponding to it, but that reason alone could reliably draw the conclusion that here the great divide between ideas and realities is necessarily bridged and the idea is reflected perfectly in reality. This special idea is, of course, the idea of God.

Anselm believed that God was best understood as "That than which no greater can be conceived." Most philosophers have interpreted this to mean that the idea of God is to be thought of as the idea of "the greatest possible being." Others, in the same vein, have followed in the footsteps of Anselm and have said that God is to be thought of as an absolutely perfect being. This was the approach taken by the later philosopher Descartes.

> *If therefore that than which nothing greater can be conceived exists in the understanding alone, then this thing than which nothing greater can be conceived is something than which a greater can be conceived. And this is clearly impossible. Therefore, there can be no doubt at all that something than which a greater cannot be conceived exists in both the understanding and in reality.*

— Saint Anselm (1033-1109 *Proslogion*)

Whenever God is defined as an absolutely perfect, or unsurpassable, being, an interesting line of reasoning can be generated. I want to present only a sample version. An ontological argument for the existence of God:

1. God is the one and only greatest possible being. (By definition)

2. A greatest possible being has the greatest form of existence possible, which is necessary existence, or existence in all possible circumstances. (By definition)

3. It is at least possible that there is a God. (There is a God in some possible set of circumstances, whether they are actual circumstances, or fictional, yet possible, ones)

4. A God who exists in any possible circumstances exists in all. (From premise 2)

Therefore,

5. God exists in the actual world. (In the circumstances in which we actually find ourselves)

It is necessary to assume something which is necessary of itself, and has no cause of its necessity outside itself but is rather the cause of necessity in other things. And this all men call God.

— Saint Thomas Aquinas (c.1225-1274)

This is wild. The ace card here is the idea of necessary existence, or existence in all possible circumstances. God, according to this conception, is definitive of the realm of possibility. Any being that could exist in some circumstances and fail to exist in others is a less than absolutely perfect being. A perfect being must be so great and must have a form of existence so strong that it could not possibly fail to exist. God must necessarily exist.

Remarkable. Intriguing. And, for some philosophers, incredibly irritating. Critics have claimed that there must be something wrong here. But they haven't been able to agree on exactly what is wrong. Nor have they been able to make any clearly compelling case for anything at all being wrong.

There are two kinds of people in the world: the conscious dogmatists and the unconscious dogmatists. I have always found myself that the unconscious dogmatists were by far the most dogmatic.

— G. K. Chesterton

The most controversial part of the argument, for philosophers who resist it, is Step 3. This link in the reasoning alleges that, whether we think there actually is a God or not, we should at least acknowledge that it is possible that there is a God. Some defenders of this premise have claimed that as long as the concept of God as a greatest possible being is logically consistent and contains no two properties that contradict each other, then God is at least a possible being and Step 3 is true. Others have suggested that the concept of possibility operative here requires more than that. But it is our usual procedure in philosophy, as in life, to proceed on the basis of "innocent until proven guilty." Here, the application of this presumption would be that we should treat the concept of God as consistent, coherent, or possible unless we have some good reason to do otherwise.

Philosophers continue to disagree over what to think of ontological arguments for the existence of God. These arguments have defenders who support them with the assistance of truly mind boggling complexities in logic and metaphysics. And they have critics who wade through all those complexities and still insist that they must all fail.

The whole concord of the world consists in discord.

— Seneca

No end of this discussion over the ontological argument is even remotely in sight. The debate rages on. What do you think? Or maybe you want to take a couple of aspirin and lie down and perhaps get back to me later on that one.

Cosmology and God

Wonder is the basis of worship.

— Thomas Carlyle

One of my favorite professors at Yale was Paul Holmer, professor of philosophical theology at the Divinity School. I recall one class — I think it was on the thought of Sören Kierkegaard — when he broke into an uncharacteristically personal story about his vacation house on a lake in Minnesota. The house was on an island, out in the middle of nowhere. He told us that, on evenings when the sky was clear, he loved to go outside late at night, get into a small boat, and row out some distance onto the lake. He'd stop and lie back against the hull and just look at the sky. The blackest of backdrops allowed thousands of stars to sparkle and shimmer at him. He'd take it all in and feel overcome with the incredible wonderment of it all. This world, this universe, this unlikely placement of such a small and intensely curious consciousness in the midst of it all left to muse philosophically on the why and how.

He said that he was always struck with the sheer improbability of all this existing, this vast expanse of being. He would feel pierced to the heart by the cosmological question: Why is there something rather than nothing? And its cousin: Why all this?

Wonder is a state of mind in which . . . nothing is taken for granted. . . . Each thing is a surprise, being is unbelievable. We are amazed at seeing anything at all; amazed not only at particular values and things but at the unexpectedness of being as such, at the fact that there is being at all.

— Abraham Joshua Heshel (1907-1972)

The questions did not just sit in the water or sink into his heart unanswered. He reported that he always felt overcome with the grandeur of the theistic vision. All this is meant to be. All of this was created by an intelligence much greater than that required to ask the question and grope for its answer. The only alternative is unimaginably opaque and endlessly unsatisfying.

It is this sentiment that launches what philosophers have called the cosmological argument. Why indeed is there something rather than nothing? How could all this profusion of being come to exist at all? There could have been nothing, for all we know when we begin to reflect on the mystery of being. Eternal nothingness. A universal void. But there is light. And there is matter. Incomprehensibly much matter and energy, extravagantly arrayed and flung into space.

Why?

This is the ultimate philosophical question.

All arguments for the existence of God other than ontological arguments are explanatory in nature. The basic idea behind all explanatory arguments is that the existence of our contingent universe needs an explanation, and only the sort of being that religious people describe as God could possibly provide a suitable explanation.

Cosmological arguments for the existence of God are lines of reasoning that begin with the fact that a cosmos, or orderly universe of being, exists. And they contend that the only adequate explanation for that fact would be the existence of a being very different from anything in that universe, with properties that uniquely allow its existence, unlike that of the physical universe, to be self-explanatory.

Why ask why?

— Question asked by skeptics and recent beer commercials

The theist asks "Why?" and insists that there must be a reason for our existence. But the atheist, or at least the atheist who appears impervious to cosmological wonderment and wants to resist the theist's reasoning, typically responds as follows: "Well, why not? Why should we marvel at the mere fact of existence or at the profusion of being? Doesn't this just assume that without some special explanation, there would be nothing? And why assume that? Can't existence just be a brute fact, without any explanation, and without the need of any?"

The more unintelligent a man is, the less mysterious existence seems to him.

— Arthur Schopenhauer

In reply to the atheist's point, the theist can launch a full blown cosmological argument. Look at one modern example.

A modern cosmological argument:

1. The existence of something is intelligible only if it has an explanation. (By definition of intelligibility)

2. The existence of the universe thus either

    (a) is unintelligible, or

    (b) has an explanation. (From Step 1)

3. No rational person should accept 2-a. (By definition of rationality)

4. A rational person should accept 2-b: The universe has an explanation. (From Steps 2 and 3)

5. There are only three kinds of explanation:

    (a) Scientific: Explanations of the form C+L->E (independent initial physical Conditions, plus relevant Laws, yield the Event explained)

    (b) Personal: Explanations that cite the desires, beliefs, powers, and intentions of some personal agent.

    (c) Essential: The essence of the thing to be explained necessitates its existence or qualities.

6. The explanation for the existence of the whole universe can't be scientific. (There can't be initial physical conditions and laws independent of what is to be explained)

7. The explanation for the existence of the whole universe can't be essential. (The universe is not the sort of thing that exists necessarily.) Therefore (hold onto your chair),

8. A rational person should believe that the universe has a personal explanation.

9. No personal agent but God could create an entire universe.

    Therefore,

10. A rational person should believe that there is a God.

It is impossible to account for the creation of the universe without the agency of a Supreme Being.

— George Washington (1732-1799)

Quite an argument! I've tried to put in parentheses, throughout, what the justification is for each step, but here's more explanation:

✔ **(1) The existence of something is intelligible only if it has an explanation. (By definition of intelligibility)**

The first premise of the argument says that something is intelligible only if it has an explanation. Explanations put things into a context in terms of origin or dependence relations. You come to understand why something is, or why it is as it is, by seeing what brought it about, why it came to be, or how its dependence on something else dictates that it had to be what it is. Example: You wake up in a hospital room with a cast on your leg. You don't understand. The situation is rendered intelligible to you when someone explains that you were in an automobile accident and that a crushed door broke your leg. Given those conditions and the operation of the relevant laws governing mass, force, bone density and the like, your situation came about.

✔ **(2) The existence of the universe thus either**

(a) is unintelligible, or

(b) has an explanation. (From Step 1)

The second step of the argument follows quickly from the first. Anything, including the whole universe, will then fall into one or the other of two categories. Either it will have an explanation, or it will be unintelligible. Our second premise applies that fact to the existence of the universe.

✔ **The third step, perhaps surprisingly, claims that no rational person should accept the statement that the existence of the universe is just unintelligible.**

Notice the word *should*. This claim is not meant to be a sociological report on what people, independently identified as rational, will or will not be expected, as a matter of fact, to do. It is meant rather to be a conceptual implication of rationality. It could thus have been stated as "No rational person can, as rational, accept 2-a" or "Rationality itself forbids an acceptance of 2-a." Why? Because it is in the essential nature of rationality to expect and seek explanations everywhere they can possibly be sought.

At least on the macro-level, with respect to events and situations involving large-scale objects such as socks, shoes, cars, toothpicks, skin cells, planets, and electric guitars, a rational person doesn't ever think that things could even possibly just happen without any explanation whatsoever. If my car is not where I left it parked an hour ago, I will not even entertain for a second the possibility that there is no explanation whatsoever for its disappearance. Rationality intrinsically involves an expectation, or even demand, of intelligibility, and thus of explanations.

The history of modern science and technology is a history of the increasing satisfaction of this expectation throughout the sweep of human experience.

✔ **(4) A rational person should accept 2-b: The universe has an explanation. (From Steps 2 and 3)**

Step 4 just draws the logical implication of what has come before. If it is in the nature of rationality to look for explanations wherever they can possibly be found, then the rational person will not just accept the existence of the physical universe as a brute fact that allows of no explanation. The rational person will assume there is an explanation and will look to discover what it is.

Reason commands us far more imperiously than a master; in disobeying the latter we are made unhappy, in disobeying the former, fools.

— Pascal

✔ **(5) There are only three kinds of explanation:**

  (a) **Scientific: Explanations of the form C+L->E (independent initial physical Conditions, plus relevant Laws, yield the Event explained)**

  (b) **Personal: Explanations that cite the desires, beliefs, powers, and intentions of some personal agent.**

  (c) **Essential: The essence of the thing to be explained necessitates its existence or qualities.**

This independent premise of the argument arises out of an analysis of what counts as an explanation. It seems that there are three fundamentally different types of explanations that we accept as conferring intelligibility.

Suppose that a rock flies through your front window, smashing the glass. You hear muffled laughter outside and shouts. You run outside and see a group of kids looking guilty. You point at the window and say, "What's the explanation for this?" One skinny kid in thick glasses steps up and says, "Well, given the mass, velocity, and trajectory of the stone, along with the fragility of glass, it was inevitable that massive fracturing occur." My guess is that this is not the sort of explanation you'd be seeking. You'd be after a totally different sort of explanation: "Oh, and Billy hates your guts. He did it on a dare." That would explain the situation in the manner sought.

All things and events are foreshown and brought into being by causes; but the causation is of two Kinds; there are results originating from the Soul and results due to . . . the environment.

— Plotinus (c. 205-270)

There are indeed two very different types of causal explanation at work here. Scientific explanations cite independently existing natural conditions and the operation of distinct natural laws to causally account for the state or condition to be explained. Personal explanations operate in a different mode, citing intellectual, attitudinal, emotional, and volitional states (intentions) of persons. The third and more unusual type of explanation is the kind used when someone asks why a triangle has three sides. The answer is that it is of the nature or essence of a triangle to have three sides. Triangles necessarily have three sides. It could not be otherwise. And this is all the explanation we need. Likewise, if it's asked why a batch of water contains hydrogen, the explanation is an essential one: It is the essence of water to contain hydrogen and oxygen. That's just what water is. And that's just the sort of explanation needed. There do seem to be three different types of explanation to render things intelligible. Step 5 seems right.

(6) The explanation for the existence of the whole universe can't be scientific. (There can't be initial physical conditions and laws independent of what is to be explained.)

Step 6 is the first big surprise to most people. Don't scientists go around all the time explaining the existence of the whole universe? After all, what else is the Big Bang Theory but an explanation of how the universe got to be here?

Only a fundamental misunderstanding of the range and scope of physical cosmology offers this objection to Step 6. The Big Bang Theory describes an explosion from what scientists call a singularity, or singularity point, into the array of objects we now know of as the physical universe. But where that singularity itself came from and where the laws came from in accordance with which it exploded outward is a set of questions science cannot answer.

The whole universe, with its entire history, is an entity that is utterly comprehensive on a natural scale. It is the sum total of all natural conditions and all natural laws. In order to be able to give a scientific explanation of its existence, you'd need to be able to get an Archimidean point outside the whole system, with natural conditions and laws not included in what needed explaining, as the basis for your explanation. But if the universe is just all natural conditions and laws, there can be no initial natural conditions or laws outside it. Therefore there can be no scientific explanation for the existence of the universe.

The usual approach of science of constructing a mathematical model cannot answer the questions of why there should be a universe for the model to describe. Why does the universe go to all the bother of existing?

— Stephen Hawking

This conclusion generates a "Wow!" response in many people, a deeply furrowed brow in others. Be careful with your response. Frequently furrowed brows — an endemic risk in philosophy, a sort of occupational hazard — can lead to permanent wrinkles and the premature appearance of excessive wisdom.

✔ **(7) The explanation for the existence of the whole universe can't be essential. (The universe is not the sort of thing that exists necessarily.)**

Step 7 requires some comment. Why can't it just be the essential nature of the universe to exist? Maybe the physical cosmos is itself just a necessarily existent entity, and no further explanation is required. But this suggestion seems very dubious.

The universe is just composed of contingent objects, objects that themselves might not have existed or might have been far different from what they are. It is the consensus of contemporary physicists that if initial conditions or laws in the Big Bang had been any different from what they were, then very different results would have ensued, to the extent of disallowing large-scale structures at all. But if any and every object in the universe could have failed to exist, then it seems natural to suppose that the sum total of those objects, an entity just composed of them as parts, surely could itself have failed to exist. And we can certainly imagine its not existing. We can imagine nothing ever having existing in the physical realm. An eternal void instead of a whizzing, whirling, buzzing cosmos. Therefore, the universe is not the sort of thing that can exist essentially or necessarily. The explanation for its existence must lie elsewhere.

✔ **(8) A rational person should believe that the universe has a personal explanation.**

This logically follows from what has come before. If rationality demands that the universe have an explanation, and there are only three possible sorts of explanations, scientific, essential, and personal, and if it is indeed impossible for that explanation to be scientific, and implausible to think it's essential, then rationality does seem to demand that we believe the universe to have a personal explanation. But this is the OUCH point for many people who may have sought to avoid anything remotely like theism. Once you get this far, the remainder of the argument just rolls right out.

✔ **(9) No personal agent but God could create an entire universe.**

We are talking about a person who is not part of the universe at all, and who is powerful enough to bring a universe into being out of nothing. Who else would qualify? Therefore,

✔ **(10) A rational person should believe that there is a God.**

And this is the conclusion the theist desires.

There is nothing which God cannot effect.

— Cicero

The most prominent objection that is ever raised against a form of cosmological argument like this consists in asking, "Then what is the explanation for God's existence?" This is most effective when done with a smugness of tone and deliberate emphasis on the word "God."

The objector usually means to imply here that the cosmological argument will generate an *infinite regress* of explanations. To explain the existence of God, by the reasoning just used, it would seem that we need to postulate the existence of a Super-God. But then that being's existence would need explaining by the activities of a Super-Duper-God, and on and on, *ad infinitum* and *absurdum* (to infinity and absurdity).

This objection seems to just assume that God's existence does not have a scientific or personal explanation, then it is unintelligible. But it should be obvious by now what a defender of the argument will say to this.

The existence of God is intelligible not because it was caused by anything or anyone, but because it flows from his essence. This was the claim that the ontological argument made about God (see previous section). God cannot fail to exist. God exists necessarily. It is God's essential nature to exist. And in this regard, God is very different from anything in the universe. God's existence logically follows from God's essence. No other explanation for God is either necessary or possible. Thus, we don't have to worry about postulating (theoretically supposing the existence of) other deities in an infinite regress (or infinite mess) of explanatory postulations.

God, as the ontological argument told us, is fundamentally different from the universe. The very concept of God, it contends, precludes God's not existing. So we cannot even imagine God's not existing and know with full detail what we are imagining, without contradiction. But we can with the universe. It does not seem to be at all the sort of thing whose essence is to exist. Its concept does not logically imply its reality in all sets of possible circumstances. And that is different from the concept of God as a greatest possible being.

Notice that the conclusion of this version of the cosmological argument is not "Therefore, there is a God." It is just that, if we are rational, we should believe that there is a God. But this in itself is a surprise to many people who associate religious belief not with rationality but instead with the irrational side of life. This argument contends not just that it is rational to believe, but that it is irrational not to believe.

The principle of sufficient reason

A closely related traditional form of cosmological argument starts with a philosophical principle known as The Principle of Sufficient Reason (PSR), which says, "There must be an explanation (a) for any being, and (b) for any positive fact. Using PSR, a theist can reason,

1. Every being is either dependent or self-existent.

2. Not every being can be dependent.

Thus,

3. There is a self-existent being.

Because of PSR, Step 1 rules out there being anything that is explained by nothing. A dependent being is explained by something else. A self-existent being is self-explanatory, or necessary.

Step 2 results from this reasoning: If all beings were dependent, then there would be one positive fact — that these beings exist at all — that would have no explanation, and this is ruled out by PSR also; that fact can only be explained by a nondependent being; thus 2 is true.

And Step 3 follows from 1 and 2. There is no reason to think that anything in the universe, or the total composed of these things, is self-existent, thus there must be a God outside the system of dependent beings who created them.

A Designer Universe?

I find in the universe so many forms of order, organization, system, law, and adjustment of means to ends, that I believe in a cosmic intelligence and I conceive God as the life, mind, order, and law of the world.

— Will Durant

Have you ever walked along the beach and discovered an astonishingly beautiful seashell? The markings can be breathtaking. Or how about the artwork to be found in a field of flowers? Sometimes, it looks as if nature has been contrived by an incredibly powerful artist — and at other times, by a very witty jokester.

There is another family of theistic arguments that seek to explain not the mere existence of a universe at all, but the existence and nature of the remarkable one that we find ourselves in. These are usually called arguments from design or sometimes just design arguments for the existence of God.

One traditional form of this sort of argument arose at about the time that mechanisms like clocks and watches were capturing the attention and admiration of many intelligent people in Europe. In the 18th century, English philosopher William Paley (1743-1805) gave this reasoning a classic expression. I want to adapt Paley's reasoning in a slightly different form for our use here.

Imagine that you're walking along in a field, and you come upon a watch on the ground. You pick it up and admire its complexity, apparently contrived by an intelligent designer for a particular purpose — that of telling time. It would not occur to you to imagine that such an object had literally been there forever and had never been brought into existence at all. That would be ludicrous.

Nor would it enter your mind that such a complex set of interworking parts just happened to come into their structural relationship and thus come into being as a watch merely by the outworkings of chance.

You'd assume instead that the mechanism had been designed and assembled by a highly intelligent and very skilled being — a person — and that it was such a being who most likely was responsible in some way for its being in the field (Okay, well, maybe not in this case a highly intelligent and skilled person, but a fairly stupid or inattentive Klutz who either dropped it and didn't notice, or set it down and forgot, and will rue the day when he gets home and hears the words, "Honey, did you pick up my watch like I asked you to?" — but you get my point).

From this beginning, philosophers like Paley have directed our attention to the fact that the natural world around us contains many apparently complex and seemingly well-designed working structures that appear to serve well various purposes. They ask us to realize that it would be just as improbable for these natural processes and structures to have just been around forever, or else to have been produced by blind chance, as it would be for the watch to either lie in the field forever, or else to have just come together by chance there. The conclusion is that there is a divine watchmaker — a divine designer — behind the mechanisms of nature and responsible for the designs we see there.

> *As a house implies a builder, and a garment a weaver, and a door a carpenter, so does the existence of the Universe imply a Creator.*
>
> — Akiba (C.140- C.185) in *Midrash*

Let's put this into a clear and simple argument form.

A traditional design argument:

1. So far as we are able to determine, every highly complex object with intricate moving parts is a product of intelligent design. (The only such objects whose ultimate origin we are sure about are artifacts designed by people.)

2. The universe is a highly complex object with intricate moving parts. (From observation)

   Therefore,

3. Probably, the universe is a product of intelligent design. (From Steps 1 and 2)

4. No one could design a universe but God. (It's a big job)

Therefore,

5. Probably, there is a God. (From Steps 3 and 4)

In a sense, this can look like no more than an argument by analogy. There are a lot of things that we know to have been designed by intelligence. But then some things we don't know to be designed are analogous in some ways to those designed things. They are complex and have intricate moving parts that seem to serve a purpose. Therefore, by analogy, they are probably designed, too.

Maybe. But how analogous to a Rolex, or a Timex, is the human body? How analogous to a BMW 740iL is the entire universe? Yes, they're both impressive, quite spacious, and low maintenance, and if either required major repairs, I'd hate to see the bill, but do they really have enough in common to get a theistic argument off the ground? I mean, — and any 740 owner will confirm — truly intelligent design would surely have produced much better cup holders.

Critics of the traditional design argument reason that the analogy is too weak, and that the theory of evolution has demonstrated a mechanism for the production of complex organic life forms with apparently well-functioning, purposive parts that requires no reference whatsoever to the design of an intelligent, purposive being. And yet, the very existence of such mechanisms of development in the universe, processes productive of higher and more complex life forms that are finally themselves capable of embodying conscious intelligence, is itself a launching point for a newer version of the design argument.

The visible order of the universe proclaims a supreme intelligence.

— J. J. Rousseau (1712-1778)

I want to present very briefly a version of design argument that is based on modern scientific confirmation theory. I'll keep it as simple as possible here, but, as you might imagine by now, the philosophy can get as complicated as you like, or can stand. I'll first introduce some of the basic vocabulary.

The study of confirmation is the study of how theories gain support from positive evidence or suffer defeat from contrary evidence. When evidence counts in favor of the truth of a theory, it *confirms* that theory or offers it *confirmation*. When evidence counts against the truth of a theory, it *disconfirms* the theory or offers it *disconfirmation*. The ideal end point of confirmation is *verification,* or proof. The ideal end point of disconfirmation is *falsification*, or disproof.

How to decide whether evidence confirms or disconfirms a theory is a matter of *expectation*. We ask: If the theory were true, what evidence would we expect to find? And, are our expectations satisfied? Let me lay this out just a bit more formally. The basic idea is very simple, but we need to be as precise as we can here.

Imagine that we are considering two rival scientific hypotheses or theories, H1 and H2. For any such competing hypotheses or theories as H1 and H2, and any body of evidence E, if E would be more expected or likely if H1 were true than if H2 were true — if the truth of H1 would lead you to expect the discovery of E more strongly than the truth of H2 would — and E is in fact discovered, then E confirms H1 relative to, or over, H2.

Let E be the evidence of a friend walking into the building with an umbrella, totally soaking wet. H1 can be the hypothesis that it's raining outside. H2 can be the hypothesis that it's a sunny day. E would be more expected on H1 than on H2. Therefore E confirms H1 over H2. It's most likely raining.

It's not that E and H2 are incompatible. Perhaps it is a sunny day after all, and your friend was just bringing an umbrella into work for use when it did rain, and a jokester watering plants outside, seeing this, decided to hose him down. That is a possible scenario making E compatible with H2. But this scenario is unlikely. H1 is vastly more probable, given just E.

Confirmation theory in science formally captures certain ways of thinking that we all engage in naturally and mostly unconsciously all the time as we try to discern what's true and false in the world. Chemists, astrophysicists, and police detectives use many of the same forms of thinking as moms and dads do when they try to figure out what the kids are up to. We are always assessing evidence and evaluating rival hypotheses for our belief.

Now we can apply the simplest ideas of confirmation theory to the question of whether there is a God or not. Let H1 be the hypothesis of theism: There is an intelligent, moral, spiritual being who created the world. Now let H2 be naturalism: Nothing exists but natural laws and physical conditions. And, finally, let E be the existence in this world of intelligent, moral, and spiritual beings. Also allow E to encompass the fact that the laws of nature in our universe are such that large-scale structures could come into existence and support organic life to the point of allowing the growing complexity that would result ultimately in people with theistic tendencies of belief.

> *All things speak of God.*
>
> — Edward Young (1683-1765)

Would E be more likely to be observed given H1 or H2? The theist will suggest that, if we are intellectually fair-minded, we will allow that E could possibly come about if H2 were true. Given infinite space or time, any crazy thing might happen within a physical universe. E thus could arise on H2, however unlikely that might seem to be. But on H1, something like E would be much more strongly expected. E is the kind of creaturely evidence that might well be expected to result from the activities of a divine creator interested in things personal, moral, and spiritual. But if the probability of E would be higher on H1 than on H2, then E confirms H1 relative to H2.

> *God is our name for the last generalization to which we can arrive.*
>
> — Emerson

Many theists, including some who are themselves practicing scientists, think that it is just too strange that our universe operates in accordance with certain precise fundamental physical magnitudes and laws that seem to be fine-tuned to produce an orderly cosmos hospitable at some point to the development of something so different from bare matter as life and consciousness. Personhood just seems so qualitatively different from atoms whizzing through the void that its production in such a world seems the work of intentional contrivance. It looks like the ultimate plan of a God.

> *The visible marks of extraordinary wisdom and power appear so plainly in all the works of the creation that a rational creature who will but seriously reflect on them, cannot miss the discovery of a deity.*
>
> — John Locke (1632-1704)

As you can imagine, philosophers who are of a contrary bent can raise objections to this argument, either contending that theism for some reason is so inherently improbable that even if this evidence did raise its probability relative to naturalism, it is still more reasonable to be an atheist. Other critics point out that if we enlarge our evidence base from just that of the existence of intelligent, moral, spiritual beings, and the laws that allow them to exist in this world, to other facts about the universe, such as that evil exists, we may come away with a different conclusion.

I save the problem of evil for Chapter 21. The point to be made now is that design reasoning has reverberated through the centuries with proponents and critics. It has taken on different forms, and it seems to be able to keep up with the developments of modern science. It postulates the existence of an intelligent designer behind the universe, but some theists claim that they really don't need a postulation or an inference to God's existence. They say they believe because of their personal experience of God.

Religious Experience

> *I myself believe that the evidence for God lies primarily in inner personal experiences.*
>
> — William James

THE THINKER

Novelist Reynolds Price speaks out

A Southern novelist, who has faced both cancer and paralysis, has recounted in a couple of recent books the basis of his ongoing religious belief. I want to quote from the most recent of those books, to illustrate how a highly intelligent and sensitive individual can view the texture of his own experience:

"My belief in a Creator derives largely from detailed and overpowering personal intuition, an unshakable hunch, and a set of demonstrations that go far back in my consciousness — well before I began to comprehend the details of the world of deeply held but unoppressive Christian faith in which my parents had been formed, and in which they raised me. What I've called *demonstrations* have come in a very few experiences of my own, beginning when I was six years old.

"Starting on a warm afternoon in the summer of 1939, when I was wandering alone in the pine woods by our suburban house in piedmont North Carolina, I've experienced moments of sustained calm awareness that subsequent questioning has never discounted. Those moments, which occurred at unpredictable and widely spaced intervals till some thirteen years ago, still seem to me undeniable manifestations of the Creator's benign, or patiently watchful, interest in particular stretches of my life, though perhaps not all of it. And each of these moments

— never lasting for more than seconds but seeming, in retrospect, hours long — has taken the form of sudden and entirely unsought breakings-in upon my consciousness of a demonstration that all of visible nature (myself included) is a single reality, a single thought from a central mind.

"To be more descriptive, in those moments or openings — which are far from exotic in humankind (Wordsworth's accounts, in The Prelude and other poems, of similar findings in his youth are the classic description, as I learned years after my own began) — I've heard what amounts to a piercingly direct harmony that appears to come from the heart of whatever reality made us and watches over our lives.

"There've been no shows of light, no gleaming illusory messengers, almost no words; and the music that underlies each moment is silent but felt in every cell like a grander pulse beneath my own. Almost simultaneously, I've been assured that this reality is launched on a history that's immensely longer than any life span I can hope to have and that it's designed to end in some form of transformation and eternal entry into the presence of that central mind, God."

— From Letter To A Man In The Fire (Scribner, 1999)

I have frequently felt what presents itself as the presence of an unseen, loving intelligence guiding me. I have sometimes felt the absence of this. And then I screw up royally. But it always comes back. I have occasionally felt it vividly.

The most vivid religious experience of my life happened in front of the math building on the campus of the University of North Carolina when I was a student there. I was just walking back to my dorm after a class one day early in the afternoon, and there on the sidewalk, midstride, I had an overwhelmingly vivid and completely unexpected sense of suddenly receiving marching orders for life. An overarching, or undergirding, unseen presence spoke to me out of both the sky and the cells of my being. A sort of surround sound, divine stereo experience, except that the message came without tone or timbre. It has echoed in my heart and mind through the decades since.

I'm by nature a skeptic, and I'm very oriented to the senses, and whatever sense experience tells us about reality. I tend to insist on evidence and always crave proof. But the apertures to something more that occasionally have entered my life have defeated those tendencies and tamed that orientation. The craving, of course, lives on. And that's probably a good part of the reason that I'm a philosopher.

One of our greatest American philosophers, William James, wrote a book that continues to be read with profit over a hundred years after its publication, *The Varieties of Religious Experience*. The title itself captures an important point. There is a great variety to religious experience in our world. A good deal of it is most likely delusory. But a great deal, I think, is real.

I have come to believe that religious experience, in some form, is the most common grounding for the theistic vision. Most of us would not find a postulated being whose reality was just inferred by elaborate argument to be very relevant to how we live our lives. And yet it's still a good thing that the arguments are there. They help us to understand. But here, as in all other aspects of our lives, some form of experience, however subtle, seems to be important.

> *It is the heart which experiences God, and not the reason.*
>
> — Pascal

But how do we know that experiences of something so different as a God would presumably be are even remotely reliable, and thus can be trusted? And aren't there any contrary experiences that count against the apparent genuineness of religious experiences and thus against the truth of religious beliefs grounded on that experience?

Those are questions relevant to the topic of Chapter 21.

Chapter 21

The Problem of Evil

In This Chapter

▶ Understanding the implications of theism

▶ Laying out the main argument against the existence of God

▶ Examining answers to evil

Not only is there no God, but try getting a plumber on weekends.

— Woody Allen

*E*vil is the dark shadow that has kept many modern intellectuals from being able to embrace any version of the theistic vision. In this chapter, we look at the argument from evil that can be constructed for the conclusion that there is no God. We look at some traditional, inadequate responses to the argument, and then we develop and scrutinize some much more promising lines of thought.

Expectations of Theism

Theists claim that there is a perfect being who created the world and watches over it. Critics wonder how that can be so, given the nature of the world. They ask, "If a perfect being were watching over us, what then should we expect the world to be like? Does this expectation match up with what our world as a matter of fact is like?"

Would we expect a world created by a perfect being to be so imperfect as to contain cancers that torment untold thousands of people a day, viruses that make otherwise healthy people miserable, horrible birth defects, insanity, starvation, war, murder, torture, plane crashes, and killer storms that wipe out entire towns?

When I was a little boy, perhaps about the age of seven, I desperately wanted a pet. A dog was uppermost in my mind. Even a cat was a possibility. But my mother thought a dog would be too much trouble. And she didn't like cat hair. So she took me to a store where I could look at other possibilities.

There were cages of canaries that merely sat on their perches and would never really look me in the eye, and some bowls of fish that just swam around constantly. Nothing pettable there. A few small turtles finally caught my eye. They would crawl around slowly, and every now and then peer up at me, as if they were actually taking notice of my presence. Okay, turtles you can hold. And maybe you can talk to them. They'd never fetch the paper or sit up and beg, but they had some potential as daily companions. Did I mention that I was an only child?

So, that day, we bought two turtles. Tommy and Timmy the turtles. I also bought them a clear plastic bowl type home. Not the simple, plain, ordinary model, but a turtle paradise. It had an island in the middle. And on that island, a real, green, plastic palm tree. Club Med for turtles. I gave them clean water and even some little turtle toys. I wanted them to be happy. We put them on a table where I could view them every day and where they'd have plenty of daytime light. We kept them well fed with the finest of turtle food and cleaned their water regularly.

Tommy and Timmy lived a blissful turtle existence until the day my mother, while cleaning the bowl, accidentally flushed them both down the toilet. A great tragedy in turtle land. But I had done my best.

The critic of theism doesn't think that this world looks like it was brought into existence by a Creator God who did his best. It doesn't seem to be the kind of environment that was custom-designed by an all powerful and perfectly loving God for creatures he really cares about. If, as a seven-year-old boy, I was so careful to create the perfect life for my little turtles, the critic wants to know why we human beings don't have much better conditions for our existence. Was God sleepwalking through the process of creation? Was he utterly careless about our ultimate well-being? Did he not care?

> *The First Cause worked automatically like a somnambulist, and not reflectively like a sage.*
>
> — Thomas Hardy

We suffer all sorts of deprivations, insults, injuries, and pains during our time here, and then eventually all get flushed down the cosmic toilet to boot. And this is supposed to be the creation of a supremely perfect being? The critic of theism is not convinced. This world often seems to be a chaotic realm of looming tragedy, not an expression of divine love.

The strongest argument against believing that there is a God is rooted in what has been widely known as the problem of evil. Why would a perfect, and perfectly loving, being create, or even allow, a world so full of pain and suffering? That is the question that many critics of theism say that religious believers cannot satisfactorily answer.

> *If it turns out that there is a God, I don't think he's evil. The worst thing you can say about him is that, basically, he's an underachiever.*
>
> — Woody Allen

The Argument from Evil

> *We live in a world that is bursting with sin and sorrow.*
>
> — Samuel Johnson

There is a simple argument at the core of most atheistic belief. We can begin our look at the problem of evil by examining each of its steps.

The main argument against theism

The main argument against believing that there is a God is surprisingly simple on the surface. It has only three steps.

The atheist's main argument:

1. If there were a God, there would be no evil in the world. (From the concept of God)

2. There is evil in the world. (By observation)

   Therefore,

3. There is no God.

This is a valid argument. That just means that if both its premises are true, then so is its conclusion. So we need to examine its premises with care. I want to look at each of the two premises in reverse order.

Premise 2 is meant to report the obvious fact that there is pain, suffering, and wrongdoing in our world. As such, it seems clearly true. In our world, hunger abounds. Disease strikes people of every age. Accidents happen that injure and maim. It would be absurd to deny the simple claim made by Premise 2.

> *The world, as a rule, does not live on beaches and in country clubs.*
>
> — F. Scott Fitzgerald

Premise 1 is more complicated. It is a conditional statement meant to present one logical implication of any exalted concept of God. The atheist means to suggest in this premise that there is an incompatibility between the existence of God and the reality of evil.

But why should a theist, or an honest inquirer, accept this claim of incompatibility? Why does the atheist? Why should anyone accept Premise 1? For this crucial premise of the main argument, there is an interesting supporting argument. We can't appreciate the force of the main argument without appreciating it as well.

The alleged incompatibility of God and evil

The first premise of the atheist's main argument against the existence of God needs support. It claims that a God would never allow evil in the world. The supporting argument that is available for this claim goes as follows.

Supporting argument for Premise 1:

A. A morally good being prevents all the evil that he has the power and opportunity to prevent. (By definition of goodness)

B. An omnipotent being has the power to prevent all evil. (By definition of omnipotence)

C. An omniscient, omnipresent, and eternal being who is the creator of all has the opportunity to prevent all evil. (By definition of all the operative concepts)

D. God is, by definition, omnipotent, omniscient, omnipresent, eternal, and is creator of all else. (By the standard, developed concept of God)

Therefore,

E. If there were a God, there would be no evil in the world. (And this conclusion is identical to Premise 1 of the main argument, which was in need of support)

We should examine this argument's premises out of proper order, too, starting with the ones on which it is easiest to comment. First, though, a general point. Careful reflection will show that this argument's form is such that, if all its premises are true, then so is its conclusion. Because of that, it is important to give each premise careful scrutiny.

Premise *D* offers a standard explication of the concept of God and is acceptable to all theists being challenged by the argument. Premise *B* follows from a standard definition of omnipotence. The truth of it can be seen quite simply by reflecting on the straightforward truth that an omnipotent being could have prevented all evil by seeing to it that nothing was created at all. That would do the trick. And if there is a creation, it surely seems that an omnipotent being could so arrange things as to prevent any evil's arising at all. So we can grant this premise as well.

> *God, the ruler of all.*
>
> — Tacitus

Premise *C* follows from the concept of opportunity, together with the concepts of omniscience, omnipresence, and eternity. A person has an opportunity to do something if he is in the right place at the right time and can know of his access in such a way as to be able to act. A being who is omnipresent exists in all places. One who is eternal exists at all times. And one who is omniscient knows all that can be known. Thus, a being who had all three of these extraordinary attributes would never lack the opportunity to do anything. The truth of *C* follows from this.

The remaining premise is the controversial one. Premise *A* purports to offer a truth following from the nature of goodness. It says simply that a good person will prevent all the evil he has the power to prevent. And that, on the surface, surely seems true. Good people strive to rid the world of poverty, disease, war, and unsafe working conditions. A good person will give of his time, energy, and money to prevent bad things from happening to others. So surely Premise *A* is right, isn't it?

Strictly speaking, Premise *A* is false. But it is close enough to the truth to sound right on first glance, and even on second glance. But, oh, that third glance is a doozie. The third glance is a specialty of philosophers. So I want to use the next section to look at this crucial premise again.

Moral justification for allowing evil

We can best proceed by considering a question. Can a good person ever be justified in allowing, or even in bringing about, an instance of pain, or an instance of suffering? What do you think?

> *All God's creatures are his family; and he is the most beloved of God who does most good to God's creatures.*
>
> — Muhammad (c. 570-632 A.D.)

If you are a dentist or a surgeon, or know a nice one, you may have realized instantly that, despite the knee-jerk reaction we all have to say "No!" here, we actually have to say "Yes." A good person can on occasion be morally justified in bringing about or allowing an instance of pain or suffering if that pain or suffering is somehow necessary for the prevention of a worse evil or the attainment of a greater good. Take the pain inflicted by a surgeon, who has to operate on a person to save his or her life. We don't hold surgeons morally reprehensible for the post-operative pain that their actions inflict, as long as that pain is reasonably judged to be the result of actions that were necessary to prevent worse evil or to attain great good, such as that of restored health or a normal appearance. A surgeon who cut unnecessarily or inflicted pain carelessly would indeed be censured. But one who does only what is necessary is morally blameless for any pain that unfortunately and unpreventably results.

Philosophers like to be precise about things like this. Defining "evil" in the most neutral sense we can, to be any instance of pain, suffering, or wrongdoing, we can offer the following philosophical principle.

Moral justification in the face of evil:

A moral agent A is morally justified in bringing about or allowing an evil E if, and only if, either:

- E is necessary for the prevention of some greater evil

  or

- E is necessary for the occurrence of some greater, overweighing good

  or

- A's bringing about or allowing E is itself, as an action, necessary for the occurrence of some greater good or the prevention of some worse evil.

This is just a complex conditional statement for a widely recognized set of qualifications. A parent can punish a child in a reasonable way or allow the child to endure a minor deprivation in order to teach an important lesson. Coaches and military trainers push their charges through drills that cause fatigue and muscle pain, for the sake of a greater good. Yet, sadism is never permissible.

> *No gains without pains.*
>
> — Benjamin Franklin (1706–1790)

Evil is never justified unless it is necessary in the ways outlined. And that doesn't turn it into good. It is still evil, and it may still be unfortunate and regrettable, but if it is necessary, and it, or its allowance, participates in bringing about a morally more preferable result than would otherwise have happened, it is not unredeemed evil incompatible with the existence and oversight of a morally good being who could have prevented it.

Moral justification and the atheist's argument

A morally good being can be justified in allowing or even bringing about instances of pain and suffering. What this discovery means is that the atheist's argument, to have all true premises, must be changed. Recall the first premise of the supporting argument that we are still evaluating:

A. A morally good being prevents all the evil that he has the power and opportunity to prevent. (By definition of goodness)

In order to be a completely true statement, (A) needs to be rewritten as:

A*. A morally good being prevents all the morally unjustified evil that he has the power and opportunity to prevent.

The original premise implies logically that a surgeon cannot be a morally good being and yet perform operations, and this is just false. The newly revised premise acknowledges that a morally good being need not seek to prevent all instances of evil. He can even bring about instances of pain that are morally justified.

But once we revise this first premise of the supporting argument, we have to revise the conclusion, too, if we want the argument to be a valid one:

The original conclusion was

E. If there were a God, there would be no evil in the world.

Now, all that follows from the revised first premise, along with the supporting premises, is

E*. If there were a God, there would be no morally unjustified evil in the world.

But this is not identical to the first premise of the atheist's main argument from evil. And that was the premise that needed proof. The original argument then also needs to be revised in accordance with our new insights. The first premise can now just signal an incompatibility between God and morally unjustified evil.

But then Premise 2 will have to be changed accordingly as well. The subject of the conversation has shifted from evil to morally unjustified evil, and that must be reflected in the new second premise. So this is what we have as a result.

The atheist's main argument revised:

1. If there were a God, there would be no morally unjustified evil in the world. (From the concept of God)

2. There is morally unjustified evil in the world. (By purported observation)

   Therefore,

3. There is no God.

Here's the problem. We all know that there is evil in the world, if evil is just defined as pain, suffering, and wrongdoing. We can see it all around us. But do we know that there is morally unjustified evil in the world? Can we know that there is at least one instance of evil in the world that is never somehow redeemed, and thus justified? Is this the sort of thing that can be known by just looking around? Or is it the sort of claim whose defense would take much more than the casual observation sufficient for the original second premise, whose only claim was that there is evil in the world?

The theist's claim

The theist can suggest, and in fact must claim, that God is morally justified in allowing or bringing about every instance of evil in the world. Nothing can slip through the net. A single instance of pain or suffering whose occurrence, or whose allowance, had absolutely no moral justification whatsoever would, by the revised argument from evil, be enough to show that there is no God, or at least no Creator like the one that classical theism claims.

> *What we call evil is only a necessary moment in our endless development.*
>
> — Franz Kafka

Because we are representing the atheist as giving an argument here against the existence of God, the burden of proof, with respect to the persuasiveness of this argument, is on the atheist to show us the truth of his second premise. But what can he do? The most he can accomplish in this regard is to remind us of the horrific nature of some of the evils in this world and appeal to our moral intuitions to judge that they could not possibly be morally justified under any conceivable circumstances.

The theist insists that this life is only an infinitesimal segment of an overall existence of infinite duration, and reminds us that there may be spiritual factors involved in shaping the nature of this life whose outlines we cannot here even vaguely discern. But if that is even possibly true, then it will be very difficult for the atheist to provide any good reason for us to believe the revised second premise of his argument — his claim that there is evil in the world which not even the most exalted Creator God would be justified in allowing.

Such a God, whose many plans we might not be able to even begin to fathom, could, for all we know, have an ultimately perfect reason for allowing the world to be as it is.

The created world is but a small parenthesis in eternity.

— Sir Thomas Browne

Or could it be that the burden of proof is instead on the theist? After all, it is the theist's claim that there is a God that is ultimately responsible for this whole debate. The theist makes a claim, and then the atheist attacks it. What sense does it make to say that the whole burden of proof for determining the ultimate nature of the evil in our world rests on the atheist? The theist is committed to holding that the evil in our world is all somehow ultimately justified, however horrible, and that it is thus all compatible with the existence of a morally good and perfect Creator. Doesn't the theist have to justify this extraordinary claim? How can any honest seeker after truth be persuaded that theism is the correct world view unless the theist addresses this issue?

God is subtle but he is not malicious.

— Albert Einstein (1879–1955)

Most theists seem to have agreed and have offered a variety of responses to the problem of evil. We need to look at several of the most common of these lines of thought. We can start with what is currently the least popular of the responses and then move on to more commonly used forms of argument. It is important to understand all the main lines of argument that can be used with any significant plausibility.

The Great Theodicies

A *theodicy* (pronounced "thee-odd-issy") is an attempt to answer the challenge of evil by outlining a set of considerations that would show that there can indeed exist a God who is just in allowing the evil that we find in our world.

The word theodicy comes from two Greek roots: *Theos,* for God, and *Dike* ("Deekay"), for justice. Any solution to the problem of evil that offers a specific explanation for why God allows evil counts as a theodicy.

There are three classic theodicies that have had many adherents over the centuries. Each can be given in an extreme, or comprehensive, form, or in a limited version. The extreme form in each case tries to explain all the evil we find in the world. The limited form of each attempts to explain only some of the evil in the world.

The punishment theodicy

The punishment theodicy makes use of a notion of cosmic justice and divine punishment. It will be interesting to look first at the most extreme claim that has been made along these lines.

The extreme version: All suffering is punishment for sin

You can find indications throughout the Bible that God disciplines those he loves, as well as punishing wrongdoers for their deeds. So some theists have tried to claim that all pain and suffering is justified punishment for sin.

Punishment is a vital need of the human soul.

— Simone Weil

Before evaluating this claim, we should note that there are at least three different conceptions of what punishment is.

- ✔ **The Social Utility View** says that the purpose for punishing wrongdoers is to protect society from crime and evil.
- ✔ **The Rehabilitation View** says that the purpose of punishment is the rehabilitation, or training, of the wrongdoer.
- ✔ **The Retributive View** says that the purpose of punishment is to reestablish justice in the universe.

The concept of retribution is this: When a wrongdoer commits an evil deed, he is taking something for himself that is not his for the taking. This creates an imbalance in the overall state of justice in the cosmos. The only way that can be redressed is for the wrongdoer to be given something he does not want (incarceration or suffering), or to have forcibly taken from him something he does not want to give (his freedom or his life).

One day brings the punishment which many days demand.

— Publilius Syrus

Most punishment theodicies take for granted the retributive view, but a punishment theodicy can be constructed that involves rehabilitation and perhaps even social utility.

Criticism: The main problem with The Punishment Theodicy in any extreme form is the problem of the apparently innocent sufferer. If all suffering is punishment for sin, then why, as the Psalmist once repeatedly asked, do the wicked sometimes prosper and the good suffer? Why do babies experience pain and sometimes suffer deformities?

Some punishment theodicists have tried to claim that suffering can be punishment for sin committed in a previous life. But a belief in previous lives is not a part of most versions of Judeo-Christian theism. Others claim that infants can suffer for the sins of their parents. And while this is obviously true when interpreted in a causal way, it is far from obvious when interpreted in terms of justice.

> *Punishment follows close on guilt.*

> — Horace

One problem for any punishment theodicy offered as an explanation for the whole realm of evil is the question of why God would allow sin in the first place. And an answer to this question takes us to the next theodicy (see the following section, "The free will theodicy").

The limited version: Some evil is punishment for wrongdoing

A limited version of The Punishment Theodicy can escape the problem of the apparently innocent sufferer. It may be that God allows some of the pain and suffering in the world as justified punishment for wrong doing. But a limited version of this theodicy by definition cannot act as a complete answer to the problem of evil. More will be required. Something will be needed on the topic of sin, and more will be needed on suffering.

The free will theodicy

> *With man, most of his misfortunes are occasioned by man.*

> — Pliny the Elder (23–79)

The free will theodicy turns attention away from God and on to us. It says that it is not God who is responsible for the pain and suffering in the world, but we human beings who bring it about by misusing our free will. God is justified in wanting the universe to contain the great good of free-willed creatures, because freedom alone can produce virtue, but it is then necessary that God leave us free to do wrong as well as right. A being prevented from ever going wrong does not freely do good. God could have created us as robots or divine puppets, but he did not. He justifiably wanted creatures who could freely share love with each other as well as with their Creator. And while evil is not necessary for free will, the possibility of it is. And the actuality of it is something that God can't control without robbing us of our freedom.

The extreme version: All evil is the result of the misuse of free will by God's creatures

Nature, in her most dazzling aspects or stupendous parts, is but the background and theatre of the tragedy of man.

— John Morely (1871–1908)

This extreme version of the theodicy attributes all evil to the misuse of free will.

Criticism: What about natural disasters? Earthquakes? Tornadoes? Hurricanes? How in the world could these things be due to the misuse of free will by God's creatures?

Some theists have gone so far as to suggest that all natural disasters are the result of the misuse of free will by powerful nonhuman, demonic beings. Tornadoes that careen across the Midwest? Demonic bowling for Hoosiers.

Ridiculous. Absurd. Meteorologically ludicrous. A solution to the problem of evil has to be credible. And this is not. But some theists have suggested that the suffering inflicted by natural disasters can after all be traced to the misuse of human free will. This claim is made in two very different ways. The more believable claim is that, without people in the way, a natural disaster is just a rearranging of natural structures. It is human misjudgment or carelessness, or sometimes just stubbornness, that keeps us in tornado alley, in hurricane-prone beach areas, or living on fault lines. Most of the people in Los Angeles want to be in L. A. despite the near certainty of an eventual killer earthquake. And most of the rest of the country want those people to be there, too. (I'm kidding.) Can it be that if we were closer to our Creator, more attuned to inner spiritual guidance, that we would mostly, or entirely, avoid the suffering that natural disasters effect? We could certainly reduce our risk, even if we just listened to common sense. But it's hard to believe that flawed human decision-making can be held responsible for all pain and suffering that comes from the forces of nature.

Of man's first disobedience, and the fruit
Of that forbidden tree, whose mortal taste
Brought death into the world, and all our woe.

— Milton (1608–1674) *Paradise Lost*

A more bizarre historical claim has it that due to the sin of the first humans, evil entered the world in the form of natural disaster. But, in addition to clashing with any modicum of natural science whatsoever, this move makes no theological sense. Would a good and loving God design the world in such a way as to minimize the impact of evil, or set things up in such a way that one sin would result in thousands of years of natural evil? A loving being would most likely be a minimizer, not a maximizer. So, this strategy is unconvincing.

Is much of the suffering in human history due to the misuse of free will? Most certainly. Think of all the wars, the murders, the tortures, the mental suffering that human beings inflict on each other. If all human beings had always lived as moral saints, a great proportion of the evil that has afflicted humankind would not have come into being at all. It is our fault. And if free will is important enough, valuable enough, for God to want it and to be willing to tolerate all this to have it, well, it must be pretty important.

Few men are sufficiently discerning to appreciate all the evil they do.

— La Rouchefoucauld (1613–1680)

That last remark has been for many philosophers the basis of an objection. How can free will be so valuable? If we human beings see someone about to misuse his free will by shooting into a crowd, wouldn't we tackle him and restrain that freedom? Don't we then judge that his freedom is not so important as to override the negative impact of his intended actions? If we are justified in restraining him, then why wouldn't God be just as justified in stopping him? But too often such people are not stopped by anyone, human or divine. If there is a God, then why are such people allowed such egregious misuses of free will? How could Hitler's freedom be so precious as to outweigh the torture and murder of millions of people? Wouldn't you have stopped him if you could? Then if there is a God, why didn't God? The theist may reply that God did stop him, eventually. Perhaps. But not soon enough.

This objection shows that it is very difficult to see how the free will theodicy alone can be used as a total solution to the problem of evil. Perhaps nothing more than a more limited version will strike any sensitive person as plausible.

The limited version: Some evil is justifiably allowed as the price of free will

This is a more plausible claim. But, as in the case of a limited version of the punishment theodicy (see the section earlier in this chapter), this version of the free will theodicy cannot stand alone. It will need augmentation. Perhaps those two claims can work together. Some sin is allowed as the price of free will. And some suffering is punishment for sin.

It is a sin to believe evil of others, but it is seldom a mistake.

— H. L. Mencken

The soul-making theodicy

The soul-making theodicy claims that God has provided the conditions necessary for character development and growth among his creatures. God's intent in creating the world was not to provide a paradise of heaven on earth.

God wanted to provide an environment in which beings with moral and spiritual potential could develop and grow in the direction of completeness. But this requires that we be able to cultivate virtues that can't result from a trouble-free existence. Thus God had to allow trouble into the world. The purpose of this world is soul-making. And that is an enterprise that results from grappling with sin, suffering, and pain.

> *Happiness is not the end of life: character is.*
>
> — Henry Ward Beecher (1813–1887)

This theodicy claims that four distinct factors are required for soul-making.

- ✔ **There must be free-willed beings.** Moral character cannot be stamped on a person from outside. It must be freely cultivated.

- ✔ **There must be an environment in which these beings can exercise their freedom in morally significant ways.** That means there must be real moral choices. And there must be stable natural laws as the backdrop and stage for moral decision making. A world in which the laws of nature changed all the time would not be a context in which rational decisions could be made about how to act. How could you help a thirsty man if a glass of water might any second burst into flames? How could you know what was needed to feed the hungry if at any second a sandwich could morph into a poisonous snake or a stone? Stability provides for moral decision making and moral action. But in a stable world, wrong choices can have bad results.

- ✔ **There must be challenges to the characters of the free beings who have been created.** In a morally frictionless universe, no one would grow. We grow through conflict and difficulty. So problems must exist.

- ✔ **There must be opportunities for these free beings to respond virtuously as well as viciously to their challenges.** The suffering in the world can't thus all be utterly overwhelming. And we can't be led by the hand, metaphysically speaking. We need elbow room for making mistakes as well as for doing the good.

> *Every evil to which we do not succumb is a benefactor.*
>
> — Emerson

This theodicy, like the others, comes in two versions (see the following sections to discover what they are).

The extreme version: All evil is necessary for the great enterprise of soul-making

To understand this claim, we can make some distinctions. Designate as first-order good any good that we can enjoy apart from any evil at all. The feeling of a cool breeze on a warm day, or of a hot bath on a cold day, might be an example. The pleasure of a friend's company might be another. First-order evil would be any evil that can simply come into our lives unbidden and create some form of pain or suffering. I stump my toe on a chair, and it hurts. You get a bad cold and feel miserable for a week. I feel endangered by a situation and worry.

There is no question why a good God would allow first-order good into the world. It is pleasant and good to experience. But the question is why God would allow first-order evil. The soul-making theodicist explains that first-order evil is allowed in order to provide for the possibility of a higher order good. So we need to distinguish a second-order level of good, which consists in virtuous responses to first order evil, and which thus could not exist without that first-order evil. Consider patience, which is a virtuous response to potentially irritating or frustrating circumstances. Or think of courage, which is a virtuous response to danger. There is also the virtue of long-suffering, which is, by definition, a response to suffering. Various virtues could not exist unless the world contained evils and challenges to which they can be the response.

Although the world is full of suffering, it is full also of the overcoming of it.

— Helen Keller

To allow us to be free, God has to allow us to respond badly as well as virtuously to these challenges in our environment. People can react to evil callously. Or they can react manipulatively. Charity is a virtuous response to need. Phony charities are vicious responses to circumstances of need. We could call this second-order evil. The critic of theism wants to know what justifies God in allowing second-order evils, but the answer is straightforward. We couldn't be free unless they were allowed. Now, some of them also lead to third-order goods, which are virtuous responses to second-order evils. But this is not necessary for their justification.

This is a powerful line of thought. We were not created to be coddled but to be challenged to become the best we are capable of being. We are undergoing soul-making, which is sometimes a painful enterprise. But can this be a complete response to the problem of evil? Is all evil allowed because that is somehow necessary for the enterprise of soul-making?

Pain was not given thee merely to be miserable under; learn from it, turn it to account.

— Thomas Carlyle (1795–1881)

There seems to be a problem of inefficiency. Not all evil seems to present an opportunity for soul-making. Some harm is overwhelming. Some accidents kill. Not all sins seem justifiably allowed just because they are part of a process of growth and development for human beings. Some people become so hardened in evil that there seems no real prospect of their turning around. Perhaps God sees it differently. But how plausible is this in all cases?

This problem is avoided or at least mitigated by backing off the extreme version of the theodicy, which attempts a complete explanation of evil, and contenting ourselves with a more modest claim.

The limited version: Some evil is necessary, or necessarily allowed, for the great enterprise of soul-making

The limited version is more plausible and can be used in combination with the limited versions of the other theodicies to create a composite theodicy.

> *Either the human being must suffer and struggle as the price of a more searching vision, or his gaze must be shallow and without intellectual revelation.*
>
> — Thomas De Quincy (1845)

Soul-making is a profound process and should never for a moment be underestimated. A friend of mine, a prominent American philosopher, went to England for a visit and, while there, ventured to go see a man, a British philosopher, who, in midlife, had undergone a terribly tragic accident. This individual had been an extraordinarily active and fit person who was very athletically inclined. Yet, in an instant, he had been rendered quadraplegic. Totally paralyzed, he was in tremendous pain and confined to bed. He could speak only very slowly. Agonizingly slowly. He continued to do his philosophical work by laboriously dictating his books to a secretary who sat by his bedside and patiently awaited the words as they were slowly formed and uttered. Despite his horrible condition, this gentleman continued, however slowly, to produce work of the highest quality published by such prestigious institutions as Oxford University Press.

> *A wounded deer leaps highest.*
>
> — Emily Dickenson

At the end of my friend's visit, this remarkable philosopher told him that, if he had his life to live over and could choose whether to undergo this extraordinary and trying ordeal, he would go through it all over again because of what it had taught him. What he had been allowed to see because of it, he confided, could never be fully put into words, but was so precious as to be worth all the agony and loss.

> *Adversity is the first path to truth.*
>
> — Byron

A fourth combination theodicy

This fourth option, a combination of the limited versions of the three most classic approaches, may be the most plausible strategy of all. It can be constructed from the notions of cosmic justice and punishment, free will, and soul-making and can be deployed in such a manner as to go a long way toward answering the question of why a good and perfect God would allow all the evil of our world. As such, it may display a quality often seen in biology, *heterosis* — the superior strength that can be found in properly created hybrids, where individual strengths can be retained and weaknesses avoided.

> *What's wrong with this world is, it's not finished yet.*
>
> — William Faulkner (1897–1962)

And yet, even a combination of all these notions can seem to fall short. Especially in the face of a particular instance of evil. A friend's baby falls sick and dies. A terrible accident happens to a wonderful person. Do we know why? Can we know why? Must a theist know why, or be able to suggest why with a high degree of probability?

The Element of Mystery

> *You cannot plumb the depths of the human heart, nor find out what a man is thinking; how do you expect to search out God, who made all these things, and find out his mind or comprehend his thoughts?*
>
> — Apocrypha Judith 8:14

The most famous religious text on the problem of evil, the Book of Job (pronounced with the long "o" sound, as in "Oh, no!"), does not try to answer the question of why there is evil. It rather questions the questioner. Who are we to think we can understand? Where were we when the foundations of the earth were laid? How can we presume to fathom all the intentions and goals of a perfect creator? We must allow for some mystery to remain, after we have constructed all our theodicies.

The claim here is that we can indeed make great progress in thinking through the problem of evil, but we must remember our condition. If we think that we can use our three-pound brains to plumb all the mysteries of creation, we are just being silly. A tiny infant cannot understand the life and work of Albert Einstein. Nor can a beginning school child. But God is much more different from Einstein, and the rest of us, in intelligence and wisdom than Einstein is different from the small child. So we should not expect to understand it all.

Every conjecture we can form with regard to the works of God has as little probability as the conjectures of a child with regard to the works of a man.

— Thomas Reid (1710–1796)

The Book of Isaiah also reports God issuing a reminder about this: "For my thoughts are not your thoughts, neither are your ways my ways," declares the Lord. "For as the heavens are higher than the earth, so are my ways higher than your ways, and my thoughts than your thoughts." It is good for us, now and then, philosophers that we are, to be put in our place.

Any response to the problem of evil that does not allow an active role for a concept of mystery doesn't grasp the magnitude of the issues under consideration. If we couldn't offer any possible explanations for why God might be allowing evil in our world, we couldn't justify at all using the concept of good in application to God. And yet it doesn't follow at all that we must be able to tell an utterly complete story about what a Creator of the entire universe is up to in all ways.

A comprehended God is not God.

— John Chrysostom (345–407)

I believe in the incomprehensibility of God.

Honore de Balzac (1799–1850)

Any theism that didn't ultimately point to mystery would not be a very believable world view. So we must not regret our final use of the concept of mystery. It is not an unfortunate, desperation ploy but a necessary part of any exalted theism.

Do we have enough here to defend the claim that there is a God? Do we have a sufficient response to the atheistic argument from evil? What do you think?

Part VIII
The Meaning of
Life

The 5th Wave   By Rich Tennant

"I think you're on to something here."

In this part . . .

In this part, we figure out the meaning of life. No joke. Why not? Does life have a meaning? Does your particular life have a meaning? Is life one huge gamble? What is a successful life in this world?

Chapter 22

What Is the Meaning of Life?

In This Chapter

▶ Asking the biggest question about this life

▶ Distinguishing related questions about meaning, value, and importance

▶ Suggesting what the meaning of life really is

Here we are in this wholly fantastic universe with scarcely a clue as to whether our existence has any real significance.

— E. F. Schumacher (1911–1977)

What is the meaning of life? This has often been said to be the deepest question that can be asked about life in this world. But there is a deeper question: Is there any meaning to life? When we ask merely what the meaning of life is, we are presupposing that it has a meaning. And it is just this presupposition that many intellectuals began to question in the early 20th century.

In this chapter, we address both questions. First, we ask the more fundamental of the two, and then — not to give too much away — I'll find good enough reason to ask the less fundamental one as well. And to answer it.

The Questions We Can Ask

We can distinguish several different fundamental questions about life that are all somehow related:

✔ Is there any meaning to life?

✔ Does life have any purpose?

✔ Is there any value to life?

✔ Does life have any importance?

I can ask any of these questions about life in general or about my life in particular. Usually, the reason I might find myself asking any of these about life in general is that I want to gauge the implications for my life in particular. These questions are thus rarely asked in a purely theoretical mode, but more often to get our bearings in the world.

These are what philosophers call *existential* questions. They concern how we exist in the world, how we should view existence, and how we ought to exist. In another phraseology, they are all *existentially central* questions, probing at the core of what it is to be alive and be human in this world. They are thus very different from the *existentially peripheral* matters that we, unfortunately, tend to spend most of our time thinking about and discussing.

> *The continual pursuit of meanings — wider, clearer, more negotiable, more articulate meanings — is philosophy.*
>
> — Suzanne K. Langer

These are the questions most fundamental to getting our bearings and finding our way. How do we decide what it's really important to pursue in this life? What is truly worth our time and energy? Existentially peripheral matters can be enjoyable entertainments, pleasant diversions, or irritating distractions. We just should never let them dominate our lives. Only the existentially central questions we can raise and contemplate will give us ultimate guidance in life.

What is truth? Is there an objective moral order? Are we really free and responsible beings? Is there a soul? Can we survive bodily death? Is there a God? These are all existentially central questions. They are crucially relevant to understanding who we are and what our lives are all about.

> *You can't do without philosophy, since everything has its hidden meaning which we must know.*
>
> — Maxim Gorky (1868–1936)

We don't ask fundamental questions often enough, once we're out of school. And even there, we learned to treat almost everything theoretically. Camus said this, Sartre said that, and these three ideas came from Kierkegaard. Yes, but what do they mean for us now? We need to retake the territory of our own minds and give ourselves the time to think through the truly important issues, like those surrounding the question of the meaning of life.

I give talks to business groups all over the country. Sometimes to thousands of people at once. You would not believe how many people come up to me after some of these talks and tell me that they're "closet philosophers." Even some of the toughest characters in modern American corporate life secretly harbor an urge they cannot shake to get their considerable intellects around the ultimate questions. But they rarely have time. Or an impetus that can help them launch such thoughts in a productive direction. That's one of the reasons I decided to write this book. To help all my closet philosophy friends and acquaintances to begin to grapple with these issues in a productive way.

> *At best, a true philosopher can fulfill his mission very imperfectly, which is to pilot himself, or at most a few voluntary companions who may find themselves in the same boat.*
>
> George Santayana (1863–1952)

With that in mind, let me make a few clarifications concerning how we should think about the questions in this chapter. First, there are indeed several distinct ideas that are at stake here: Value, importance, purpose, and meaning, to name again the most crucial.

When I ask whether life has ultimate value, or whether my life has value, I can be probing toward two different things. The first is what philosophers call *extrinsic value* — value that is conferred on something by something or someone else. What we call sentimental value is a form of extrinsic value. An ordinary-looking item can have great sentimental value, great extrinsic value of this sort, because of its involvement in my life, or in events that matter a great deal to me. I endow it with that value.

> *Life has a value only when it has something valuable as its object.*
>
> — Hegel

The most common form of extrinsic value may be that of instrumental value: Something is valuable instrumentally because it produces or leads to something else that is of value. Aspirin is instrumentally valuable because it can lead to the cessation of a headache or to the avoidance of a heart attack. My car has instrumental value due to its ability to get me places and to get me there in style and comfort (especially with the top down). Because of all the great experiences I've had in connection with that car, it has also begun to have sentimental value as well. But that won't mean much at trade-in time. The sales manager won't care how many beautiful sunsets or sparkling stars it has given my wife and me when he makes an offer. I may care, though, when I weigh it.

A second form of value — *intrinsic value* — is the value that a thing or quality has in and of itself, regardless of whether it leads to anything else of value, and regardless of how it is viewed. When you pursue something that is of intrinsic value, you seek it not merely for any benefits it might bring you, but just because you think that it is important in and of itself. The great moral traditions have held that human beings, as individuals, have intrinsic value. Even people who can't do anything of value are something of value.

Happiness has intrinsic value. It is not, and need not be, pursued for the sake of anything else beyond it. Love has intrinsic value. And, theistic philosophers have said throughout the centuries, the ultimate intrinsic values are to be found in God, and in union with God.

> *Life's values originate in circumstances over which the individual has no control.*
>
> — Charles A. Lindbergh

When I ask whether life has ultimate value, and in this context, whether my life has value, I am interested in questions of both intrinsic and extrinsic value.

When I ask whether life has a purpose, or in this context, whether my life has a purpose, I am asking a distinct, though related, question. Purpose has to do with aims, goals, or missions. Purpose is a distinctively teleological notion (from the Greek *telos,* or target). I can certainly set goals for my life, but I obviously have no such power concerning the universal phenomenon of life itself. But when most people find themselves asking deep existential questions about purpose, they are not asking whether it is within their own power to create purposive activities. They tend rather to be probing into whether there may be some purposes for life and for their own lives that are preordained, or provided independently of their own wills. This is clearly a question about the ultimate context of life in this universe and straightforwardly connects up with questions about theism and naturalism. Are we here because of a greater purpose? Or is our existence without plan or purpose?

> *The idea of life having a purpose stands and falls with the religious system.*
>
> — Sigmund Freud

Purposes are connected with values. We aim our activities at goals that we value, whether extrinsically, because they in turn lead on to other things, or intrinsically, because we view them as good in themselves. Our lives are purposive if they are directed toward the pursuit of important values. And it is the pursuit and attainment of important values that most clearly would give my life itself importance. We can immerse ourselves in trivialities in this world, or we can seek to embody and achieve values of importance in what we do. Or we can mix it up a little. In the philosophical or cosmic sense, importance has much less to do with fame, or celebrity, or any form of public recognition than it does with basic value. My life has dignity if it has true importance, which is to say, if it is lived purposively, in accordance with the highest values, even if it is imperfectly so lived. Again, this has nothing directly to do with worldly status. It is much deeper than that.

> *Human dignity . . . can be achieved only in the field of ethics, and ethical achievement is measured by the degree in which our actions are governed by compassion and love, not by greed and aggressiveness.*
>
> — Arnold J. Toynbee (1889–1975)

When most people ask, in their heart of hearts, whether their own lives are of any importance, they most often mean to be asking either of two things. One question is whether they will be able to make a real difference for good before they depart this world. If this is the question, then they are hoping that their lives will attain this sort of extrinsic value. They want to be tools of goodness in the grand enterprise of life.

The other question is whether their lives themselves, regardless of their impact on the world around them, have any form of intrinsic value, or else extrinsic value that was not wholly of their own making. Anyone, for example, who believes that he is on a mission from God feels a sense of importance to his life, regardless of his own personal success in carrying out that mission. Mother Theresa was once asked how she could devote her life to helping dying people who were eventually going to die anyway. She said that she believed that she was not called by God to be successful, but just to be faithful. And, yet, faithfulness itself is a form of success. A theist can feel a sense of the importance of life, and of his or her own life, because of its divine origin and intent.

It could also be possible for a naturalistic philosopher to feel a sense of dignity and cosmic importance because of her overall role in focusing the universe's long march to conscious intelligence in her own person. This would not be a role of her own choosing, but could be viewed as a role contextually, and cosmically, determined. A person who has a sense of importance about her life generally is more likely to see her life as meaningful.

> As far as we can discern, the sole purpose of human existence is to kindle a light in the darkness of being.
>
> — Carl G. Jung

Meaning has to do with purpose, value, and importance. And it is most often the focal notion used to appraise life as a whole. As such, the following section focuses on it, while keeping in mind the related notions that necessarily will function in understanding it.

So let us ask: Is there a meaning to life?

Meaning and This World

To answer the question "Is there a meaning to life?" we first need to see, however briefly, the ways in which philosophers have attempted to answer this question without making any sort of religious commitment whatsoever. Then we can see what difference a religious stance can make to the nature of the answer.

It is the acme of life to understand life.

— George Santayana

Our question is whether life has any meaning. In this section, we look at the two most prominent answers that have been given from a this-worldly perspective.

Nihilism: The ultimate negativity

At any street corner, the feeling of absurdity can strike any man in the face.

— Albert Camus

The nihilist's answer to the question of whether life has meaning is a simple and emphatic No. Life itself has no meaning. Your life has no meaning. My life has no meaning. Existence is without meaning of any kind. There is a void of significance to everything. There is no purpose to life. No plan. No reason. There are no ultimate values that we are here to embrace or embody. And nothing is finally of any importance whatsoever. So, party on if that's your inclination, or else you could work very hard to forget your cosmic plight. Or you could choose to opt out of it all. But nothing really matters in the end.

The *existentialists* are a collection of, mainly, early 20th-century philosophers who are thought of in connection with this answer. But there are probably more novelists, poets, rock musicians, and filmmakers who represent the nihilist point of view than there are philosophers. And of that fact I am very glad. Because I think of nihilism as bad philosophy.

> *The moment a man questions the meaning and value of life, he is sick, since objectively neither has any existence.*

— Sigmund Freud (A Bad and Very Sick Philosopher)

I need to point out something very important, first off. The nihilist has a basic problem. There is no way to prove that life has no meaning. There is in fact no way to even marshal common human intuitions and observations in such a way as to support an overall world view in which it must be said that life has no meaning. There is no principle of rationality that offers clear support for nihilism. And part of the reason for that is that nihilism is by its nature a universal denial, what philosophers sometimes call a *negative universal existence judgment,* and this is the hardest sort of claim to justify, regardless of the subject matter.

Suppose I say, "There is no snake in this room." This is *a negative particular existence claim,* ranging over a limited domain — the room I'm in. I could justify my claim by an extensive search of the room, moving around chairs and table and looking under everything. The evidence at some point would be sufficient to ground my statement. But if I said, "There are no, and never have been, any beings in this universe with three heads and eight arms, weighing over 200 pounds," how could I ever prove it? This is a negative universal existence claim ranging over a potentially unlimited domain. Where am I going to have to go to check all the relevant evidence? It's impossible. There is nothing I could do that would be sufficient to justify that sort of claim.

The claim that there is no meaning to life is a negative universal existence claim ranging in principle over an unlimited domain. How then could anyone demonstrate that it is true? I've never found a nihilist who could answer that question convincingly.

> *Life has to be given a meaning because of the obvious fact that it has no meaning.*

> — Henry Miller (novelist, 1891–1980)

Some nihilists think that it's just obvious that life has no meaning. They view the world as a purely physical phenomenon, starting from, perhaps, unimaginably weird strings of pure energy and building itself up into a material cosmos in a blind process born of necessity and chance. There is no room in a naturalistic universe for meanings. What would be the status of a meaning? What would it be made of, where would it come from, where and how would it exist? In a reality consisting only of matter in motion, it's hard to see what the ultimate status of anything as different from an atom as a meaning would be. And if we think that we can give anything meaning, we are fooling ourselves, according to a consistent development of this world view. Any attempts to create meaning are themselves nothing more than empty, meaningless gestures in a universe that just doesn't care.

> *I don't wanna take no year's sabbatical and go see some guru in the Himalayas to learn the secret of life. I don't think there's too many secrets to life, really.*

> — Charlie Daniels (Southern Rock Country Boy Guru)

This grounding of nihilism would make it obvious to us only if the naturalistic world view that gives rise to it were itself obvious, and, as you can see in earlier chapters, it's not. A naturalistic philosophy of the world is just one contender for our consideration, and not a wildly attractive one. The fact that it has been popular in the past century is no recommendation of it. Cigarettes and bell-bottom pants have been popular in the past century.

Some nihilists try to claim that meaning is a linguistic phenomenon — only words have meanings — and that because life is not a linguistic item, it can't have a meaning. Nonsense. Body movement can have meaning. We can make meaningful discoveries. We can give meaningful looks. And there is no syntax or semantics sufficient to justify the claim that there is really a linguistic phenomenon operative in every such case. A meaningful experience need not refer, or modify, or express action. It is not a category mistake to ask whether life has meaning. It is not nonsense to suppose it does.

Other philosophers explicitly say that life could have a meaning only if there were a God, and they are convinced that there is none. Perhaps they are impressed by the problem of evil. It could be that they believe that they have not themselves had any religious experiences sufficient to ground a belief in any God. For whatever reason, they are nonbelievers and are convinced that meaning goes down with the ship. No God, no meaning. Why would they think this? Stay tuned. In the next section, I show why.

Some other atheistic and agnostic philosophers have given a very different answer to the question of whether life has any meaning. It is a positive viewpoint that has come to be a major perspective for a philosophy of life in the modern world.

The do-it-yourself-approach to the meaning of life

Many philosophers have claimed that, within the confines of a this-worldly approach — without making any reference to the question of whether there is a God or not — we can provide a strong positive answer to the question of whether this life has any meaning. The answer is Yes, if you give it meaning.

> *There is no meaning to life except the meaning man gives his life by the unfolding of his powers, by living productively.*
>
> — Erich Fromm (1900–1980)

Nothing has meaning unless it is given meaning. But we have it within our power to endow our lives with meaning by structuring them around purposes, values, and desires that we choose to pursue. I call this The Do-It-Yourself-Approach to the Meaning of Life because it holds each of us responsible for answering the question of meaning with action, not speculation.

We need to take a closer look at this common answer to our question. First, it is based on a thesis about meaning:

The Endowment Thesis: Nothing has meaning unless it is endowed with meaning (purpose, value, or importance) by an intelligent agent.

And a corollary to this thesis is the following proposition:

The Meaning of Life Corollary: Life has no meaning unless it is endowed with meaning.

> *It has always been difficult for man to realize that his life is all an art.*
>
> — Havelock Ellis

But when we try to apply the Endowment Thesis to the overall phenomenon of our lives, and suppose that we can successfully act on it here, we run into a problem. Something can be endowed with meaning only if an agent has some requisite degree of control over it. I cannot endow the words of the French language with new meanings today at noon. I don't have the requisite control. I can't endow your life with meaning. And you can't give mine meaning. Neither of us has the necessary scope of control when it comes to another person's life. But here is the problem. Much of our own lives we have no control over. I do have control over many of the things in my life. I can act in such a way as to rid myself of some problems, and I can make decisions that bring me new opportunities. But there are several crucial things about my life that I have little or no control over.

> *Life's uncertain voyage.*
>
> — Shakespeare

I do not have control over:

- ✔ The basic circumstances of my birth
- ✔ Many of the formative features of my life
- ✔ The fact that I will undergo suffering in this world
- ✔ The reality that I must face death

I did not choose to be born in 1952 instead of 1945 or 1612. If I had been born in a very different historical period, in a different culture, or to very different parents, I would have been a very different person in many ways. I would have had a different life. And these would surely be differences relevant to the meaning of what I do.

I did not choose the neighbors of my childhood, or my relatives, or who would attend the schools where I was a student. I did not get to pick my teachers, or my doctor, or what city I would live in as I grew up. I did not have within my control the people I would meet as I came of age and the person I would find to marry. Yet these are all crucial matters for the continued formation of a personality and of a life.

> *The life of a man is like a game with dice; if you don't get the throw you want, you must show your skill in making the best of the throw you do get.*
>
> — Terence (c. 190–160 B.C.)

I cannot choose to forego suffering in this world. I can seek to avoid it. But I can't just opt out altogether. It is something that is, in the most fundamental sense, beyond my control. I can live cautiously, and I can to some extent influence what sort of sufferings I will, or may, endure throughout my life, but so much of this side of existence is just simply beyond my control. And it is important to how I judge my life's meaning.

Finally, I have no control whatsoever over the question of whether I will die. It's a given, like it or not. And the reality of death poses in the most dramatic of ways the question of life's meaning. This is not because a life without end would necessarily be meaningful. An infinite existence could be just as void of significance as a 20-year span, in principle. It's just that an absolute boundary like death psychologically causes us to ask questions about what is on this side of it, as well as questions about death itself, and whether there is anything at all on the other side. Meaning questions are fundamental among these.

> *Life is short and we have never too much time for gladdening the hearts of those who are traveling the dark journey with us. Oh, be swift to love, make haste to be kind!*
>
> — Henri Amiel (1821–1881)

These are just four important matters that are beyond our control. They show us that there are things in life over which we lack sufficient control for meaning endowment. I cannot therefore endow the entirety of my existence with meaning. I can establish islands of meaning within my life. But I am without the requisite power to give meaning to the whole of my life. And you are in exactly the same quandary.

No being could give meaning to the whole of any human being's life, or to life itself, unless that being had the requisite sort of control over matters of birth, life, suffering, and death. But no being could have that sort of power except the sort of being that religious people call God.

Thus, the question as to whether life as a whole, or my life as an entirety, has meaning ends up connecting directly with the question of whether there is a God. (See Part VII.)

> *I do not know whether there are gods, but there ought to be.*
>
> — Diogenes

God and Meaning

I suspect that many theists would say that the best answer to the question of whether life has meaning is not the qualified, and demonstrably limited, affirmative answer of The Do-It-Yourself-Approach (see preceding section), but an unconditional yes flowing out of theistic belief.

> *To believe in God means to see that life has a meaning.*
>
> — Ludwig Wittgenstein (1889–1951)

Theists believe that God created the universe for certain purposes, and that the Creator in turn brought about our existence within the cosmos for distinctive purposes as well. On the theistic vision of the world, there are objective values rooted in the nature of God, and there is a source of importance for our lives and activities that comes from far above or below the sweep of our natural surroundings, whichever vertical metaphor you prefer.

There is an objectivity of meaning that is provided for us. But within the overarching context of this meaning, which is both objective and provided for us, we are free to endow our days with meaning in pursuit of the projects and values that best reflect our own natures and talents. Theists don't need to hold that the meaning of our lives is altogether provided for us, so that we are merely passive in relation to it. The meaning of life is not an off the rack suit that we must just wear without alteration. We can tailor to fit. But it is designer couture, so there are limits. Believers in God can endorse what is good and sensible among the basic presuppositions and premises of The-Do-It-Yourself-Approach, while avoiding the limitations it has when it attempts to be a solo answer to the question of meaning.

A question naturally arises at this point. If there is an objective meaning provided to life itself, and to our lives, by a God, according to the theistic vision, then what is it? What could it be? Many theologians and religious philosophers who assure us that God provides meaning never venture to say exactly what it is.

In analyzing the views of the world's great theistic philosophies and religions, I have come to believe that the objective, overarching meaning of life is closely reflective of the nature of the theistic God. It is creative love, or loving creativity. As long as our activities flow in that direction and are consistent with that vision, they are good and meaningful, and our lives are purposive, meaningful, and important.

> *Men must live and create.*
>
> — Camus

We are each free to structure our lives around any values we choose. We can be ambitious for wealth. We can be greedy for power. We can indulge in trivial pursuits of pleasure to the exclusion of almost anything else. But we will be living truly meaningful lives only if we structure them in accordance with creative love, or loving creativity. This is the touchstone. This is the standard.

I have developed this point in connection with the most pressing issues of life and work in my book *If Aristotle Ran General Motors: The New Soul of Business,* and so I won't repeat myself to elaborate on it any more here. But it is important to point out that this approach to the question of meaning goes far beyond any standard, this-worldly version of The Do-It-Yourself-Approach, while yet incorporating its legitimate insights.

The theist will say that life does have meaning. And the theist can suggest what that meaning is. Without theism, however, it is very difficult to see how life as a whole could ever be judged meaningful. It is hard to see how our individual lives could ever be meaningful through and through. In fact, in a thoroughly naturalistic universe, it would be hard to see how any of our gestures toward meaning could be efficacious in any way at all. For this reason, the debate about the existence of God is never just an intellectual controversy. It is of the greatest existential significance. And it puts everything else in perspective.

The meaning of life as a whole is tied to the existence of God. And this is just one of the more important instances where we can see that, in philosophy, ultimately, everything is tied to everything else.

Is there, then, total meaning available for our lives or not? What do you think? Chapter 23 talks more fully about what is at stake. And it looks at one of the most ingenious arguments ever discovered to help us answer our ultimate questions.

Some philosophical comments on God and meaning

Many great minds have connected the issue of meaning with the existence of God:

The smallest details of this world derive infinite significance from their relation to an unseen divine order.
— William James

Man's only legitimate end in life is to finish God's work — to bring to full growth the capacities and talents implanted in us.
— Eric Hoffer (1902–1983)

Man's perfection would be the fulfillment of his end; and his end would be union with his Maker.
— William James

The highest aim of man: the knowledge of God.
— Moses Maimonides

God is. That is the primordial fact. It is in order that we may discover this fact for ourselves, by direct experience, that we exist. The final end and purpose of every human being is the unitive knowledge of God's being.
— Aldous Huxley (1894–1963)

The meaning of life consists in the love and service of God.
— Leo Tolstoy (1828–1910)

The supreme value and highest good is not life as such, but spiritual life rising up to God — not the quantity, but the quality of life.
— Nicholas Berdyaev (1874–1948)

Chapter 23

Pascal's Wager: Betting Your Life

● ●

In This Chapter

▶ Considering life as a gamble

▶ Presenting Pascal's Wager for religious belief

▶ Working through the debate over the wager

▶ Thinking of world views as wagers

● ●

Let us weigh the gain and loss, in wagering that God is. Consider these alternatives: If you win, you win all; if you lose, you lose nothing. Do not hesitate, then, to wager that He is.

— Pascal

In this chapter, we look at one of the most fascinating philosophical arguments ever devised. It has persuaded many people to change their lives, and it has monumentally irritated others. Most scholars think of it as an argument for the rationality of believing in God, or even more, as an argument that the only rational choice to make on ultimate matters of world view is to cast your lot with the theists. But if you read this chapter through, you can see that it's much more than an argument concerning religious belief. It is an argument for believing that there is overall meaning to life.

Blaise Pascal: Philosopher-Genius

Blaise Pascal (pronounced *"Blaze Pass CAL"*) was born in a provincial town in France in 1623. His father educated him, but in the early years withheld one subject as too titillating and overwhelmingly exciting for young minds. Wanting to protect little Blaise from anything that would overstimulate his budding intellect and deflect him away from the study of anything else, his father decided to lock up all the math books in the house. But you know how kids are. They find a way to discover whatever it is that we most want to keep away from them. It is said that the boy discovered on his own the elements of Euclidean geometry when he was 12 years old. The early glimmerings of his genius were easy to see.

At age 13, Blaise attended discussion groups with his father, featuring some of the greatest intellects of the day — scientists, mathematicians, and philosophers argued their ideas in an open forum and showed Blaise the nature of rational debate. At age 16, he wrote a paper on a topic in projective geometry on the basis of which many people started to say that he was already the smartest man in Europe. At 19, he began the work that led to his invention of a calculating machine, which is often cited as a precursor of modern computers. He laid the foundations for decision theory and made important contributions to our understanding of probability, as well as devising experiments that helped push early modern science in fruitful directions.

I was once at a gas station getting a fill up, and I was wearing a Pascal T-shirt, with a picture of the great thinker emblazoned across the front. The gas station attendant came up to the window and, seeing my shirt, said in astonishment, "You know who Pascal is?" I replied, in equal surprise, "*You* know who Pascal is?" Blaise wasn't exactly a household name. The guy said, "Yeah, we had to learn about him in auto mechanics school — you know, hydraulics, pneumatics, stuff like that — Pascal was *the man,* dude!" He was, dude.

> *Pascal is one of those writers who will be and who must be studied afresh by men in every generation.*
>
> — T. S. Eliot

Blaise Pascal was also an incredible philosophical intellect and religious thinker. Born into a Catholic family, he never cared about religion until one night in his early 30s when he had an unexpected and unsought mystical experience, an experience so powerful that it completely changed his life, his priorities, and his interests. He decided to use the rest of his days on earth to write in support of what he had come to think of as ultimate truth. He wanted to write a book in defense of religious belief that would appeal to all his atheistic and agnostic friends. But he died before he could complete the project. His notes were published shortly after his death and have become one of the world's perennial bestsellers, as the book *The Pensées*, or The Thoughts.

Many years ago, I decided to read and reread his notes in order to come to a deeper understanding of his whole philosophy. For eight summers, I taught a seminar sponsored by The National Endowment for the Humanities called Faith, Reason, and the Meaning of Life, based on a careful reading of his text. Some of the best and most remarkable school teachers in America came to Notre Dame and lived together for a month each summer to talk with me about the issues Pascal raised. I was amazed to see how this man, who died at the age of 39, was able to get under the skin of people over 300 years later. It is no exaggeration to say that I saw Pascal change people's lives. Years later, some of these Pascalians are still in touch with me and report the ongoing relevance in their lives of what he once wrote.

I decided to go through his notes again and again and to write the book that I think he could have, or should have, and indeed might have written if he had lived longer and had been somehow acquainted with the best of the philosophy that came after him. In the book that resulted, *Making Sense of It All: Pascal and the Meaning of Life*, I tried to bring together all his best insights, while feeling free to say when I thought he was wrong. The remarkable thing is, in my opinion, how seldom he was wrong. But the single most controversial idea in the entire sweep of his *Pensées* is the argument we examine in this chapter. It has been praised and condemned by countless philosophers in the past three centuries. And it will continue to be studied far into the future. It is an argument known as *Pascal's Wager*.

The Wager

Life, Pascal believed, is a gamble. We're always placing our bets. Very little is certain in this world. We live and breathe probabilities. We are constantly making rational calculations as to what we need to do, and how we should structure our lives, in order to secure the goals that we value. We are always wagering our time and energy on one strategy or another in pursuit of our own hopes and dreams.

> *To be alive at all involves some risk.*

> — Harold MacMillan

Life is process. Pascal was right that we are always pursuing goals and placing our bets on what will work and what's not worth our trouble. We are engaged in that process every day. But, Pascal believed, we are also typically engaged in avoidance behavior concerning some of the things that really matter most. We use the daily demands of work and family life to keep our distance from some of the deeper issues that ultimately matter most and provide us with the most fundamental context for understanding our work and doing family life right. We are hurtling forward as fast as we can go, and we are headed for the edge of a cliff, without ever pausing to think through what it's all about.

Pascal believed that there are diseases of the soul that are much worse than the diseases of the body. We sleepwalk through too much of life. Or we sleep run. We are automatons in high gear. And we are out of touch with the deepest and most important issues we need to address. We cut ourselves off from the deepest sources of wisdom and guidance and then complain about how our lives are going.

> *Diseases of the soul are more dangerous and more numerous than those of the body.*

> — Cicero

Pascal's night of fire

We do not know exactly what happened to Pascal on his night of fire, but we know that it was an experience so vivid that it turned his life around. After his death, a servant was going through his clothes and found a note sewn into the lining of his coat. It was a memorial of his mystical experience that he had carried with him since the night it happened. The parchment was dated, and at the top of the page, the word for fire was written. In that note he records not what he experienced, but what his heartfelt responses to it were. It was the secret that gave him the final clue to his life's meaning.

Pascal wanted to reconnect us to those sources. He had come to believe that the deepest reality is spiritual. We can live on a physical level, and even on an intellectual level, and miss it completely. The physical is the level of the body, the intellectual is the level of the mind. But the spiritual is the level of the heart, that core capacity we all have where thought and feeling and will all come together.

On the night of November 23, 1654, Pascal underwent what historians call his "Night of Fire," a religious experience that apparently lasted hours, and that turned him around and convinced him that there is a living God who should be the focus and inspiration of all our lives. He saw all around him that accomplished people were disconnected from this Source and too busy in their various pursuits to notice or care. So he set it as his task to construct a rational argument that would appeal to them, get their attention, and point their lives in a theistic direction.

Pascal rooted his argument for religious belief in the view of life as one huge game. It's like a horse race between two thoroughbreds, theism and naturalism. Is there a God or not? There is evidence and argument that can be marshaled in either direction, as we have seen. Many people find this confusing and are sincerely unsure what to believe. Pascal hit upon a line of reasoning that he thought would break the tie and turn the tables.

> *If a man will begin with certainties, he will end with doubts, but if he will be content to begin with doubts, he shall end in certainties.*
>
> — Francis Bacon

How does a rational gambler place his bets? Not always on the contender most likely to win, surprisingly enough. Not always on the option with the highest purse. Pascal discovered that a rational gambler seeking to maximize his gains over the long run tends to place his bets in accordance with what is known now as *expected value* and is determined by the formula:

Bet: (Chance × Payoff) – Cost = Expected Value

Let me explain this. Imagine a very simple horse race between Greta and Annie. Suppose that they have run together ten times before, and that Greta has won six of these races. If you bet on Greta and she wins, you win $10. It costs $5 for a ticket on Greta. If you bet on Annie, it costs only $3, because she is less likely to win. But if she does win, you get $20. How do you bet?

Using the formula, we get the assignments in Table 23-1.

Table 23-1	An Example of a Bet to Illustrate the Expected Value Formula			
Bet	**Chance**	**Payoff**	**Cost**	**Expected Value**
Greta	.6	$10	$5	$1
Annie	.4	$20	$3	$5

According to Pascal, a rational gambler seeking to maximize his gains over the long run will bet on Annie here, because she has associated with her the highest expected value. Now, expected value is not the amount you expect to win. That is the payoff. It is an abstract quantity calculated to represent what value should be factored in association with this betting option, all things considered. Rational wagering is not always in accordance with chance only, or with payoff only, or even with cost only. It is a function of all three.

Now, Pascal would have us consider the cosmic race and apply what we have just discovered (see Table 23-2).

Table 23-2	The Issue of Theism and Atheism Cast as a Gambling Situation			
Bet	**Chance**	**Payoff**	**Cost**	**Expected Value**
Atheism	.5 or so	Finite	Finite	Finite
God	.5 or so	Infinite	Finite	Infinite

As long as the evidence is balanced, or even remotely roughly balanced, Pascal would have us reflect on these other relevant considerations and wager accordingly.

What's the cost of betting on God? Well, to know this you have to know what it means to place this particular bet. The ultimate form of betting on God involves being a believing theist and centering your life on a receptive openness to divine leading. But a person who is not already a believing theist can't just decide to believe while still thinking that the evidence is ambiguous. For such a person, betting on God would involve preliminary activities and attitudes. Pascal believed that betting on God could involve just turning your attention more openly to spiritual things, attempting to pray, trying to live in accordance with the moral tradition associated with theistic belief, and actively seeking God and God's will for your life. The personal cost of all this is real but limited — some time, some energy, some effort. But it is a finite cost.

The cost of betting against God is also finite. You'd just avoid any of the activities and attitudes associated with the alternative bet that you choose not to engage in. You'd live without a certain sort of hope. But you wouldn't have to give up much else. Even atheists can go to church if they like and enjoy Handel's *Messiah* in the appropriate season.

If the probabilities are even, or remotely even, and the costs are comparable, the most crucial place in the formula will be the payoff column. If you bet on atheism and win, then what do you win? Not much. Perhaps any sense pleasures that you indulged yourself in within the confines of this life that you would have avoided for moral reasons if you had been making the contrary bet. But, in the end, you wouldn't even know that you won. So you won't even have the pleasure of knowing you were right.

If you bet on theism and win, then what do you gain? Pascal says eternal life. Infinite reward. An endless positive payoff. And if you lose, he adds, you lose nothing. For any pleasure you gave up, there was an acceptable one to substitute. The theistic wager need not be seen as one involving asceticism and refusal. And if you bet on God and lose, then presumably you won't survive death to discover that you lost. And so you won't even suffer the frustration of discovering that you were wrong on such a major issue.

> *Our Creator would never have made such lovely days, and have given us the deep hearts to enjoy them, unless we were meant to be immortal.*
>
> — Nathaniel Hawthorne

We have here an interesting asymmetry between theism and atheism. If you bet on any form of developed traditional theism and are right, then you'll survive the trauma of bodily death to discover that you were right. If you were wrong, then there will be no occasion after death to be forced to realize that you were wrong. Either death will be the total end, in which case you won't survive to have to confront your world view mistake. Or you will enter somehow naturalistically into another life, in which there will be enough misleading apparent evidence of a Creator (supporting the standard arguments for the existence of God) that you, again, will not be forced to see that you were wrong. If on the contrary you bet on atheism and are right, then you'll never live to see for certain that you were right. Either death will end your experience altogether, or — much less likely — you'll enter another ambiguous existence by some natural mechanism of survival and still won't know that you were right. If you bet on atheism and are wrong, then, according to the claims of traditional theists, you'll know you were wrong.

If this reasoning is plausible, then there is associated with the bet on atheism an ultimate, epistemological No-Satisfaction Guarantee, and with the bet on God, an ultimate epistemological No-Dissatisfaction Guarantee.

Which bet should be made? Pascal thinks that a rational person should bet on God. When our formula is used for guidance, the expected utility associated with atheism is finite, and the one associated with theism is infinite. There is no greater difference possible than that between an infinite quantity and a finite one, however large. A rational person will bet in accordance with the highest expected utility. Therefore, a rational person will bet on God.

Is Pascal right? I've never met anyone who told me that he or she believed in God because of the ontological argument. I've met only a few people whose minds clearly were made up by a consideration of the cosmological argument. Several more have reported to me that they have found something like a design argument persuasive. (See Part VII for more on these arguments.) But I've met a great many people who, in explanation of their religious belief, offer some version of Pascal's Wager.

Wise venturing is the most commendable part of human prudence.

— Marquis of Halifax (1633–1695)

In one of my summer seminars, a tough-looking guy sat back in his chair from day one with his arms crossed and looked very skeptical about everything that I said concerning either Pascal or philosophy. He was a sports guy. He betted on horse races. And other things. He was more comfortable with a brewski in his hand than a philosophy text. I could tell that he might be a hard sell on the value of philosophy. After a couple of weeks of intensive work, we got to the wager. At the end of our first two-hour session presenting the argument, he came up to me and said, "Pascal understood the ponies. For the first time, it all made sense to me today. This Pascal was a pretty smart guy."

The wager has been a strong persuader ever since it was articulated. And yet it has had many critics as well.

Criticisms of the Wager

I want to look at five prominent and common objections to Pascal's Wager. I will present each as persuasively as possible and then indicate briefly how Pascal might respond.

The immorality objection

The philosopher William James, a man very sympathetic with religious belief, once said that if he were God, he'd take particular pleasure in sending to hell anyone who believed in him on Pascalian grounds. James thought the whole idea of betting on God for the sake of infinite personal gain was utterly abhorrent. It was the exaltation of gross selfishness to a cosmic scale. And it confused true religion with religious play-acting engaged in sheerly for the possibility of external rewards. James was offended. And other critics have been as well.

Some put the criticism like this. Any God who would reward a crass, self-seeking, aggrandizement strategy like the one recommended by Pascal is an immoral being. Any universe in which sincere atheism is punished and insincere religious activity engaged in only for the sake of some payoff is rewarded, is an immoral universe.

Pascal wants his argument, in principle, to appeal to as many people as possible. So the argument connects up with the one thing that everyone is guaranteed to have in common with everyone else: Self-interest. And self-interest is in no way an immoral or unworthy attitude. It is only the exaltation of self-interest over every other sort of interest that is morally repugnant. In addition, Pascal can argue that his wager is the one appeal to self-interest that will get people moving in a direction where such interest will come to play its proper subordinate role in their lives, as they submit themselves to the possibility of something greater than themselves.

Was Pascal supposing that God will reward a charade of self-interest posing as piety? Not at all. Pascal was a shrewd psychologist. He understood human behavior. He wanted to construct an argument that would lead people to change their lives, in the knowledge that concrete actions often lead to real attitudes in human life, and that an actual search, however launched, would position people better to see the realities that were objectively there to be seen.

> *The spiritual life is a grand experiment which ends in an experience; but it is not merely a leap in the dark.*
>
> — Dean W. R. Inge

Pascal didn't think of wagering as a leap into the dark. He believed that a greater openness in thought and an effort at prayer would issue in a change of perception and, ultimately, a change of heart. It is not necessary to view the payoff of the wager as a literally external reward that will almost contractually be given to the person who places the right bet. We can envision the payoff as the ultimate culmination of a proper self-development, an intrinsic reward of a life suitably well formed in the right direction. A wagering person,

Pascal thought, is eventually much more likely to become a person of real faith, and it is this sort of person who properly and naturally enters into the everlasting communion with God that is promised to all who embrace it. This is the payoff.

> *Heaven means to be one with God.*
>
> — Confucius

Is there any possibility that a sincere atheist nonetheless eventually could participate in the eternal life of good that the great theistic religions announce? Pascal's argument could allow for that possibility. But, especially if entry into another form of existence centered on communion with God is not thought of as some sort of external reward, but rather as an interior completion of a process begun in this life, it is extremely unlikely, on all reasonable construals of spirituality, that it could ever be possible without something like a movement toward real faith. Eternal life may be a gift, but it can be given only to someone capable of receiving it. Wagering preliminaries of action and attitude can lead to a real receptivity and, finally, to an authentic belief. And if this is eventually going to be needed, why not launch out on it now? The rational response still seems to be that of wagering. And there need be no unjust portrayal of the universe or of divine behavior lying behind the argument that we all should wager.

> *The only certainty is that nothing is certain.*
>
> — Pliny the Elder (c. 23–79)

The probability assignment objection

Some critics object to using a formula for expected utility (see the section "The Wager," earlier in this chapter) here at all because of a problem they have with talking about probabilities when it comes to ultimate issues like this. What's the probability of there being a God? Is it .5, or .4, or .37256? What sense does this make? That's the concern. How would we assign probability values nonarbitrarily to such a question?

The problem is generated by a certain picture of probability assignment. When you flip a coin, there are two sides. The probability of each side showing at the end of the flip is, in principle, one out of two, or .5. The probability of heads is thus .5, and the probability of tails is equal to that. Likewise, with a six-sided die, the probability of any given side showing after a toss is one out of six. We were able to assign probabilities to Greta and Annie (see the section "The Wager," earlier in this chapter) because of their past races. There have not been ten universes, five of which were created by a God and five of which were not. Just because theism and atheism seem like polar opposites, like heads and tails, it doesn't follow that each should be assigned a probability of one out of two.

Pascal's argument need not be taken to assign probabilities at all on the basis of a simple partitioning of the options, as if the mere fact that there were two options presented determines that the chance of each being true should be one out of two. Pascal's argument can be taken to be based in a very different source of probability assignment. In everyday life, we are often prepared to give rough numerical probability assignments to reflect the preponderance of evidence that we have for a given eventuality. That's how we can be told that there is a 40 percent chance of rain tomorrow. Pascal's argument can be thought of as deriving its probability assignments in exactly the same way.

Almost all human life depends on probabilities.

— Voltaire

The wager is an argument devised for a person who views all the arguments and evidences concerning a naturalistic world view and a theistic alternative, and thinks that there is enough to be said in either direction that it's not clear what to believe. At that stage, from that perspective, it could be said that the evidence is roughly balanced, and that can be reflected by probability assign-ments of roughly .5 for atheism and .5 for theism. It doesn't matter whether the evidence is precisely balanced, but it does matter that it is balanced enough so that the answer to the question of whether there is a God is not just obvious from the evidence alone.

Now, if it is obvious to you that there is a God, or if it's clear enough on the basis of evidence or experience, then you don't need the wager, except as something to offer your friends. At least, you don't need it for yourself now. But in the lives of many believing theists, there can come a time when dark-ness seems to fall, and the experience and evidence once relied on may not seem as clear as it once did. At that juncture, the wager may keep you on target or get you back on track. The proper progress of wagering always involves opening yourself more and more to a vision of the divine at work in and beyond our world.

When you have succeeded in enshrining God within your heart, you will see Him everywhere.

— Swami Shivananda (1887–1963)

The many claimants objection

But there are many religions. Many purported Gods. If I plug into the formula the Judeo-Christian God, I get the result that I should wager on him. If I plug in the Hindu God, I get the consequence that I should wager in the Hindu way. And so on for every religion claiming everlasting life and eternal bliss for the faithful. Can you hedge your bets by betting on them all? But some exclude others and so disallow this. What can you do?

Pascal knew that there were many religions and many claimants for our belief. But he did not offer the wager argument for just any claim associated with an infinite payoff. He meant it as a tie-breaker. He had in mind the stand-off between classic Western Judeo-Christian theism and atheism. The argument was meant only to break any tie in evidential considerations, and it can be argued that its use is legitimate only in such situations.

In principle, the formula would indeed generate infinite expectation for any such cosmic possibility. But then we'd be forced back to the chance column. And to the cost column. Among the proclaimers of infinite payoff, which can be backed up with the most evidence and argument? Which makes the most sense? Which is associated with the most reasonable cost? Pascal thought that only the Judeo-Christian tradition qualified. You might disagree with his assessment. But it's hard to argue with his basic reasoning. We should seek the longest term developmental path that we can pursue, compatible with what reason and prudence require. Why be content with anything less?

While I was at Yale, there was an unusual looking graduate student who entered the Department of Religious Studies the year after I did. He was very short and had extremely long brown hair, half way down to his bare feet. He never wore shoes, even on the coldest Connecticut days. He had an intense gaze in his light blue eyes, and was silent much of the time. But when he did speak, it was clear that he was very smart. But there was one catch. He believed that he was God Incarnate. He was the return of the Messiah. He had come back. He kept the messianic secret for a couple of months and then called together three of Yale's top theology professors so that as they broke bread over dinner, he could announce his true identity.

> *Madness is man's desperate attempt to reach transcendence, to rise beyond himself.*
>
> — Abraham Joshua Heshel

He had come to study theology, in particular Christology. For him, it was an exercise in self-knowledge. He had written a 600-page senior honors thesis in college on the problem of evil. How could the existence of all the pain and suffering in the world be compatible with his existence? That was ultimately the concern. He had disciples in New Haven. He married people in his name. He was crazy.

This young man promised his few disciples eternal life if they would give up everything and follow him. A graduate student from Wales, who had come to Yale after a Cambridge University degree, told me that he had felt true evil for the first time in his life, in the presence of this man and two of his followers.

I don't know what ever happened to him. I don't even remember his name. And I don't really want to know. He was real. But he is also a type. Does Pascal's Wager apply to his claims? Should we follow such people just because, on the unbelievably minuscule probability that they are who they say they are, the formula tells us that there is infinite expected utility associated with their claims? No. Pascal would direct us back to the chance and cost considerations and insist that we avoid such people like a plague. It is not an implication of his argument that any crazy claimant of infinite reward deserves our attention or allegiance.

Probabilities direct the conduct of the wise man.

— Cicero

The single case objection

Other critics object to using the formula for an essentially single case scenario. The claim is this. Considerations of expected utility are meant to apply to repetitive wagering situations. They give guidance concerning long term expectation. They are not meant to apply to situations where only one bet will be placed. If I am placing one and only one bet, the critic goes on to say, then surely I want to win that specific bet. I'm not concerned to perhaps go for a long shot because over the long run doing so on occasion will be associated with overall winnings maximization. I want to win now. I want to win this one. So only the evidence matters. Which is most likely to win? Or, in the case of theism and atheism, which is likelier to be true? If the evidence is balanced, I'll wait until more is forthcoming.

The wager is for people who do not judge the purely evidential or argumentative support for theism or atheism to be in itself convincing one way or the other. It is a line of reasoning to direct them along a specific path. It says, in effect, that it is not reasonable to wait and wait for more evidence. Right now, Pascal said, you are either wagering for God or against God. If you are praying, seeking God's presence and will for your life, and trying to view the world through theistic spectacles, you are wagering for God. If you are not praying, not seeking God's will for your life, and not trying to see things in the light of eternity, then you are living as if there is no God. And that just means that you are right now wagering that there is no God. Which wager is best? You must wager one way or the other on any given day. It is Pascal's argument that is meant to convince you which wager is best.

The fact that it's a single case changes nothing. What are we supposed to do if the evidence is indeed unclear? What other considerations are there than what we are calling cost and payoff? The formula is inevitable. So, place your bets.

Religion consists in the simple feeling of a relationship of dependence upon something above us and a desire to establish relations with this mysterious power.

— Miguel de Unamuno (1864–1936)

Choosing a World View Right for You

Philosophers can sometimes give us the impression that there is a whole cafeteria line of Big Questions that they deal with, and that we can pick and choose which ones to investigate ourselves. I have come to believe that philosophy is very different from that. As I've said before, throughout this book, I have become convinced that, in philosophy, everything is connected with everything else. What we are offered are more like package deals.

The main theistic package:

- An objective moral order
- Free will
- A soul
- Life after death
- God
- Meaning
- Bliss

This is one alternative world view. But there is also its major rival to consider.

The main naturalistic package:

- Quick description: None of the above
- No objective moral order
- No free will
- No soul
- No life after death
- No God
- No meaning
- No hope

Of course, this is not a popularity contest. Nor is it the ultimate consumer opportunity. We can't just say "wow" to one and "yuck" to the other and sign on to whatever is most desirable. We need to weigh evidence. And we need to place our bets as intelligently as we can.

> *Why do you hasten to remove anything which hurts your eye, while if something affects your soul, you postpone the cure until next year?*
>
> — Horace

Was Pascal right? There is a cosmic wager going on. You and I are living and thinking in one way, or in another. Which bet are you placing? Pascal wanted to insist that it matters.

But on this side of the most ultimate issues, there are plans to be made, things to do, and things to avoid. What is the domain within which our decisions affect how we view the meaningfulness of our lives and activities day to day? Chapter 24 looks at how we think about success and happiness in this world. Philosophy always keeps us mindful of the ultimate issues. But not all are of cosmic significance. Some are personal. And are also important.

You have talents. You have values. And you have desires. How can you make your way forward in this world that undoubtedly does exist, regardless of what you decide about a next world? Read the next chapter to find out.

Chapter 24

Success and Happiness in Life

• •

In This Chapter

▶ Asking what is enough for happiness

▶ Probing the concept of success

▶ Mastering the seven universal conditions for success

• •

> *Pursue some path, however narrow and crooked, in which you can walk with love and reverence.*
>
> — Henry David Thoreau

In this chapter, we look at the elements for a philosophy of human success. It takes us in some familiar, and perhaps some surprising, directions. Philosophers don't just talk about the outer limits of life and the hidden essence of being alive. We reflect on the practical daily issues as well. It is some of that practical reflection that absorbs us in this chapter.

When philosophers talk about the practical demands of daily life, we always want to talk about context and perspective. The philosopher Francis Bacon once said that knowledge is power. And that's true. But wisdom is perspective. And that's even more important than power.

A prominent and unusually creative television producer once told me that he believes most people these days waste their lives chasing the wrong things. Are you? Am I? How can we know?

What is Enough? The Race for More

We live in an acquisitive culture. We have more, and we want more, than ever before. We live in a time of boundless opportunity. But we also live in an age filled with lives out of control. We spend all our time and energy chasing things that won't satisfy us. Why?

The greatest case of mistaken identity in the modern world has involved the four markers of public success: Money, fame, power, and status. These four things just may have been the most widely shared dreams and the most ardently pursued goals in the past century. Yet, as an ancient philosopher might say, they can make very good servants, but are themselves very bad masters.

Money, fame, power, and status can be good and useful as resources, but they are very problematic as focal goals. When they are pursued as focal targets, the concept of "enough" can't get a grip at all. What amount of money is enough? Everyone I know who has a little wants more. But it's even more interesting that everyone I know who has a lot wants even more. A reporter once asked John D. Rockefeller how much money it takes for a man to be happy. He replied, "A little bit more than he's got."

> *Money's easy to make if it's money you want. But with few exceptions people don't want money. They want luxury and they want love and they want admiration.*

— John Steinbeck

What is enough? The concept of enough is, of course, a relative concept. Any question of what would be enough begs the follow-up question "Enough for what?" And this just shows that the concept of enough applies only to things that are of instrumental value, valuable only insofar as they lead to or produce something else (something that itself either also has instrumental value, or else has intrinsic value, value in and of itself).

Put simply, the question of enough applies only to things that are in some sense resources. When money, fame, power, and status are viewed as resources, the question of enough does have application. Enough money is the amount of money it takes to complete a project, or pay off debts, or maintain a lifestyle. Enough power is the amount it takes to get a job done. Even fame and status can work this way. For an actor, enough fame is the amount that gets him invited to work in good movies for healthy fees and then gets public attention for his work. A certain level of status in a community can be judged enough for playing a particular role in community affairs or for producing a certain degree of receptivity in people concerning a project or process that needs support.

Enough is a relative concept. More is absolute. There can always be more. And that's a problem for many people. We live in a very competitive culture, so we live in a culture of more. It's nearly heretical to suggest that bigger is not always better and faster is not always an improvement. I don't need a Ferrari to get me home from the grocery store. Ice cream doesn't melt *that* fast. How big should a company be? How powerful a computer do I need? How many items of clothing are enough? Or, closer to home for me, how many guitars do I actually need to own? Are there lines to be drawn? In a culture of more, it's often hard to see or set limits.

There is more to life than increasing its speed.

— Gandhi

There are two different forms of dissatisfaction in human life. There is first the dissatisfaction of acquisition. This is when you're not satisfied with what you have. You want more stuff. More money. More power. A bigger house. Another house. A more luxurious car. Or a faster car.

The second form of dissatisfaction is the dissatisfaction of aspiration. This is when you are not satisfied with what you are and want to become something better. You want to be wiser, to know more, to experience more, to develop more talents, to be a better person. You want to deepen yourself spiritually. You want to connect better with your world. You want to have a deeper impact for good on your children, on your community, or in your work. You aspire to a richer, more fulfilling being-in-the-world.

The dissatisfaction of acquisition feeds on itself in an almost cancerous way. The more you give in to it and try to satisfy it, the more it can grow, until it is literally out of control. There are people who can fully enjoy owning the new Mercedes convertible that they long lusted for only to the moment when that new red Ferrari pulls up beside them at a stoplight. The dissatisfaction of acquisition can become an unhealthy, impossible, tyrannical demand.

> *Ambition makes the same mistake concerning power that avarice makes concerning wealth: she begins by accumulating power as a means to happiness, and she finishes by continuing to accumulate it as an end. Ambition, in fact, is the avarice of power.*
>
> — C. C. Colton (1780–1832)

The dissatisfaction of aspiration can be quite different. Contentment is not supposed to be the same thing as apathy. Contentment is emotionally accepting your present as being what it is, without being filled with resentment, frustration, or irritation at anything you are undergoing. But that is thoroughly compatible with wanting the future to be quite different. You aspire to be better or to accomplish more. You are not satisfied to stay where you are existentially, with no further growth and no further effects for good on your world. You want to be and do more. This is the dissatisfaction of aspiration. It can be a very healthy goad to personal growth and fulfillment.

> *Be always displeased at what you are, if you desire to attain to what you are not.*
>
> — Saint Augustine (354–430)

Is there a certain number of books, such that, having read that many, you will have read enough? Is there a total number of ideas such that, having had that many new thoughts, you will be able to say, "Enough, already"? Isn't personal growth and aspiration at least in principle open-ended in a way that acquisition is not? I have enough tennis shoes. I have enough suits. I have enough computers. But, in the confines of this life, I'll never be wise enough. And that's no tragedy at all. I'm a joyful guy, but I'll never have my fill of joy — I'll never be joyful enough. But don't feel sorry for me about that.

In fact, it is the materially well off among us who feel wise enough already, but want much more stuff, who are living the philosophical tragedy of our times. To those men and women I want to say: Learn when enough is enough and when it isn't. The external things that we accrue can be great resources for the inner journey we are on, as well as for making our outer mark on the world, if we have enough guidance along the way to know what it's worth our time and energy to pursue.

The hope of the world lies in what one demands, not of others, but of oneself.

— James Baldwin (1924–1987)

The prominent national newspaper *USA Today* recently ran a cover story in their *Life* section on country music singer Alan Jackson. This is a man who, at the time, had sold 25 million records, had been named Country Music Association Entertainer of the Year, and lived in a 30,000 square foot mansion. The article was not about his career accomplishments or financial success, though; it was an account of his recent bout of "almost suicidal" depression, and how he is in the process of saving a marriage that had been in free fall from a storybook beginning, careening toward a textbook divorce.

Jackson told *USA Today:* "I'd always been the type person who didn't understand people who'd commit suicide. I thought that was the stupidest thing in the world — that if it got that bad, why didn't you just change it and move on?" But then he found himself confronted with what seems to have been an almost Tolstoyan, gut-wrenching struggle with the meaning of his success and why it wasn't making him happy. He came to realize that, in a deeply important way, he had been taking the wrong approach to life, and that his innermost attitude toward what he was doing wasn't taking him to where he wanted to be as a person.

He commented: "What was happening was, I couldn't be happy. I kept trying to let everything else make me happy." And then he said, with the sort of perceptiveness that makes for a good twist in a reflective country ballad, "Maybe that's why I'm a success. I worked so hard to get all this stuff to make me happy. Then that didn't do it. It actually got worse."

Success has ruined many a man.

— Benjamin Franklin

Here's the question: Do we often, and maybe even inevitably, do good things for what are really the wrong reasons? Is outer success in the world often the result of an inner need for happiness that cannot be satisfied by external things? Wouldn't it be an odd truth about the world if only the intrinsic rewards of a job — the sense of good that comes from a worthy task well done — truly satisfy us, but only the extrinsic rewards we anticipate — the money, or power, or recognition — typically motivate us to work as hard as it takes to really make our mark in the world? The question is, Do we tend to be motivated by the things that can never fully satisfy? And, if so, can we turn that around?

The great novelist Leo Tolstoy recounts in his famous book *Confession* that at the peak of his own success, he started to ask some of these same questions, issues that were forced on him by a sudden depression amidst accomplishment, a bout of negativity that he could not fully understand. As a young man, he chased money and fame. And he got both, in large measure. He married and then pursued the security, comfort, and physical well-being of his family. But when all the externals were finally in place, he began to ask the deeper questions of why he was doing any of the things that had come to dominate his day.

Alan Jackson needed to begin to come to terms with some of these issues before he could turn his life around and recover from a tailspin that no one but a philosopher might have expected. And his example leaves us all with a question that each of us should ponder:

What really and deeply motivates me in what I'm doing, the inner sense that I'm doing something worthy, noble and good, or the outer goods that might result?

What puts a twang in my heart?

> *It is the nature of every man to err, but only a fool perseveres in error.*
>
> — Cicero

True Success

True success is not about external acquisition. It's about what I like to call The 3-D Approach to Life:

- ✔ Discover your positive talents.
- ✔ Develop the most meaningful and beneficial of those talents.
- ✔ Deploy your talents into the world for the good of others as well as yourself.

The man who was born with a talent which he was meant to use finds his greatest happiness in using it

— Johann Wolfgang von Goethe (1749–1832)

I say that it is important to discover your positive talents. By "positive," I mean talents that can make a positive, meaningful, beneficial contribution to your life, or to the lives of others. I mean talents whose exercise will reflect the best about life and cohere with all that we know to be good and important. I specify also that you should develop the most meaningful and beneficial of those talents. Life is short. Time is precious. Energy is limited. We should all focus on the highest of our talents, if we want true success in our lives.

The great German philosopher Leibniz (1646–1716) tells a story about a man who cultivates expertise at throwing peas and skewering them on pins. A person might have a talent for doing this, but it doesn't follow automatically that he should spend a lot of time cultivating *that* skill. It is a waste of time. You might have a talent for insulting people, but it's not one you should cultivate, or even discover. Insulting people is not a positive, meaningful, beneficial talent. We should discover and cultivate what is best within ourselves. And we should spend significant time on only those talents that can be put to work somehow for the good of others as well as ourselves.

Does that mean that my talent for playing tennis, or yours for fly fishing, has to benefit others directly, or it shouldn't be cultivated? Not at all. Its benefits can be indirect. Tennis may relax me and refresh my mind to return to the philosophy by which I best serve others. A weekend of golf or fishing may restore your soul and make you a better companion for your friends and family. The talents involved can certainly count as positive, meaningful, and beneficial, as long as they are used well, and in such a way as to allow for a suitably balanced life.

Too many people worry about making a splash or amassing a fortune. They crave acceptance and see fame as the ultimate version of satisfying that real need. They cultivate only those talents they have that might somehow lead to wealth or celebrity. And in thinking like this, they are making a fundamental philosophical mistake.

Either there is a God or naturalistic atheism is the ultimate truth about reality. On either world view, this endless craving for externals is misguided.

If atheistic naturalism or naturalistic atheism (we can say it both ways) is true, then any craving to make a splash, get the cash, or win over the multitudes is fundamentally misguided. In a naturalistic universe, working toward any external thing like that is meaningless because the end result is meaningless. Importance is an illusion. Of course, in a naturalistic universe, everything may just be equally meaningless. But the implication of that is "Why bother?"

If theism is true, the quest for external fame and wealth is fundamentally misplaced. Such externals should never be our focal goals. Our importance is to be traced to our divine origin and purpose. Our sense of self-worth is to be found in our relation to our Creator, not in our renown or in our material holdings. We are here on a mission of creative love, or loving creativity. We are to be discovering the meaningful talents with which we've been endowed, developing those talents, and putting those talents to work for the good of other people as well as ourselves. And this is exactly what all perceptive people find to be the most satisfying way to live their lives, whether they are atheists, Baptists, Catholics, or agnostics.

> *A true measure of your worth includes all the benefits others have gained from your success.*

> — Cullen Hightower

Why do most people find the chase for external things to be ultimately unsatisfying? Is it because naturalism is true, and none of those things has any value at all? Or is it because theism is true, and none of those things has the right sort of value to alone support a meaningful life? One of those world views is on target. And regardless of which one it is, chasing externals seems misguided.

But something deeper can be said. There is a natural human tendency to strive for excellence. It can be worn away from our lives by an improper upbringing and by a lack of immediate cultural support (think "slacker"), and it can be misinterpreted in terms of world conquering, but it is there. Why? Does it have survival value, in an evolutionary sense? But it does not aspire to mere survival. It hankers after something much greater — human flourishing.

Tolstoy discovered, at the end of his mid-life crisis, a new meaning for his life. It centered on the importance of service to others. Many other people have come to realize the same thing. The greatest fulfillment comes from our relationships to others and comes most deeply when we are living in creative, loving service to those other people. Why? Theists say that this is what we were created for. Theism sees love and creativity at the core of why there is a universe at all. It offers an ultimate explanation for why people of almost any world view imaginable find these things to be the most satisfying and most fulfilling. And so our experience of struggling to understand what success in this world really is may also be relevant to understanding the ultimate context for life in this world as well.

> *There is no greater satisfaction for a just and well-meaning person than the knowledge that he has devoted his best energies to the service of the good cause.*

> — Albert Einstein

True success is deeply satisfying success. True success is sustainable success. It is a form of achievement that nurtures the whole person. It is not self-destructive or essentially detrimental to others. It will have different forms for different people. But it will always involve the 3-D approach at its core.

The Universal Conditions of Success

From Plato and Aristotle to the present day, the wisest people who have ever thought about success and excellence have left us bits and pieces of powerful advice for attaining true success in our lives. I have put them all together as this framework of seven universal conditions, which I call *The 7 Cs of Success (A New Framework for Excellence)*.

For the most deeply satisfying and sustainable forms of success in our lives, we need to bring into any situation, relationship, or enterprise:

- A clear **conception** of what we want, a vivid vision, a goal clearly imagined.

- A strong **confidence** that we can attain that goal.

- A focused **concentration** on what it takes to reach the goal.

- A stubborn **consistency** in pursuing our vision.

- An emotional **commitment** to the importance of what we're doing.

- A good **character** to guide us and keep us on a proper course.

- A **capacity to enjoy** the process along the way.

Most of these 7 Cs of Success will sound familiar to you, if you've read or thought about success at all. Any success that you've already had in your life will have been produced by following at least most of these conditions. Whenever I find myself confronting any stubborn difficulties in business or life, it is always due, to some extent, to my forgetfulness of, or failure to live in accordance with, at least one of these seven conditions. The whole framework is like a penetrating diagnostic tool for understanding where we are, where we need to be, and how we should start the process of getting there.

I've developed these seven conditions at length in a book called *True Success: A New Philosophy of Excellence,* and so will limit what I say here. But I do want to clarify each of them briefly and say a few words about how they interrelate.

The greatest advice from philosophers

Thales said it. Socrates repeated it. It was inscribed in marble at the most revered of ancient Greek sites, the Oracle at Delphi: "Know Thyself." This is the simplest, most practical, most profound, most famous, and most difficult piece of advice ever given by philosophers. Self-knowledge requires time, thought, humility, objectivity, openness, and living. It is acquired as we move forward in life. But to gain it, we have to reflect on what we experience, and examine how we think. What do you love? What do you like? What do you hate? What do you dislike? What would really satisfy you? What wouldn't be worth the trouble? Only by knowing yourself can you answer these questions. But the effort of asking them and trying to answer will yield a clearer self-understanding and the knowledge the Greeks recommended.

A clear conception of what we want, a vivid vision, a goal clearly imagined

In any challenging situation, we need to think through exactly what we want to see happen as the consequence of our efforts. What do we want to accomplish? What's the ultimate goal? To be able to answer such questions requires self-knowledge, one of the most difficult things for most of us to attain. And yet it's the prerequisite for any rational road to success.

True success always starts with an inner vision, however incomplete it might be. That's why most of the books on success by famous coaches, business stars, motivational consultants, and psychologists begin with chapters on goal setting. The world as we find it is just raw material for what we can make it. Life is indeed meant to be all about loving creativity, or creative love. We are meant to be artists with our energies and with our lives. We are here to create. And the only way to do that well is to structure our energies around clear goals.

> *This world is but a canvas to our imaginations.*

> — Thoreau

Some people wonder how we can rationally set either personal or business goals in changing times. How can we take aim when the targets around us are always moving? Our goals will certainly have to change on occasion as our circumstances change. We can never know at the beginning of a process all that we should know to be able to anticipate everything that will need to happen, and everything that we'll need to do, to bring about the accomplishment of our ultimate goals. And what we do experience as we seek to realize our goals may lead us to set different goals than the ones that got us underway. Goal setting is meant first and foremost to focus us and to move us forward in life. And as we move forward, we learn. Then we can set new goals more intelligently, with a more complete grasp of what's available, and what's desirable, than we ever could have at the outset of the process, or without such a process at all.

We need to fight for clarity and imaginative vividness in the areas of our lives where the challenges are greatest and the opportunities are biggest. We need a vision to steer us forward and inspire us to greater efforts. We also need to be inspired ourselves if we want to have a chance of inspiring others to help us in our endeavors. And, given the reality that almost nothing worth doing can be done entirely alone in this world, it is of vital importance to be able to inspire others to share in our own visions of what is possible.

A strong confidence that we can attain that goal

Inner attitude is often the most important key to outer results. When considering goals to pursue, we need to be aware that it is important to launch out only into enterprises in which we will be able to have some significant measure of confidence. William James' conception of precursive faith (developed in Chapter 6) is operative here. In any new enterprise of importance, we need an up-front faith in what we are doing. We need a belief in our own competence to do it and in the worthiness of the endeavor. Sometimes we have to work hard to generate an attitude of inner confidence. But it always facilitates success.

> *Very often the only way to get a quality in reality is to start behaving as if you had it already.*
>
> — C. S. Lewis

Confidence in ourselves is such a basic ingredient for facilitating any form of accomplishment that it is shocking to see how rare it apparently is in the world today. One of the greatest struggles in modern times is self-confidence. But it shouldn't be such a surprise. Especially in rapidly changing contexts, it's natural to be unsure that the personal attributes that served us well in the past will do so now and into the future. And when we are confronted every day with success stories brought into our homes by all the mass media, it's difficult not to find the competitive level of modern times a bit daunting.

Is confidence a strictly necessary condition for success? No, it's possible to just get lucky however high or low your self-confidence. But to the extent that persistence seems to be one of the most important traits in human life, confidence is needed for it, and gains its own importance instrumentally, in service to that trait of persistent pursuit. A strong confidence is no guarantee of success. But it is among the chief facilitators of it.

A focused concentration on what it takes to reach the goal

All the world's great religions and philosophies emphasize the importance of what we attend to and what we focus on in our lives. Big dreams just lead to big disappointments when people don't learn how to plan their path forward. Success at anything interesting is always the result of planning your efforts and then enacting that plan.

> *Determine that the thing can and shall be done, and then we shall find the way.*

> — Abraham Lincoln (1809–1865)

Gestalt psychologists long ago taught us that a new mental focus can generate new perceptual abilities. Focusing your energy in a new direction, toward a new clear goal, you will begin to see things all around you that you might have missed before, things that are relevant to your goal and that can help you attain it. A focused concentration is an interpretive grid that can help any of us spot what we need for getting where we want to go.

The process of moving from an envisioned goal to a reality accomplished is one of flexible firmness — an underlying firmness of commitment augmented by a flexibility of attitude and tactics that can allow you to adjust as you go and adapt as you learn.

The most important thing I've learned about success as I've studied the great thinkers and worked with very successful people is the extraordinary importance of an action orientation to life. But unplanned, blind action is never a prescription for success. The formula is plan and act. Prepare first and then get things going. Don't wait for success to come to you. Go get it. Even a flawed plan can get you moving in such a way as to lead you to see what would be a better plan. Planned action is the key.

> *Everything has to be rethought.*

> — Elias Canetti (1905–1994)

A stubborn consistency in pursuing our vision

The single most pervasive cause of failure in modern, developed countries is self-imposed, self-sabotage — people acting inconsistently with their own goals and values. It happens in governments, in families, and in businesses. It happens in people's souls. But why would anyone act in a direction contrary to what they really want and value? The answers are surprisingly simple. Stress. Pressure. Fear. Temptation. Distraction. Miscalculation.

Whatever the reason, inconsistent behavior always exacts a cost. It gets us off track. At worst, it causes us to self-destruct. At best, it delays our progress.

The word *consistency* comes from two Greek roots, a verb meaning "to stand" and a particle meaning "together." Consistency is all about standing together. Do my actions stand together with my words? Do my reactions and emotions stand together with my deepest beliefs and values? Do the members of my family stand together? Do the people I work with stand together? This is what consistency is all about. It's a matter of gathering all available energy and focusing efforts in a unified direction. Inconsistency defuses power. Consistency moves us toward our goals in the most efficient ways possible.

> *A straight path never leads anywhere but to the objective.*
>
> — André Gide (1869–1951)

I could go on about this condition at great length, because it's the one that I have struggled with the most in my life. I'm a spontaneous personality, and I have to reign myself in tightly sometimes to see to it that I'm using my time and energy in the way most consistent with my overall goals and values.

An emotional commitment to the importance of what we're doing

Passion is the core of extraordinary success. It is a key to overcoming difficulties, seizing opportunities, working far beyond the call of duty, and getting other people excited about your projects. Too much goal setting in the modern world has been an exercise of the intellect and not also the heart.

Desire is the key to extraordinary effort and creative success. The tighter a connection that you can see between your daily activities and your long-term dreams, the more you can remind yourself of how the difficult work of today will lead to the securing of your own most cherished values in the future and the easier it is to maintain that emotional commitment that is of the essence of sustainable success.

A strong desire for any object will ensure success, for the desire of the end will point out the means.

— William Hazlitt

Too many people sleepwalk through their days on emotional cruise control, not feeling the importance of their lives or of their jobs. Routine has anesthetized them, or the turbulence of change has shocked them into an emotional stupor that is not conducive to creativity or personal fulfillment. Philosophers always appreciate the role of rationality in human life. But we also know that it's not just the head, but also the heart, which can guide us on to those tasks that are right for us and keep us functioning at the peak of our abilities. The scientist, mathematician, and philosopher Blaise Pascal (see Chapter 23) is perhaps best known for his statement that "The heart has its reasons of which reason knows nothing." We all need to get in touch with those deepest reasons that will motivate us in whatever we are doing.

A good character to guide us and keep us on a proper course

It's well known that good character inspires trust. And trust is the foundation for people to work together well. Character thus is a condition for all good collaboration. In a world in which partnerships and collaborative synergies are increasingly important, the moral foundations for people working well together will become increasingly important.

A good character actually does a lot more than just provide for interpersonal trust. It has an effect on the individual's freedom and insight. Evil not only corrupts, it blinds. A person whose perspective has been deeply skewed by selfishness or patterns of deception cannot understand the world in as clear and insightful a way as the person whose mental and emotional dispositions are well formed by morally sound decisions and actions.

Character is power.

— Booker Washington (1856–1915)

But many people wonder about character being a universal condition for success. Can't a bad character sometimes have significant, even flamboyant, success? For a while. In a limited domain. And at the expense of what really matters in life. But unethical success is always self-destructive in the long run. The unethical manipulator may take advantage of people over a period of time, but eventually they are all out there ready to bring him down. And they will.

Good character is built on individual virtues. And virtues, in the end, create both inner harmony and outer harmony. This makes sustainable success all the more likely.

The one great requisite is character.

— Talmud

A capacity to enjoy the process along the way

Condition 7 is the one most easily forgotten amid the pressures of contemporary business and society. But it is just as important as the other six. The best people in every domain of human activity, in all of human history, have been people who loved what they were doing. Some very accomplished people were miserable in other departments of their lives, but when it came to the sphere of their main talent, a love of the process always produced an excellence in the results that they sought.

It has often been remarked that it's not the destination but the journey that is of utmost importance in human life. Life is a process. And if you can't enjoy the process of your life as it is, then you need to make a change and find something that you can enjoy. Because only then will you be positioning yourself for the deepest, most satisfying, most enduring forms of success.

The more you are enjoying the process, the easier it will be to set creative goals. Confidence will come more naturally. It will be easier to focus your concentration on what needs to be done. Consistency will not be such a battle. The emotional commitment will flow. And issues of character will not be as difficult to manage.

Actor Geena Davis on meaning and success

In a recent interview for a major magazine, popular movie star Geena Davis caught herself beginning to wax philosophical and said, a bit apologetically:

"Listen to me talk about the meaning of life. I'm only trying to say that I view life as a journey. It's not so much having some goal and getting to it. It's taking the journey itself that matters. The process, each step along the way, is the important thing — the moment you're in right now. Taking seriously the opportunity to be responsible for yourself as a person, for who you are and what you believe. I don't think life is about arriving somewhere and then just hanging out. It's expanding and expanding and trying and trying to get somewhere new and never stopping. It's getting out your colors and showing them."

Likewise, the more careful you are about character issues, the easier it will be to truly enjoy the process. Strength of character facilitates consistency. And doing only what you know to be good and right allows for a less troubled confidence. See how these conditions are deeply interconnected? They are a unified framework of tools with which we can work our way toward the most fulfilling forms of success in our world.

Nothing is worth more than this day.

— Goethe

A Concluding Note on Happiness

Happiness is just as widely misunderstood in our time as success. And that's no surprise to me, because they are deeply related notions. The concept of success is often associated with the concepts of wealth, fame, power, and status. (See the section "What is Enough? The Race for More," earlier in this chapter.) It ought to be associated with another family of concepts altogether. It is better ensconced in the neighborhood of excellence, fulfillment, satisfaction, and happiness.

Happiness does not consist in pastimes and amusements, but in virtuous activities.

— Aristotle

Happiness is not the same thing as pleasure. And it's not the same thing as personal peace. It is, as Aristotle believed, an activity. It is participation in something that brings fulfillment. It is engagement in a worthy enterprise. It is connected with creative love, or loving creativity. It involves pleasure and peace. But it goes beyond these states. It is, ultimately, productive. And it requires very little. I know very wealthy people who are extremely unhappy and very poor people who are blissful. Money is not a curse, nor is the lack of it a blessing. It is just not at the core of the issue at all.

Happiness depends more on the inward Disposition of mind than on the outward Circumstances.

— Benjamin Franklin (1706–1790)

Consider this interview exchange in *The New York Times* between the writer Orville Schell, and George Lucas, the father of *Star Wars*.

Schell: Would you say that you're now leading the good life?

Lucas: I would say that I'm happy. The interesting part of that — and I hate to say it because it's such a cliché — the good life has nothing to do with the money thing and fortune.

Schell: Since you have money, you're probably not quite the right person to say such a thing.

Lucas: No, I am the right person! I've been there! I've done it! . . . I've got just about as much money as you can get, and I was just as happy 30 years ago. As long as I could make a movie, I was happy. And as long as I can still make movies, I'll still be happy.

Remember this, that very little is needed to make a happy life.

— Marcus Aurelius (121–180)

Happiness is about doing something you love with people you respect. It is an ongoing result of discovering your best talents, developing those talents, and deploying them into the world for the good of others as well as yourself. Sound familiar? I hope so. That 3-D Approach to living (see the section "True Success," earlier in this chapter) is just as fundamental to happiness as it is to success.

Happiness is not achieved by the conscious pursuit of happiness; it is generally the by-product of other activities.

— Aldous Huxley (1894–1963)

As we seek to make a difference for good in the world, we position ourselves for the great good of personal happiness. And as we get in touch with the deepest resources we have, we protect ourselves from being buffeted about and being thrown off the track of true happiness. Durable bliss is an unnecessarily rare thing in our world. I hope that, as you continue to philosophize about your life, you will experience happiness in your own heart, as I have in mine. Philosophy need not be a gloomy enterprise. And philosophers can be admirably happy. If we point ourselves in the right directions. And if we use well the wisdom of those who have come before us.

Understanding is joyous.

— Carl Sagan (1934–1996)

Part IX
The Part of Tens

In this part . . .

Ten great philosophers! Ten great questions! Greatness, greatness everywhere! In this part, we hit some of the highest of the highlights. If you can remember what you read in this part ten years from now, you'll know as much as the average philosophy major ten years after graduation. But shhhhh. They paid a lot more than the price of this book for their degrees. So don't rub it in. Just give them a copy of this book, and they'll know.

So if this part is equivalent to an undergraduate major (ten years later), what is the whole book equivalent to? With the What-Is-Remembered-Ten-Years-Later proviso, at least a master's degree. But don't get cocky. You have to *remember* it! You want stuff to impress people with at parties? Then read this part.

Chapter 25

Ten Great Philosophers

A man's mind is known by the company it keeps.

— James Russell Lowell (1819–1891)

In this chapter, we take a snap shot look at ten of the greatest philosophers in history. Some that I profile would be on anyone's list. Some are just my peculiar choice. All have something to teach us.

Socrates

The name Socrates almost rhymes with "Opera tease." Fifth century B.C., Greek. Think: Toga. Easy trivia question: Who came first, Socrates or the Pre-Socratics?

Socrates was the big-city philosopher in ancient Athens. Accused and convicted of corrupting the youth, his only real crime was that of having embarrassed and irritated a number of important people, although some say he had a criminally ugly face. His punishment was the death penalty. When asked what he thought he deserved, he suggested free food and lodging. He didn't get the free food, but they did give him a free cell for a short time and something to drink — the poison hemlock.

Famous quote: "The unexamined life is not worth living."

Having the fewest wants, I am nearest to the gods.

— Socrates

Socrates didn't write books; he just liked to ask probing and sometimes humiliating questions, which gave rise to the famous Socratic Method of Teaching. This street corner philosopher made a career of deflating pompous windbags. When he was told that the oracle at Delphi had declared him to be the wisest man in Athens, he claimed to be very perplexed. To understand what the oracle might mean by this, he began questioning the citizens of the city in an attempt to find someone wiser than himself. The surprising discovery: He was the wisest! They all believed they had a wisdom they didn't have. Socrates was the only one who realized he knew nothing, and so he was the wisest after all. Or so this original wise guy himself claimed, before his philosophical career was concluded so abruptly.

Plato

Pronounce the name Plato like "Play toe"; mid-fifth century to mid-fourth century B.C., Greek. An aristocratic man with plenty of money and a superb physique, Plato at one time won two prizes as a championship wrestler. Actually, the man's real (and little known) name was Aristocles; Plato was just a nickname given to him by his friends, whose original connotation made reference to his broad shoulders.

Plato became an enthusiastic and talented student of Socrates and wrote famous dialogues featuring his teacher verbally grappling with opponents. Our wrestler believed in the pre-existence and immortality of the soul, holding that life is nothing more than the imprisonment of the soul in a body. In addition to the physical world, there is a heavenly realm of greater reality consisting in Forms, Ideals, or Ideas (such as Equality, Justice, Humanity, and so on).

> *Beloved Pan, and all ye other gods who haunt this place, give me beauty in the inward soul; and may the outward and inward man be at one. May I reckon the wise to be the wealthy, and may I have such a quantity of gold as none but the temperate can carry.*
>
> — Plato

Well-known image — Plato's cave. Plato suggested that we are all like men shackled in a cave, staring at a wall, seeing only reflections and shadows and mistaking them for the real thing — the substantial realities are *outside* the cave, beyond what our senses can now show us. As his crowning achievement, he wrote a famous treatise *(The Republic)* on the ideal society, in which he expressed the thought that it is a philosopher, of all people, who should be king (big surprise!).

Aristotle

Fourth century B.C., Greek. Plato's best student, who went on to become the very well-paid tutor of Alexander the Great. Probably the highest paid philosopher in history (up until now — but buy more copies of this book for your friends and maybe we can do something about that), Aristotle started his own philosophical school when he was 50 years old. He lived only ten more years, but amazingly produced nearly a thousand books and pamphlets, only a few of which have survived.

All men by nature desire knowledge.

— Aristotle

Of course, we all know that the author of *Ecclesiastes* in the Old Testament speaks the truth when he says, "The writing of many books is endless, and excessive devotion to books is wearying to the body." Aristotle knew this, too, and so we are told that when he sat writing, he held a metal ball in one hand while he wrote with the other. When he became tired and began to nod off, the ball would drop to the floor and loudly awaken him back to philosophy.

This great thinker was called a *peripatetic* philosopher (*peripateo* = "to walk around") because he liked to lecture to his students while taking a walk. Another group of philosophers were called stoics because they preferred sitting around on porches (stoa) when they shot the breeze.

A key theme in Aristotle's thought is that happiness (*eudaimonia*, pronounced "you day mow nee ah") is the goal of life. Aristotle was a good deal less other-worldly than Plato. He voluntarily went into exile from Athens when conditions became a bit politically dangerous for him, in his words, "lest Athens sin twice against philosophy" (see the preceding section on Socrates).

With regard to excellence, it is not enough to know it, but we must try to have it and use it.

— Aristotle

The founder of logical theory, Aristotle believed that the greatest human endeavor is the use of reason in theoretical activity. One of his best known ideas was his conception of "The Golden Mean" — "avoid extremes," the counsel of moderation in all things. His famous student, the great and over-achieving Alexander, obviously never got this point.

Saint Thomas Aquinas

Italian, 13th century. The Godfather of Catholic philosophy. A very, very large Dominican, Aquinas was one of the heaviest thinkers at a time when the greatest minds were often housed in the largest, most corpulent bodies, a time not inappropriately known as the "middle" ages. Corroborating the medieval metaphysical principle that effects resemble their causes, his literary output is often described as "enormously voluminous."

Aquinas was probably the single greatest Christian thinker of all time. One of his most famous contributions has come to be known as The Five Ways — five arguments for the existence of God. The most famous is known as The Cosmological Argument (we cover a related version of the argument in Chapter 20).

Aquinas was definitely a late bloomer: his teachers and fellow students called him "the dumb ox." Only one teacher was perceptive enough to dissent from this opinion, Albert the Great. Albert once announced, "You call him a Dumb Ox; I tell you that the Dumb Ox will bellow so loud that his bellowing will fill the world."

> *There are three things necessary for the salvation of man: to know what he ought to believe; to know what he ought to desire; and to know what he ought to do.*
>
> — St. Thomas

When Aquinas first announced to his family that he wanted to become a simple friar, his brothers took him by force and locked him away in a castle. Once, as he was seated by the fire, they sent in a beautiful prostitute to lure him away from his religious intentions. It is reported that he chased her out of his cell, perhaps with logical conundrums.

William of Ockham

William of Ockham's name can also be spelled Occam and rhymes with "rock 'em" and "Sock 'em," appropriately enough, because he was an intellectual fighter known as "The Invincible Doctor;" 14th-century English Franciscan. Ockham decided that Universals, like Plato's Forms (see the Plato entry in this chapter) — such things as Justice, Equality, Chairness and dogginess — don't really exist as abstract entities which should be counted among the furniture of reality, and are rather just the tangled outgrowth of metaphysical speculation. He shaved away this Plato's Beard with his famous principle known as Ockham's Razor — "Do not multiply postulated entities without necessity." This principle has also been known as the original principle of simplicity, or parsimony, the first "Keep it simple, stupid" injunction.

> *Plurality should not be posited unnecessarily.*

> — Ockham

Ockham became infamous for the extreme claim that whatever God does is by definition good, regardless of what it is. He believed that there are no objective values apart from God's commands and once even went so far as to say that "If God had commanded his creatures to hate himself, hatred of God would have been praiseworthy."

Ockham got into big trouble with the Pope for condemning some dubious church policies. He expressed extreme disapproval of the enormous sums of money being lavished on a building being erected in honor of Saint Francis of Assisi, the founder of his own Order, and wrote a powerful Defense of Poverty opposing the Pope. He was jailed, but unlike Socrates, he broke out and sought refuge with the Emperor of Germany, saying "You defend me by the sword and I will defend you by the pen."

The result? He was excommunicated, but not executed. Spiritually inked out, not physically cut off.

William of Ockham has the enduring distinction of being the only great philosopher whose place of burial is marked by a plaque in a parking garage in Germany. He is, however, more remembered for his logical skills than for his eternal parking spot.

René Descartes

Pronounce the name René Descartes like "Wren-ay DAY cart"; 17th century, French. Often called the Father of Modern Philosophy, Descartes spent most of his life searching for a way to unify all of human knowledge; but in his last few years he was mostly captivated by the problem of how to keep his hair from turning gray.

In the midst of his life of searching, Descartes once declared that a beautiful woman, a good book, and a perfect preacher were, of all the things in the world, the most difficult to find.

> *It is not enough to have a good mind. The main thing is to use it well.*

> — Descartes

This philosopher began his most famous work with skeptical questioning in search of one indubitable truth to use as a foundation for all of knowledge. The truth? *"Cogito ergo sum"* ("I think, therefore I am," originally expressed by him in French, not Latin, as *"je pense, donc je suis"*). That discovery, and the conviction that "God is not a deceiver," helped him stop worrying that life is all a dream or a deception cooked up by an evil genius.

For most of his life, Descartes had a famous habit: He stayed in bed meditating every day "until midday." He then made the mistake of taking a position with the Queen of Sweden as her personal philosophy tutor, for which he was required to rise well before five each morning. He was dead within months.

Descartes believed that humans have minds and experience, but animals don't. This is said to have led one of his followers to kick his own dog repeatedly in amazement that it could act so much like it was in pain when it didn't have a mind with which to feel pain. It's sometimes bewildering to see the consequences of a philosophical thought.

Immanuel Kant

The *a* in Immanuel Kant's last name is pronounced in either of two ways: as in "father" or in "ant"; 18th century, German.

Kant is probably the most famous of many famous verbose and complex German philosophers. As a young man and a student, he lived a life of poverty and deprivation. He often went hungry, but preserved his health by "breathing only through my nose in the winter and keeping the pneumonia winds out of my chest by refusing to enter into conversation with anyone." Barely five feet tall, he was to become one of the giants of philosophy.

Reading the works of Scottish philosopher and skeptic David Hume awakened him, he said, from his "dogmatic slumber." His best known book is *The Critique of Pure Reason,* sometimes described as a nearly unreadable masterpiece of philosophy. Kant himself described it as "dry, obscure, contrary to all ordinary ideas, and on top of that prolix." He was right. He once sent the completed manuscript to a friend, who was himself an eminent scholar. The man read some of the book but returned it unfinished, explaining, "If I go on to the end, I am afraid I shall go mad."

Born in Konigsberg, Prussia, Kant never left town. He took a walk every day with such regularity (at 3:30 in the afternoon) that people could set their clocks by him. In his philosophical work, he tried to restrict reason to make room for faith. He believed that theoretical reason can't reach beyond the world of experience, and so he disliked the traditional "proofs" of the existence of God. He wanted instead to make religious belief a matter of "practical reason."

Kant chose philosophy over marriage because of a medical problem that makes me cringe, so we won't discuss it. His most famous distinction: The phenomenal world (things as they appear to us) and the noumenal world (things as they are in themselves).

> *Morality is not properly the doctrine of how we may make ourselves happy, but how we may make ourselves worthy of happiness.*

> — Kant

His well-known and unduly severe conception of morality: acting on the motive of duty alone. His principle of universalizability in ethics is often alluded to by the common question: "What if everybody did it?" But to this, I have often heard the common rejoinder: "They don't."

Immanuel Kant has to be one of the most influential and unreadable of all the theoretical philosophers in history. But getting through philosophy graduate school without studying him is nearly impossible. Perhaps this is a reason to go to business school instead.

G.W.F. Hegel

G.W.F. Hegel's real name — George. But like most of the other great thinkers, he is typically called only by his last name. The name rhymes with "bagel;" late 18th, early 19th century, German. Harder to read than Kant.

Hegel is thought by many to have been only the second major philosopher after Socrates to be married. The first? Another George, the Irish philosopher George Berkeley (pronounced "Barkly"). Hegel is also thought by many to have been very confused. For some reason, this is not incompatible with philosophical renown.

Interestingly, like his married Irish predecessor, Hegel was a famous Idealist philosopher who believed that all that really exists must be mental. He was convinced that there isn't, ultimately, any independent material stuff at all (there is more on this in Chapter 13).

According to Hegel, the history of the world is the history of the Absolute Spirit concretizing itself (whatever exactly that means), and is a history of development. Hegel gave us the idea of a "dialectical development" — one thing happens (a *thesis*), the opposite happens (its *antithesis*), and from a dynamic tension, a higher resolution (a *synthesis*) arises.

> *What is rational is real and what is real is rational. On this conviction the plain man like the philosopher takes his stand, and from it philosophy starts in its study of the universe of the mind as well as the universe of nature.*
>
> — Hegel

Art and religion are, according to Hegel, like science, forms of thought. The highest form of thought? You guessed it, philosophy.

On his deathbed, Hegel complained, "Only one man ever understood me." He fell silent for a while and then added, "And he didn't understand me."

Sören Kierkegaard

Pronounced (I know, it's hard to believe, but trust me) as "Cur-cagore", or "Keer-ca-guard" (the Americanized pronunciation); 19th century, Danish.

A profound religious writer who often published his work pseudonymously, Kierkegaard constantly made fun of the eminent philosopher Hegel (see preceding section). He was a great philosophical wit, as well as being the Father of *Existentialism* (the movement of sometimes dreary thinkers focused on what it means to be in the world), a combination many people find surprising.

The idea of "a leap of faith" was one of Kierkegaard's best known contributions to philosophical and religious thought. The importance of subjective engagement was another of his important themes. An inspired as well as an inspiring writer, he once wrote a 100-page book *(Philosophical Fragments)* and later published a postscript to it of over 500 pages *(Concluding Unscientific Postscript)*.

> *The greatest hazard of all, losing one's self, can occur very quietly in the world, as if it were nothing at all. No other loss can occur so quietly; any other loss — an arm, a leg, five dollars, a wife, etc. — is sure to be noticed.*
>
> — Kierkegaard

The 20th-century philosopher Wittgenstein, himself no existentialist, at one time expressed the opinion that Kierkegaard was the greatest thinker of his century, but added in criticism of his writing style: "He is too long-winded; he keeps on saying the same thing over and over again. When I read him I always wanted to say, 'Oh all right, I agree, I agree, but please get on with it.'" As an example of his views on philosophy, the following passage is typical:

"The difference between 'popular' and philosophical is the amount of time a thing takes. Ask a man: do you know this or do you not know it — if he answers immediately, then the answer is popular, he is an undergraduate. If it takes ten years for the answer to come, and if it comes in the form of a system, if it is not quite clear whether he knows it or not, then it is a philosophical answer and the man a professor of philosophy — at least that is what he ought to be."

Lest it be thought that Kierkegaard favors the popular in all ways, his remarks on the most active purveyors of popular learning and taste should also be quoted: "God knows that I am not blood-thirsty and I think I have in a terrible degree a sense of my responsibility to God; but nevertheless, I should be ready to take the responsibility upon me, in God's name, of giving the order to fire if I could first of all make absolutely and conscientiously sure that there was not a single man standing in front of the rifles, not a single creature, who was not — a journalist. That is said of the class as a whole." (Note to all potential reviewers: The opinions expressed are only those of the existentialist, and not of the author.)

Bertrand Russell

British, 20th century (1872-1970). Equally renowned for his work in logic and his many romantic escapades, Russell was a fertile thinker who changed his mind a lot and was enormously influential.

Russell began to express his intense curiosity about the world from the time that he was three days old, as we know from his mother's writing then: "He lifts his head up and looks about in an energetic way." Told at the age of five that the world is round, he refused to believe it, but began digging a hole outdoors to see whether he would end up, bottom end up, in Australia. As it turns out, he didn't get to Australia until his late 70s.

Early on, Russell became fascinated with mathematics, a study which awakened his philosophical interests. Later in life, he once summed up his intellectual history by saying that when he became too stupid for mathematics, he took to philosophy, and when he became too stupid for philosophy, he turned to history.

Russell did write on a wide variety of topics and often had quite interesting things to say: Democracy, for example, has at least one merit. Elected officials cannot be more stupid than the electorate, for the more stupid the official is, the more stupid yet the people were to vote for him.

Once asked by a publisher to write a complimentary foreword to a book by a philosopher whom Russell thought always stole his ideas, Russell replied: "Modesty forbids."

> *It is preoccupation with possession, more than anything else that prevents men from living freely and nobly.*
>
> — Russell

In his late 60s, he was offered a position at the College of the City of New York, but because of a taxpayer's suit filed by a Brooklyn dentist's wife to annul the appointment, he was legally ruled morally unfit to teach New Yorkers, and was prevented from accepting such a position. In the suit, his books were described as "lecherous, salacious, libidinous, lustful, venerous, erotomaniac, aphrodisiac, atheistic, irreverent, narrow-minded, untruthful, and bereft of moral fibre." The philosopher Wittgenstein, Russell's former student, commented when he heard about this that if anything was the opposite of aphrodisiac it was Russell writing on sex.

Russell predicted that only inhabitants of Tierra del Fuego (at the southernmost tip of South America), and perhaps a few Australians, would survive the next major war. He went on to win a Nobel Prize for Literature (because there isn't one for philosophy, and I want to know *why not?*).

Chapter 26

Ten Great Questions

In This Chapter

▶ Asking ten of the great philosophical questions

▶ Attempting a few answers

A man, though wise, should never be ashamed of learning more, and must unbend his mind.

— Sophocles

In this chapter, we take a quick look at ten great philosophical questions.

Is Philosophy Practical?

Philosophers seem to have argued endlessly about issues we can never finally resolve. If I say that a blue car is outside and you say that you didn't see any such car, we can go look. If I say that a God exists and you say that you don't think so, there is no easy way to go look. At least, not a way that I'm in a hurry to take. Do philosophers just spin their mental wheels fixating on things we can't know? And, if so, isn't philosophy the most impractical thing imaginable?

What is it for something to be practical? Something is practical if it helps you to realize your goals. If your goals include knowing who you really are, what life in this world is all about, and what's ultimately important, then philosophy is eminently practical. If these things are not among your goals, well, then you need new goals.

Everything is useful for something.

— Tacitus

Can philosophers argue endlessly over ultimate issues? Sure. But that doesn't mean that there are no answers or that the answers don't matter. People can argue endlessly over financial planning and investment strategies. But a good investment still beats a bad one any day. Politicians argue endlessly over issues of government. Some policies still work better than others. There is wisdom to be had in life even where strict proof is not available. And philosophy is the search for that wisdom.

Can We Ever Really Know Anything?

Yes. We can. Is there survival of death or not? You may think you know the answer to this question, or you may think you don't. What you do know, however, is that either there is or there isn't. And this is enough to demonstrate logically that we can really know something. It's certainly not enough to know only such truths as this sort of either-or. That obviously won't help you plan your life. But, being capable of some knowledge, we can know much more than logical trivialities. And we can know beyond the reach of proof — which is, in itself, *something* well worth knowing.

We know plenty of things about the matters of daily life. We know how we like to be treated. We know that our time is an extremely limited commodity. We know what it feels like to be busy. We know what it feels like to suffer. Philosophy is the attempt to build on those ordinary things that we all realize we know and to come to some extraordinary conclusions about fundamental issues that we don't usually contemplate in the frantic rush of daily life.

Knowledge does not require universal agreement. It doesn't even require that everyone I respect should agree with me. Sometimes you or I can be privy to a fact or an inkling of truth that is not universally recognized. A lack of clear-sightedness or perspective on anyone else's part, though, can never undermine the ability that you have to attain real knowledge by your own means.

> *When someone opposes me, he arouses my attention, not my anger. I go to meet a man who contradicts me, who instructs me. The cause of truth should be the common cause for both.*
>
> — Montaigne (1533–1592)

In fact, the existence of disagreement between ourselves and others is something that can spur us on to further knowledge. If we are open-minded enough to learn from it what is there to be learned. And then we increase our knowledge.

Skeptics are right to question on a broad scale. But they are rarely right to deny on a broad scale. Knowledge is one of the capacities, and fundamental powers, of human life. (See Chapters 4, 5, and 6 for more on knowledge and skepticism.)

Is There Ultimately an Objectivity to Ethics?

People hold different values, and we clearly sometimes disagree on ethical judgments. But that does not imply that there is no objective truth of the matter to be known. The realities of ethics are there to be seen if we just put on the right lenses.

> *Our whole life is startlingly moral.*
>
> — Thoreau

Epistemology should not dictate metaphysics. You have my permission to quote that at parties. Put another way, a lack of agreement on what we know does not determine ultimately what there is. Problems in knowing do not logically imply any lack of reality in what we are trying to come to know. Physicists disagree. Economists disagree. But there is an objective physical universe, however hard it is sometimes to know. And there are ongoing economic realities, whether they can be adequately captured in the economists' categories or not.

The same is true of ethics. Knowing and being are sometimes different. When you look at the deepest practical levels of ethical thought across cultures, you find surprising agreements underneath all the surface differences. There are universal truths concerning human nature.

There may be areas where we'll never be sure about what the ethical truth is. And there may even be ethical territories that we must just colonize through convention and agreement, areas where there is no determinate notable landscape apart from our human constructions. But for the most part, the realities of ethics and morality are there, or rather, here, before we ever start drawing up laws and promulgating rules.

> *The great secret of morals is love.*
>
> — Shelley

Who Am I?

Who wants to know? Just kidding. The question of personal identity, in the deepest sense, is one of the most crucial to answer, and one of the most difficult questions that human beings can take on. And isn't that ironic? You'd think that self-knowledge would be fairly easy. After all, we have constant and immediate access to the quarry of our investigations. But appearances are often different from realities. Self-knowledge ends up being one of the most profoundly difficult quests in human life.

We grow up hearing from other people who they think we are. But we must each engage in a process for ourselves that is one part discovery, one part invention. Some of this question is engaged by taking on the big metaphysical questions that we broach in the body of the book, having to do with the objectivity of morality (Part III), the reality of freedom (Part IV), the existence of the mind (Part V), our attitudes toward death and questions about life after death (Part VI), God (Part VII), and meaning (Part VIII). How you react to these issues constitutes a deep part of who you are. But another part of the identity question is broached only when we face the practical issues concerning success in this world, in our daily lives.

What are your talents? What are your values? What do you really, most deeply care about? What is your mission in life? What legacy would you most want to leave the world?

These are questions of self-knowledge. And it's only rarely that they can all be answered early in life. We grow in our understanding of the questions, and in our vision of their answers, as we live and experiment with different possible paths. Life is supposed to be a series of adventures — adventures of self-knowledge and self-creation. As we explore the outer world, we form and learn more about our own inner worlds.

> *To know oneself, one must assert oneself.*
>
> — Albert Camus

"Who am I?" is less a question to answer than it is one to live with and use. It should always be connected up with another question: "What am I becoming?" In the end, each of us is responsible for what we do with the talents and opportunities that we are given. Each of us has the chance to do things that will make a positive difference in the world and that will express well who we are. But to accomplish this, we must use the freedom that we have to find our own way forward in life. Benefiting from the wisest counsel we can find, each of us has the responsibility to develop our own wisdom and put it into action. Only the process itself will finally answer the question of who we are.

Is Happiness Really Possible in Our World?

Yes. It sometimes seems as illusive as anything you can imagine, but it is available in this world. Happiness should never be confused with self-indulgence or even with gleeful giddiness. It is, in the end, less an emotional state than a total state of being. Evil makes it difficult. Suffering tries to hold it at bay. It sometimes seems that so many things hold us hostage in this world that we can never shake free to be truly happy. It's easy to feel that you can't be happy unless your spouse is, and your children are, and even your own parents, and at least your closest friends, and on, and on. And how can I be happy today, not knowing what tomorrow will bring? Again, without even worrying about the future, the past itself may weigh on you and hold you back from the happiness you crave.

The most insightful philosophers have made it clear that the only moment we ever really possess is the present. And yet the past and the future are constantly trying to assert ownership over us. One of the most important forms of liberation to be attained in this world is freedom from the times that we do not really possess. Haunted by the past or held by hopes of the future, most people never really experience the present moment in all its fullness. And yet this is the foundation for experiencing true happiness.

The great philosophers have made it clear that engagement in a process of working toward worthy objectives, along with other good people — a process that you can enjoy along the way — is a fundamental key to the universally sought state of personal happiness. It is not, for most people, attainable as a solitary pursuit. And it can't be bought or borrowed. It must be created as the byproduct of loving, creative activities that make a difference for good in the world.

> *We may fail of our happiness, strive we ever so bravely; but we are less likely to fail if we measure with judgment our chances and our capabilities.*
>
> — Agnes Reppler

There are happy people in this world. Actually, there are many. Sometimes you have to move a bit outside the normal spheres of your daily activity to find them. But finding one of them can be an inspiration for life. Being one of them allows you to inspire others for life.

Is There, After All, a God?

Even though we cover this question fairly extensively in Part VII, glance briefly at Table 26-1 for a big picture of the typical reasons for and against believing in God.

Table 26-1	Is There a God?
Main Reasons for Believing	**Main Reasons for Not Believing**
Ontological argument	Conceptual difficulties
Cosmological argument	Problem of evil (Chapter 21)
Design argument	Dislike for religious institutions
Religious experience	Worry that it's not scientific
(All in Chapter 20)	
Pascal's wager (Chapter 23)	

What makes the most sense, overall, of the facts of existence and of your experience? If theism is true, it is subtle. But if atheism is true, why do we exist?

Most of the great philosophers have been, in some way or other, believers in a Creator God. In our list of ten great philosophers in Chapter 25, only one was an atheist — the most recent one, Bertrand Russell. Only in the past hundred or so years has secularism, and either agnosticism or atheism, been fashionable among philosophers and teachers of philosophy. Yet, a few years ago, I once asked a number of prominent, active philosophers to tell the story of their own spiritual adventures, and together we produced a book called *God and the Philosophers* (Oxford Press) that helped signal a significant turn-around among at least a sizable minority of highly respected, contemporary academic philosophers. There is a new openness to the question of God and a new wave of commitment to theism among philosophers. This may still be considered a minority movement among current professors of philosophy, but it is a noteworthy return to the great theistic traditions of the past, with an addition of distinctive insights from the present.

Many prominent fiction writers of the past century, as distinct from university philosophers, have been concerned to understand the human condition at the deepest possible levels of experience in this world. And a number of them, like Flannery O'Connor, Walker Percy, and Reynolds Price, have been believers in God. Again, many novelists are not theists. But some of those who have probed most deeply, in my estimation, and have lived most sensitively, have been.

What can be seen on earth indicates neither the total absence, nor the manifest presence of divinity, but the presence of a hidden God. Everything bears this stamp.

— Blaise Pascal

But, in the end, this is a question that is left for each of us to grapple over, given the indicators of our own experience. What makes the most sense of the whole evidence that we have to work with? What touches us as true?

Like the question Who am I? this is a question that sometimes can be answered only by the process of living. Isn't that interesting?

What Is the Good Life?

The good life is not one in which kids take guns to school and kill school mates. It's not a life where people are tortured and large groups exterminated because of their ethnic background. Nor is it one in which greed brings nations into conflict.

The good life is not first and foremost about acquisition, power, luxury, or status. It is not about celebrity. And it's not an existence of unbridled, self-indulgent excess.

Our will is always for our own good, but we do not always see what that is.

— Jean Jacques Rousseau

The life that is good must be founded on an attitude of respect and nurture toward the intellectual, aesthetic, moral, and spiritual needs of every human being. It begins in an inner circle of family, extends to friends and coworkers, and finally reaches out across all artificial and natural boundaries to all of life on this earth.

The good life involves freedom, love, work, pleasure, challenge, friendship, community, service, and the sort of resources that can be used creatively.

There is nothing about humble surroundings in a small town that, in itself, prevents a living of the good life. And there is nothing about the upper east side of Manhattan that, in itself, prevents a living of the good life. The greatest obstacles to the good life are not external things at all, but are those inner vices that have been identified and understood since the time of the ancient philosophers. Envy, resentment, bitterness, malice, mendacity, and prejudice are all enemies of the good life and obstacles to its being lived.

The best life is a meaningful, creative, open adventure that brings opportunity, learning, laughter, and joy into the lives of other people. It's a life that connects up with the deepest realities and aspires toward the highest possibilities.

> *Happiness is not best achieved by those who seek it directly; and it would seem that the same is true of the good.*
>
> — Bertrand Russell

The good life will differ in its particularities for each of us. But its general outlines are universal.

Why Is So Much Suffering in the World?

There is so much suffering because there is so much *sentience*, or experience. We are sentient beings. We feel as well as think. We experience life on many levels. Because of that, we can live deeply. But because of that, we can suffer tremendously.

The smarter you are, the more you can suffer. Until you really wise up. Then you can put things into a bigger perspective and endure what before would have been unendurable.

But, again, why is there so much suffering? Our freedom is so powerful, we can create enormous suffering for each other. And we do. That explains part of it. Some of that is intentional evil. Some is just stupidity. But even apart from malice and thoughtlessness, suffering enters our lives.

We can't always say why. We can't always understand the suffering that we see around us. And this frustrates us. But we can respond to it better than we typically do. And here is a fascinating fact about human life that I've noticed. The people who respond to suffering the best — take Mother Theresa as a paradigm here — seem puzzled and frustrated by it the least. And this itself is something well worth philosophizing about.

> *He knows not his own strength who has not met adversity.*
>
> — Ben Jonson (1573–1637)

If a Tree Falls in the Forest....

"If a tree falls in the forest and there is no one around to hear it, does it make a sound?" You thought we were going to get through the whole book without this one? Here's a sad fact. If you ever had a philosophy course in college, then ten years later this is the one question you're likely to remember, but with no idea whatsoever about why it was asked, and what it was doing in a philosophy course.

A fool sees not the same tree that a wise man sees.

— William Blake (1757–1827)

This question is about the role of an observer in reality. Or about the nature of reality apart from observers. It can be taken to be a question about what some philosophers call primary and secondary qualities. A primary quality is a characteristic that an object has in itself, like its physical mass. A secondary quality is one that is had only in relation to an observer. If in the entire universe, there were no beings with eyes and the sense of sight, there would be no colors. There would be light waves and wavelengths, but no color. Colors result from the processing of light waves by brains. That, at least, is the claim made by philosophers who draw a hard and fast distinction between primary and secondary qualities. The tree scenario can just be a test case to see whether you accept this distinction and think of sound as a secondary quality.

Or the tree question can be meant to elicit intuitions about basic ontology — about our most basic theory of being or existence. Is a sound the sort of thing that is essentially listener dependent, so that it cannot exist unheard, or can it have objective existence in and of itself?

Can you believe that philosophers ask questions like this? And we do. My best philosophy buddy in graduate school once entertained me for an afternoon with the question of whether the gleam of light bouncing off a chrome automobile bumper on a sunny day has its own ontological status. We philosophers want to know what sorts of things really exist, what purported things are really fictions, and what sorts of things have only a dependent form of reality.

Bishop Berkeley believed that all apparently material things have only a dependent reality (See Chapter 13). On his form of idealism, according to which only minds and ideas in minds actually exist, it follows that, without an observer, not only does the sound of the falling tree not exist, but the tree doesn't either.

When we are not observing things, according to Berkeley, God must be, or they wouldn't exist. Ronald Knox once formulated this limerick to convey Berkeley's philosophy:

> There was a young man who said, "God
> Must think it exceedingly odd
> If he finds that this tree
> Continues to be
> When there's no one around in the Quad."

> REPLY
> Dear Sir:
> Your astonishment's odd:
> I am always about in the Quad.
> And that's why the tree
> Will continue to be,
> Since observed by

> Yours Faithfully,
>   God.

Bishop Berkeley speaks

> Some truths there are so near and obvious to the mind, that a man need only open his eyes to see them. Such I take this important one to be, to wit, that all the choir of heaven and furniture of earth, in a word all those bodies which compose the mightily frame of the world, have not any subsistence without a mind, that their being is to be perceived or known; that consequently so long as they are not actually perceived by me, or do not exist in my mind, or that of any other created spirit, they must either have no existence at all, or else subsist in the mind of some eternal spirit: it being perfectly unintelligible and involving all the absurdity of abstraction, to attribute to any single part of them an existence independent of a spirit. To be convinced of which, the reader need only reflect and try to separate in his own thoughts the being of a sensible thing from its being perceived.

> — (From *A Treatise Concerning The Principles of Human Knowledge*)

The tree question can be used to elicit intuitions to lead us in Berkelyan directions. If a sound is listener-dependent and color is viewer-dependent, then many other things may be, in the broadest possible sense, observer dependent.

> If a man speaks in the forest, and there is no woman around to hear him, is he still wrong?

> — Sign at a local hot dog stand run by women

Recent science has indeed had a harder time than most of us imagine separating observers from realities observed. In a number of discoveries in modern physics, and in principles articulated to accommodate these discoveries (such as the well known problem of measurement) we human beings just gotten more and more deeply implicated in the nature of what we are trying to describe. Where is the dividing line between us and the rest of nature? It's just not as easy to say as we once thought.

So what's the answer to the tree question? Hey, I didn't promise to answer them all, just to lay them out.

What's Stronger in Human Life, Rationality or Irrationality?

No contest. Nonrational forces are stronger than rational thought and can cause us sometimes to do very irrational things. But nonrational forces are not themselves irrational. The heart leads us in a way that the mind can't. Emotions are more powerful than reason. And within the realm of the mind, it is the imagination that is much stronger than the logical intellect.

But a horse can be much stronger than his bridle. A dog may be much stronger than his leash. And yet, if they are trained properly, the horse and the dog can benefit from submission to the guidance that may only be possible with that bridle or leash.

Reason must be our last judge and guide in everything.

— John Locke (1632–1704)

Logic can give us guidance. Reason can provide direction. But only the nonrational forces in human life can ultimately provide the motivation, the inspiration, and the energy for moving us forward productively. Yet, unbridled by reason, these same forces that are capable of producing great good in our lives can lead to terrible tragedy. Life without logic would be no better than groping in the dark. Rationality can illumine our paths. But we must grasp our ultimate goals with a perceptiveness greater than what the mind alone can offer.

Reason itself is a matter of faith. It is an act of faith to assert that our thoughts have any relation to reality at all.

— G. K. Chesterton

Irrationality often prevails in human life. But that is no reason to despair. It is only that much more reason for those of us who value rationality to see to it that we spread its influence within our own lives, and as far as we can through all our activities.

Index

• E •

IDG BOOKS WORLDWIDE
BOOK REGISTRATION

We want to hear from you!

Register This Book and Win!

Visit **http://my2cents.dummies.com** to register this book and tell us how you liked it!

✔ Get entered in our monthly prize giveaway.

✔ Give us feedback about this book — tell us what you like best, what you like least, or maybe what you'd like to ask the author and us to change!

✔ Let us know any other *...For Dummies*® topics that interest you.

Your feedback helps us determine what books to publish, tells us what coverage to add as we revise our books, and lets us know whether we're meeting your needs as a *...For Dummies* reader. You're our most valuable resource, and what you have to say is important to us!

Not on the Web yet? It's easy to get started with *Dummies 101*®: *The Internet For Windows*® *98* or *The Internet For Dummies*®, 6th Edition, at local retailers everywhere.

Or let us know what you think by sending us a letter at the following address:

...For Dummies Book Registration
Dummies Press
7260 Shadeland Station, Suite 100
Indianapolis, IN 46256-3917
Fax 317-596-5498

™

BESTSELLING
BOOK SERIES